ANTIQUITÉ
ET SCIENCES
HUMAINES

LA TRAVERSÉE DES
FRONTIÈRES

9

DIRECTEURS DE COLLECTION

Corinne BONNET
Frederik VERVAET

COMITÉ SCIENTIFIQUE

Zainab BAHRANI
(Columbia University, New York)

Nicola CUSUMANO
(Università degli Studi di Palermo)

Erich GRUEN
(University of California, Berkeley)

Nicholas PURCELL
(St John's College, Oxford)

Aloys WINTERLING
(Humboldt Universität, Berlin)

GODS IN THE HOUSE
Anthropology of Roman Housing – II

Edited by
Alexandra DARDENAY
and Laurent BRICAULT

BREPOLS

© 2023, Brepols Publishers n.v., Turnhout, Belgium.

All rights reserved.
No part of this publication may be reproduced,
stored in a retrieval system, or transmitted,
in any form or by any means, electronic, mechanical,
photocopying, recording, or otherwise
without the prior permission of the publisher.

D/2023/0095/143

ISBN 978-2-503-60169-4

e-ISBN 978-2-503-60170-0

DOI 10.1484/M.ASH-EB.5.130867

ISSN 2466-5916

e-ISSN 2565-9200

Printed in the EU on acid-free paper.

CONTENTS

Alexandra Dardenay & Laurent Bricault
Gods in the House: An Anthropological Approach to Ancient Divinities and Domestic Cults   7

I
GODS OF THE HOUSE

Heather F. Sharpe
Domestic Aphrodite, Goddess of Desire and Seduction   21

Nicolas Amoroso
Dédoublements de divinités dans les laraires romains : polymorphie des images et multiplicité des champs d'action   51

Françoise Van Haeperen
Honorer Mithra en contexte résidentiel. Réflexions à partir des exemples de Rome et d'Ostie   81

Carla Sfameni
Divine Guests: Religious Identities and Groups of Deities in Roman Domestic Shrines   105

II
GODS IN THE HOUSE

Eric M. Moormann
Sacraria ou 'chapelles' religieuses à Pompéi : culte domestique ou vénération publique ?   139

Maddalena BASSANI
Morphologies of Sacra Privata *in the Roman House: Architecture, Furnishings, Cults*   171

Alexandra DARDENAY
Herculaneum's Insula V *Domestic Cult Places: Reflections on Typology, Locations and Fields of Action*   209

III
TOWARDS AN ANTHROPOLOGICAL ANALYSIS OF SPACES AND RITUALS

Marin MAUGER
Domestic Religion and the Anthropology of Space in the Entrance to the Roman House   241

Anna-Katharina RIEGER
From Routines to Rituals in Pompeian Houses – How Layout and Image-objects of Household Shrines Shape Religious Knowledge   267

Emmanuel PUI
Les pratiques cultuelles dans les villas gallo-romaines du Haut-Empire   307

Aude DURAND
Réflexion sur le devenir et la propriété des sacraria *en contexte domestique*   333

INDEX RERUM   359

INDEX DEORUM   361

INDEX LOCORUM   365

ALEXANDRA DARDENAY & LAURENT BRICAULT

GODS IN THE HOUSE: AN ANTHROPOLOGICAL APPROACH TO ANCIENT DIVINITIES AND DOMESTIC CULTS

All of Rome, whether it was in the private or public sphere, had to be in harmony with the religious order of the world, and the home was no exception to this rule. Was not the city itself viewed as a vast dwelling, with its hearth in the temple of Vesta and the presence there of the divine Penates, which according to legend Aeneas had conveyed to Italy after having saved them from the burning of Troy?

However, despite the structural role that it undoubtedly had at the heart of Roman society, domestic religion[1] has been largely neglected in the scholarly works of the past fifty years.[2] The great historiographical currents – even the most recent ones – have generally pushed it to the side in order to concentrate on official cults and, notably, civic religion.[3] Whether proponents of *Polis*

---

[1] This expression in most modern languages has replaced "private religion" or "private cults," which were in use until recently, in part to avoid the risk of an opposite reading with respect to the concept of public/private, which did not apply to the same areas as in our contemporary societies.

[2] More than a century ago, A. De Marchi devoted two volumes to this theme that remain a remarkable source of references: *Il culto privato di Roma antica: I, La religione nella vita domestica. Iscrizioni e offerte votive*; *II, La religione gentilizia e collegiale*, Milan, U. Hoepli, 1896-1903.

[3] With rare exceptions. See, for example, H. J. ROSE, "The Religion of a Greek Household," *Euphrosyne* 1 (1957), 95-116; D. ORR, "Roman Domestic Religion: The Evidence of the Household Shrines," *ANRW* 2.16.2, Berlin – New York, 1978, p. 1557-1591; A. DUBOURDIEU, *Les origines et le développement du culte des Pénates à Rome*, Rome, EFR, 1989 (Collection de l'École française de Rome 118); K. BOWES, *Private Worship, Public Values and Religious Change in Late Antiquity*, Cambridge, CUP, 2008; J. BODEL, S. OLYAN (eds.), *Household and Family Religion in Antiquity*, Malden, Blackwell, 2008; M.-O. LAFORGE,

Religion[4] or devotees of *Lived Ancient Religion* – concerned with giving a proper account of the full complexity of ancient religious life, and reproachful of the *Polis Religion* model for not doing so – neither the former nor the latter have truly looked into domestic religion.[5] Both groups have come up against the same stumbling point: the scarcity of sources. The traditional raw material of historians – namely literary, epigraphical and numismatic sources – is not rich in information on domestic cults: the literary texts, which were written by and for the Roman elites, give scarce attention to private worship; inscriptions with religious character that come from the private sphere are quite rare; and, the coins issued by the authorities (civic, royal, Republican, Imperial) say nothing about cults practiced inside the home.

For John Scheid, this broad historiographical view is explained by the fact that, for most historians, it was within the institutional framework of the city that the religions of the Greco-Roman world developed, and it is for this reason that so-called public cult provides most of the information on religious practices. Domestic religion would not be distinguished from this,[6] which has led Jörg Rüpke to write that "There was no *religion privée*, no 'domestic religion' in Roman antiquity."[7] However, anxious to fill this gap partly, or at any rate to draw attention

---

La religion privée à Pompéi, Naples, Centre Jean Bérard, 2009; W. VAN ANDRINGA, *Quotidien des dieux et des hommes: La vie religieuse dans les cités du Vésuve à l'époque romaine*, Rome, EFR, 2009 (Bibliothèque des Écoles françaises d'Athènes et de Rome 337); C. W. PERSON, *Household Shrines and Cults in Roman Achaia: A New Approach to Examining Cultural Change under the Roman Empire*, PhD diss., Bryn Mawr College, 2012 (online); H. F. SHARPE, "Bronze Statuettes from the Athenian Agora: Evidence for Domestic Cults in Roman Greece," *Hesperia* 83 (2014), p. 143-187.

[4] See the seminal paper of C. SOURVINOU-INWOOD, "What is Polis Religion?," in R. BUXTON (ed.), *Oxford Readings in Greek Religion*, Oxford, OUP, 2000, p. 13-37, first published in O. MURRAY, S. PRICE (eds.), *The Greek City from Homer to Alexander*, Oxford, Clarendon Press, 1990, p. 295-322.

[5] In the rich volume edited by R. RAJA, J. RÜPKE, *A Companion to the Archaeology of Religion in the Ancient World*, Chichester – Malden, MA – Oxford, 2015, the most relevant paper is the one written by K. BOWES, "At Home", p. 209-219.

[6] See, for example, in this volume, the contributions of E. Moormann, p. 139-169, and A. Durand, p. 333-357, on the *sacraria*.

[7] J. RÜPKE, *Pantheon: A New History of Roman Religion*, Princeton, NJ, Princeton University Press, 2018, p. 255.

to it,[8] Scheid devoted his final year of teaching at the Collège de France to the question of *sacra privata*.[9] And yet, once again, specific attention was not given to the form and structure of domestic cults, but rather to the place of the individual in private religion, while analyzing the type of behavior in which individuals could engage outside of civic religion.[10] It therefore was not a matter of describing private religious life, or even a single aspect or another of it. What Scheid has essentially sought to do is to examine whether the devotion that was shown to the gods in this setting, in which they were considered to be closer to people, was of a different type from that demonstrated in the city's spaces, with its forum, festivals and public rites.

A renewal of the question prompted by archaeology and iconography

It is through archaeology and iconography that domestic religion invites fresh examination by historians of the ancient world.[11] In effect, the inclusion of archaeological data in this area of study has made it possible to overcome the impasse in which scholars had been stuck due to the poverty of the ancient literary sources. In this volume we will see, in particular, how an approach combining the studies of textual sources and archaeology, iconography and epigraphy has permitted a profound renewal of the traditional heuristic approach to Roman cults from a more anthropological perspective. And rather than approaching *sacra privata* merely as a part of the history of religions, we shall instead approach them from the perspective of the study of the Roman house as *household*,[12] so as to place in evidence the structural role

---

[8] His own manual on *Religion romaine* (4 editions) hardly addresses the question.

[9] J. SCHEID, "*Priuatim deos colere*. Réflexions sur les cultes privés à Rome et dans le monde romain occidental", *Cours du Collège de France* 2014-2015 (http://www.college-de-france.fr/site/john-scheid/course-2014-2015.htm). See also J. SCHEID, *Les Romains et leurs religions. La piété au quotidien*, Éditions du Cerf, Paris, 2023.

[10] See J. SCHEID, "Religion collective et religion privée," *DHA* 39.2 (2013), p. 19-31.

[11] See RAJA, RÜPKE, *Companion*.

[12] See BODEL, OLYAN, *Household and Family Religion*.

of cults in the organization of the household, the daily lives of the individuals composing it, and the internal hierarchies.[13]

Little is known about the forms and organization of domestic cults before the Augustan era.[14] It was then that they took the form by which they were known during the Imperial Period, with an apparent crystallization of key elements such as the *genius* of the *paterfamilias*, the Lares, and the Penates. This is, in any case, the way that they are found in the cities of Campania, where better than anywhere else one can approach the material study of domestic life during the Imperial Period. As always, due to the disproportionate impact of the sources provided by the remains of Pompeii, one must be cautious in interpreting this documentation as reflecting a norm with regard to one or more domestic cults. Emphasis should be placed on a necessary confrontation between the rich Campanian dossier and that of other sites that might concern the Latin West as much as the Greek-speaking East, even if the work on these other parts of the Mediterranean is sparse, to say the least.[15]

The objective of this volume is to envision the phenomenon of *sacra privata* evenly over the long term, which the corpus of Vesuvian sources alone obviously does not make possible. Expanding the chronological and temporal areas of study widely seems to us essential for a proper understanding of the specificities of domestic cults.

It is generally thought, in effect, that there did not exist a *single* domestic cult, but rather *multiple* domestic cults, just as there was not a single cult of Mercury or Mithras.[16] This does not mean, of course, that each *paterfamilias* was given the freedom to create domestic rituals that were specific to his family. Today it has been well established – and not only by Scheid drawing,

---

[13] A. Dardenay, N. Laubry (eds.), *Anthropology of Roman Housing*, Turnhout, Brepols, 2020 (Antiquités et sciences humaines : La traversée des frontières 5).

[14] M.-O. Charles-Laforge, "Les cultes privés chez les Romains (IIIe s. avant – IIIe s. après J.-C.)," *Pallas* 111 (2019), p. 171-197.

[15] See, in this volume, the contribution of H. Sharpe, p. 21-50.

[16] See the title of the recent book of L. Bricault, P. Roy, *Les cultes de Mithra dans l'Empire romain*, Toulouse, PUM, 2021. About Mithras in a domestic perspective, see, in this volume, the contribution by F. Van Haeperen, p. 81-103.

notably, from Cato the Elder[17] – that the rituals performed within the framework of *sacra publica* were not fundamentally different from those undertaken in a domestic context. It is more than likely that when at home the *paterfamilias* did not perform rituals and sacrifices that were all that different from those he performed (if he held a priestly office) or saw being performed in public ceremonies.[18]

Anthropology of the Roman home and its domestic cults

Analysis of domestic cults proves central from the perspective of an anthropological study of Roman housing. *Sacra privata* in effect played a structural role for the *familia*, by uniting the group of individuals living under a single roof around the figure of the *paterfamilias*, whatever their status may have been – *ingenui*, slaves or freedmen, minors or adults, men or women. It was quite probably one of the only occasions that there would be an opportunity for members of a household all to share time and an activity together. Thus, the organization of domestic life did not *a priori* allow for daily meals that brought together all of the members of the *familia*, or at any rate it did not normally do so.[19] Adults and children probably would eat separately, not to mention that the slaves would certainly take their meal separately. Therefore, domestic cults probably would have been seen, in most households, as presenting a unique opportunity for col-

---

[17] J. Scheid, *Quand faire c'est croire*, Paris, Aubier, 2005, chapter 5, p. 129-160; see also M.-L. Hänninen, "Domestic Cult and the Construction of an Ideal Roman Peasant Family," in S. Katajala-Peltomaa, V. Vuolanto (eds.), *Religious Participation in Ancient and Medieval Societies: Rituals, Interaction and Identity*, Rome, Institutum Romanum Finlandiae, 2013 (Acta Instituti Romani Finlandiae 41), p. 39-49.

[18] J. Scheid (ed.), *Pour une archéologie du rite : Nouvelles perspectives de l'archéologie funéraire*, Rome, EFR, 2008 (Collection de l'École française de Rome).

[19] K. Bradley, "The Roman Family at Dinner," in I. Nielsen, H. S. Nielsen (eds.), *Meals in a Social Context. Aspects of the Communal Meal in the Hellenistic and Roman World*, Aarhus, Aarhus UP, 1998, p. 36-55; P. M. Allison, "Everyday Eating and Drinking in Roman Domestic Contexts," in B. E. Parr, A. Di Castro, C. Hope (eds.), *Housing and Habitat in the Mediterranean World. Cultural and Environmental Responses*, Louvain, Peeters, 2015 (*BABesch* Supplements 26), p. 265-279.

lective opportunity for what is today "together time". Moreover, by placing the figure of the *paterfamilias* at the top, their structure made it possible for the authority of the *dominus* to be established and for him to recall the patriarchal foundations of Roman society on a daily basis. Thus the establishment of the superiority of the *dominus* over the rest of the members of the *familia* seems to have been one of the motivations for the *sacra privata* having been deeply rooted, as Cicero writes in *De Officiis*, Book 1:

> [54] For since the reproductive instinct is by Nature's gift the common possession of all living creatures, the first bond of union is that between husband and wife; the next, that between parents and children; then we find one home, with everything in common. And this is the foundation of civil government, the nursery, as it were, of the state. Then follow the bonds between brothers and sisters, and next those of first and then of second cousins; and when they can no longer be sheltered under one roof, they go out into other homes, as into colonies. Then follow between these, in turn, marriages and connections by marriage, and from these again a new stock of relations; and from this propagation and aftergrowth states have their beginnings. [55] The bonds of common blood hold men fast through good-will and affection; for it means much to share in common the same family traditions, the same forms of domestic worship, and the same ancestral tombs.[20]

What could be more instructive for a child, a spouse or a slave than day after day to contemplate the spectacle of the *paterfamilias*, invested with the power to communicate with the gods, and serving as intercessor in the dialogue between the family and the gods? What better proof of his legitimacy to rule as master of the household?

---

[20] Translation Walter Miller, Loeb Classical Library. 54. *Nam cum sit hoc natura commune animantium, ut habeant libidinem procreandi, prima societas in ipso coniugio est, proxima in liberis, deinde una domus, communia omnia; id autem est principium urbis et quasi seminarium rei publicae. Sequuntur fratrum coniunctiones, post consobrinorum sobrinorumque qui cum una domo iam capi non possint, in alias domos, tamquam in colonias exeunt. Sequuntur conubia et affinitates ex quibus etiam plures propinqui; quae propagatio et suboles origo est rerum publicarum. Sanguinis autem coniunctio et beneuolentia deuincit homines et caritate.* 55. *Magnum est enim eadem habere monumenta maiorum, iisdem uti sacris, sepulcra habere communia.*

From this perspective, the presence of the *genius* of the *paterfamilias* alongside the Lares in domestic shrines has a particular resonance, even if in reality we are unaware of the importance of the influence of this figure in domestic cults. In effect, if at Pompeii the *genius* quite often seems to be associated with the Lares, to the point of forming a virtual triad, in contrast it is virtually absent from the *lararia* of Herculaneum, where the Lares, when they are present, appear alone or with the serpents.[21] This difference between the two sites – revealed through the contributions of C. Sfameni and A. Dardenay in this volume – necessarily asks if it is necessary to see here a bias in the sources, with the Pompeian documentation being much more abundant, and if it is a reflection of local or social specificities. The apparent absence of the *genius* at Herculaneum is certainly intriguing, especially since it appears – albeit in a sporadic manner – at other Roman sites, for example in Gaul and Spain.[22] Sfameni, in her contribution on groups of divinities, thus shows that the traditional association of *Genius* and Lares is typical of Pompeii, and that outside of Campania images of the serpents and the Lares – together or apart are not frequently attested. To be sure, the state of iconographic documentation, so scattered beyond the Vesuvian sites, does not permit one to generalize. This is why highlighting the most glaring differences between the Pompeian and Herculanean corpora remains our best tool for putting this question into perspective at the current time. Therefore, Sfameni analyzes in the broadest manner possible the makeup of the groups of divinities attested in Roman domestic shrines, taking into account the relative size of the Pompeian corpus and permitting its paradigmatic character to be called into question. This approach enables her to reveal – on a broad spatio-temporal scale – the existence of more regional or social dynamics in the development of these groups of divinities. The results of this study are extended by those in the contribution of E. Pui, who

---

[21] See, in this volume, the contributions of C. Sfameni, p. 105-135, and A. Dardenay, p. 209-237.

[22] M.-O. Laforge, "Lares, Génie et Pénates : les divinités du foyer, figures identitaires?", in M. Blandenet, C. Chillet, C. Courrier, *Figures de l'identité: naissance et destin des modèles communautaires dans le monde romain*, Lyon, 2010, p. 195-221.

– in examining the cult practices at villas in Gaul and Germany – shows a form of transversality among the domestic cults at the regional level. In effect, the choice of divinities honored, as well as the cultic materials used, transcended social classes and belonged to a cultural heritage mixing both native and Roman elements.

Richness and diversity in the domestic pantheons

Thus archaeology has made it possible to bring to light, in Italy and the whole of the Greek and Roman worlds, domestic pantheons whose diversity and originality necessarily call for investigation.[23] The divine powers that would be called upon by the *patres* certainly varied from one region to another and even at the micro-territorial scale, from one house to another, according to the religious preferences of the master of the house, who was always concerned over the proper functioning of his affairs, be they domestic or professional.[24] Two- or three-dimensional images of the selected gods populated inhabited spaces in various ways that are increasingly better understood.[25] Thus, in the contribution of F. Van Haeperen, the examination of *Mithraea* established in a residential context suggests that in certain rich families Mithras was the object of a cult – one that was not exclusive but coexisting with that of other domestic divinities – in *ad hoc* shrines often located beneath the house. The *paterfamilias* presided over ceremonies for which there would be assembled a community composed of his sons, slaves, and freedmen,

---

[23] See SHARPE, *Bronze Statuettes*.

[24] V. HUET, S. WYLER, "Association de dieux et d'images dans les laraires de Pompéi", in S. ESTIENNE, V. HUET, F. LISSARRAGUE, F. PROST (eds.), *Figures de dieux : Construire le divin en images*, Rennes, PUR, 2014, p. 195-221. See, in this volume, the contributions of H. Sharpe, p. 21-50, N. Amoroso, p. 51-79, F. Van Haeperen, p. 81-103, and C. Sfameni, p. 105-135.

[25] D. JAILLARD, "'Images' des dieux et pratiques rituelles dans les maisons grecques : L'exemple de Zeus *Ktésios*," *MEFRA* 116 (2004), p. 871-893; P. BONINI, "Le tracce del sacro. Presenze della religiosità privata nella Grecia romana," in M. BASSANI, F. GHEDINI (eds.), Religionem significare: *Aspetti storico-religiosi, strutturali, iconografici e materiali dei sacra privata*, Roma, Quasar, 2011 (Antenor Quaderni 19), p. 205-228; D. ANELLI, "Il culto dei Lari in Grecia," *Annuario della Scuola Archeologica Italiana di Atene e delle Missioni Italiane in Oriente* 96 (2018), p. 137-148.

and perhaps also some relatives, peers or friends. Similar to other domestic cults, the cult of Mithras observed in the great dwellings of Rome, especially during the fourth century, therefore itself appeared to be an instrument for the cohesion of the familial community – at least its male members – around the figure of the *paterfamilias*.

Topography of the sacred in the home

Another major contribution of archaeology concerns, moreover, the sacred topography of the house.[26] While, in theory, Lares and Penates were present throughout a dwelling, it is generally held that their cult was centered in small domestic shrines.[27] Their typology varied, with a simple niche representing the most modest end of the spectrum and a masonry sanctuary the most luxurious, not to mention a range of shrines made of wood, the size and mobility of which varied.[28] An examination of these *sacraria* (structures or shrines), proposed in the contribution of E. Moormann in this volume, suggests that the link between these domestic installations and monumental sacred architecture is rather thin, with regard to both architectural forms and ornamentation. *Lararia* cannot be considered, from a formal point of view, miniature temples.

The position of the domestic shrine or shrines in the house was supposed to enable the divinities to keep watch on most of the rooms, and even the entranceway. This function was even one of the main attributes of the Lares, in their role of appointed protectors of the whole area covered by the dwelling, all the way up to each boundary. This last point, which is also an issue raised

---

[26] BASSANI, GHEDINI, Religionem significare.

[27] T. FRÖHLICH, *Lararien- und Fassadenbilder in den Vesuvstädten: Untersuchungen zur "volkstümlichen" pompejanischen Malerei*, Mainz, von Zabern, 1991; A. KAUFMANN-HEINIMANN, *Götter und Lararien aus Augusta Raurica: Herstellung, Fundzusammenhängen und sakrale Funktion figürlicher Bronzen in einer römischen Stadt*, Augst, Römermuseum 1998; M. BASSANI, Sacraria: *Ambienti e piccoli edifici per il culto domestico in area vesuviana*, Padua, Libreria Universitaria, 2008 (Antenor Quaderni 9).

[28] See, in this volume, the contributions of A. Dardenay, p. 209-237, M. Bassani, p. 171-208, and M. Mauger, p. 241-266.

in this volume, and its associated problems are examined from different points of view by A. Durand and M. Mauger.

Between permanent and temporary arrangements, the locations for domestic cult could be found in different parts of the home. It was not, in fact, rare to come across a multiplicity of cult places in a single dwelling, but their positioning undoubtedly was not a function of chance. In fact, the hypotheses formulated in the contributions of M. Bassani regarding the placing of domestic shrines inside and outside the house and of Dardenay regarding the link between the areas for the divinities' activities and the locations of their shrines together suggest that the positioning of domestic shrines often responded to preoccupations associated as much with the ergonomics of the home as with the master of the house's concern with self-representation. The study of archaeological traces left by changes in ownership on the morphology or even the location of *sacraria* in Durand's contribution emphasizes that this question of location was not lacking in challenges for the owner. In addition, it is evident that, with the exception of shrines in the cooking area whose main function was undoubtedly associated with the protection of the food storage area and preparation of meals, domestic shrines were generally situated on the main circulation paths both within and within/without the home. This suggests that it was essential not only that the divinities would see everything and everyone, but also that they would be as visible as possible, including sometimes from outside the home.

Connection between domestic cults and modes of living

This question regarding visibility might seem elementary, but it is fundamental. In considering the question of the protection of the door to the home, Mauger emphasizes the extent to which the dangers facing the family were taken seriously. The entranceway was viewed as a flaw in the protective envelope around the house. It was this fear over its unreliability that prompted inhabitants to engage in rites and place apotropaic images around this opening. Several examples developed in contributions to this volume show that it was common for the shrines and images of divinities to be arranged in such a way as to be viewed from outside the home.[29] Thus the gods were certainly everywhere in the house, but they were especially present in certain strategic locations (*atrium*, kitchen, windows and entrances), so as to maximize their visibility and ability to provide surveillance, but also to maintain purity in the face of external defilement.

The question of visibility – and more precisely the direction of gaze and the ability to be seen and watching, which is related to the location of the *sacraria* in the household – is likewise considered in depth by A.-K. Rieger in her contribution. *Sacraria* and divine images help us to envision the perspective of the fixed nature of daily routines. From an anthropological point of view, this question of routines is intrinsically linked to that of the organization and cohesion of the family unit.

One of the principal phenomena that emerges from the contributions collected in this volume is, in effect, the capacity for strengthening the familial bond that was created by these domestic religious rituals, whether they were routine or associated with exceptional circumstances. And this unifying nature also characterizes the divine images populating the home. Essentially, while being shared by all members of the family unit, they could be interpreted and experienced in as many ways as there existed individuals in the household. As H. Sharpe shows for the figure of Aphrodite, it is vain to seek a single explanation for the extraordinary presence of this goddess in the domestic context. Many attributes are associated with her, whether erotic or matrimonial, or linked to fertility, beauty or dress, which attest to the crucial place that she occupied in many aspects of daily life. This is the reason why she took on religious and social significance for the different members of the household. Therefore, the repetition of images of a single divinity in the home, a crucial question that N. Amoroso has looked into, makes it possible to clarify the function of divine images in domestic cults. Possessing several

---

[29] One shall not forget that the gods of the household could also appear on the exterior walls, especially in the case of commercial or craft shops. See on this subject: J. R. CLARKE, *Art in the Lives of Ordinary Romans: visual representation and non-elite viewers in Italy, 100 B.C.-A.D. 315*, Berkeley, University of California Press, 2003, p. 87-94, p. 105-112, and J. HARTNETT, *The Roman street: urban life and society in Pompeii, Herculaneum, and Rome*, Cambridge, Cambridge University Press 2017.

images of a single divinity – and, it must be asked, was it the *same* divinity, despite the apparent similarities in the iconographic designs? – perhaps responded to functional or ritual preoccupations, or even both at the same time.

Since it is difficult to precisely restore the unfolding of the rituals, other anthropological approaches can therefore be considered. It is once more the approach emphasized by Rieger – which starts from the premise that the inhabitants of a house interacted with one another each day, and sometimes even unconsciously with the images of the domestic divinities – that seeks to understand how the "visualization" of all of this imagery functioned. The question of the perception and reception of divine images, and of their power of suggestion, is in effect inseparable from questions regarding their spatial positioning in the ergonomics of the home and the power that was attributed to them.

Lastly, another approach makes it possible to identify, thanks to the materials and arrangements revealed by archaeology, the human actions and practices conducted in a domestic setting in particular. It is with such an approach that Durand investigates in particular the traces left by a change in ownership on the evolution of domestic cults in a residence. This "archaeology of gesture" [30] provides rich and previously unpublished material regarding the manner in which individuals both invested themselves in and shaped domestic spaces, how they lived with gods at the heart of their dwellings, and which rituals they practiced on a daily basis.[31]

---

[30] W. Van Andringa, *Archéologie du geste : Rites et pratiques à Pompéi*, Paris, Hermann, 2021.

[31] See, in this volume, the contributions of A.-K. Rieger, p. 267-305, and E. Pui, p. 307-332.

I
GODS OF THE HOUSE

HEATHER F. SHARPE

DOMESTIC APHRODITE, GODDESS OF DESIRE AND SEDUCTION

1. *Introduction*

One of the most preeminent goddesses found in Greek and Roman houses was Aphrodite. As the goddess of love and physical desire, her presence in domestic contexts appears quite fitting, but attempts to ascribe specific reasons behind her popularity and the exact nature of her sphere of influence have only briefly been explored. Attempts to categorize the purpose of such imagery as "decorative" or "religious" have proven difficult, and in recent years scholars have instead sought a more nuanced approach to understand how sculpture and other imagery might have been viewed and utilized by various members of a given household. The intention of this paper is to examine a sampling of Aphrodite sculptures from Greek domestic sites, review the archaeological contexts in which they were found, consider religious-cultic and decorative functions of such imagery, reflect on modes of display, and lastly consider how viewers, in particular women, might have responded to images of her. This paper takes inspiration from recent studies of Aphrodite, which focus on the female viewer with consideration of how Aphrodite imagery served the religious, social, and personal needs of women in the Greek world.[1]

---

[1] C. M. HAVELOCK, *The Aphrodite of Knidos and Her Successors: A Historical Review of the Female Nude in Greek Art*, Ann Arbor, University of Michigan Press, 1995; N. BOYMEL KAMPEN, "Epilogue: Gender and Desire", in A. O. KOLOSKI-OSTROW, C. L. LYONS (eds.), *Naked Truths: Women, Sexuality, and Gender in Classical Art and Archaeology*, London, Routledge, 1997, p. 267-277; K. SEAMAN, "Retrieving the Original Aphrodite of Knidos", *Atti della Accade-*

Material in this survey will include representations of Aphrodite in terracotta, marble, and bronze found in domestic contexts from the middle of the Hellenistic period to the Greek Imperial period. Attention will focus predominantly on sites located in the eastern Mediterranean in an effort to elucidate reasons for the goddess's popularity among inhabitants of the Greek East and to provide some insight into the origins of her appearance in domestic contexts.

2. *Aphrodite and household cult*

According to ancient sources, there were numerous gods venerated within the Greek house. Chief among them were Zeus Herkeios, Zeus Ktesios, Hermes (primarily in the form of herms), Apollo Patroos, and Hestia, and each had a particular role to play in the security and prosperity of the family and household.[2] By comparison, references to Aphrodite are seldom found. There is an intriguing passage in Theophrastus' *Characters*, in which the Athenian writer describes 'a superstitious man,' who concerns himself overly much with appeasing the gods, including buying myrtle boughs and frankincense to sacrifice to the Hermaphrodite.[3] In his discussion of the passage, Herbert Rose assumes that the Hermaphrodite may have been a double herm with the two deities portrayed back-to-back; however, pairs of

---

mia Nazionale dei Lincei 15 (2004), p. 531-594; A. HEINEMANN, "The Cave, the Gaze, the Bride, and her Lover: The Constraints of Narrating Desire on a Hellenistic Mirror", in E. WAGNER-DURAND, B. FATH, A. HEINEMANN (eds.), *Image – Narration – Context: Visual Narration in Cultures and Societies of the Old World*, Heidelberg, Propylaeum, 2019, p. 335-351.

[2] For a summary of the literary and archaeological evidence, see M. NILSSON, "Roman and Greek Domestic Cult", *Opuscula Romana* (1954); H. ROSE, "The Religion of a Greek Household", *Euprhosyne* 1 (1957), p. 95-116; C. KUNZE, "Die Skulpturenausstattung hellenistischer Paläste", in W. HOEPFNER, G. BRANDS (eds.), *Basileia. Die Paläste der hellenistischen Könige*, Mainz, von Zabern, 1996, p. 109-129. C. A. FARAONE, "Household Religion in Ancient Greece", in J. P. BODEL, S. M. OLYAN (eds.), *Household and Family Religion in Antiquity*, Malden, Blackwell, 2012, p. 210-228; D. BOEDEKER, "Family Matters: Domestic Religion in Classical Greece", in BODEL, OLYAN, *Household and Family Religion*, p. 229-247.

[3] Theophr. *Char.* 16.10. For a discussion of the passage, see H. ROSE, "The Religion of a Greek Household", p. 108-109.

small lead herms of a male and female deity placed side by side on a single base have been found at Olynthus, and perhaps this is the arrangement to which Theophrastus is referring.[4] Less enigmatic is an epigram by the third-century BC Syracusan poet Theocritus, who describes how a woman, Chrysogone, set up a statue of Ourania (Aphrodite) in the house of her husband Amphikles directly connecting it to the children and life she shared with her husband.[5]

In the Hellenistic period, while ancient sources barely mention Aphrodite's role in household cult, statuettes of the goddess begin to be found in ever greater numbers at sites such as Priene and Delos. In his analysis of the terracotta figurines from Priene, Frank Rumscheid provides an extensive analysis of Classical and Hellenistic statuettes of Aphrodite found at Greek domestic sites and demonstrates that her appearance was closely connected to the household cult; however, the display of sculpture would increasingly take on a more decorative role.[6]

Some of the changes that appear to have taken place regarding the selection of gods on display in Hellenistic Greek households undoubtedly were impacted, or in some cases popularized, by cult practices sponsored by Hellenistic rulers, in particular with their promotion of deities tied to ancestral and dynastic cults. Literary, numismatic, and archaeological evidence attest to the veneration of deities in connection with ancestral worship and the Hellenistic ruler cult, and it is worth considering whether the popularity of Aphrodite and Dionysos in domestic contexts was in part propagated by the veneration of these deities by Macedonian

---

[4] ROSE, "The Religion of a Greek Household", p. 108-109. For the small lead herms from Olynthus, see D. M. ROBINSON, *Excavations at Olynthus, Part X. Metal and Minor Miscellaneous Finds*, Baltimore, Johns Hopkins Press, 1941, p. 6-14, pl II-III.

[5] Theoc. *Epigr.* 13 (*AP* 6, 340): "This is no vulgar Venus. Addressing her in prayer, Call her celestial. Chaste Crysogona set her up here in the household of Amphicles whose life she was happy to share and whose children she bore." D. HINE, *Theocritus: Idylls and Epigrams*, New York, Atheneum, 1982. See passage discussed by V. J. HARWARD, "Greek Domestic Sculpture and the Origins of Private Art Patronage", diss. Harvard 1982, p. 95.

[6] F. RUMSCHEID, *Die figürlichen Terrakotten von Priene: Fundkontexte, Ikonographie und Funktion in Wohnhäusern und Heiligtümern im Licht antiker Parallelbefunde*, Wiesbaden, Reichert, 2006, p. 338-344.

and later Ptolemaic rulers.[7] The association of Hellenistic rulers with Dionysos and, more importantly here, between Hellenistic queens and Aphrodite would evolve further under the Ptolemies. Ptolemy II and his sister/wife Arsinoë II were the *Theoi Adelphoi*, and while Ptolemy associated himself with Dionysos, a new cult tradition began with Arsinoë II, in which she was equated to Aphrodite.[8] The choice of Aphrodite appears to have been particularly appropriate, as among her various incarnations she was a goddess of marriage, fertility and, as Aphrodite Euploia, she alluded to the maritime ventures of the Ptolemies.[9] One of the ways in which Ptolemy II and Arsinoë II reinforced their associations with Dionysos and Aphrodite was through the visual arts. The Pavilion of Ptolemy in Alexandria, described by Athenaeus, contained elaborately decorated dining rooms decorated with Dionysiac imagery.[10] This tradition was continued by their descendants, and of note is the elaborate decoration of Ptolemy Philopator's Thalamegos or royal pleasure barge. The luxury ship was said to have been fitted with private rooms for the royal couple and their court as well as a series of elaborate banqueting rooms, including one dedicated to Dionysos and two others located on either side of a small round shrine for Aphrodite, complete with a marble statue of the goddess.[11] While there was likely a strong ritual component to the Dionysiac and Aphrodite imagery in these royal banqueting rooms, the adoption of these same sculptural trends in private settings of Hellenistic houses may have been for decorative reasons in addition to religious ones.[12]

---

[7] Kunze, "Skulpturenausstattung".

[8] S. B. Pomeroy, *Women in Hellenistic Egypt: From Alexander to Cleopatra*, Detroit, Wayne State University Press, 1990, p. 29-38.

[9] Pomeroy, *Women in Hellenistic Egypt*, p. 29-38.

[10] Ath. *Deipn.* 5.196a-202f; E. Calandra, *The Ephemeral and the Eternal: The Pavilion of Ptolemy Philadelphos in the Court of Alexandria*, Tripodes 13, Athens, Scuola Archeologica Italiana, 2011, p. 139-140.

[11] Ath. *Deipn.* 5.204d-206d; F. Caspari, "Das Nilschiff Ptolemaios IV", *JDAI* 31 (1916), p. 1-74; Kunze, "Skulpturenausstattung", p. 126.

[12] Kunze, "Skulpturenausstattung", p. 126. The connection between art works depicting Aphrodite and members of her circle with dining and banqueting spaces and sympotic activities has alternated between viewing such works as either decorative or religious-cultic. Martin Kreeb and Frank Rumscheid have in general proposed a religious-cultic function but have also indicated that a decorative intent should also be considered. Kreeb in particular proposes that the same

Aphrodite and her son Eros may have assumed more decorative functions in Late Hellenistic (and subsequently with Italic Roman) houses, but this doesn't mean that the goddess was fully secularized. During the Hellenistic and Greek Imperial periods, there is a marked increase in the appearance of small-scale sculptures of the goddess in the eastern Mediterranean, principally from Egyptian and Syrian sites (Fig. 1).[13] Few have been found in situ, but we should imagine that most came from either domestic or funerary contexts.[14] Bronze statuettes show the goddess wearing crowns and other attributes of Egyptian deities, and thus she is most likely an amalgamation of Aphrodite, Isis, Nechbet, and Astarte. According to Christine Havelock and Wendy Cheshire, the growth in popularity of this syncretistic goddess in the private realm may be associated with the power and influence of Hellenistic queens (e.g. Arsinoe II), who were linked or assimilated with these goddesses either during their lifetime or after their death.[15] Most of these bronze statuettes were found in Egypt and Syria, and thus their popularity appears to have been concentrated in former Ptolemaic and Seleucid territories. I will return to these statuettes later in the paper.

With the influx of Romans (and Roman cult practices) to Greece, Aphrodite may have received additional impetus for worship in the private sphere. Under Emperor Augustus, the goddess Venus was quickly adopted into Roman household cult practices as demonstrated by her frequent appearance in *lararia* of Pompeii and Herculaneum.[16] In the Greek East, there is evidence of

---

sculpture could serve different functions according to where it was displayed. F. RUMSCHEID, *Die figürlichen Terrakotten*, p. 126-131; KREEB, *Untersuchungen zur figürlichen Ausstattung delischer Privathäuser*, Chicago, Ares, 1988, p. 68.

[13] A. HEKLER, "Alexandrinische Aphroditestatuetten", *ÖJh* 14 (1911), p. 112-120; E. R. WILLIAMS, "A Bronze Statuette of Isis-Aphrodite", *JARCE* 16 (1979), p. 93-101; M.-O. JENTEL, "Quelques aspects d'Aphrodite en Égypte et en Syrie à l'époque héllenistique et romaine", in C. AUGÉ, L. KAHIL (eds.), *Mythologie gréco-romaine, mythologies périphériques : études d'iconographie: Paris, 17 Mai 1979*, Paris, Éd. du CNRS, 1981, p. 151-155.

[14] WILLLIAMS, "Bronze Statuette", p. 99.

[15] HAVELOCK, *The Aphrodite of Knidos*, p. 126-129; W. A. CHESHIRE, "Aphrodite Cleopatra", *JARCE* 43 (2007), p. 151-191.

[16] See Dwyer on Aphrodite's function as either decorative or cultic in Pompeian houses: E. DWYER, *Pompeian Domestic Sculpture: A Study of Five Pompeian Houses and Their Contents*, Rome, 1982, p. 124.

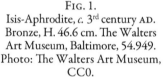

Fig. 1.
Isis-Aphrodite, *c.* 3rd century AD. Bronze, H. 46.6 cm. The Walters Art Museum, Baltimore, 54.949. Photo: The Walters Art Museum, CC0.

Fig. 2.
Aphrodite, late 2nd - early 3rd century AD. Bronze, H. 19.5 cm. Agora Museum, Athens, B 409. Photo: American School of Classical Studies at Athens: Agora Excavations.

what we might refer to as traditional Roman cult practices, demonstrated by the appearance of Roman *lararia* figures. For example, an Aphrodite/Venus bronze statuette found in the Athenian Agora (Fig. 2) explicitly testifies to her role in household cult practices due to the presence of a Roman *lar* statuette among the finds; the presence of the *lar* statuette suggests that the assemblage may have belonged to a Roman *émigré* who, like so many others, settled in Greece during the Hellenistic and Imperial periods.[17]

---

[17] H. SHARPE, "Bronze Statuettes from the Athenian Agora: Evidence for Domestic Cults in Roman Greece", *Hesperia* 83 (2014), p. 143-187; H. SHARPE, "The Paramythia Bronzes: Expressions of Cultural Identity in Roman Epirus", in J. M. DAEHNER, K. LAPATIN, A. SPINELLI (eds.), *Artistry in Bronze: The Greeks and Their Legacy. XIXth International Congress on Ancient Bronzes, Los Angeles*, Los Angeles, The J. Paul Getty Museum and Getty Conservation Institute, 2017, p. 134-143.

In an increasingly cosmopolitan Roman Empire, there is likely to be greater variety as well as increased amalgamation of religious cult practices. Between Hellenistic Greek household cult traditions and those introduced by Romans who settled in the Greek East, it may be difficult to distinguish whether a goddess on display is Aphrodite, Venus, or a syncretization of related deities.[18]

In summary, while ancient sources rarely include Aphrodite among the traditional Greek household deities, archaeological evidence does indicate that during the Hellenistic and Greek Imperial periods, she was the recipient of household cult worship. On the other hand, this doesn't mean that she didn't serve other functions within the Greek house.

3. *Aphrodite in androns?*

During the Hellenistic period, Aphrodite appears in domestic contexts in considerable numbers, most notably at Priene and Delos. Justifications for her presence in Greek households have ranged from decorative to religious/cultic to varying degrees of the two combined. Based on limited archaeological evidence from Priene, where some statuettes of the goddess were found in *androns*, it has been suggested that Aphrodite's presence in Hellenistic houses alluded to the erotic and pleasurable activities of the symposium.[19] Yet, how often was she associated with

---

[18] Providing a notable exception, statuettes of Aphrodite, Dionysos, and Athena discovered in a first-second century AD house on Samos strongly suggest Greek rather than Roman cult practices: M. KOSMA, "A Group of Terracotta Figurines from Samos: A Case for Domestic Cult?", in E. LAFLI, A. MULLER (eds.), *Figurines de terre cuite en méditerranée grecque et romaine, vol. 2 : iconographie et contextes*, Villeneuve-d'Ascq, Presses universitaires du Septentrion, 2015, p. 281-287.

[19] J. RAEDER, *Priene: Funde aus einer griechischen Stadt*, Berlin, Mann, 1984, p. 22-25, 33-38; R. AMMERMAN, "The Religious Context of Hellenistic Terracotta Figurines", in J. P. UHLENBROCK, D. BURR THOMPSON, R. MILLER AMMERMAN (eds.), *The Coroplast's Art: Greek Terracottas of the Hellenistic World*, New York, Caratzas, 1990, p. 37-46 (p. 38); J. P. UHLENBROCK, "The East Greek Coroplastic Centers in the Hellenistic Period", in UHLENBROCK, BURR THOMPSON, MILLER AMMERMAN, *The Coroplast's Art*, p. 72-80, (p. 78); F. RUMSCHEID, "Sandalen-Geschichten", in K. STEMMER (ed.), *In den Gärten der Aphrodite*, Berlin, Bnb, 2001, p. 125-137.

dining/banqueting rooms? Could she be found in any other areas of the house? A brief survey of some of the sites and finds might provide greater clarification.

3.1. Priene

Priene has played an important role in forming general conceptions of the display of small sculpture – mostly of terracotta but some of marble – in Hellenistic Greek houses.[20] In his 2006 study, *Die figürlichen Terrakotten von Priene*, Frank Rumscheid catalogued over 400 terracotta figurines and figurine fragments, yet a significant number have no specific findspot recorded.[21] Of the roughly thirty-nine marble and terracotta figurines identified as Aphrodite, only fourteen can be assigned to a specific room within a house. Of those, five are marble statuettes, rare discoveries from Priene houses, which likely account for the care in recording their findspot.[22]

One of the largest assemblages of marble and terracotta statuettes was discovered in House 33 East in a relatively small room located in the southeastern corner of the property (Fig. 3). The roughly eighteen square-meter room contained nine marble statuettes (measuring between approximately 40 and 70 cm), thirty-three terracotta figurines (the largest of which measures 27 cm), in addition to a large collection of course-ware bowls, jugs, *unguentaria*, and the remains of a bronze lamp-holder or *thymiaterion*.[23] Among the finds, Aphrodite and Eros are especially prominent: three marble statuettes (Figs. 4-5) and three

---

[20] W. HOEPFNER, E. L. SCHWANDNER. *Haus und Stadt im klassischen Griechenland*, München, Deutscher Kunstverlag, 1994, p. 188-225.

[21] RUMSCHEID, *Die figürlichen Terrakotten*, p. 34-38.

[22] T. WIEGAND, H. SCHRADER, *Priene: Ergebnisse der Ausgrabungen und Untersuchungen in den Jahren 1895-1898*. Berlin, Reimer, 1904, p. 366-374, Abb. 465-470; RUMSCHEID, *Die figürlichen Terrakotten*, p. 52, cat. nos I.2, I.3, I.5 and I.8.

[23] WIEGAND, SCHRADER, *Priene*, p. 326-327; RUMSCHEID, *Die figürlichen Terrakotten*, p. 51-56. Rumscheid provides a succinct inventory of the statuettes: marble and terracotta statuettes of Aphrodite, terracotta statuettes of Eros, one marble statuette of Dionysos with a panther, and a sampling of other minor terracotta figures, including miscellaneous standing female figures, a herm, a satyr, various grotesques, and genre figures.

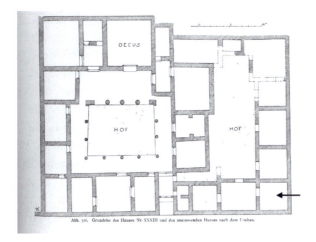

Fig. 3.
Plan of House 33/House 33 East, Priene.
WIEGAND, SCHRADER, *Priene*, p. 297, Abb. 316. Copyright expired.

Fig. 4.
Aphrodite from House 33 East, Priene.
Berlin, Antikensammlung, SK 1533.
Marble, H. 61.5 cm. Photo: bpk
Bildagentur / Antikensammlung,
SMB / Johannes Laurentius.

Fig. 5.
Aphrodite from House 33 East,
Priene. Istanbul Archaeological
Museum, 1052. Marble, H. 51 cm.
Photo: Mendel (Jahrunbekannt).
DAI-Istanbul. Neg. R 24615.

terracotta statuettes of Aphrodite and four terracotta statuettes of Eros in addition to fragments of at least seven others. In his assessment of the finds and archaeological context, Joachim Raeder proposed that the room served as an *andron*, a designation seemingly supported by the numerous examples of Aphrodite and Dionysiac-themed sculptures that alluded to the drinking and erotic activities that characterized Greek symposia.[24] A reassessment of the context and finds by Rumscheid, however, has brought into question the reasons behind the deposition of items and subsequently the function of the room in House 33 East. The considerable diversity of objects deposited in the room, the incomplete nature of some of the finds (e.g., some marble sculptures are missing their bases), the lack of appropriate symposium ware, and the sheer number of objects gathered in such a small space speaks for a room function other than an *andron*. Frank Rumscheid presents reasons for and against attributing the space as an *andron*, and his reasons for designating the space as storage of a household's collection of figurative sculpture while in the midst of renovations is most compelling.[25]

This does not discount the appropriateness of Aphrodite statuettes on display in banqueting rooms. In House 13, a marble statuette of an Aphrodite Anadyomene was found in the *andron* along with the feet of two *klinai*.[26] In House 14, a terracotta statuette of Aphrodite with a dolphin was discovered in room a, identified as the *andron*, along with fragments of a satyr statuette, a large terracotta krater, two inscribed drinking vessels, and bronze *klinai* feet and fittings.[27] Rumscheid admits that some of the room's contents may have fallen from the upper story, but believes that the Aphrodite and satyr statuettes are appropriate to the erotic Dionysiac atmosphere of a banquet room.

---

[24] RAEDER, *Priene*, p. 22-25, 33-38.

[25] RUMSCHEID, *Die figürlichen Terrakotten*, p. 51-56.

[26] WIEGAND, SCHRADER, *Priene*, p. 321-322, 371, Abb. 467; RUMSCHEID, *Die figürlichen Terrakotten*, p. 339.

[27] The terracotta Aphrodite statuette and the satyr statuette, which might have been of marble considering its recorded height of 50 cm, are currently missing. In the neighboring room, identified as the *oikos*, were found *klinai* feet and a bronze horse-head fulcrum. WIEGAND, SCHRADER, *Priene*, p. 322; RUMSCHEID, *Die figürlichen Terrakotten*, p. 44.

A somewhat ambiguous scenario is created by the finds discovered in House 29. Marble and terracotta statuettes were discovered in two basement rooms located to the south of the court and consist of a marble statuette of a nude youth, a marble semi-nude female seated figure wearing a stephane (Aphrodite?) (Fig. 6), a large (52.2 cm) terracotta statuette of a draped female figure wearing a stephane (a possible Aphrodite according to Rumscheid), and a slightly smaller naked Aphrodite terracotta statuette.[28] Considering the modest nature of these two southern rooms, Wiegand proposed that the sculptural finds fell from more formal rooms located on the second story.[29]

FIG. 6.
Aphrodite from House 29, Priene.
Istanbul Archaeological Museum, 746. Marble, H. 34 cm.
Photo: Mendel (Jahrunbekannt). DAI-Istanbul. Neg. R 19750.

[28] RUMSCHEID, *Die figürlichen Terrakotten*, p. 50, cat. no. 20. The second terracotta Aphrodite statuette has not been identified among the Priene finds. See also WIEGAND, SCHRADER, *Priene*, p. 321, Abb. 416 (terracotta draped female), Abb. 461 (nude youth), and Abb. 468 (marble seated female figure).
[29] WIEGAND, SCHRADER, *Priene*, p. 321.

3.2. Delos

In his study *Untersuchungen zur figürlichen Ausstattung delischer Privathaüser*, Martin Kreeb demonstrated that Aphrodite was one of the most popular deities found in (or associated with) Delian houses.[30] Statuettes of Eros were similarly widespread, although unlike the strong preference for marble for depicting Aphrodite, the winged god was typically rendered in terracotta.[31] Unfortunately, in spite of the wealth of material finds preserved on Delos, few works of sculpture were found in situ. The violent attacks incurred on the island's inhabitants in 88 and 69 BC and the resulting looting and destruction of property meant that much of the household contents were heavily disturbed and thus many artifacts, if not carried away by fleeing inhabitants or plundered by invaders, were unlikely to have been discovered in situ by excavators. Of the approximately forty small-scale sculptures of Aphrodite found in the city, only six were recorded as having been discovered in a house while the rest are listed as stray finds discovered in the vicinity of particular houses or recorded as having been found in one of the island's residential quarters.[32]

The House of the Herms provides some of the best evidence regarding the disposition of Aphrodite statuettes in the city residences. To the north of the peristyle court, a large hall (oikos d) was outfitted with two statue bases, one of which contains a partial inscription that appears to name Aphrodite and the other potentially records the name of Praxiteles as maker.[33] As described by Kreeb, the statue bases (and corresponding statues) were prominently displayed so that they were easily visible to visitors upon first entering the house and peristyle court. This and other evidence of statuary display in Delian houses led Kreeb to propose

---

[30] KREEB, *Untersuchungen*, p. 58-59.

[31] KREEB, *Untersuchungen*, p. 60.

[32] KREEB, *Untersuchungen*, p. 11. The following are the marble statuettes as inventoried by Kreeb: S 19.2, Peribolos St., House C; S 24.1, House of the Herms, peristyle court; S 24.12, House of the Herms, stairwell landing; S 25.2, Inopos House; S 42.1 and S 42.2 (statuette base), Haus Th VI O room d; S 46.4, Theater quarter, House VIII A. I am excluding the sculptural finds from the Establishment of the Poseidoniastes as it functioned more as a clubhouse than a traditional residence.

[33] KREEB, *Untersuchungen*, p. 37-39, cat. nos S 24.9 and S 24.12.

that a number of sculptural works were carefully arranged to be prominently and aesthetically displayed in the more visible house areas, in particular the courts, suggesting that domestic sculpture increasingly blurred the lines between functionality and decoration.[34]

There is some evidence that artistic works may have fallen from rooms located on the upper floors and include not only sculpture but mosaics and paintings as well. From the House of the Herms, fragments of a second marble statuette of Aphrodite along with pieces of a small marble sculpture of Artemis were discovered in the peristyle court and appear to have fallen from the upper floor.[35] Found in room d of House Th VI O were fragments of two marble statuettes – a torso from an Aphrodite Anadyomene and remnants of a second female figure possibly representing Aphrodite loosening her sandal or another Anadyomene – that can't be excluded as coming from one of the rooms on the second floor.[36] On the other hand, there is reliable evidence that mosaics and paintings of Aphrodite and Eros adorned a variety of rooms, including those located on the upper floors, suggesting continued expansion of the use of decoration to suit various needs of household members.[37]

3.3. Ephesos

The city of Ephesos offers a clearer picture of the use of sculpture in Greek houses, albeit predominantly from the first three centuries AD. Excavations of the Terrace Houses have uncovered a tremendous amount of architectural and sculptural material, and it's not feasible to review all the sculptures of Aphrodite found at the site for this current study. Instead, I will focus on a few assemblages and rooms that can best provide useful information regarding the contexts and possible functions of Aphrodite sculptures in late Hellenistic and Roman Ephesian houses.

---

[34] KREEB, *Untersuchungen*, p. 33-43.
[35] KREEB, *Untersuchungen*, p. 50. Cat. no. S 24.1: nude torso of Aphrodite, possible Medici type; cat. no. S 24.2: Artemis.
[36] KREEB, *Untersuchungen*, p. 15-17, cat. no. S 42.1 and S 42.2.
[37] KREEB, *Untersuchungen*, p. 51-57; Tables V, VIII, and IX.

In one of the earlier levels beneath Terrace House 1, excavators discovered the remains of a Late Hellenistic peristyle house. Among the finds were terracotta figurines and a smaller number of marble statuettes from some of the rooms surrounding the peristyle.[38] The ground floor rooms of the peristyle house apparently were used for storage, and therefore the collection of statuettes and other furnishings likely fell from the second floor during the destruction of the house, which might have occurred during an earthquake in 23 AD.[39] A large collection of objects was found in the debris of the upper floor of room 1, including two terracotta statuettes of Aphrodite loosening her sandal (Figs. 7-8) and two Eros and Psyche figurines.[40] Additional terracottas were found: fragments of female figurines, a torso of a male "puppet," and masks, as well as a small terracotta *thymiaterion* and the remains of an elaborate marble table. The excavators suggest that the upstairs room, decorated with a white tesserae floor, white painted walls, and filled with terracotta figurines displayed on an ornate marble table, alluded to the world of Aphrodite and Eros and would have been used for leisure and social occasions; however, the presence of the *thymiaterion* within the assemblage suggests a cultic character to the group of figurines.[41]

At the same time, it is evident that larger sculptures of Aphrodite were utilized in more conspicuous areas of the Terrace Houses, signifying an increased interest in decorative displays similar to what Martin Kreeb demonstrated with his study of Late Hellenistic sculpture on Delos. Although not found in situ, a 49 cm marble statuette of Aphrodite (Fig. 9a-b) discovered in Stiegengasse 2 just outside of Residence 3 of Terrace House 1,

---

[38] For a discussion of the finds, see C. LANG-AUINGER et al., *Hanghaus 1 in Ephesos: Funde und Ausstattung*, FiE VIII/4, Wien, Verlag der Österreichischen Akademie der Wissenschaften, 2003, p. 153-208, 209-252.

[39] E. RATHMAYR, "Sculptural Programs of Specific Residential Units of Terrace House 1 and 2 in Ephesos", in M. AURENHAMMER (ed.), *Sculpture in Roman Asia Minor: Proceedings of the International Conference at Selçuk, 1st-3rd October 2013*, Sonderschriften OAI 56, Wien, Holzhausen, 2018, p. 129-145 (p. 129-130). For a reassessment of the finds, see RUMSCHEID, *Die figürlichen Terrakotten*, p. 116-118.

[40] C. LANG-AUINGER et al., *Hanghaus 1*, p. 213-220, cat. no. TK 3 – TK 6.

[41] C. LANG-AUINGER et al., *Hanghaus 1*, p. 217; RUMSCHEID, *Die figürlichen Terrakotten*, p. 116-119.

FIG. 7.
Aphrodite loosening her sandal,
early 1st century AD. Terracotta,
H. 30.8 cm. Archaeological Museum,
Ephesus, 34/75/92.
Photo: OeAW-OeAI / Niki Gail.

FIG. 8.
Aphrodite loosening her sandal, early
1st century AD. Terracotta, H. 13 cm.
Excavation house storage, Austrian
Archaeological Institute in Ephesus.
Photo: OeAW-OeAI / Niki Gail.

FIG. 9a-b.
Aphrodite fountain figure from Stiegengasse 2, Terrace House 1, Ephesus.
Late Hellenistic. Marble, H. 49 cm. Archaeological Museum, Ephesus, 1909.
Photo: OeAW-OeAI / Niki Gail.

was used as a fountain figure and was equipped with a hole in her breast to allow water to spring forth.[42] Water features were clearly in evidence in some of the other residences and it is easy to imagine the small Aphrodite fountain figure decorating a fountain in one of the peristyle courts.[43]

More impressive are the sculptural finds from Terrace House 2, Residence 6. This large residence underwent a series of major renovations and additions during the early to mid-second century AD, most likely initiated by the homeowner Gaius Flavius Furius Aptus who, according to inscriptions found within the house, served as a priest of Dionysos but likely held other prominent civic and religious offices in the city.[44] While numerous marble and terracotta sculptures of Aphrodite were found throughout the house, she was perhaps most prominent in Room 36, one of the opulent reception rooms located south of the peristyle, which provided access to the luxuriously appointed Marble Hall 31 and Apsidal Hall 8. During the middle of the second century AD, Furius Aptus installed a large water basin in Room 36 and on either side of the stepped entryway to Apsidal Hall 8, erected two statues, of which only their inscribed statue bases survive.[45] The inscriptions mention both Gaius (Flavius Furius

---

[42] M. AURENHAMMER, "Sculptures of Gods and Heroes from Ephesos", in H. KOESTER (ed.), *Ephesos: Metropolis of Asia: An Interdisciplinary Approach to Its Archaeology, Religion and Culture*, Cambridge, Harvard University Press, 2010, p. 251-280 (p. 261); M. AURENHAMMER, "Skulpturen aus Stein und Bronze", in C. LANG-AUINGER et al., *Hanghaus 1*, p. 153-208 (p. 189 and 208, cat. no. S 125).

[43] For sculptures on display in gardens, see B. S. RIDGWAY, "The Setting of Greek Sculpture", *Hesperia* 40 (1971), p. 336-356 (p. 352-353); and G. MERKER, *The Hellenistic Sculpture of Rhodes*, Studies in Mediterranean Archaeology 40, Göteborg, Aström, 1973, p. 15. From the Casa Romana on Kos, four Aphrodite marble statuettes were excavated from the two peristyles, all of which were said to have been found in the vicinity of two water basins: M. ALBERTOCCHI, "An Example of Domestic Garden Statuary at Cos: The Casa Romana", in I. JENKINS, G. B. WAYWELL (eds.), *Sculptors and Sculpture of Caria and the Dodecanese*, London, British Museum Press, 1997, p. 120-126.

[44] For the sculptural program of Terrace House 2, House 6, see RATHMAYR, "Sculptural Programs", p. 135-137; H. THÜR et al., *Hanghaus 2 in Ephesos: Die Wohneinheit 6: Baubefund, Ausstattung, Funde*. FiE VIII/9, Wien, Verlag der Österreichischen Akademie der Wissenschaften, 2014, p. 386-387, 391-396.

[45] RATHMAYR, "Sculptural Programs", p. 135-137; THÜR et al., *Hanghaus 2*, p. 391-392.

Aptus) and Aphrodite, who is effusively honored with accolades to her beauty and beneficence, with prominence given to her divine birth from the sea.[46] The reference to Aphrodite's birth and in particular a suggestion that the goddess is wringing sea water from her hair led Elisabeth Rathmayr to propose that the two missing statues depicted Aphrodite Anadyomene and were arranged for decorative effect as pendant figures on either side of the entryway to Apsidal Hall 8. In addition to the water basin and statues in Room 36, water features were also installed in both Apsidal Hall 8 and Marble Hall 31, which not only heightened the illusion of Aphrodite's association with the sea but created an impressive opulent atmosphere meant to convey the wealth and status of the homeowner.[47]

The sculptures of Aphrodite from the Terrace Houses at Ephesos offer a unique opportunity to assess the goddess's appearance in domestic contexts over a lengthy chronological period. Terracotta and marble representations of the goddess (in addition to depictions of Eros) are found in the earliest Hellenistic inhabitation levels and were prevalent in rooms grouped around the peristyle court.[48] The use of terracotta figurines persisted into the Roman period and as the houses grew in size and grandeur, they could be found in a greater variety of rooms. According to the excavators, terracotta and marble sculptures in general (and particularly those of Aphrodite) could serve a religious-cultic

---

[46] Thür et al., *Hanghaus 2*, p. 343, cat no. IST 2-3. For the Greek text and English translation by Stefan Hagel, see Rathmayr, "Sculptural Programs", p. 136, fn. 60. Eastern base: Ζηνὸς καλλιγόνοιο καὶ εὐτέ- / κνοιο Διώνης ἀβροτάτη / μακάρων χαῖρε θεὰ θύγατερ. / ὄντως φρογενής τε καὶ ἐκ πόν- / τοιο βέβηκας χαιτάων παλά- / μαις κύματα πεμπομένη (Daughter of fair-siring Zeus and Dione, mother of beauty, tenderest always of all blissful divinities, hail! Truly born in foam and out of the sea thou arrivest, sending with your arms surges of waves from your hair. Translation by Stefan Hagel/IKAnt-OeAW). Western base: Γάϊον καὶ Περικλῆα σάω πολύολβε / Κυθήρη ἠμὲν ἐπὶ ξεινῆς ἠδ' ἄρ' / ἐνὶ σφετέρῃ / ξεῖνον ξεινοδόχον τέ. σὲ γὰρ περί- / αλλα θεάων τείουσιν προφρόνως / πάντα σεβιζόμενοι. (Gaius and Pericles, o Cythera, provider of riches, guard, both when they're abroad and when they stay in their homes, both as guests and as hosts. For it's you of all goddesses whom they honour foremost and first, paying you worship and awe).

[47] Rathmayr, "Sculptural Programs", p. 135-173.

[48] E. Rathmayr, "Terrakotten aus dem Hanghaus 2 in Ephesos", in Lafli, Muller, *Figurines de terre cuite en Méditerranée*, p. 274.

or decorative function (or a combination of both); however, distinguishing their exact purpose necessitates a more precise understanding of their original contexts.[49] Thus, while the assemblage of terracottas from the Hellenistic peristyle house in Terrace House 1 suggests a more private religious veneration of Aphrodite and Eros, the installation of two pendant Aphrodite statues (either life-size or smaller) with accompanying inscriptions honoring Furius Aptus in the larger and more luxurious Residence 6 of Terrace House 2 not only pays homage to Aphrodite and her gifts but also acts to reflect the status and wealth of the houseowner.[50]

3.4. Summary of Evidence

In this limited survey, I hope to have demonstrated, that while sculptures of Aphrodite were occasionally found in *androns*, banqueting rooms, and other highly visible spaces such as peristyle courts, she also could be found in other less visible areas of the house, namely rooms on the second floor; however, determining the functions of upstairs rooms is problematic.[51] Based on scant references in ancient sources, it has been assumed that the second floor was the location of the *gynaikon*, but the idea that the Greek house could easily be separated into men's and women's quarters has been challenged by Michael Jameson and Lisa Nevett.[52] According to these recent studies, the distribution of artifacts does not support separation of the sexes as implied by the Greek terms *gynaikon* and *andron*, but rather suggests a more

---

[49] THÜR et al., *Hanghaus 2*, p. 370-371 and 377-387; RATHMAYR, "Terrakotten", p. 276-277.

[50] LANG-AUINGER et al., *Hanghaus 1*, p. 213-220; RATHMAYR, "Sculptural Programs", p. 135-137.

[51] M. TRÜMPER, "Differentiation in the Hellenistic Houses of Delos: The Question of Functional Areas", *BSA Studies* 15 (2007) p. 323-334.

[52] M. JAMESON, "Private Space in the Greek City", in O. MURRAY, S. PRICE, *The Greek City from Homer to Alexander*, Oxford, Clarendon Press, 1990, p. 171-198. L. C. NEVETT, "Separation or Seclusion? Towards an Archaeological Approach to Investigating Women in the Greek Household in the Fifth to Third Centuries B.C.", in M. P. PEARSON, *Architecture and Order: Approaches to Social Space*, London, Routledge, 1994, p. 98-112.

fluid use of domestic space.⁵³ While upper-story rooms may not have served as the *gynaikon*, it is natural to assume that whatever the purpose of these rooms, women would have been familiar with the spaces and with the imagery/sculpture on display there. It has been suggested that the second floor was utilized for sleeping by various members of the household, and if so, Aphrodite figurines located upstairs may have served different social or religious functions than the erotic-themed decoration appropriate to the symposium.⁵⁴

At this point, it is worthwhile to review the types of Aphrodite statuettes found in Greek domestic contexts. At Priene, Delos, and Ephesus, we see a clear preference for distinct types. Aphrodite loosening her sandal, Aphrodite Anadyomene, and the Knidia were most widespread, followed by Aphrodite leaning on a pillar; however, this last type was heavily favored on Delos, which skews our perception of her popularity. The version known as Aphrodite Pseliumene was slightly less numerous, and rather surprisingly the Crouching Aphrodite is represented by only a few examples. Clearly, some types were favored over others, which leads to the question of why. Two predominant types – Anadyomene and Knidia – typically represent the goddess nude in erotically charged poses. The first shows Aphrodite rising from the sea with hands raised to arrange or wring water from her hair (a pose that draws attention to the curves of her body). The second, based on Praxiteles' famous sculpture, depicts the goddess at her bath. Intriguingly, the most popular type appears to have been Aphrodite loosening her sandal, which depicts the goddess in a convoluted posture, but again one that draws the viewer's gaze to her body, particularly her smooth back and rounded buttocks. What was the appeal of these statue types? This rather straightforward question can't be fully answered here, but it should be noted that all these versions reference either the

---

[53] JAMESON, "Private Space"; L. C. NEVETT, "Gender Relations in the Classical Greek Household: The Archaeological Evidence", *BSA* 90 (1995), p. 363-381; L. C. NEVETT, *House and Society in the Ancient Greek World*, Cambridge, Cambridge University Press, 1999, p. 53-79.

[54] In *Thesmophoriazusae* (481), Aristophanes describes how a newly married couple sleeps upstairs.

goddess's sea-born birth or the act of bathing, both of which portray the goddess either nude or partially nude, highlighting the beauty and sensuality of Aphrodite's body.

4. *Aphrodite in Syria and Egypt*

If we look to related imagery of the goddess from Egypt and Syria, we see a similar trend in the preference for certain Aphrodite types. From Syria, a considerable number of bronze statuettes of Aphrodite (or a hellenized version of Astarte) were discovered in the nineteenth century, many of which ended up in the de Clercq Collection (Fig. 10).[55] The most prevalent types include the Knidia, Anadyomene, and versions showing the goddess adorning herself with jewelry, commonly referred to as Aphrodite Pseliumene.[56] Anton de Ridder, who published the de Clercq Collection, mentions an ancient tradition whereby women in Syria were buried with a statuette of Aphrodite (or Astarte) beneath her head.[57] Based on the high number of well-preserved Aphrodite/Astarte statuettes reputed to have been found in Syria, it is very likely that most came from tombs based on their excellent state of preservation. These bronze statuettes from Syria are often associated with a series of bronze figurines said to have been manufactured in Egypt, which similarly depict Aphrodite (or more precisely Isis-Aphrodite) adorning herself with jewelry (Pseliumene) (Fig. 11).[58] A clue to understanding these bronze statuettes from Syria and Egypt may be found in the ancient town of Karanis in Lower Egypt, where excavators discovered a number of Aphrodite figurines, in marble and bronze, from some of the houses once occupied by an ethnically diverse

---

[55] Most said to be from Sidon and Tartus: A. DE RIDDER, *Collection De Clercq, Tome 3: Les bronzes*, Paris, Leroux, 1905.

[56] Plin. *HN* 34.69; Tatianus, *Ad Gr.* 33.35; 34.36; N. FRANKEN, "Statuette der Aphrodite Pseliomene nach Praxiteles", *Stiftung zur Förderung der Hamburgischen Kunstsammlungen* (2011-2012), p. 46-49; R. FLEISCHER, "Eine Gruppe syrisch-phönikischer Bronzestatuetten-Basen", *DM* 1 (1983) p. 31-42.

[57] RIDDER, *De Clercq*, p. 3; E. PIOT, "Vases peints athéniens", *GazArch* 4 (1878) p. 55-59 (p. 57, n. 1).

[58] JENTEL, "Quelques aspects d'Aphrodite", p. 151-155. See also A. HEKLER, "Alexandrinische", p. 112-120.

DOMESTIC APHRODITE, GODDESS OF DESIRE AND SEDUCTION

FIG. 10.
Aphrodite, 1st-2nd century AD.
From Syria. Bronze,
H. 28.2 cm. Louvre Museum,
Paris, BR 4420. Photo
by Hervé Lewandowski:
© RMN-Grand Palais / Art
Resources, NY.

FIG. 11.
Isis-Aphrodite, 2nd century
AD. From Lower Egypt.
Bronze, H. 57.5 cm.
Louvre Museum, Paris, BR 12.
Photo by Tony Querrec:
© RMN-Grand Palais /
Art Resources, NY.

FIG. 12.
Aphrodite from Karanis,
Egypt, 2nd-4th century AD.
Bronze, H. 34 cm. Kelsey
Museum of Archaeology,
University of Michigan, KM
10728. Photo courtesy Kelsey
Museum of Archaeology.

population of Egyptians, Greeks, and Romans.[59] The Aphrodite statuettes depict the goddess either nude or semi-nude, and residents displayed a strong preference for Anadyomene versions with one example in bronze of Aphrodite Pseliumene (Fig. 12).[60] The majority of the statuettes were found in contexts dating from the mid-first to fourth century AD, but a few of the figurines may date considerably earlier.[61] As to the function of these Aphrodite statuettes, marriage contracts preserved on papyri from various sites in Lower Egypt, particularly Ptolemais and Naucra-

---

[59] E. K. GAZDA, *Guardians of the Nile: Sculptures from Karanis in the Fayoum (c. 250 BC – AD 450)*, Ann Arbor, Kelsey Museum of Archaeology, 1977.

[60] GAZDA, *Guardians*, cat. nos 16-20; 39-40; 48. Also found were a number of Eros statuettes (cat. nos 41-45).

[61] GAZDA, *Guardians*, cat. nos 16 (second or first century BC) and 18 (second century BC).

tis, may provide an answer.⁶² The marriage contracts, typically written in demotic or Greek, range in date from the end of the fourth century BC to the sixth century AD, but critical to the topic at hand are contracts that date to the second to third century AD, which specifically mention bronze statuettes of Aphrodite as part of the dowries the brides will bring to their new home.⁶³ Thus, we should imagine that many of the Syrian-Egyptian goddess statuettes were once originally on display in houses, perhaps in household shrines or even in private spaces such as bedrooms. Whichever the case, it is clear that these statuettes were closely tied to the women of the house in their roles as brides and mothers.

5. *Aphrodite and the new bride*

Although Aphrodite's appearance in Greek domestic contexts appears sudden, she in fact had long been associated with pivotal moments in the lives of women, particularly at the time of their marriage. During the Archaic and Classical periods, Athenian vase painting is rich in imagery illustrating the pivotal events that comprise the ancient wedding ceremony. Appropriately, the vases used in those very rituals provide us with visuals that flesh out the description of weddings preserved in literary sources.⁶⁴ Additionally, vases closely connected to a woman's domestic life, for example *pyxides*, *lekythoi* and *unguentaria*, which she might have received at the *epaulia* after the wedding, were frequently decorated with wedding imagery and could have been used throughout her lifetime and, at her death, interred in her grave.⁶⁵

---

⁶² F. BURKHALTER, "Les statuettes en bronze d'Aphrodite en Égypte romaine d'après les documents papyrologiques", *RA* 1 (1990), p. 51-60; POMEROY, *Women in Hellenistic Egypt*, p. 83-124; M. PARCA, "The Women of Ptolemaic Egypt: The View from Papyrology", in S. L. JAMES, S. DILLON (eds.), *A Companion to Women in the Ancient World*, Malden, Wiley-Blackwell, 2012, p. 316-328.

⁶³ POMEROY, *Women in Hellenistic Egypt*, p. 84; BURKHALTER, "Les statuettes en bronze", p. 55.

⁶⁴ For a summary of these sources, see J. H. OAKLEY, R. H. SINOS, *The Wedding in Ancient Athens*, Madison, University of Wisconsin Press, 1993.

⁶⁵ In Athens, vases typically decorated with wedding scenes were *loutrophoroi* and *lebetes gamikoi*; however, at least in the case of *loutrophoroi*, they were usually

Vase painting scenes associated with the wedding ritual commonly focus on the preparations of the bride, including the prenuptial bath, dress and adornment, and the bride's transportation to her new house. An Attic red-figure *pyxis* in the Metropolitan Museum of Art (Fig. 13) highlights some of the stages of this process: a nude figure of the bride kneels besides Eros who assists in rinsing her hair; next a woman with long flowing hair, presumably the bride, adjusts her gown and again is attended by Eros, who holds a small chest; two other women (attendants) decorate a *loutrophoros* with ribbons, followed by a woman (bride?) who looks out at the viewer as she arranges her hair. The scene appears to culminate with a separate scene, set off by two architectural columns; as described by John Oakley and Rebecca Sinos, on the left is the bride, seated on a *klismos* with an Eros perched on her lap, followed by Aphrodite seated in the center, and a third woman who perhaps represents Peitho (persuasion).[66] In some respects, the New York *pyxis* is representational of standard Greek wedding scene imagery: the themes of bathing, dressing, and adornment are repeated over and over. Eros is a frequent participant, assisting in enhancing the beauty and desirability of the bride, proffering chests and vessels, adorning her with jewelry, or holding wreaths and sashes. Elsewhere, Eros flutters about the heads of the bride and groom, serving as a visual symbol of the desire instilled in the groom by the bride's appearance (Fig. 14).[67] Less common is the scene where the bride is outfitted with *nymphides*, her wedding sandals. An Attic red-figure *lekythos* in the Boston Museum of Fine Arts (Fig. 15) shows a bride preparing for her wedding: attendants assist her with a necklace and her bridal crown, while Eros kneels beside her tying her *nymphides*.

In the fourth to third century BC, we see a further development of female bathing and grooming imagery appearing on Greek bronze mirrors, this time explicitly depicting nude bathers

---

dedicated to the Sanctuary of the Nymphe after the wedding: OAKLEY, SINOS, *Wedding*, p. 43.

[66] OAKLEY, SINOS, *Wedding*, p. 17, figs. 20-21.

[67] R. F. SUTTON JR., "Nuptial Eros: The Visual Discourse of Marriage in Classical Athens", *JWalt* 55/56 (1997/1998), p. 27-48.

Fig. 13.
Attic red-figure pyxis decorated with bridal scene (drawing), *c.* 420-400 BC.
H. 17.5 cm. Metropolitan Museum of Art, New York, 1972.118.148.
Bequest of Walter C. Baker, 1971.
Photo © The Metropolitan Museum of Art. Image source: Art Resource, NY.

Fig. 14.
Attic red-figure loutrophoros with wedding scene, *c.* 400 BC. H. 54.3 cm. Metropolitan Museum of Art, New York, 75.2.15. Gift of Samuel Ward, 1875. Photo © The Metropolitan Museum of Art. Image source: Art Resource, NY.

Fig. 15.
Attic red-figure oil flask (lekythos) in the form of an acorn with scene of bridal preparations. In the manner of the Meidias Painter, *c.* 410-400 BC. 16.2 × 6 cm. Museum of Fine Arts, Boston, Anonymous gift, 95.1402. Photo © 2022 Museum of Fine Arts, Boston.

Fig. 16.
Greek folding mirror (interior): Pan and nymph, *c.* 300-280 BC.
Bronze, D. 13.5 cm. Berlin, Antikensammlung, SMB Misc. 8148.
Photo: bpk Bildagentur / Antikensammlung, Staatliche Museen zu Berlin /
Johannes Laurentius / Art Resources, NY.

often identified as nymphs.[68] In his study of some of these mirrors, Alexander Heinemann describes how the nymph imagery would especially appeal to a new bride as the Greek word *nymphe* refers to both nymph and bride. Furthermore, these bathing nymphs often adopt poses derived from Aphrodite iconography, particularly Crouching Aphrodite and variants of the Knidia.[69] In the Berlin Antikensammlung, the engraved lid of an early third-century BC Greek folding mirror (Fig. 16) depicts a female nude crouching in a cave in the act of bathing. As she washes her hair, she appears oblivious to the figure of a lustful Pan who reacts to her naked beauty; his head protrudes from the cave wall as does his genitalia which functions as the fountain, providing as it were the water for the bathing nymph. As with the wedding vase imagery discussed above, the newlywed bride was surely meant to see herself in these bathing and grooming scenes. The imagery both reflects the ideal behavior of the young bride

[68] HEINEMANN, "The Cave, the Gaze, the Bride"; A. STEWART, "A Tale of Seven Nudes: The Capitoline and Medici Aphrodites, four nymphs at Elean Herakleia, and an Aphrodite at Megalopolis", *Antichthon* 44 (2010), p. 12-32.

[69] STEWART, "A Tale of Seven Nudes".

and reinforces the reasons why such bathing and beautification rituals are necessary: to enhance the desirability of a new wife.[70]

Similar to the vase imagery and mirror decoration discussed above, sculptures of Aphrodite found in Greek domestic contexts must have served as exemplars for Greek brides.[71] As described in the *Homeric Hymn to Aphrodite*, the goddess's elaborate bathing and beauty rituals were undertaken to entice her lovers.[72] Vase imagery depicting young women at their bridal toilette closely mirror Aphrodite's own seductive preparations; the incorporation of Eros into these bridal scenes also blurs the boundaries between myth and reality.[73] As well, sculptural representations of Aphrodite bathing and those alluding to her birth at sea, including the Knidia, Anadyomene, and Crouching Aphrodite, directly reference ritualistic bathing practices specifically associated with sexual intercourse: the prenuptial bath and one taken after intercourse.[74] In her study of the Aphrodite of Knidos, Kris Seaman clearly describes how the act of bathing and adornment enhanced the goddess's desirability and induced fertility.[75] Aphro-

---

[70] HEINEMANN, "The Cave, the Gaze, the Bride". For the use of repeated images in defining femininity, see N. BOYMEL KAMPEN, "Women's Desire, Archaeology, and Feminist Theory", in D. B. COUNTS, R. R. HOLLOWAY, A. TUCK (eds.), *Koine: Mediterranean Studies in Honor of R. Ross Holloway*. Oxford, Oxbow Books, 2009, p. 207-215 (p. 210).

[71] W. NEUMER-PFAU, *Studien zur Ikonographie und gesellschaftlichen Funktion hellenistischer Aphrodite-Statuen*, Bonn, Habelt, 1982, p. 55-60; N. BOYMEL KAMPEN, "Gender Studies", in *Contextualizing Classics: Ideology, Performance, Dialogue: Essays in Honor of John J. Peradotto*. Lanham, Rowman and Littlefield, 1999, p. 269-283 (p. 277); BOYMEL KAMPEN, "Epilogue", p. 269-270.

[72] *Homeric Hymn to Aphrodite*, 53-201.

[73] There appears to be deliberate conflation between images of Aphrodite, mythological women, and those representing mortal women: R. KOUSSER, "The World of Aphrodite in the Late Fifth Century B.C.", in C. MARCONI (ed.), *Greek Vases, Images, and Controversies: Proceedings of the Conference Sponsored by the Center for the Ancient Mediterranean at Columbia University, 23-24 March 2002*, Leiden, Brill, 2004, p. 97-112; R. F. SUTTON, JR., "Female Bathers and the Emergence of the Female Nude in Greek Art", in C. KOSSO, A. SCOTT (eds.), *The Nature and Function of Water, Baths, Bathing, and Hygiene from Antiquity Through the Renaissance*, Leiden, Brill, 2009, p. 61-86; S. HUYSECOM-HAXHI, "Aphrodite, Coming of Age and Marriage: Contextualisation and Reconsideration of the Nude Young Woman Kneeling in a Shell", in G. PAPANTONIOU, D. MICHAELIDES, M. DIKOMITOU-ELIADOU (eds.), *Hellenistic and Roman Terracottas*, Leiden and Boston, Brill, 2019, p. 259-271.

[74] SEAMAN, "Retrieving the Original Aphrodite", p. 561-562.

[75] SEAMAN, "Retrieving the Original Aphrodite", p. 561-568.

dite's origin story, born from the cast off genitals of Ouranos, strongly links her birth with fertility; moreover, for Aphrodite, bathing is equated with sex, either in preparation for marriage (or seduction) or for refreshment and ritually cleansing after intercourse.[76] Just as Aphrodite is anointed with oils, dressed in luxurious purple and gold garments, and bedecked in jewelry decorated with precious stones to aid in her seduction of Anchises, a bride is likewise cleansed, garbed in beautiful clothing, and adorned with necklaces and a crown to instill sexual desire in her husband.[77]

Finally, some comments should be said regarding the widespread popularity of the Aphrodite loosening her sandal type, with twenty-five known examples from Priene, Delos, and Ephesus.[78] By and large, many of the Aphrodite statuettes discovered in Greek domestic contexts reference either the goddess's birth or one of her ritual baths in association with marriage and/or seduction. The act of removing her sandal appears to be rather non-descript and doesn't seem to relate to any particular myth.[79] Rather, it has been suggested that the type was developed as a new and innovative way to yet again show the goddess in the act of undressing, perhaps in preparation for a bath.[80] Yet, if we can associate many of these Aphrodite statue types found in domestic contexts with the marriage ritual, the sandal loosening motif might reference the new bride undressing for her husband and removing her *nymphides* (wedding sandals) in preparation for the wedding night.

---

[76] HAVELOCK, *The Aphrodite of Knidos*, p. 23-24.

[77] R. F. SUTTON, JR., "Female Bathers", p. 68; HUYSECOM-HAXHI, "Aphrodite", p. 268; OAKLEY, SINOS, *Wedding*, p. 15-21. For Aphrodite's seduction of Anchises: *Homeric Hymn to Aphrodite*, pp. 53-201.

[78] The sandal loosening type (also referred to as the sandalbinder) has been extensively studied. Attempts to discern an "original" version have been inconclusive. For a discussion of the type with references to earlier bibliography, see L. LESSWING, "An Aphrodite Sandalbinder Statuette in the Princeton University Art Museum", *Record of the Art Museum, Princeton Museum* 74 (2015), p. 38-54.

[79] L. LESSWING, "An Aphrodite Sandalbinder", p. 45.

[80] For the statue type in association with *hetairai*, see F. RUMSCHEID, "Sandalen-Geschichten", in K. STEMMER (ed.), *In den Gärten der Aphrodite*, Berlin 2001, p. 125-137.

A critical change that seems to have taken place between the Classical period, when vases and bronze mirrors were most evident, and the Hellenistic period, when figurines of Aphrodite become increasingly common, is the locations of these objects within the Greek house. While the vases and mirrors may have been used and viewed primarily by women in more secluded spaces, sculptures of Aphrodite begin to appear in more prominent areas of the house and thus were visible to a wider spectrum of the house inhabitants, namely both men and women. As a goddess of marriage, Aphrodite had a pivotal role in bringing a husband and wife together in marital harmony, particularly as the purpose of marriage was for reproduction and the begetting of legitimate children.[81]

6. Conclusion

In the Greek world, the goddess Aphrodite was worshipped in many guises: as Aphrodite Pandemos, her powers were implored to join together groups of people as well as men and women in marriage; in her guise of Aphrodite Ourania, her powers of fertility were invoked; and as a sea-born goddess, she was venerated as Euploia (good sailing) and Limenia (of the harbor). Thus, to search for just one reason behind her extraordinary prevalence in Greek domestic contexts is ill-conceived. To male viewers her appearance in the *andron* may have communicated messages of the erotic pleasures embodied by the goddess; *hetairai* as well, who looked upon Aphrodite as their patron goddess, saw within her ways in which they could utilize erotic power and seductive charms to beguile men.[82] Aphrodite also had a critical role to play for women in general. She long held great importance to the lives of women, especially in regard to their personal experiences as young women, new wives, and mothers. Rather than see Aphrodite as a goddess newly introduced to Hellenistic households, the goddess in fact had long been present in Greek houses, notably

---

[81] Plut. *Amat.* 23 (76); POMEROY, *Women*, p. 31-32.
[82] SEAMAN, "Retrieving the Original Aphrodite", p. 567; M. LEE, "Other 'Ways of Seeing': Female Viewers of the Knidian Aphrodite", *Helios* 42 (2016), p. 103-122.

through her appearance on items closely associated with women, including nuptial and toilette vases and personal items such as mirrors and jewelry. As a fertility goddess, particularly one associated with physical desire and fecundity, she played a critical role in a successful marriage, the primary purpose of which was the production of legitimate offspring.[83]

Aphrodite iconography of the Classical period, specifically relating to bridal scenes of bathing and adornment on red-figure toilette vases and decorative bronze relief mirrors, objects closely connected to the domestic lives of women, may have provided the impetus behind the appearance of some sculptural types in houses of the Hellenistic and Greek Imperial periods. Yet, it is with the appearance of innovative sculpture types beginning in the fourth century and continuing into the Hellenistic period that seems to have accelerated the trend.[84] Just as a woman may have contemplated the female-centric mythological imagery on her vases and jewelry, so too might she have looked upon a statuette of Aphrodite and seen the goddess as both an inspiration and a role-model for female desirability.[85]

As to whether the terracotta and marble statuettes of Aphrodite were the object of traditional cult activities involving prayers, libations, and offerings, determination should be made on a case-by-case basis. The Aphrodite and Eros terracotta statuettes from the Late Hellenistic peristyle house beneath Terrace House 1 at Ephesus certainly appear to have been the focus of cult ritual, but we might look upon such imagery with an eye towards degree rather than as purely religious-cultic or decorative. It is doubtful that sculptures of Aphrodite and Eros were ever purely decorative in the sense that only the aesthetic properties of the artworks were important. Judging from the prevalence of Aphrodite in Greek domestic art, the goddess served an essential role

---

[83] Xen. *Oec.* 7.18-17.41; Dem. *Neaer.* 59.122; Men. *Sam.* 726-727.

[84] NEUMER-PFAU, *Studien zur Ikonographie*; H.-H. VON PRITTWITZ UND GAFFRON, *Der Wandel der Aphrodite: Archäologische Studien zu weiblichen halbbekleideten Statuetten des späten Hellenismus*. Bonn, Habelt, 1988; HAVELOCK, *The Aphrodite of Knidos*.

[85] The role of the female viewer in connection with images of Aphrodite is prominent in the work of Natalie Boymel Kampen: BOYMEL KAMPEN, "Epilogue: Gender and Desire"; BOYMEL KAMPEN, "Gender Studies", p. 269-283; BOYMEL KAMPEN, "Women's Desire", p. 207-215.

in overseeing the domestic, social, and religious needs of diverse members within the household. The dearth of literary sources on private domestic cult practices in general may account for our incomplete understanding of Aphrodite's presence and function in the private sphere, but more likely it is due to the meager evidence we have of the experiences of ancient Greek women, an omission which is belied by the widespread popularity of Aphrodite imagery in the home and the fundamental role the goddess played in women's daily lives.

NICOLAS AMOROSO

DÉDOUBLEMENTS DE DIVINITÉS DANS LES LARAIRES ROMAINS : POLYMORPHIE DES IMAGES ET MULTIPLICITÉ DES CHAMPS D'ACTION *

Si le riche dossier des laraires pompéiens montre à quel point la religion domestique romaine s'articule sur le culte des Lares, d'autres divinités domestiques – dont le nombre varie d'une *domus* à l'autre – prenaient place dans les sanctuaires des maisons et jouaient un rôle tout aussi important. Tantôt « fixes » lorsqu'elles sont représentées en peinture ou « mobiles » dans le cas des figurines, les images de ces divinités devaient refléter les préférences religieuses du maître de maison. De la découverte des cités vésuviennes aux fouilles les plus récentes, l'archéologie nous fait ainsi connaître une importante série de panthéons miniatures en bronze figés à un moment donné par une destruction ou un abandon. Parmi ces ensembles, inventoriés et documentés par nos prédécesseurs[1], nous observons un phénomène qui n'a toutefois jamais été étudié de manière isolée : celui du dédoublement

---

* Nos remerciements les plus vifs sont adressés aux éditeurs de ce volume pour leur proposition de contribution. Nous souhaitons aussi remercier les collègues qui nous ont autorisé à publier les photographies des objets de leurs collections : Madame Sophie Bärtschi Delbarre (Conservatrice, Site et Musée romain d'Avenches), Madame Clara Agustoni (Conservatrice, Musée romain de Vallon), Madame Marion Veschambre Patrac (Chargée des collections, Musée Bargoin, Clermont-Ferrand), Madame Claudine Massard (Régisseuse, Musée d'Autun), Madame Dominik Kimmel (Bildarchiv, Römisch-Germanisches Zentralmuseum, Mainz).

[1] En particulier, l'étude de référence d'Annemarie Kaufmann-Heinimann sur les bronzes trouvés à Augst/*Augusta Raurica* à laquelle est annexé un inventaire des ensembles de statuettes en bronze des laraires du monde romain. Cf. A. KAUFMANN-HEINIMANN, *Götter und Lararien aus Augusta Raurica: Herstellung, Fundzusammenhänge und sakrale Funktion figürlicher Bronzen in einer römischen Stadt*, Augst, Römermuseum, 1998 (Forschungen in Augst 26).

d'une ou de plusieurs divinités à l'intérieur d'un même panthéon domestique. Si de telles configurations peuvent a priori constituer les témoins d'une dévotion particulière envers l'une ou l'autre divinité, seul un examen approfondi des statuettes permet de cerner davantage le fonctionnement de ces images divines dans le contexte des cultes domestiques.

Le phénomène n'est manifestement pas limité aux cités vésuviennes puisqu'il est attesté ailleurs en Italie, mais aussi dans les provinces romaines, en particulier en Gaule et en Germanie. En se fondant sur les données quantitatives (nombre d'occurrences) et qualitatives (types de divinité), notre approche vise à analyser les rapports fonctionnels entre ces objets qui reproduisent – au moins par deux fois – l'image d'une même divinité dans un laraire. Place privilégiée octroyée à un dieu particulier ou volonté de se constituer une collection, les raisons de ces dédoublements sont certainement multiples. Bien qu'elles soient intégrées dans une même catégorie divine, les statuettes se distinguent toutefois par leur taille, leur style et leurs particularités iconographiques. Ces caractéristiques nous invitent à adopter une approche méthodologique ancrée sur une sélection d'études de cas déterminée à partir des données archéologiques. En effet, avant d'amorcer notre enquête, il a fallu identifier les dédoublements effectifs et fonctionnels au sein des laraires en les différenciant des ensembles de figurines divines rassemblées a posteriori dans un dépôt secondaire et hétérogène. Notre étude se fonde sur un corpus de 25 ensembles de petits bronzes (listés en annexe) qui peuvent être associés à des sanctuaires « privés ». Sans être normée, la pratique du dédoublement semble ainsi être partagée dans de nombreux contextes géographiques (de l'Italie à la Germanie) et archéologiques (*domus*, villas ou *tabernae*). Notre discours s'articule sur l'analyse croisée du contexte vésuvien et des témoignages mis au jour dans les provinces de Gaule et de Germanie. L'enjeu est de proposer, dans un essai de synthèse, une nouvelle lecture des images divines en bronze qui composent les laraires du monde romain.

1. *Le contexte vésuvien : Pompéi et Herculanum*

Dans la lignée des travaux de nos prédécesseurs, notre recherche relative aux cultes domestiques romains s'ancre en premier lieu sur les données fournies par l'archéologie vésuvienne. Une rapide lecture du corpus des panthéons domestiques pompéiens *intra et extra muros* permet de mesurer le large éventail des combinaisons divines et la diversité du « répertoire imagé » des dieux et déesses à l'échelle d'une cité provinciale, fouillée aux deux tiers. Parmi cet inventaire formé de 43 ensembles de statuettes de laraires[2], huit groupes témoignent d'un dédoublement des divinités domestiques. Avant d'amorcer notre analyse, il est important de préciser que les traces matérielles des laraires pompéiens témoignent d'une complémentarité des images, comme l'illustre parfaitement le sanctuaire domestique installé dans l'*atrium* de la *Casa di un flamine* donnant sur la rue de Nola (V 4, 3). Trois petits bronzes représentent le Génie et les Lares – trouvés dans l'armoire d'une pièce adjacente à l'*atrium*[3] – prenaient place

---

[2] Une donnée quantitative établie à partir des répertoires de petits bronzes publiés antérieurement. Cf. G. K. BOYCE, *Corpus of the lararia of Pompeii*, Roma, American Academy in Rome, 1937 (Memoirs of the American Academy in Rome 14) ; T. FRÖHLICH, *Lararien- und Fassadenbilder in den Vesuvstädten: Untersuchungen zur Volkstümlichen pompejanischen Malerei*, Mainz, 1991 (Mitteilungen des Deutschen archäologischen Instituts. Römische Abteilung 32) ; KAUFMANN-HEINIMANN, *Götter und Lararien* ; A. CORALINI, *Hercules domesticus: immagini di Ercole nelle case della regione vesuviana: I secolo a.C. - 79. d.C.*, Napoli, Electa, 2001 (Studi della Soprintendenza archeologica di Pompei 4) ; A. KAUFMANN-HEINIMANN, « Statuettes de laraire et religion domestique à Pompéi », in *Contributi di archeologia vesuviana III : I culti di Pompei*, Roma, L'Erma di Bretschneider, 2007, p. 151-157 (Studi della Soprintendenza archeologica di Pompei 21) ; M. BASSANI, *Sacraria. Ambienti e piccoli edifici per il culto domestico in area vesuviana*, Roma, Quasar, 2008 (Antenor Quaderni 6) ; M.-O. CHARLES-LAFORGE, *La religion privée à Pompéi*, Naples, Centre Jean Bérard, 2009 (Études du Centre Jean Bérard 7) ; V. GASPARINI, « Il culto di Giove a Pompei », *Vesuviana* 6 (2014), p. 9-93 ; N. AMOROSO, « The roles of Isis in Roman Domestic Cults: A study of the Isis-Fortuna bronze statuettes from the Vesuvian Area », *Archiv für Religionsgeschichte* 18/19 (2017), p. 37-74. Voir aussi la contribution de Carla Sfameni dans ce volume.

[3] Selon une hypothèse de BOYCE, *Corpus of the lararia*, p. 40. Voir aussi S. ADAMO MUSCETTOLA, « Osservazioni sulla composizione dei larari con statuette in bronzo di Pompei e Ercolano », in U. GEHRIG (éd.), *Toreutik und figürliche Bronzen römischer Zeit, Akten der 6. Tagung über Antike Bronzen, Berlin, 13-17 Mai 1980: Madame G.-M. Faider-Feytmans zum Gedächtnis*, Berlin, Staat-

dans une niche encadrée par une décoration peinte, datée entre 62 et 79 ap. J.-C.[4] et composée de deux registres réunissant huit divinités[5]. Le premier niveau présente Bacchus, Vénus Pompéienne et Éros à gauche, tandis que Fortuna et Jupiter sont placés à droite. Au second registre se suivent Mercure, Victoria aux pieds de laquelle court un porcelet, Hercule et Minerve tenant une patère au-dessus d'un autel. Dans ce contexte, dieux de bronze et divinités peintes forment un panthéon complémentaire associant ici le culte ancestral des Lares aux grandes figures des temples publics de Pompéi[6]. En outre, pour interpréter l'association de ces images, il faut tenir compte des différences matérielles entre le support pictural et la petite plastique en bronze : le premier, s'il semble offrir plus de libertés, résulte d'une « fixation » des intentions du commanditaire[7], tandis que la seconde catégorie, issue d'une production dite standardisée et répétitive[8], suit une typologie beaucoup plus limitée et procède par « accumulation »[9].

Commençons notre analyse par le laraire à *aedicula* de la *Casa delle Pareti Rosse* (VIII 5, 37). De manière analogue au contexte précédent, ce sanctuaire est placé dans l'*atrium* mais il s'inscrit dans une logique inverse puisque le groupe du Génie et des Lares

---

liche Museen Preussischer Kulturbesitz, Antikenmuseum, 1984, p. 26-27, fig. 25 ; KAUFMANN-HEINIMANN, *Götter und Lararien*, p. 218, GFV23, fig. 163 ; CORALINI, *Hercules domesticus*, p. 182, P.054 (avec fig.).

[4] Selon FRÖHLICH, *Lararien- und Fassadenbilder*, p. 272, qui suit l'avis de A. MAU, « Ausgrabungen von Pompeji », *RM* 16 (1901), p. 320 signalant la présence d'une décoration du IVe style nettoyée lors de la dernière phase d'occupation avant 79 ap. J.-C.

[5] FRÖHLICH, *Lararien- und Fassadenbilder*, p. 271-272, L52, pl. 33,1.

[6] V. HUET, S. WYLER, « Association de dieux et d'images dans les laraires de Pompéi », in S. ESTIENNE, V. HUET, F. LISSARRAGUE, F. PROST (éd.), *Figures de dieux. Construire le divin en images*, Rennes, PUR, 2014, p. 203.

[7] Si elles pouvaient être modifiées, restaurées, etc., les peintures de laraire doivent avoir été conçues comme une unité cohérente, Cf. HUET, WYLER, *Association de dieux*, p. 209.

[8] ADAMO MUSCETTOLA, *Osservazioni sulla composizione*, p. 10.

[9] En effet, nombreux sont les ensembles de statuettes qui rassemblent des pièces de style et de chronologie différentes, témoignant à la fois d'une acquisition diversifiée des objets (productions locales et importations) et d'une constitution d'une collection sur la longue durée.

est peint[10] et associé à un petit panthéon de bronze (Fig. 1)[11]. Cet ensemble intègre aussi des statuettes de Lares qui encadrent des figurines du dieu Hercule, d'Apollon et de Mercure qui est représenté deux fois. Deux divinités pompéiennes ancestrales sont ici associées au dieu du profit et des gains, lequel devait a priori jouir d'une vénération particulière. Toutefois, un examen détaillé des deux statuettes invite à nuancer cette affirmation. En effet, si le plus petit bronze (haut de 15,7 cm) montre Mercure nu, tenant la bourse, coiffé du pétase, les endromides aux pieds, une chlamyde ramenée sur l'avant-bras droit, la seconde représenta-

Fig. 1.
Laraire de la *Casa delle Pareti Rosse* (Pompéi, VIII, 5, 37).
© Römisch-Germanisches Zentralmuseum, Mainz / n° T_1972_03264 et T_1972_02989.

[10] Boyce, *Corpus of the lararia*, p. 77, n° 371 ; Fröhlich, *Lararien- und Fassadenbilder*, p. 291, L96, pl. 31 ; F. Giacobello, *Larari pompeiani: iconografia e culto dei Lari in ambito domestico*, Milano, LED, 2008, p. 202-203, cat. 94.
[11] Kaufmann-Heinimann, *Götter und Lararien*, p. 222, GFV37, fig. 169.

tion se distingue par ses dimensions – 22 centimètres de hauteur, soit la plus grande de l'ensemble – son iconographie et son style. En effet, la statuette représente un jeune homme debout vêtu d'une chlamyde qui couvre le corps, portant des sandales, tenant la bourse de la main droite, la gauche devait recevoir un caducée fondu séparément. L'absence du pétase, la pose polyclétéenne, corrélées aux traits fortement individualisés du personnage a incité Stefania Adamo Muscettola à reconnaître l'empereur Auguste, en tant que *filius Maiae*[12]. S'il n'est pas utile de discuter cette interprétation ici, nous préciserons que d'autres petits bronzes présentent des caractéristiques physiques propres aux portraits impériaux de l'époque julio-claudienne[13], tandis que des représentations d'empereurs sont attestées dans d'autres laraires[14]. Parallèlement, Suétone précise dans la *Vie d'Auguste* que l'empereur Hadrien possédait parmi ses *Lares cubiculi* une statuette en bronze d'Auguste adolescent offerte par l'auteur lui-même[15]. Ces Lares « des chambres à coucher » étaient installés dans des espaces personnels, comme semble l'illustrer un groupe de statuettes de divinités en bronze dans le *biclinium* n° 2 de la *Casa a Graticcio* à Herculanum (III 14/15)[16]. L'emplacement de ce groupe de bronzes le distingue des *sacraria* placés dans l'*atrium* ou le péristyle, puisqu'il s'agit ici d'une pièce « privative », et non d'un espace de représentation au sein de la maison.

Le laraire de la *Casa delle Pareti Rosse* a ainsi livré deux statuettes, issues d'un même répertoire iconographique, qui ren-

---

[12] ADAMO MUSCETTOLA, *Osservazioni sulla composizione*, p. 17-20.

[13] Citons un petit bronze de 11 cm trouvé à Saint-Cizy et conservé au Musée Saint-Raymond de Toulouse. Il représente le dieu Mercure nu, dont les traits du visage et le style de la coiffure renvoient aux portraits de l'époque julio-claudienne. Cf. P. CAPUS, « Un petit bronze de Mercure, nouvelle acquisition pour le Musée Saint-Raymond », *Antiquités Nationales* 50/51 (2020/2021), p. 21-33.

[14] Citons en particulier deux ensembles mis au jour à Cos : le premier, dans une maison proche de l'agora, a livré un buste en bronze de Caligula, tandis que le second, dans ladite *Casa dei bronzi*, intègre le buste en bronze d'un Sévère. Cf. KAUFMANN-HEINIMANN, *Götter und Lararien*, p. 308-309, GF114 et GF115, fig. 275-276 (avec bibliographie précédente).

[15] Suétone, *Vie d'Auguste*, 7.1.

[16] Ensemble de huit statuettes de divinités en bronze : couple de Lares en paire inversée, Lare, déesse Panthée coiffée du *basileion*, Harpocrate, Jupiter, Esculape, Fortuna, Minerve et Diane, cf. KAUFMANN-HEINIMANN, *Götter und Lararien*, p. 210, GFV3.

voient à des réalités différentes mais complémentaires. Rappelons que Mercure est l'une des divinités les plus représentées à l'intérieur de l'écrin domestique[17], tant en peinture qu'en sculpture. En tant que dieu des gains, on le rencontre en bronze dans les laraires pompéiens où il peut être associé à Hercule et Vénus[18], à Hercule et Apollon[19], à Minerve[20], à la triade capitoline[21] et aux divinités du cercle isiaque[22]. Le répertoire de ses représentations peintes témoigne aussi de la diversité des combinaisons divines. On le rencontre souvent dans les boutiques, « agissant » en partenariat avec le dieu Bacchus. Tel est le cas d'une peinture d'un laraire installé dans une *caupona* bien connue de la rue de l'Abondance (I 8, 8)[23] où le binôme encadre le Génie et les Lares à l'intérieur d'un décor de temple. Les découvertes archéologiques associées – 3 kg de monnaies de bronze et plusieurs amphores – soulignent ce rapport entre le dieu des gains et celui du vin, selon une association propice aux espaces de production et de commerce[24].

Poursuivons notre analyse en citant l'exemple de la *Casa del Citarista* (I 4, 5) qui a livré, dans une pièce adjacente au grand

---

[17] Le cas de la *Casa delle Pareti Rosse* n'est pas isolé. Deux statuettes de Mercure ont été trouvées dans le péristyle d'une maison anonyme (IX 6, g). Ces objets ne sont toutefois pas localisables aujourd'hui. Cf. KAUFMANN-HEINIMANN, *Götter und Lararien*, p. 224, GFV42.

[18] Maison dite de *Trebius Valens* (III 2, 1), première moitié du Iᵉʳ siècle ap. J.-C. ; KAUFMANN-HEINIMANN, *Götter und Lararien*, p. 216, GFV15, fig. 159 ; CORALINI, *Hercules domesticus*, p. 174-175, P.045.

[19] *Casa delle Pareti Rosse* (VIII 5, 37), voir *supra* et l'annexe du présent article.

[20] *Casa del Cenacolo* (V 2, h), laraire constitué d'une niche stuquée et décorée d'une peinture d'Hercule (IVᵉ style) dans laquelle ont été trouvées une statuette de Mercure en bronze et de Minerve en terre cuite ; cf. KAUFMANN-HEINIMANN, *Götter und Lararien*, p. 218, GFV21, fig. 162 ; CORALINI, *Hercules domesticus*, p. 177-178, P.049.

[21] Maison des Amours Dorés (VI 16, 7), cf. KAUFMANN-HEINIMANN, *Götter und Lararien*, p. 220, GFV27, fig. 165-166 (avec bibliographie précédente).

[22] Villa *rustica*, Contrada Civita di Nitto, Fondo Imperiali, cf. KAUFMANN-HEINIMANN, *Götter und Lararien*, p. 210-211, GFV2, fig. 146 (avec bibliographie précédente).

[23] FRÖHLICH, *Lararien- und Fassadenbilder*, p. 252-253, L8, pl. 2,1.

[24] W. VAN ANDRINGA, *Quotidien des dieux et des hommes : la vie religieuse dans les cités du Vésuve à l'époque romaine*, Paris, 2009 (BEFAR 337), p. 294, fig. 224.

FIG. 2.
Deux statuettes de Minerve trouvées dans la *Casa del Citarista* (Pompéi, I, 4, 5).
© Römisch-Germanisches Zentralmuseum, Mainz / n° T_1972_03131
et T_1972_03039.

péristyle, deux statuettes de Minerve[25] (Fig. 2). Ces deux objets présentent les attributs habituels de la déesse, à savoir le casque à cimier et l'égide ici cerclée de serpents, mais ils se différencient par la forme de la base, les dimensions, le drapé et surtout la position des bras et leurs attributs. L'une des figures tient une patère dans la main droite, tandis que la main gauche est ouverte, avec le bras le long du corps ; elle devait sans doute être en appui sur un bouclier, comme le suggère la pose du personnage. L'autre statuette devait tenir un attribut disparu – lance ou bouclier – alors que le bras droit est levé et replié vers le visage, la main tenant un petit serpent. Bien qu'il soit moins précis que le précédent, ce contexte montre ainsi deux images différentes d'une

---

[25] KAUFMANN-HEINIMANN, *Götter und Lararien*, p. 214, fig. 151, GFV7.

même divinité : la première peut être qualifiée « d'active » car elle évoque les pratiques rituelles par la patère – un attribut habituellement tenu par le *Genius*, les Lares et d'autres divinités [26] – tandis que l'autre associe une arme au serpent, l'animal symbolique de Minerve. Rappelons que ces objets mobiles ont pu être exposés à des moments distincts et/ou dans différentes pièces de la maison. Nous reviendrons plus loin sur cet aspect majeur pour l'interprétation de la présence « multiple » d'une même divinité.

Le dédoublement caractérise d'autres ensembles de figurines trouvés dans les *villae* de l'*ager pompeianus*. Tel est le cas d'une villa datée du Ier siècle ap. J.-C. et fouillée entre 1907 et 1908 dans la *Contrada Civita di Nitto*, à Boscoreale. Bien qu'aucun plan détaillé n'ait été réalisé au moment des fouilles, le mobilier archéologique a été soigneusement inventorié en 1908 et rassemblé dans un catalogue exhaustif publié par Grete Stefani en 1994 [27]. Grâce à ce travail, nous savons que la pièce n° 6 de la *pars urbana* (dont la fonction reste inconnue) a livré un lot de huit statuettes de laraire en bronze [28] parmi lesquelles Isis [29] et Harpocrate [30] apparaissent deux fois, accompagnés par Sérapis [31], Diane, Minerve et Mercure. Dans un même ensemble statuaire, la déesse Isis est représentée une première fois avec le gouver-

---

[26] Notons que le même rapport est attesté dans un groupe de statuettes en bronze de laraire (aujourd'hui disparues) découvertes à Rome dans les *Horti Domitiae* : le groupe intègre deux figurines d'Apollon à la lyre, dont l'une tient une patère dans la main droite. Cf. KAUFMANN-HEINIMANN, *Götter und Lararien*, p. 314, GF121, fig. 282.

[27] G. STEFANI, *Vecchi scavi sconosciuti: la villa rinvenuta dal marchese Giovanni Imperiali in località Civita (1907-1908)*, Roma, L'Erma di Bretschneider, 1994 (Soprintendenza archeologica di Pompei. Monografie 9).

[28] KAUFMANN-HEINIMANN, *Götter und Lararien*, p. 210, GFV2, fig. 146.

[29] La première statuette (H. 8 cm, inv. 2/2370) montre Isis debout avec son costume noué sur la poitrine, tenant un sistre et des épis de blé, tandis que la seconde (H. 11 cm, inv. 20274) montre la déesse coiffée du *basileion* tenant *cornucopia* et gouvernail, cf. STEFANI, *Vecchi scavi*, p. 35-36, cat. 57 et cat. 59.

[30] La seconde statuette (H. 5,5 cm, inv. 2/2368) a été détruite lors du bombardement de 1943, cf. STEFANI, *Vecchi scavi*, p. 35, cat. 56.

[31] Cet objet (H. 10 cm, inv. 2/2365) a été détruit lors du bombardement de 1943. La description reportée par STEFANI, *Vecchi scavi*, p. 34, cat. 55, indique que le dieu était représenté debout, nu, tenant un sceptre et une patère. La coloration « isiaque » attribuée à l'objet tient de son association aux statuettes d'Isis et d'Harpocrate.

nail et la corne d'abondance, et une seconde fois vêtue du nœud isiaque et agitant le sistre. De dimensions et de style différents, ces deux figurines devaient certainement être complémentaires au sein d'un même répertoire d'objets, en illustrant ainsi la diversité des compétences de la déesse[32]. La forte coloration isiaque de l'ensemble est renforcée par la présence d'un sistre en bronze mis au jour dans le même espace. Cette combinaison n'étonne guère puisque nous connaissons plusieurs laraires peints consacrés aux divinités du cercle isiaque[33]. Enfin, une peinture qui ornait la paroi orientale de l'une des cours de la *pars rustica* de cette même villa identifie un second laraire car elle conservait au premier registre les deux serpents de part et d'autre d'un autel, surmontés au second registre par un couple de Lares[34].

L'ensemble de statuettes en bronze d'une villa anonyme du Ier siècle ap. J.-C.[35], fouillée en 1903 dans le *Fondo d'Acunzo* à Boscoreale, offre un intéressant parallèle au cas qui vient d'être exposé. Un espace dédié aux cultes domestiques a été identifié dans la *pars rustica* de cette villa de l'*ager pompeianus* à proximité de la cuisine (pièce n° 8). Celui-ci présente un podium sur lequel ont été trouvées *in situ* sept statuettes en bronze (Fig. 3). Aujourd'hui conservées au Walters Art Museum de Baltimore, elles montrent des représentations du *Genius*, de Jupiter (deux fois), de Mercure, de Sol et d'Isis. Dans ce contexte, la déesse est attestée deux fois, parée du gouvernail et de la *cornucopia*. La répétition d'Isis au gouvernail confirme « le caractère popu-

---

[32] Sur cet aspect, voir N. AMOROSO, *Les petits bronzes d'Isis au gouvernail et à la corne d'abondance*, Bordeaux, Ausonius (Suppléments à la Bibliotheca Isiaca 2) (sous presse).

[33] Pour une synthèse des données, cf. AMOROSO, *Ibid.*

[34] STEFANI, *Vecchi scavi*, p. 82-83, pl. IX, 1-2 ; GIACOBELLO, *Larari pompeiani*, p. 228-229, cat. 16.

[35] M. DELLA CORTE, « Villa rustica, esplorata dal sig. Ferruccio De Prisco nel fondo d'Acunzo, posto immediatamente a mezzogiorno del piazzale della stazione ferroviaria di Boscoreale, l'anno 1903 », *Notizie degli Scavi di Antichità* (1921), p. 336-442 ; BOYCE, *Corpus of the lararia*, p. 100 ; FRÖHLICH, *Lararien- und Fassadenbilder*, p. 356 ; KAUFMANN-HEINIMANN, *Götter und Lararien*, p. 210, GFV1, fig. 145 ; BASSANI, Sacraria, p. 212-213, cat. 26. Voir aussi le commentaire de Maddalena Bassani: M. BASSANI, « Gods and Cult Objects in Roman Houses. Notes for a Methodological Research », in R. BERG, A. CORALINI, A. KAISA KOPONEN, R. VÄLIMÄKI (ed.), *Tangible Religion. Materiality of Domestic Cults practices from Antiquity to early Modern Era*, Rome, 2021, p. 104-107.

Fig. 3.
Laraire d'une villa *rustica*, *Fondo d'Acunzo* à Boscoreale
© The Walters Art Museum.

laire de cette déesse[36] » à l'intérieur du panthéon domestique[37]. De nouveau, il convient de préciser que ces deux objets sont issus de deux types différents et qu'ils ont pu intégrer cet ensemble à des moments distincts[38]. Aussi, la différence dans l'agencement du drapé pour ces deux figurines pourrait ici être significative. En effet, dans le premier cas, les références iconographiques au type de l'Aphrodite au pilier permettent de proposer une lecture polysémique de l'objet. Ce dernier pouvait être « activé » de deux manières différentes en fonction des pratiques du culte domestique : l'iconographie permet de reconnaître, selon les circonstances, Vénus, la déesse poliade pompéienne, ou Isis, en tant que divinité de l'abondance et protectrice des récoltes de la villa. Le même schéma peut être appliqué à la seconde statuette isiaque puisque le type renvoie à des modèles exploités pour représenter

---

[36] Van Andringa, *Quotidien des dieux et des hommes*, p. 259, à propos de ce laraire.
[37] Sur la notion de panthéon, voir J. Rüpke, *Pantheon: A new history of Roman religion*, Princeton University Press, 2018.
[38] Toutefois, ces types iconographiques circulent dans l'ensemble du monde romain, entre le I{er} et le III{e} siècle ap. J.-C. Rien n'exclut que les statuettes aient été intégrées au même moment, cf. Amoroso, *Les petits bronzes*.

la déesse Junon[39]. Ces différences entre les deux statuettes tendent à montrer qu'il ne s'agit pas d'une accumulation d'images identiques. Au contraire, elles témoignent d'une complémentarité qui rendait possible différentes combinaisons divines. Laurent Bricault a récemment proposé d'y reconnaître une référence aux deux champs d'action de la déesse Isis, sur la terre et sur la mer[40].

La même logique permettrait d'expliquer la double présence de Jupiter dans ce laraire. De manière analogue à la *Casa del citarista* mentionnée plus haut, le dieu est représenté une première fois trônant et vêtu du *Hüfmantel*, tenant le sceptre et la patère, tandis que la seconde statuette le montre debout et nu, tenant le sceptre de la main gauche et le foudre de la dextre. La première statuette n'est pas sans rappeler le laraire de la *Casa degli Amorini dorati*, où un Jupiter du même type est associé à Junon et Minerve trônant pour matérialiser la triade capitoline[41]. En représentant le dieu effectuant une libation, cette figurine pourrait évoquer la divinité capitoline et son temple sur le forum de Pompéi ; la seconde statuette montre une image « générique » du dieu avec ses attributs caractéristiques, en particulier le foudre. Ce sont, de nouveau, deux champs d'action distincts mais complémentaires dont ces statuettes se font l'écho.

Dans les sanctuaires domestiques pompéiens, l'iconographie est en étroite corrélation avec les images cultuelles telles qu'elles figuraient dans les lieux de cultes publics[42]. Elle constitue donc une forme de représentation adressée à un public qui partage une culture religieuse commune, à l'échelle de la cité[43]. En outre, les dédoublements observés jusqu'ici, s'ils s'articulent autour d'images complémentaires, rendaient efficientes une pluralité de configurations des panthéons au sein de l'habitat. Une telle lecture peut encore être appuyée par la composition du laraire trouvé dans le *biclinium* n° 2 de la *Casa a Graticcio* à Hercu-

---

[39] Prenons l'exemple de la figurine de Junon qui provient du trésor de Weissenburg et qui présente des analogies « vestimentaires » avec cette statuette, cf. KAUFMANN-HEINIMANN, *Götter und Lararien*, p. 276, cat. GF 66.

[40] L. BRICAULT, *Isis Pelagia: Images, Names and Cults of a Goddess of the Seas*, Leiden – Boston, E.J. Brill, 2020 (RGRW 190), p. 139-140, fig. 101.

[41] KAUFMANN-HEINIMANN, *Götter und Lararien*, p. 220, GFV27, fig. 166.

[42] VAN ANDRINGA, *Quotidien des dieux et des hommes*, p. 20.

[43] HUET, WYLER, *Association de dieux*, p. 211-213.

lanum (III 14/15)[44] mentionné plus haut : une figurine – montrant une déesse ailée coiffée du *basileion*, tenant un gouvernail et une *cornucopia*, portant le carquois – est accompagnée des Lares, de Jupiter, d'Esculape, de l'enfant Harpocrate, de Minerve, de Diane et surtout d'une statuette de Fortuna tenant elle aussi le gouvernail et la corne d'abondance. Cette composition illustre l'association d'une déesse secourable (Fortuna) et celle d'une déesse polymorphe de coloration isiaque (par le *basileion*) et aux compétences multiples, comme en attestent ses nombreux attributs. De telles combinaisons montrent à quel point les images divines pouvaient se nourrir les unes des autres, puisque leur richesse iconographique pouvait multiplier les connexions entre sphères divines et champs d'action. Parallèlement, la statuette dite « panthée » intégrait parfaitement l'ensemble, de même qu'elle pouvait être « activée » de manière isolée, tel un objet « mémoire » matérialisant la synthèse d'un panthéon domestique.

2. *Gaules et Germanies*

Plusieurs découvertes distribuées sur le territoire des Gaules et des Germanies (cf. annexes) ont livré des statuettes de laraire qui attestent un dédoublement de divinités. Associées à des villas, des *domus* ou des boutiques, ces contextes – majoritairement issus de fouilles anciennes – offrent de précieux témoignages pour confronter les observations formulées au point précédent. Parmi ce répertoire composé de 13 groupes divins, le dieu Mercure est particulièrement « répété » avec dix occurrences (cf. annexes). En Gaule romaine, nous le verrons, il peut être multiplié par cinq au sein d'un même lot de statuettes. Ce constat suscite d'emblée des interrogations. Si le dieu à la bourse est effectivement très populaire dans cette partie de l'empire – une popularité également attestée par la documentation pompéienne – cette multiplication peut-elle simplement résulter d'une accumulation d'objets sur une longue durée ou d'un rassemblement de figurines enfoui dans un moment de détresse ? Un examen des laraires intégrant d'autres divinités (Minerve, Fortuna et Jupiter) nous offre plusieurs clefs de lecture pour interpréter ce phénomène propre à la Gaule.

---

[44] KAUFMANN-HEINIMANN, *Götter und Lararien*, p. 210, GFV3.

Dans une fouille ancienne, réalisée en 1916[45], l'une des maisons du quartier n° 27 de l'antique *Aventicum* a livré un bel ensemble de statuettes de laraire (Fig. 4a). Réunies dans l'angle sud-est d'une vaste pièce interprétée comme un *atrium*, elles semblent traduire un enfouissement volontaire qui aurait précédé une phase de réaménagement du site[46], occupé jusqu'au IVe siècle ap. J.-C. Le lot se caractérise par un ensemble constitué d'un Lare disposant d'un socle finement décoré d'une guirlande de laurier, d'un Mercure nu tenant la bourse, d'une Junon tenant un sceptre de la main gauche et une patère de la dextre, d'une Victoire à la *cornucopia*, et surtout de deux Minerve. Dominant l'ensemble par ses dimensions (27,2 cm de hauteur) et datée de l'époque julio-claudienne, la première statuette (Fig. 4b) montre la déesse tenant la lance dans la main droite et sans doute un bouclier dans la gauche. Vêtue d'une tunique et d'un ample

Fig. 4a.
Statuettes du laraire d'Avenches.
© Aventicum – Site et Musée romains d'Avenches, photo Fibbi-Aeppli, Grandson.

[45] W. Cart, « Le laraire d'Avenches », *Bulletin de l'Association Pro Aventico* 13 (1917), p. 43-61.

[46] M. E. Fuchs, « Témoignages du culte domestique en Suisse romaine », in F. Fontana, E. Murgia (dir.), Sacrum Facere. *Atti del III Seminario di Archeologia del Sacro. Lo spazio del "sacro": ambienti e gesti del rito, Trieste, 3-4 ottobre 2014*, Trieste, EUT Edizioni, 2016 (Polymnia. Studi di archeologia 7), p. 105.

FIG. 4b.
Statuette de Minerve (H. 27,2 cm)
trouvée dans le laraire d'Avenches.
© Aventicum – Site et Musée romains
d'Avenches, photo Paul Lutz.

FIG. 4c.
Statuette de Minerve (H. 19,5 cm)
trouvée dans le laraire d'Avenches.
© Aventicum – Site et Musée romains
d'Avenches, photo Paul Lutz.

manteau aux plis en saillie finement détaillés, Minerve porte une égide cerclée de serpents tandis que sa tête est coiffée d'un casque dont le cimier est soutenu par une chouette[47]. Datée du IIe siècle ap. J.-C. et de dimensions moindres (H. 19,5 cm), la seconde statuette présente le même type iconographique que la précédente, à l'exception de la chouette qui n'est pas présente (Fig. 4c).

[47] Cet agencement caractérise d'autres statuettes en bronze de la déesse. Citons un exemplaire de dimensions analogues (H. 20,5 cm, sans socle) trouvé à Berlin et conservé aux Staatlichen Museen zu Berlin, inv. 31790, cf. K. A. NEUGEBAUER, « Bronzestatuette der Minerva », *AA* (1948/49), p. 63-70. Un second exemplaire, découvert à Grbavac (Croatie), est conservé au Musée de Zagreb, cf. A. RENDIC-MIOCEVIC, M. SEGVIC, « Religions and Cults in South Pannonian Regions », in J. FITZ (éd.), *Religion and Cults in Pannonia, Exhibition at Székesfehérvár, Csók István Gallery 15 May – 30 September 1996*, Székesfehérvár : Fejér Megyei Múzeumok Igazgatósága, 1998, p. 7-8, fig. 7. Ces deux figurines présentent des équivalences d'atelier avec la statuette d'Avenches.

Ce précieux contexte nous incite à soutenir la thèse d'une accumulation de deux objets d'époques diverses, renforçant l'importance de la divinité par le dédoublement d'une image pratiquement identique. La qualité plastique, en particulier celle du Lare[48], permettent d'attribuer l'ensemble à des ateliers d'Italie ou de Gaule méridionale, tandis que la composition fait directement écho aux panthéons domestiques des cités vésuviennes.

Dans le prolongement « géographique » du lot examiné, arrêtons-nous sur l'établissement romain de Vallon. Située en Germanie Supérieure à une dizaine de kilomètres d'*Aventicum*/Avenches, une villa y a été découverte de manière fortuite dans les années 1970 lors de la réalisation de travaux publics. La partie actuellement connue est datée du IIIe siècle ap. J.-C.[49] : elle regroupe trois corps de bâtiments distincts, disposés en L et reliés par un portique qui dessert une quarantaine de locaux. La pièce qui nous intéresse est localisée dans le bâtiment central et se distingue des autres par une abside. Il devait certainement s'agir d'un local important car les fouilles ont mis au jour un pavement de mosaïques montrant Bacchus et Ariane, des structures en bois carbonisées et des éléments mobiliers en bronze, notamment des charnières, des poignées, des appliques et surtout une dizaine de figurines de divinités. La fonction de la pièce a pu être interprétée à partir de ces objets qui jouent ici le rôle de précieux indicateurs du sacré, mais aussi à partir du décor et des meubles en bois qui en font « autant une salle de réception qu'un cabinet de travail muni d'une bibliothèque »[50] : on suppose en effet que les armoires devaient contenir des rouleaux de

---

[48] L'incrustation d'argent (yeux) et de cuivre (*angusti clavi*), la forme de la base, se rencontrent sur la statuette de Lare trouvée parmi le trésor des bronzes de Bavay (H. 20,2 cm, inv. 1969, Br 8), cf. A. Kaufmann-Heinimann, « Statuette de Lare », in L. De Chavagnac, B. Mille (éd.), *Nouveaux regards sur le trésor des bronzes de Bavay*, Milano, Silvana Editoriale, 2020, p. 113-114, cat. 8 (avec bibliographie précédente).

[49] S. Gardiol, F. Rebetez, F. Saby, « La villa gallo-romaine de Vallon FR : une seconde mosaïque figurée et un laraire », *Archéologie suisse* 13 (1990), p. 169-184.

[50] M. Cavalieri, « Βιβλιοθήκη/bibliotheca : le mot et la chose en Grèce et à Rome », in N. Amoroso, M. Cavalieri, N. L. J. Meunier (éd.), *Locum, armarium, libros. Livres et bibliothèques dans l'Antiquité*, Louvain-la-Neuve, Presses Universitaires de Louvain, 2017 (Fervet Opus 2), p. 55.

papyrus et des *codices* en parchemin. Les restitutions fondées sur les traces archéologiques représentent le petit temple domestique en bois sous la forme d'une *grande armarium*[51] qui s'inspire du modèle unique offert par la *Casa del sacello di legno* à Herculanum[52]. Les biens de la villa de Vallon étaient protégés par plusieurs divinités, présentes sous la forme de statuettes en bronze (Fig. 5) : un Apollon, deux Mercure, deux Diane, un Hercule et une Isis tenant le gouvernail et la corne d'abondance accompagnée de son fils Harpocrate. Le contexte de découverte montre que cette pièce et la villa ont été détruites par un incendie et

Fig. 5.
Laraire de la villa romaine de Vallon.
© Service archéologique de l'État de Fribourg.

---

[51] Selon l'expression utilisée par Pétrone lorsqu'il décrit le laraire de Trimalchion (*Satyricon*, XXXIX). Cf. Fuchs, *Témoignages du culte*, fig. 23 et fig. 25.
[52] E. De Carolis, *Il mobile a Pompei ed Ercolano. Letti, tavoli, sedie e armadi. Contributi alla tipologie dei mobili della prima età imperiale*, Roma, L'Erma di Bretschneider, 2007, p. 139, fig. 104.

successivement abandonnées, entre la fin du IIIe et le début du IVe siècle ap. J.-C. ; cette datation se fonde sur les monnaies trouvées *in situ* qui fournissent un *terminus post quem*[53].

En se fondant sur le calice consacré par une certaine Paterna aux *Suleviae*[54] découvert dans la salle du laraire de Vallon à proximité du bronze isiaque, Annemarie Kaufmann-Heinimann[55] identifie un laraire de caractère « officiel », non pas réservé *stricto sensu* à une famille, mais à une audience plus large, ce que confirment le nombre et la diversité des divinités qui intégraient ce panthéon de bronze. Cet ensemble a pu être associé à un buste d'empereur (ou d'ancêtre ?) – dont il reste une mèche de cheveux et une oreille – installé dans une niche de cette même salle[56]. Diane (présente deux fois) et Isis munie du gouvernail et de la corne d'abondance (la plus grande statuette de l'ensemble) y occupaient une place prédominante. Précisons que cette image de la déesse d'origine égyptienne est connue par une centaine de petits bronzes qui proviennent de l'ensemble du monde romain[57]. Parallèlement, l'une des représentations de Mercure (ou peut-être les deux) est caractéristique du territoire des Gaules où le dieu apparaît accompagné d'animaux (coq, bouc, bélier, tortue), découverts ici de manière isolée. Citons, par comparaison, l'exemple d'une maison d'artisans de Kaiseraugst (Région 17, E, maison 1), dans la basse-ville d'*Augusta Raurica*/Augst, qui rassemble des statuettes – rangées dans une caisse ou une armoire – représentant un Lare, Hercule, le dieu *Somnus* et deux Mercure : le premier est entouré d'un bouc, d'un coq et d'une tortue, tandis que le second – dont il ne subsiste que la base – est accompagné d'un bélier et peut-être d'un coq. La première de ces statuettes, soit la mieux conservée, présente une entaille au centre de la face

---

[53] C. AGUSTONI, M. E. FUCHS, « Des bronzes dans l'incendie de la salle du laraire de Vallon », in E. DESCHLER-ERB, P. DELLA CASA (éd.), *New Research on Ancient Bronzes. Acts of the XVIIIth International Congress on Ancient Bronzes, Zürich, 3-7 September 2013*, Zürich, Chronos, 2015 (Zurich Studies in Archaeology, 10), p. 171-174.

[54] Les *Suleviae* sont « des déesses indigènes, protectrices du monde féminin honorées du lac Léman au Rhin en passant par Avenches », cf. FUCHS, *Témoignages du culte*, p. 109.

[55] KAUFMANN-HEINIMANN, *Götter und Lararien*, p. 285, GF83.

[56] FUCHS, *Témoignages du culte*, p. 109.

[57] AMOROSO, *Les petits bronzes*.

supérieure de la base. Utilisée comme une « tirelire », la statuette devait recevoir des offrandes monétaires. Cette particularité, caractéristique de la Gaule, se rencontre sur un petit corpus de statuettes où Mercure prédomine, à l'exception de rares figurines du *Genius*, de Fortuna ou encore de Vénus[58].

Un dédoublement similaire est attesté dans le laraire d'une villa de Homburg-Saar[59] : un Mercure à la bourse nu debout est accompagné par un groupe représentant Mercure assis, tenant le caducée, un coq à ses pieds, un sanglier et un bouc à sa droite, tandis qu'une entaille pour recevoir des monnaies est placée sur la face arrière de l'objet. Enfin, dans une maison du *vicus* de *Vitudurum*/Oberwinterthur, un autre groupe de statuettes en bronze devait être conservé dans une armoire en bois qui a été détruite par un incendie au IIIe siècle ap. J.-C. Une statuette de Mercure de tradition gauloise, accompagnée d'un coq et d'une chèvre, domine l'ensemble composé d'une Minerve, d'un Amour sur griffe de lion et d'un second Mercure, dont le type est attesté en Italie septentrionale et en Germanie[60].

L'examen des dédoublements de divinités dans les Gaules et les Germanies enrichit fondamentalement notre analyse puisqu'elle pose la question des rapports entre les dieux du monde romain et les divinités d'origine locale au sein des laraires. L'exemple d'un lot de petits bronzes découverts à Saarlouis-Fraulautern est significatif[61]. En effet, ce petit groupe se compose d'une statuette de Minerve et deux figurines de Jupiter : la première[62] montre le dieu

---

[58] Kaufmann-Heinimann *Götter und Lararien*, p. 168-180. Sur un Génie en bronze avec la même entaille et portant une dédicace au « Génie des *aerarii Diarenses* », soit un petit groupe de bronziers locaux, cf. J.-C. Béal, « Au Génie des bronziers de *Diar[-]* », *Revue archéologique de Narbonnaise* 41 (2008), p. 169-180.

[59] A. Kolling, « Grabungen im römischen Vicus Schwarzenacker », in *Ausgrabungen in Deutschland gefördert von der Deutschen Forschungsgemeinschaft 1950-1975*, Mainz, Verlag des Römisch-Germanischen Zentralmuseums, 1975 (Forschungsinstitut für Vor- und Frühgeschichte. Monographien 1,1), p. 439-442, fig. 4-7.

[60] C. Ebnöther, A. Kaufmann-Heinimann, « Ein Schrank mit Lararium des 3. Jahrhunderts », in E. Deschler-Erb, *Beiträge zum römischen Oberwinterthur–Vitudurum 7. Ausgrabungen im Unteren Bühl*, Zürich, Orell Füssli, 1996 (Monographien der Kantonsarchäologie Zürich, 27), p. 229-251.

[61] Kaufmann-Heinimann, *Götter und Lararien*, p. 274, GF63, fig. 236.

[62] Statuette de Jupiter en bronze, IIe siècle ap. J.-C., H. 15 cm, Saarbrücken, Landesmuseum für Vor- und Frühgeschichte.

barbu debout et nu, hormis un drapé couvrant l'épaule gauche, tenant le foudre de la main droite et un sceptre (manquant) de la gauche ; la seconde figurine[63] est différente puisque l'on y reconnaît un dieu imberbe « en mouvement », la jambe droite avancée et pliée, le foudre tenu dans la main droite levée au-dessus de la tête, tandis que la main gauche est ouverte et orientée vers le bas, elle devait tenir un attribut particulier (peut-être une roue, faisant écho à l'iconographie de Taranis). Ce petit groupe divin met ainsi en image des équivalences entre un dieu romain et une divinité d'origine gauloise, dont les champs d'action se recouvrent, chacun gardant toutefois ses particularités.

Dans son étude sur les cultes domestiques en Gaule, Jacques Santrot n'hésite pas à évoquer un « laraire mixte[64] » en mentionnant l'exemple de Clermont-Ferrand (Fig. 6). Ce dernier a été mis au jour dans une maison du IIIe siècle ap. J.-C., à l'est du *cardo*, dans une petite pièce (vestibule ?), à proximité de la porte d'accès. Le site a livré un mobilier que l'on qualifierait volontiers d'éclectique, dans lequel onze figurines de bronze sont associées à une statuette du dieu Sucellus en calcaire. Parmi les statuettes métalliques, deux objets de grandes dimensions dominent l'ensemble : une Fortuna en bronze avec des incrustations d'argent et un *Genius*. Ce groupe intègre deux autres figurines de Fortuna, une déesse de l'Abondance, Diane, Mars Ultor, Mercure, Cernunnos, un cerf et un taureau. Les divinités « gauloises » sont ici associées à des images typiquement romaines, tels Mars Ultor, le Génie et surtout les trois occurrences de Fortuna, dont la multiplication pourrait faire écho aux *matres* gauloises[65]. L'éclectisme iconographique semble ici aller de pair avec la diversité des matériaux (bronze, argent et calcaire).

---

[63] Statuette de Jupiter en bronze, IIe siècle ap. J.-C., H. 14 cm, Saarbrücken, Landesmuseum für Vor- und Frühgeschichte. Cf. F. BLANCHARD, *Jupiter dans les Gaules et les Germanies : du Capitole au cavalier à l'anguipède*, Rennes, PUR, 2015, fig. 32.

[64] J. SANTROT, « Lares en Gaule romaine, chapelles luxueuses et oratoires populaires », in F. BARATTE, M. JOLY, J.-C. BÉAL, *Autour du trésor de Mâcon. Luxe et quotidien en Gaule romaine, Actes du colloque de Mâcon, 27-29 janvier 2005*, Mâcon, Institut de recherche du Val de Saône-Mâconnais, 2007, p. 94-95.

[65] *Ibid.*, p. 95.

Fig. 6.
Laraire de Clermont-Ferrand.
© Rémi Boissau, musée Bargoin, ville de Clermont-Ferrand.

Notre examen du dossier documentaire des Gaules et Germanies ne pourrait se conclure sans mentionner le trésor de Mâcon[66]. Découvert en 1764 dans un contexte peu précis et aujourd'hui conservé au British Museum[67], cet ensemble exceptionnel de statuettes en argent se compose d'un Génie, de Jupiter, de Luna, d'une divinité panthée et de quatre Mercure (Fig. 7). Haute de 8 cm, la première figurine montre le dieu drapé d'un manteau lourd couvrant l'épaule le bas du corps et levant la main droite vers le pétase. Les deux suivantes (mesurant respectivement 6,8 et 6,3 cm) intègrent le schéma du Mercure nu tenant la bourse, tandis que la dernière, haute de 11 cm, constitue une œuvre d'une grande qualité plastique et représente le dieu accompagné d'un coq miniature. Le contexte archéologique de cet ensemble étant

---

[66] A. Kaufmann-Heinimann, « Les statuettes de Mâcon, un ensemble particulier », in *Autour du trésor de Mâcon*, p. 19-38.

[67] Statuettes en argent du trésor de Mâcon, British Museum, inv. 1824,0460.12 (Mercure), inv. 1824,0460.13 (Mercure), inv. 1824,0460.14 (Mercure), inv. 1824,0460.16 (Mercure), inv. 1824,0453.09 (Jupiter), inv. 1824,0426.5 (Luna), inv. 1824,0424.1 (déesse Panthée), inv. 1824,0438.2 (*Genius*). Pour consulter les notices en ligne des statuettes : https://www.britishmuseum.org/collection.

Fig. 7.
Trésor de Mâcon.
© The Trustees of the British Museum (licence CC BY-NC-SA 4.0).

inconnu, leur association aux cultes domestiques est hypothétique. L'archéologie vésuvienne nous fait toutefois connaître le seul ensemble de statuettes de laraire en argent. Celui-ci a été mis au jour en 1899 dans une pièce jouxtant la *cella vinaria* d'une villa de l'*ager pompeianus*, dans la localité actuelle de Scafati. Isis et Vénus sont associées au serpent – symbole du *Genius loci* – et à un taureau, interprété comme une image d'Apis[68]. Le rapport de fouilles[69] indique que cette pièce de la villa a livré un sceau au nom de Cnaeus Domitius Auctus.

Ce parallèle laisse penser que les statuettes de Mâcon ont été rassemblées pour former le contenu d'un laraire que les propriétaires auraient caché dans un moment de danger[70]. Rappelons que les figurines d'argent constituaient à la fois des objets de culte et des pièces de grande valeur[71]. La multiplication des

---

[68] V. Tran tam Tinh, *Essai sur le culte d'Isis à Pompéi*, Paris, De Boccard, 1964, p. 159, cat. 91.

[69] A. Sogliano, « Scafati. Avanzi degli scavi eseguiti negli anni 1909 e 1910 », *Notizie degli Scavi di Antichità* (1899), p. 377-418.

[70] Kaufmann-Heinimann, *Les statuettes de Mâcon*, p. 31.

[71] Citons le célèbre passage du roman de Pétrone (*Satyricon*, LX, 8-9) qui décrit la présence de trois statuettes de Lares en argent déposées sur la table au moment du banquet de Trimalchion.

Fig. 8.
Trésor de Brèves
© Musée Rolin, ville d'Autun.

représentations de Mercure, au-delà d'une lecture quantitative, témoigne de la volonté de faire varier les types statuaires pour ainsi constituer une véritable collection. De qualité moindre, le dépôt de petits bronzes découverts à Brèves[72] (Fig. 8) doit être interprété dans le même sens. Composé de cinq statuettes de Mercure et d'une Fortuna, ce groupe ne forme pas une unité stylistique. Deux lots se distinguent clairement : les deux plus grandes statuettes[73] présentent d'évidentes équivalences formelles et iconographiques, tandis que les trois autres[74], de facture moins soignée, font varier les types statuaires représentant le dieu assis et debout. Révélées par une ancienne découverte, rien ne garantit toutefois que toutes ces statuettes aient été fonctionnelles au même moment.

---

[72] Kaufmann-Heinimann, *Götter und Lararien*, p. 241-242, cat. GF 83.
[73] Deux statuettes de Mercure en bronze, H. 13,1 cm (socle H. 2,8 cm), Autun, Musée Rolin, inv. B. 314 et B. 315.
[74] Statuette en bronze de Mercure assis, H. 7,7 cm, Autun, Musée Rolin, inv. B. 316 ; Statuette en bronze de Mercure debout avec une chlamyde, H. 10,4 cm (socle H. 3,1 cm), Autun, Musée Rolin, inv. B. 313 ; Statuette en bronze de Mercure debout et nu, H. 7,5 cm (socle H. 2 cm), Autun, Musée Rolin, s. n.

3. *Essai de synthèse*

Dans l'état actuel de nos connaissances, neuf divinités distinctes ont été dédoublées parmi les ensembles de statuettes de laraires recensés dans cette étude (cf. annexes). Ces figurines intègrent le plus souvent des groupes d'au moins cinq objets qui doivent résulter d'une accumulation de statuettes sur la longue durée. De tels lots, dans leur diversité, pouvaient constituer de puissants « réservoirs » pour configurer les panthéons au gré des évènements propres à la maisonnée. Les difficultés que nous avons à identifier des ensembles concomitants témoignent en réalité d'un faux problème. Posséder deux images (ou plus) d'une « même » divinité devait répondre à des préoccupations fonctionnelles et cultuelles. Lorsqu'elles sont associées, ces statuettes pouvaient ainsi renforcer la présence et l'efficacité d'une divinité, en dévoilant toute (ou une partie de) l'étendue de son champ d'action. Parallèlement, en tant qu'objets mobiles, ces statuettes pouvaient être déplacées, notamment pour s'assurer de la protection de cette « même » divinité dans plusieurs pièces de la maison ; l'une des statuettes pouvait aussi être emportée par le *dominus*, l'autre assurant alors la protection du foyer. Rappelons que l'archéologie montre bien que ces objets n'étaient certainement pas exposés en permanence : on les retrouve plus fréquemment rangés dans une armoire ou une caisse. En exploitant la polymorphie des images réalisées en bronze ou en argent, les individus ont pu les utiliser comme de précieux médiums pour mobiliser un riche panthéon domestique.

La question de départ étant fondamentalement plurielle, les réponses que nous avons tenté d'apporter sont, en conséquence, multiples. Si les travaux de nos prédécesseurs se sont concentrés sur l'inventorisation des divinités au sein des laraires, notre étude tend à montrer qu'une analyse détaillée de chaque objet, pris individuellement, se révèle être féconde pour interpréter les lots des statuettes. En effet, à défaut d'identifier une juxtaposition et/ou une accumulation d'images, nous préférons insister sur la signification des associations divines, puisque chaque objet pouvait être « activé » en fonction de la configuration choisie par le propriétaire. L'exemple de la *Casa dei bronzi* à Cos ne témoigne pas du contraire[75] : un Mars typiquement romain et un Esculape côtoient une Isis coiffée du *basileion*, portant le nœud sur la poitrine, et deux autres figurines reproduisant les types statuaires d'une Vénus pudique (étonnement drapée) et d'une *Tychè*. Ces deux divinités sont elles aussi coiffées de la couronne isiaque. Ce trio pouvait ainsi former un ensemble complémentaire d'images témoignant des champs d'action multiples de la déesse d'origine égyptienne. Parallèlement, si elle était isolée des deux autres, la statuette de Vénus pouvait être associée à celle de Mars pour former un binôme significatif. Figés par un abandon ou une destruction, les ensembles examinés se révèlent être de précieux témoignages du « marché religieux » qui caractérise le monde romain de l'époque impériale. Si ces documents soulèvent encore de nombreuses questions, ils éclairent les fonctions des innombrables figurines décontextualisées, aujourd'hui distribuées dans les collections muséales ou privées du monde entier.

Annexes

GRAPHIQUE 1.
Nombre d'occurrences des dédoublements de divinités dans les laraires romains.

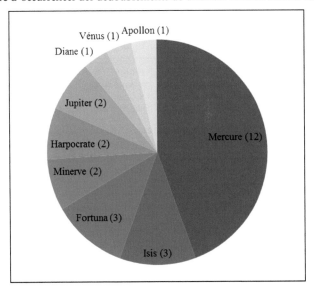

[75] KAUFMANN-HEINIMANN, *Götter und Lararien*, p. 241-242, cat. GF 83 (avec bibliographie précédente).

TABLEAU 1.
Inventaire des dédoublements de divinités dans les laraires romains

Lieu de provenance	Statuettes	Contexte archéologique	Bibliographie
Italie (10)			
Ager pompeianus Villa anonyme (Fondo d'Acunzo, Boscoreale)	Baltimore, Walters Art Museum Statuettes en bronze : Isis (2×), *Genius*, **Jupiter** (2×), Mercure et Hélios (ou les Dioscures).	Éléments d'un laraire (sur podium) placé à proximité de la cuisine Date de découverte : 1903	AMOROSO, *Roles of Isis*, p. 65-68. KAUFMANN-HEINIMANN, *Götter und Lararien*, p. 210, GFV1, fig. 145.
Ager pompeianus Villa del Fondo Giovanni Imperiali (Contrada Civita di Nitto)	Pompéi, dépôt archéologique Statuettes en bronze : Isis (2×), Sérapis, **Harpocrate** (2×), Diane, Mercure Statuette en marbre d'une déesse assise	Éléments d'un laraire trouvés dans la pièce n° 6 Date de découverte : 1908-1909	AMOROSO, *Roles of Isis*, p. 60-62 KAUFMANN-HEINIMANN, *Götter und Lararien*, p. 210-211, GFV2, fig. 146.
Pompéi *Casa del Citarista* (I 4, 5)	Naples, Musée archéologique National Statuettes en bronze : **Minerve** (2×)	Trouvées dans la pièce n° 21 (laraire ?), à l'est du péristyle Date de découverte : 1853-1861	DWYER, *Domestic sculpture*, p. 100. KAUFMANN-HEINIMANN, *Götter und Lararien*, p. 214, GFV7, fig. 151.
Pompéi Maison (V 3, 11)	Naples, Musée archéologique National Statuettes en bronze : **Harpocrate** (2×) et Vénus	Éléments d'un laraire trouvés dans une petite caisse (avec un sistre), dans la pièce B à gauche des *fauces* Date de découverte : 1902	KAUFMANN-HEINIMANN, *Götter und Lararien*, p. 218, GFV22.
Pompéi *Casa delle Pareti Rosse* (VIII 5, 37)	Naples, Musée archéologique National Statuettes en bronze : **Lare** (2×), Apollon, **Mercure** (2×)	Éléments d'un laraire peint à *aedicula* placé dans l'*atrium* Date de découverte : 1882	ADAMO MUSCETTOLA, *Osservazioni*, p. 15-20. KAUFMANN-HEINIMANN, *Götter und Lararien*, p. 222-223, GFV37, fig. 169.
Pompéi Maison anonyme (IX 6, g)	Naples, Musée archéologique National Statuettes en bronze : **Mercure** (2×)	Éléments d'un laraire (?) placé dans le péristyle Date de découverte : 1878	KAUFMANN-HEINIMANN, *Götter und Lararien*, p. 224, GFV42.
Herculanum *Casa a Graticcio* (III, 14/15)	Herculanum, *Antiquarium* Statuettes en bronze : **Fortuna** (2×), Harpocrate, **Lare** (2×), Jupiter, Minerve, Esculape, Diane	Éléments d'un laraire en bois trouvés dans le *biclinium* 2 (1er étage) Date de découverte : 9 novembre 1928	KAUFMANN-HEINIMANN, *Götter und Lararien*, p. 210-211, GFV3, fig. 147.
Herculanum *Casa del Colonnato Tuscanico* (VI, 17)	Herculanum, *Antiquarium* Statuettes en bronze : **Fortuna** (2×)	Éléments d'un laraire (?) Date de découverte : 15 mai 1961	V. TRAN TAM TINH, *Le culte des divinités orientales à Herculanum* (ÉPRO 17), Leyde, p. 66-67.

DÉDOUBLEMENTS DE DIVINITÉS DANS LES LARAIRES ROMAINS

Lieu de provenance	Statuettes	Contexte archéologique	Bibliographie
Sybaris Maison anonyme	Sybaris, Museo Archeologico della Sibaritide Statuettes en bronze : *Genius*, Hercule, **Minerve** (2×), taureau, vache allaitant un veau (Isis-Hathor ?)	Éléments d'un laraire trouvés dans la pièce 4a. Date de découverte : 1970	Kaufmann-Heinimann, *Götter und Lararien*, p. 299, GF102, fig. 263.
Rome Maison anonyme, *Horti Domitiae*	Objets volés en 1973 Statuettes en bronze : **Apollon** (2×), **Vénus** (2×), Fortuna	Éléments d'un laraire trouvés dans une maison du IIᵉ s. ap. J.-C. Date de découverte : 1960	Kaufmann-Heinimann, *Götter und Lararien*, p. 314, GF121, fig. 282.
Gaules (5)			
Anost-en-Morvan (Saône-et-Loire)	Autun, Musée Rolin Statuettes en bronze : **Mercure** (2×), Victoire (2)	Découverte fortuite dans une zone d'habitation, éléments d'un laraire (?) Date de découverte : 1896	Kaufmann-Heinimann, *Götter und Lararien*, p. 237, GF15, fig. 188. Kaufmann-Heinimann, *Statuettes de Mâcon*, p. 33-34.
Brèves (Nièvre)	Autun, Musée Rolin Statuettes en bronze : **Mercure** (5×), Fortuna	Dépôt mis au jour en bordure de la voie romaine entre Brèves et Entrains, lors de la fouille d'une maison. Éléments d'un laraire (?) Date de découverte : 1856	Kaufmann-Heinimann, *Götter und Lararien*, p. 241, GF20, fig. 193. Kaufmann-Heinimann, *Statuettes de Mâcon*, p. 33-34.
Clermont-Ferrand (Puy-de-Dôme) Fouilles de la « Confiturerie Humbert »	Clermont-Ferrand, Musée Bargoin Statuettes en bronze : *Genius*, Mars, Mercure, Diane, **Abondance** (2×), **Fortuna**, Cernunnos, taureau et cerf Statuette en argent de **Fortuna** Statuette de Sucellus en calcaire	Maison du IIIᵉ s., à l'est du *cardo*, dans une petite pièce (vestibule ?), à proximité de la porte d'accès. Éléments d'un laraire (?) Date de découverte : 1986	Kaufmann-Heinimann, *Götter und Lararien*, p. 248, GF26, fig. 199. Santrot, *Laraires en Gaule*, p. 94-95.
Mâcon (Saône-et-Loire)	Londres, British Museum Statuettes en argent : Jupiter, *Genius*, **Mercure** (4×), déesse panthée, *Luna*	Cachette domestique, éléments d'un laraire (?) Date de découverte : 1764	Kaufmann-Heinimann, *Götter und Lararien*, p. 254-255, GF33, fig. 206 Kaufmann-Heinimann, *Statuettes de Mâcon*, p. 19-35.
Homburg-Saar (Saarland) Schwarzenacker	Saarbrücken, Museum für Vor- und Frühgeschichte Statuettes en bronze : *Genius*, Apollon, **Mercure** (2×), Neptune, Victoire	Sous-sol d'une maison romaine. Les statuettes devaient être exposées à l'origine dans une pièce au-dessus de la cave. Éléments d'un laraire (?) Date de découverte : 1965	Kaufmann-Heinimann, *Götter und Lararien*, p. 270-271, GF58.

(cont.)

Lieu de provenance	Statuettes	Contexte archéologique	Bibliographie
Germanies (8)			
Augst/*Augusta Raurica* *Insula* 5/9, *taberna*	Augst, Römermuseum Statuettes en bronze : **Mercure** (2×), Minerve, pygmée assis	Éléments d'un laraire trouvés dans une *taberna* détruite au IIIe s. Date de découverte : 1966	Kaufmann-Heinimann, *Götter und Lararien*, p. 278, GF70, fig. 40-42.
Kaiseraugst, basse ville d'*Augusta Raurica* Région 17, E, maison 1	Augst, Römermuseum Statuettes en bronze : Lare, Hercule, **Mercure** (2×), *Somnus*	Éléments d'un laraire dans une caisse de chêne, trouvés dans la pièce 9. Date de découverte : 1983	Kaufmann-Heinimann, *Götter und Lararien*, p. 283, GF78, fig. 93-95. Fuchs, *Culte domestique en Suisse*, p. 104, fig. 13.
Avenches/*Aventicum* *Insula* 27, maison	Avenches, Musée romain Statuettes en bronze : Lare, Mercure, **Minerve** (2×), Junon, Victoire	Éléments d'un laraire trouvés dans l'*atrium* d'une maison détruite au IVe s. Date de découverte : 1916	Kaufmann-Heinimann, *Götter und Lararien*, p. 278-279, GF71, fig. 239. Fuchs, *Culte domestique en Suisse*, p. 105, fig. 14.
Martigny/*Octodurus*/ *Forum Claudii Vallensium* *Insula* 8, *Domus* du Génie domestique	Martigny, Office des recherches archéologiques Statuettes en bronze : *Genius*, Lare, **Mercure** (2×), Victoire	Éléments d'un laraire trouvés dans la pièce 15 (*cubiculum* ou chapelle domestique) Date de découverte : 1993	Kaufmann-Heinimann, *Götter und Lararien*, p. 282-283, GF79, fig. 244. Fuchs, *Culte domestique en Suisse*, p. 106-107.
Vallon Villa romaine	Vallon, Musée romain Statuettes en bronze : Apollon, Mars, Isis, Harpocrate, Hercule, **Mercure** (2×), Diane (2× ?), chèvre, coq, tortue et chien	Éléments d'un laraire trouvés dans la pièce à abside (*tablinum*) d'une villa détruite au IIIe s. Date de découverte : 1989	Kaufmann-Heinimann, *Götter und Lararien*, p. 285-286, GF83, fig. 248. Fuchs, *Culte domestique en Suisse*, p. 108-110, fig. 22-25.
Oberwinterthur/ *Vitudurum*	Zürich, Schweizerisches Landesmuseum Statuettes en bronze : **Mercure** (2×), Minerve, Amour	Éléments d'un laraire trouvés dans une maison détruite au IIIe s. Date de découverte : 1978	Kaufmann-Heinimann, *Götter und Lararien*, p. 288, GF86. Fuchs, *Culte domestique en Suisse*, p. 106.
Munderkingen (Baden-Württemberg)	Tübingen, Landesdenkmalamt Baden-Württemberg Statuettes en bronze : **Mercure** (2×)	Lot découvert à environ 500 m d'une villa romaine, au bord du Danube Éléments d'un laraire (?) Date de découverte : 1980	Kaufmann-Heinimann, *Götter und Lararien*, p. 272, GF60, fig. 233.
Saarlouis-Fraulautern (Saarland)	Saarbrücken, Museum für Vor- und Frühgeschichte Statuettes en bronze : **Jupiter** (2×), Minerve	Villa romaine ? Éléments d'un laraire ou d'une cachette de bronze Date de découverte : 1928	Kaufmann-Heinimann, *Götter und Lararien*, p. 274, GF63, fig. 236.
Bretagne (1)			
Exeter (Devon) Côté sud-est de l'*insula* 9	Statuettes en bronze : **Mercure** (2×), Apollon, Mars, Fortuna	Cachette de bronzes Éléments d'un laraire (?) Date de découverte : 1778	Kaufmann-Heinimann, *Götter und Lararien*, p. 229-231, GF4, fig. 178.

Lieu de provenance	Statuettes	Contexte archéologique	Bibliographie
Grèce – Dodécanèse (1)			
Cos *Casa dei bronzi*	Statuettes en bronze : Mars, Esculape, Minerve, **Isis** (3×) = Aphrodite au *basileion*, Tychè au *basileion* et Isis vêtue du nœud isiaque Buste en bronze d'un Sévère (Caracalla jeune ?)	Éléments d'un laraire, à l'étage d'une maison romaine détruite au III{e} s. Date de découverte : 1942	Kaufmann-Heinimann, *Götter und Lararien*, p. 308-309, GF114, fig. 275. Sirano, *Immagini di divinità*, p. 968-969.

FRANÇOISE VAN HAEPEREN

HONORER MITHRA EN CONTEXTE RÉSIDENTIEL
RÉFLEXIONS À PARTIR DES EXEMPLES DE ROME ET D'OSTIE

Dans quelle mesure le culte de Mithra était-il pratiqué dans un contexte résidentiel dans le monde romain[1] ? Posée dans le cadre de ce volume, cette question a donné naissance aux réflexions qui suivent. Celles-ci se veulent avant tout exploratoires ; elles ne prétendent pas épuiser la matière mais simplement poser quelques jalons en vue de recherches ultérieures. Vu l'ampleur des sources et de la bibliographie, j'ai choisi de me concentrer sur les cas de Rome et d'Ostie. Le culte de Mithra dans le port de Rome a fait l'objet de plusieurs investigations récentes et m'est familier[2]. En revanche, il est étonnant de constater que le culte de

---

[1] Sur culte de Mithra, voir par exemple M. CLAUSS, *The Roman Cult of Mithras. The God and his Mysteries*, trad. R. Gordon (éd. all. 1990), New York, Routledge, 2000 ; R. GORDON, « Institutionalized religious options », in J. RÜPKE (éd.), *Blackwell Companion to Roman Religion*, Oxford, Blackwell's Publishing, 2007, p. 392-405; L. BRICAULT, Ph. ROY, *Les cultes de Mithra*, Toulouse, PUM, 2021; N. AMOROSO, L. BRICAULT, R. VEYMIERS (éd.), *Le mystère Mithra. Plongée au cœur d'un culte romain. Catalogue d'exposition*, Musée royal de Mariemont, 2021.

Cet article, mené dans le cadre de recherches qui bénéficient de l'appui du Fonds de la Recherche Scientifique – FNRS – PDR T023419F, forme le volet d'un diptyque consacré au culte de Mithra à Rome et à Ostie, tel qu'il était pratiqué en contexte résidentiel ou associatif. L'autre volet vient de paraître : F. VAN HAEPEREN, « Honorer Mithra en contexte associatif. Réflexions à partir des exemples de Rome et d'Ostie », in C. HOËT-VAN CAUWENBERGHE, *Épigraphie romaine à l'honneur (1995-2020)*, Bordeaux, Ausonius, 2022, p. 305-321.

Je remercie chaleureusement N. Belayche, M.-Th. Raepsaet-Charlier et O. Latteur pour leurs suggestions. *Errors are mine.*

[2] L'ouvrage de G. BECATTI (*I mitrei*, Roma, Libreria dello Stato, 1954) reste une référence incontournable ; R. MARCHESINI, Sacra peregrina *ad Ostia e Porto : Mithra, Iuppiter Sabazius, Iuppiter Dolichenus, Iuppiter Heliopolita-*

ce dieu à Rome n'a fait l'objet d'aucune synthèse globale depuis la thèse publiée par Maarten Vermaseren[3]. Si la documentation, tant archéologique qu'épigraphique, est abondante – comme en témoignent le corpus de M. Vermaseren, certes vieilli mais non remplacé, ou encore les notices du *Lexicon Topographicum Vrbis Romae* –, elle se révèle cependant complexe à exploiter[4]. Les découvertes de structures, d'objets et d'inscriptions relatifs au culte de Mithra s'étalent en effet depuis le Moyen Âge jusqu'aux années 2000 et ont été documentées de manière très inégale. Si certaines structures archéologiques correspondent manifestement à des chapelles du dieu, l'interprétation d'autres vestiges n'est

---

nus, Sapienza. Università di Roma, Dottorato di Ricerca in Filologia e Storia del Mondo Antico, Anno Accademico 2012-2013 (accessible en ligne : https://iris.uniroma1.it/handle/11573/917277#.YCanVGFKhPY, consulté le 12 février 2021) ; F. Van Haeperen, *Regio I : Ostia, Portus*, Roma, Quasar, 2019 (*Fana, templa, delubra. Corpus dei luoghi di culto dell'Italia antica* [FTD], 6), *passim* ; F. Van Haeperen, « Au-delà du 'modèle missionnaire' : la topographie mithriaque d'Ostie », in F. Fontana, E. Murgia (éd.), *Sacrum facere. Atti del V Seminario di Archeologia del Sacro. Sacra peregrina. La gestione della pluralità religiosa nel mondo antico*, Trieste, Edizioni Università di Trieste, 2019, p. 81-103 ; F. Van Haeperen, *Dieux et hommes à Ostie, port de Rome (IIIᵉ s. av. J.-C. - Vᵉ s. apr. J.-C.)*, Paris, CNRS, 2020, p. 123-132.

[3] M. J. Vermaseren, *De Mithrasdienst in Rome*, Nijmegen, 1951 [*non uidi*]. A. Griffith a consacré une thèse, malheureusement inédite, à *The archaeological evidence for Mithraism in imperial Rome* (Ph.D., University of Michigan, 1993). Sur la topographie des *mithraea* de Rome, F. Coarelli, « Topografia mitriaca di Roma », in U. Bianchi (éd.), *Mysteria Mithrae*, Leiden, E.J. Brill, 1979, p. 69-79 (EPRO, 80) ; F. Van Haeperen, « Réflexions sur la topographie des *mithraea* de Rome », in F. Fontana, E. Murgia (éd.), *Il mitreo del Circo Massimo*, Trieste, Edizioni Università di Trieste, sous presse. Sur le culte de Mithra à Rome à l'époque tardive, A. Griffith, « Mithraism in the private and public lives of 4th-c. senators in Rome », *Electronic Journal of Mithraic Studies* 1 (2000), p. 1-27 (consultable au lien suivant : http://ecclesia.relig-museum.ru/Researches/sept1/griffith.htm – vu le 28/1/2020) ; V. Mahieu, « Les lieux de culte mithriaques face aux chrétiens dans la Rome tardo-antique », *RBPH* 98 (2020), p. 87-128.

[4] *CIMRM* : M. J. Vermaseren, *Corpus inscriptionum et monumentorum religionis Mithriacae*, I, Den Haag, M. Nijhoff, 1956 ; *LTVR* : *Lexicon Topographicum Vrbis Romae*, Roma, Quasar (t. I, 1993 : le *mithraeum* des *castra peregrinorum* est envisagé sous le lemme consacré à la caserne ; t. III, 1996 : 26 notices sous le lemme *Mithra*). Relevons que Rome est peu présente dans les synthèses sur Mithra (voir par exemple celles citées à la n. 1 ; fait exception l'ouvrage récent d'A. Mastrocinque [*The Mysteries of Mithras : A Different Account*, Tübingen, Mohr Siebeck, 2017], très spéculatif toutefois et peu ancré dans documentation archéologique et épigraphique [voir mon compte-rendu in *AC* 88 (2019), p. 371-372]).

pas nécessairement évidente, soit parce que ceux-ci ne sont plus visibles depuis longtemps ou peu documentés, soit parce que les restes retrouvés ne permettent pas de les identifier clairement à une chapelle du culte mithriaque[5]. Dans d'autres cas, des inscriptions témoignent de l'existence d'un lieu de culte consacré à Mithra ou d'une communauté honorant la divinité, sans qu'on puisse les rattacher à des structures connues. Ces difficultés liées à la nature de la documentation ne suffisent cependant pas, me semble-t-il, à expliquer le relatif désintérêt des chercheurs spécialistes de Mithra pour le cas de Rome et l'absence de synthèse sur le culte du dieu dans la capitale de l'Empire, qui pourtant l'aurait vu naître, de l'avis de plusieurs savants[6]. Je me demande si ce manque de considération pour le cas romain n'est pas, en bonne partie, dû au contenu même de la documentation qui ne permet d'explorer que de manière partielle les thématiques qui ont largement retenu l'attention des chercheurs intéressés par Mithra : sa théologie, ses mystères[7], ses initiations autour de sept grades, la signification astrologique des *mithraea* compris comme 'carte du ciel' – des sortes de 'normes mithriaques' que les chercheurs ont longtemps cherché à dégager[8]. Si l'un ou l'autre *mithraeum*

---

[5] Sur ces difficultés, voir VAN HAEPEREN, *Réflexions*.

[6] Voir CLAUSS, *Roman Cult*, p. 7-8, 21-22 ; R. BECK, « The Mysteries of Mithras : A new account of their genesis », *JRS* 88 (1998), p. 115-128, suivi par de nombreux chercheurs (voir entre autres, N. BELAYCHE, « Les dévots latinophones de Mithra disaient-ils leurs 'mystères' – et si oui, comment », in F. MASSA, D. NELIS (éd.), *Mystery Cults in Latin Texts*, in *Mnemosyne*, 75 (2022), p. 629-655 (je remercie l'auteure de m'avoir transmis son article alors qu'il n'était pas encore paru) ; *contra* : GORDON, *Institutionalized religious options*, p. 395-396).

[7] Dans le sillage de N. Belayche et F. Massa, dont les recherches sur les mystères s'avèrent désormais un point de départ fondamental pour toute étude sur la question, je retiens ici comme définition pour les mystères « des cérémonies réservées, non dévoilées » : N. BELAYCHE, F. MASSA (« Dossier : le 'mystères' : questionner une catégorie », *Métis* 14 (2016), avec leur article liminal « Quelques balises introductives : lexique et historiographie », p. 7-19 ; N. BELAYCHE, F. MASSA (éd.), *Mystery Cults in Visual Representation in Graeco-Roman Antiquity*, Leiden, E.J. Brill, 2020 [RGRW 194]).

[8] Comme l'ont écrit joliment M. MCCARTY, M. EGRI, A. RUSTOIU (« The Archaeology of Ancient Cult : From foundation deposits to religion in Roman Mithraism », *JRA* 32 [2019], p. 279-312 ; ici p. 281-282), les recherches sur le culte de Mithra se sont largement concentrées sur *Mithraism's thought-content and its savoir penser : beliefs, esoteric doxa, propositional claims, 'star talk'* (avec une série d'exemples à l'appui). Il convient donc, poursuivent-ils, de ne pas exclure une approche *that focuses on the cult as craft and that seeks to answer ba-*

de Rome offre de la matière pour étudier ces questions – tels ceux de Santa Prisca et des *Olympii* –, il faut bien admettre que, dans la plupart des cas, les vestiges archéologiques, iconographiques et épigraphiques de Rome n'éclairent pas ces aspects. Ils permettent en revanche d'enquêter dans d'autres directions. Où se situaient les *mithraea* ? Quels types d'activités s'y déroulaient – autres que ou bien outre les mystères et initiations chers aux savants mais peu présents dans la documentation romaine, ostienne (et d'ailleurs ...) ? Par qui étaient-ils fréquentés ? Comment étaient structurées les communautés qui s'y réunissaient[9] ?

Ce sont ici les *mithraea* implantés dans des contextes résidentiels qui vont retenir notre attention, tout comme les communautés qui les fréquentent[10]. Par contextes résidentiels, j'entends des *domus* mais aussi des contextes plus vastes, tels que des complexes comprenant notamment des *insulae* ou encore des propriétés impériales organisées autour d'un *palatium* ou de *horti*[11].

sic questions about technical know-how and the actual practices within the cult. Voir aussi les remarques critiques de P. ADRYCH, sur ce qu'elle appelle *the normative Mithraism* des modernes – qui a longtemps empêché la prise en compte de la pluralité des formes du culte (« 'The seven grades of Mithraism', or how to build a religion », in BELAYCHE, MASSA, *Mystery Cults*, p. 103-122).

[9] R. GORDON (« Mithraism and Roman Society : Social Factors in the Explanation of Religious Change in the Roman Empire », *Religion* 2 (1972), p. 92-121), suivi par d'autres (voir par exemple R. RUBIO, « Jerarquías religiosas y jerarquía social en el Mitraísmo », in L. HERNÁNDEZ GUERRA, J. ALVAR EZQUERRA (éd.), *Jerarquías religiosas y control social en el mundo antiguo, Actas del XXVII Congreso Internacional Girea-Arys IX : Valladolid, 7-9 de noviembre 2002*, Valladolid, Universidad de Valladolid, 2004, p. 459-462), a montré que la structuration hiérarchique des groupes mithriaques reproduit la hiérarchie sociale.

[10] Je ne prendrai donc pas en considération les communautés fréquentant les *mithraea* de Rome ou d'Ostie insérés dans ou à proximité de casernes ou de sanctuaires dédiés à d'autres divinités, pas plus que les chapelles du dieu implantées dans ou à proximité d'édifices thermaux ou de spectacles, ou encore dans des structures de stockage, de production ou de commerce, ou dans des sièges de collèges. Sur ces aspects, voir VAN HAEPEREN, *Au-delà du modèle missionnaire* ; VAN HAEPEREN, *Dieux et hommes*, p. 123-132 ; VAN HAEPEREN, *Réflexions* ; VAN HAEPEREN, *Honorer Mithra*.

[11] La nature des édifices dans lesquels sont implantés des *mithraea* ne peut pas toujours être établie avec certitude. Je n'évoquerai pas ici les *mithraea* insérés dans des édifices dont l'identification pose problème (comme celui de San Clemente (I. DELLA GIOVAMPAOLA, s.v. « Mithra [S. Clemens ; Reg. II] », *LTVR*, III, 1996, p. 257) ou ne peut être déterminée en l'absence de documentation (comme celui de via Passalacqua ; J. CALZINI GYSENS, s.v. « Mithra [Via Passalacqua 20 ; Reg. II] », *LTVR*, III, 1996, p. 259-260).

J'éviterai dans les pages qui suivent le terme moderne mithraïsme, le substantif mithriaste ou l'adjectif mithriaque appliqués aux *cultores Mithrae* – dont l'usage – qu'on le veuille ou non – laisse penser que le culte de Mithra est une religion et ses dévots des fidèles qui seraient uniquement attachés à cette divinité. J'utiliserai en revanche l'adjectif mithriaque pour l'appliquer aux inscriptions et objets se rapportant au culte de Mithra et le néologisme *mithraeum* pour désigner le lieu aux caractéristiques spécifiques où se réunissaient ses dévots[12].

1. Mithraea *implantés dans un contexte résidentiel et communautés qui les fréquentent*

Plusieurs *mithraea* de Rome et d'Ostie sont manifestement implantés dans un cadre résidentiel, tel qu'il vient d'être défini. Tout en présentant ces divers cas de figure, nous resterons attentifs à la question de la fréquentation de ces espaces : qui étaient les hommes qui s'y réunissaient ? Quel était leur statut juridique et social ? Appartenaient-ils nécessairement à une même *familia* (au sens antique du terme, c'est-à-dire la maisonnée, comprenant le *paterfamilias* et tous ceux et celles qui en dépendaient, fils, esclaves, affranchis) ?

Commençons par les *mithraea* implantés dans des *domus* – et plus précisément dans des espaces souterrains de celles-ci[13]. Contrairement à ce que soutenait Filippo Coarelli, plusieurs *mithraea* de Rome prennent place dans des *domus*[14]. C'est déjà le cas pour les *mithraea* du palazzo Barberini et de Santa Prisca, entre le milieu du IIe et le début du IIIe siècle, vraisemblablement aussi du *mithraeum* de l'Ospedale San Giovanni vers le milieu du IIIe siècle[15]. Des *mithraea* sont également installés au

---

[12] Sur ces questions terminologiques, voir par exemple les remarques de GORDON, *Institutionalized religious options*, p. 394-395.

[13] Sur les espaces mystériques en contexte domestique, J. ALVAR, R. RUBIO, R. SIERRA, « Religiosidad mistérica en el espacio familiar », *Arys* 1 (1998), p. 223-225.

[14] COARELLI, *Topografia*, p. 79.

[15] J. CALZINI GYSENS, *s.v.* « Mithra (Palazzo Barberini ; Reg. VI) », *LTVR*, III, 1996, p. 263-264 ; J. CALZINI GYSENS, *s.v.* « Mithra (Ospedale di San Giovanni sul Celio ; Reg. V) », *LTVR*, III, 1996, p. 261-262 ; M. ANDREUSSI,

IVe siècle dans de riches *domus*[16] (*mithraea* de la via G. Lanza[17] et des *Nummii Albini*[18] mais peut-être aussi celui des *Olympii*[19] ; quant au *specus* détruit par le préfet de la Ville, Gracchus, vers 376-377, il pourrait avoir été situé sur la propriété même de ce dernier[20]). Qu'en est-il de l'identité des dévots qui fréquentaient ces lieux de culte ? D'après les noms qui y ont été retrouvés, le *mithraeum* du palazzo Barberini semble plutôt avoir accueilli des fidèles issus du milieu des esclaves ou des affranchis (Yperanthes, Macarius et Acontio)[21]. Un tel constat peut être étendu, sur les mêmes bases, aux dévots du *mithraeum* de Santa Prisca[22],

---

s.v. « Mithra (s. Prisca ; Reg. XIII) », *LTVR*, III, 1996, p. 268-269 ; M. J. Vermaseren, C. C. Van Essen, *The Excavations in the Mithraeum of the Church of Santa Prisca in Rome*, Leiden, E.J. Brill, 1965. La *domus* dans laquelle est implanté le *mithraeum* aurait appartenu aux *priuata Traiani*, selon Vermaseren et Van Essen (*Excavations*, p. 109-110 ; voir aussi M. Vermaseren, « Nuove indagini nell'area della basilica di S. Prisca in Roma », *Mededelingen van het Nederlands Instituut te Rome* 37.2 (1975), p. 87-96, ici p. 87 et 90) ; à Licinius Sura, selon Coarelli (*Topografia*, p. 75).

[16] Griffith, *Mithraism*, p. 1-24.

[17] D. Gallo, « Il mitreo di via Giovanni Lanza », in Bianchi, *Mysteria Mithrae*, p. 249-258 ; J. Calzini Gysens, *s.v.* « Spelaeum (Via G. Lanza 128 ; Reg. V) », *LTVR*, III, 1996, p. 260 ; Griffith, *Mithraism*, p. 3-5.

[18] J. Calzini Gysens, *s.v.* « Mithra (Domus : Nummii ; Reg. VI) », *LTVR* III, 1996, p. 262 ; Griffith, *Mithraism*, p. 5-6.

[19] Voir *infra*.

[20] Mahieu, *Les lieux de culte mithriaques*, p. 90-91 (avec l'état de la question).

[21] *AE*, 1948, 100 ; *CIMRM*, 391 ; EDR 073704 (A. Carapellucci) : plaque de marbre (30 × 20 cm). Datation : IIIe s. : *Yperanthes / basem Inbicto / donum / dedit*. Voir déjà en ce sens Griffith, *Mithraism*, p. 6-7.

AE, 1980, 59a ; *CIMRM*, 395 ; EDR 077496 (A. Ferraro) : graffito : *Macarius // Macarius*.

Sur Acontio, M. Guarducci, « Quattro graffiti nel mitreo di Palazza Barberini », in Bianchi, *Mysteria Mithrae*, p. 187-192 (p. 188-190).

[22] Voir *S. Prisca*, p. 161 et p. 167 (*CIMRM*, 482e) : T[inet]lius ; *S. Prisca*, p. 162 (*CIMRM*, 481c ; *AE*, 1941, 75k ; *AE*, 1946, 83cc) : Theodorus (H. Solin, *Die Griechischen Personennamen in Rom*, Berlin – New York, De Gruyter, 2003, 78) ; *S. Prisca*, p. 162 (*CIMRM*, 481b ; *AE*, 1941, 75i ; *AE*, 1946, 83bb) : Niceforus (Solin, *Griechischen Personennamen*, p. 125-129) ; *S. Prisca*, p. 165 : Salutius ; *S. Prisca*, p. 165 : [Mar]ianus (?) ; *S. Prisca*, p. 166 : Steturstadius ; *S. Prisca*, p. 166 : Ianuarius ; *S. Prisca*, p. 167 : Saturnius ; *S. Prisca*, p. 167 : Florentius ; *S. Prisca*, p. 192 : Foebus (Solin, *Griechischen Personennamen*, p. 303-306) ; *S. Prisca*, p. 200 : Heliodorus (Solin, *Griechischen Personennamen*, p. 70-71) ; *S. Prisca*, p. 200 (*CIMRM*, 482c) : Gelasius (Solin, *Griechischen Personennamen*, p. 1365-1366).

dont les noms sont connus : ceux-ci apparaissent sur une procession de dévots, chacun d'eux étant identifié par son nom et le grade de lion – grade le plus élevé après celui de *pater*. Selon M. Vermaseren, les noms des fidèles de Santa Prisca témoignent de leur origine syrienne ; sur cette base, le savant affirmait ensuite, sans autre preuve, que ces « mithriastes » syriens avaient des connexions avec le sanctuaire de Jupiter Dolichenus situé non loin sur l'Aventin[23]. Les noms de ces dévots ne présentent toutefois aucune caractéristique typique de l'onomastique syrienne (c'est peut-être la proximité géographique du *Dolichenum* qui lui a suggéré cette hypothèse) mais sont fréquents dans l'onomastique des esclaves et des affranchis[24]. M. Vermaseren et C. C. Van Essen n'évoquent guère la question de la fréquentation du *mithraeum* de Santa Prisca[25]. Les espaces où il s'installe sont considérés comme ayant été transmis à des « mithriastes », dont ils ne précisent pas la provenance : dévots externes ou internes à la maisonnée ? Il me semble plus vraisemblable que, dans ce cas comme dans celui du *mithraeum* Barberini, la *domus* ait abrité un lieu de culte destiné à sa main-d'œuvre – à l'instar de ce qu'on peut supposer pour les *mithraea* de propriétés impériales (voir *infra*)[26]. Richard Gordon suggérait que de tels *mithraea* domestiques étaient présidés par un affranchi[27].

Quant aux *mithraea* qui ont été implantés dans de riches *domus* tardives[28], celle des *Nummii* et celle de la via Lanza, on

---

[23] Vermaseren, *Nuove indagini*, p. 92 (le point de vue est plus nuancé in Vermaseren, Van Essen, *Excavations*, p. 184-186, où les auteurs penchent davantage pour des noms « cultuels » qui auraient été donnés lors de l'initiation, sans toutefois apporter d'arguments convaincants en ce sens).

[24] À l'exception de *Tinetlius* (?) et *Steturstadius*, non attestés par ailleurs – la lecture de ces graffiti se révèle particulièrement ardue. Sur les autres noms, voir les références à Solin, dans la n. 22.

[25] Vermaseren, Van Essen, *Excavations*, p. 114.

[26] Le *mithraeum* découvert dans la villa romaine d'Els Munts (au nord de Tarragone), qui appartenait au gouverneur de la province, aurait été utilisé par les esclaves et affranchis de sa *familia* (Gordon, *Institutionalized religious options*, p. 396 ; J. Alvar, *El culto de Mitra en Hispania*, Madrid, Dykinson, 2019, p. 29-30, 168 penche pour une utilisation par les membres de la *familia*, y compris les esclaves et affranchis).

[27] Gordon, *Mithraism*, p. 104 et n. 70-71.

[28] Sur les cultes domestiques dans la Rome tardive, C. Sfameni, « Il pluralismo religioso pagano a Roma in età tardoantica attraverso le testimonianze

admet généralement qu'ils ont été fréquentés par les membres les plus éminents de la famille – famille sénatoriale dans le cas des *Nummii* – et que le *paterfamilias* en présidait la communauté, composée aussi bien de ses fils que de ses esclaves et affranchis[29]. Ces *mithraea* domestiques ont également pu accueillir des « pairs » du *paterfamilias*, également dévots de Mithra – ce qui permettait de renforcer les liens d'*amicitia*[30]. Ces hypothèses sont *in fine* fondées sur deux constats : d'une part, les inscriptions du *Phrygianum* du Vatican prouvent de manière indubitable que plusieurs sénateurs de la seconde moitié du IVe siècle étaient désormais dévots de Mithra, revêtus des plus hauts grades, et ne manquaient pas de le rappeler[31] ; d'autre part, la famille sénatoriale des *Olympii* (voir *infra*) a manifestement été à la tête d'un *mithraeum* et ce, sur trois générations[32] (que la chapelle ait été ou non implantée sur sa propriété).

En revanche, aucun *mithraeum* d'Ostie n'a été installé dans une *domus*, contrairement à une idée reçue qui circule toujours[33]. Un examen attentif des vestiges a démontré qu'il n'en était rien. Si le *mithraeum* des Parois peintes a été aménagé dans une parcelle occupée à l'époque républicaine par une *domus*, celle-ci subit de profondes transformations au IIe siècle. Au moment où y est

---

dei culti domestici », in S. Botta, M. Ferrara, A. Saggioro (éd.), *La storia delle religioni e la sfida dei pluralismi*, Brescia, Morcelliana, 2017, p. 190-202 ; plus particulièrement sur le *mithraeum* de Via Lanza, C. Sfameni, « Isis, Cybele and other oriental gods in Rome in late antiquity : 'private' contexts and the role of senatorial aristocracy », in A. Mastrocinque, C. Giuffrè Scibona (éd.), *Demeter, Isis, Vesta, and Cybele. Studies in Greek and Roman Religion in Honour of Giulia Sfameni Gasparro*, Stuttgart, Steiner Verlag, 2012, p. 120-121.

[29] En ce sens, Griffith, *Mithraism*, p. 20-21 : *The domus mithraeum could thus function as the consummate expression of its aristocratic owner's power as* pater familias *; in it he led his congregation not only with the authority of a Mithraic* pater *but also with the legal power of* patria potestas *or* dominus*, or with the social influence of a* patronus*. (...) Naturally the senator who owned his own mithraeum in his own* domus *would rise straight to the top, perhaps taking his eldest son with him (the* pater patrum *and* pater*), while other younger sons, other relatives, and various clients filled the lower ranks and the congregation.*

[30] Griffith, *Mithraism*, p. 23.

[31] Griffith, *Mithraism* ; L. Bricault, « *Gens isiaca* et identité polythéiste à Rome à la fin du IVe s. apr. J.-C. », in L. Bricault, M. J. Versluys (éd.), *Power, Politics and the Cults of Isis*, Leiden, E.J. Brill, 2014, p. 326-359.

[32] Griffith, *Mithraism*, p. 8-9.

[33] Van Haeperen, *Au-delà du modèle missionnaire*, p. 86-87.

installé un *mithraeum*, la parcelle est désormais utilisée à des fins artisanales ou industrielles[34]. Le *mithraeum* de Ménandre occupe pour sa part non une *domus* mais un édifice lié à l'artisanat ou au commerce (même s'il a pu abriter des logements de travailleurs, à l'arrière des *tabernae* donnant sur la rue)[35]. Quant au *mithraeum* des Sept sphères, il n'est pas lié à la *domus di Apuleio*. Les passages qui permettent actuellement d'accéder de la *domus* à la chapelle ont été créés lors de restaurations visant à faciliter le parcours des visiteurs. Ce *mithraeum* aurait donc pu dépendre de l'établissement industriel situé à l'ouest de celui-ci. Mais il semble plutôt avoir été implanté sur une portion de terrain appartenant à l'aire sacrée des quatre petits temples[36].

Si les *domus* d'Ostie n'ont donc pas livré de chapelles dédiées à Mithra, on trouve dans la cité portuaire des *mithraea* implantés dans de vastes ensembles résidentiels comprenant, notamment, des *insulae*[37]. C'est le cas de la chapelle installée dans la partie occidentale d'un vaste complexe qualifié de « palais impérial » dès sa découverte. Cette interprétation a depuis été battue en brèche : il s'agit bien plutôt d'un ensemble correspondant à un complexe thermal somptueux dans sa première phase d'époque antonine, avant d'être transformé, à la fin du IIe siècle, en luxueuse *insula* monumentale, composée d'appartements sur plusieurs étages, comparable à d'autres ensembles ostiens[38]. C'est aussi dans un vaste ensemble comprenant des logements, des cours et des thermes qu'est aménagé le *mithraeum* des Animaux[39]. Enfin, le *sacellum* des trois nefs, correspondant vraisemblablement aussi à un *mithraeum*, est également implanté dans un complexe résidentiel, le *Caseggiato degli Aurighi*[40]. Il est très vraisemblable que

---

[34] Van Haeperen, *Regio I : Ostia*, p. 174-177 (https://books.openedition.org/cdf/6571).

[35] *Ibid.*, p. 170 (https://books.openedition.org/cdf/6559).

[36] *Ibid.*, p. 185-187 (https://books.openedition.org/cdf/6592).

[37] Van Haeperen, *Au-delà du modèle missionnaire*, p. 87-88.

[38] Van Haeperen, *Regio I : Ostia*, p. 171-174 (https://books.openedition.org/cdf/6565).

[39] *Ibid.*, p. 153-155 (https://books.openedition.org/cdf/6528).

[40] *Ibid.*, p. 118-120 (https://books.openedition.org/cdf/6402). Sur l'identification de cette chapelle à un *mithraeum*, voir M.-L. Caldelli, N. Laubry, « compte rendu de Françoise Van Haeperen, *Fana, templa, delubra. Corpus dei*

ces *mithraea* aient avant tout été fréquentés par des individus vivant ou travaillant dans ces vastes complexes. Quoi qu'il en soit, les communautés qui s'y réunissaient devaient donc dépasser le cadre familial.

L'archéologie n'a pas révélé de *mithraea* romains implantés dans des ensembles résidentiels comparables à ceux d'Ostie. Ce constat tient vraisemblablement au fait que de telles structures ne sont presque pas documentées sur le terrain dans l'*Vrbs*[41].

Des chapelles dédiées à Mithra ont par contre été installées au sein de propriétés impériales, qu'il s'agisse de palais ou de jardins. Si de tels *mithraea* n'ont pas été mis au jour à Rome, l'épigraphie atteste leur existence. Ainsi, une épitaphe livre le nom d'un affranchi de Septime Sévère, Caracalla et Géta, Lucius Septimius Archelaus, qualifié de *pater et sacerdos Inuicti Mithrae domus Augustanae*[42]. Ce *pater* et prêtre de Mithra invaincu était donc à la tête d'une communauté de dévots s'assemblant dans un *mithraeum* aménagé au sein du palais impérial qui occupe, dès la fin du Ier siècle, la partie orientale du Palatin.

Selon une inscription trouvée via Sicilia 180 au fond du puits d'un complexe thermal, deux affranchis des empereurs Septime Sévère, Caracalla et Géta ont installé à leurs frais une statue du dieu Mithra invaincu, ont fait construire à leurs frais l'antre du dieu[43] et l'ont consacrée après son achèvement[44]. L'inscription,

---

luoghi di culto dell'Italia antica (FTD) 6. Regio I. Ostie, Porto, Roma (Edizioni Quasar), 2019 », *Archeologia Classica* 10 (2020), p. 813-814, avec un réexamen convaincant de la question.

[41] En témoigne le nombre réduit de pages du *LTVR* consacrées à des *insulae* dont plusieurs sont attestées par des sources autres qu'archéologiques (III, 1996, p. 96-98, 101-103). Une de ces *insulae* était placée sous la tutelle de Bona Dea, comme l'indique la dédicace d'un *simulacrum* et d'un autel (C. LEGA, *s.v.* « Insula Bolani », *LTVR*, III, 1996, p. 96).

[42] *CIL* VI, 2271 ; *ILS*, 4270 ; *CIMRM*, 511 : *D(is) M(anibus) / L(ucius) Septimius Auggg(ustorum) lib(ertus) Archelaus / pater et sacerdos Inuicti / Mithrae domus Augustanae / fecit sibi et Cosiae Primitiuae / coniugi bene merenti libertis liberta/busque posterisq(ue) eorum*.

[43] Le terme *antrum* apparaît ailleurs en contexte mithriaque (*CIL* VI, 754 [*mithraeum* des *Olympii*] ; cf. Stace, *Theb.* 1, 719 ; Porphyre, *antr.* 6, 5).

[44] *AE*, 1926, 48 ; *CIMRM*, 407 ; EDR 073001 (M. Giovagnoli) : plaque de marbre (172 × 48 × 6 cm) ; entre 198 et 211 : *Pro salute et reditu{m} / et uictoria{s} Impp(eratorum) Caess(arum) / L(uci) Septimi Seueri Pii Pertin(acis) / Aug(usti) Arab(ici) Adzab(enici) Part(hici) max(imi) / et M(arci) Aureli Antonin(i) Aug(usti) / [[[et P(ubli) Septimi Getae Caes(aris)]]] / [[[fil(ii) et fratris]]]*

sur plaque de marbre, précise que la dédicace est faite pour le salut, le retour et la victoire des trois empereurs. Or, la zone où a été retrouvée l'inscription appartenait à la propriété impériale des *horti Sallustiani*. La présence d'affranchis impériaux, fondant une chapelle mithriaque, pour le salut des empereurs régnants, n'étonne donc pas.

Qui étaient les membres de ces communautés mithriaques du Palatin et des *horti Sallustiani*, présidée ou fondée par des affranchis impériaux ? Il est fort vraisemblable que ceux-ci se recrutaient parmi les esclaves et affranchis de la maison impériale.

Un *mithraeum* d'Ostie, découvert à la fin du XVIIIe s., au nord-ouest de la ville, se situait dans la *crypta* d'un *palatium* correspondant vraisemblablement à une résidence impériale[45]. Plusieurs reliefs portant des inscriptions y ont été retrouvés. Une des inscriptions nous fournit une information particulièrement intéressante : la *crypta* du *palatium* a été concédée au *pater* et prêtre de Mithra par un Marcus Aurelius dont le *cognomen* manque[46]. Certains y reconnaissent Commode (malgré l'absence de titres impériaux), d'autres un citoyen ou affranchi impérial, ce qui semble davantage plausible[47]. On peut supposer que les fondateurs des autres *mithraea* installés dans des propriétés impériales ou bâtiments privés ont dû recevoir l'accord formel des propriétaires des lieux – ou de leur représentant – ou à tout le moins bénéficier de leur tolérance tacite.

Augustorum nn(ostrorum) / *totiusque domus diuinae* / *deum Inuict(um) Mithr(am)* / *Aurelius Zosimion et* / *Aurelius Titus Augg(ustorum) lib(erti)* / *suis impendiis conlo/cauerunt item antrum* / *suis sumptibus* / *exstructum fecerunt* / *item consummatum* / *consacrauerunt.* Voir Coarelli, *Topografia*, p. 72-73 ; J. Calzini Gysens, *s.v.* « Mithra. Antrum (horti Sallustiani ; Reg. VI) », *LTVR*, III, 1996, p. 264.

[45] Van Haeperen, *Regio I : Ostia*, p. 159-161 (https://books.openedition.org/cdf/6538).

[46] *CIL* XIV, 66 = *ILS*, 4227 : *C(aius) Valerius Heracles pat[e]r e[t] an[tis]/tes dei iubenis inconrupti So[l]is Inuicti Mithra[e]* / *[c]ryptam palati concessa[m] sibi a M(arco) Aurelio* / *[---]*.

[47] Pour la bibliographie, Van Haeperen, *Regio I : Ostia*, p. 159-161 (https://books.openedition.org/cdf/6538).

2. *Dédicaces familiales à Mithra*

Plusieurs inscriptions mithriaques de Rome mentionnent des membres d'une même famille – père et fils[48]. Celles-ci proviennent-elles pour autant d'un *mithraeum* implanté dans une *domus* ou dans une *insula* ? Ou témoignent-elles plutôt du fait que des représentants de telle ou telle famille fréquentaient ensemble un *mithraeum* utilisé par une communauté plus large, non limitée aux membres de la *familia* (et à leurs éventuels invités) ? On peut en outre se demander – même si la question pourrait paraître iconoclaste – si toutes les dédicaces (familiales ou non d'ailleurs) à Mithra proviennent nécessairement d'un *mithraeum* ?

Appliquons ces questions à l'un ou l'autre dossier, afin de mettre en lumière différents cas de figure qui peuvent se présenter et la complexité de la problématique des inscriptions mithriaques dans lesquelles sont cités des membres d'une même famille.

Une première difficulté consiste à s'assurer que les personnes nommées dans l'inscription appartiennent effectivement à la même famille et que les termes père ou frère se rapportent à la famille et non pas à des liens militaires, associatifs ou religieux. Cette vérification est d'autant plus nécessaire que le plus haut grade du culte de Mithra était le *pater* et que, selon plusieurs savants, les membres d'une communauté mithriaque pouvaient s'appeler entre eux *fratres*.

Ainsi, Marcus Aurelius Stertinius Carpus fait une dédicace à Mithra, en acquittement d'un vœu, pour le salut de Commode, avec Carpus, *pater*, procurateur *(fisci) castrensis* – il supervisait donc le « service chargé de gérer les fonds provenant du *patrimonium* et affectés par le prince à l'entretien de sa propre *domus* »[49], et Hermioneus et Balbinus, qualifiés de *fratres*[50]. Le *cognomen*

---

[48] Sur les relations familiales dans le culte de Mithra, voir ALVAR *et al.*, *Religiosidad mistérica* ; A. GRIFFITH, « Amicitia in the cult of Mithras : The setting and social functions of the Mithraic cult meal », in K. MUSTAKALLIO *et al.* (éd.), *Passages from Antiquity to the Middle Ages III : De Amicitia : Social Networks and Relationships*, Rome, Quasar, 2010, p. 63-77 (*Acta Instituti Romani Finlandiae*, 36) (ici p. 73, avec quelques exemples romains peu développés).

[49] J. FRANCE, « Un dispensator [f(isci) k(astrensis) ?] des trois Augustes dans le port Romain de Toulon (Telo Martius) », *ZPE* 125 (1999), p. 272-276 (ici p. 275).

[50] *CIL* VI, 727 ; *CIMRM*, 510 ; EDR 129704 (L. Benedetti 2) : base de marbre : 117,5 × 74 × 37,8 cm : *Soli Inuicto / Mithrae / pro salute Commodi /*

que partagent le dédicant principal et le procurateur permet de lever le doute qui pourrait surgir quant au sens à donner au terme *pater* : il s'agit bien de son père biologique. On notera en outre que les dévots de Mithra revêtus du grade de *pater* n'apparaissent pas en position subordonnée dans des dédicaces (sauf si leur mention, à l'ablatif, correspond en quelque sorte à une datation éponyme[51]). Le substantif *fratres* doit dès lors aussi être compris dans son sens biologique, d'autant plus qu'il n'apparaît que très rarement dans l'acception 'frère en religion', en contexte mithriaque[52]. Carpus père est généralement considéré comme un affranchi par les chercheurs ; peut-être était-ce aussi le cas de son fils M. Aurelius Stertinius[53]. Ni le texte ni le contexte de la découverte – l'inscription n'a pas été trouvée *in situ* – ne fournissent d'indice direct quant au lieu d'exposition de cette offrande. Les dimensions de la base, relativement imposante, pourraient plaider en faveur d'un emplacement dans un espace qui ne fût pas trop exigu.

Un deuxième dossier permet de poursuivre la réflexion sur les dédicaces mithriaques familiales. Il s'agit de trois offrandes (bases de statue ou autels de marbre)[54], chacune accompagnée d'un

Antonini Aug(usti) domini n(ostri) / M(arcus) Aurel(ius) Stertinius / Carpus una cum Carpo / proc(uratore) k(astrensi) patre et Her/mioneo et Balbino / fratribus / u(otum) s(oluit) f(eliciter).

[51] Voir F. MITTHOF, « Der Vorstand der Kultgemeinden des Mithras. Eine Sammlung und Untersuchung der inschriftlichen Zeugnisse », *Klio* 74 (1992), p. 275-290 ; VAN HAEPEREN, *Honorer Mithra*.

[52] BELAYCHE, *Dévots latinophones*.

[53] FRANCE, *Dispensator*, p. 275, n. 18, avec la bibliographie antérieure ; GRIFFITH, *Amicitia*, p. 73 ; notice EDR.

[54] Le nombre exact de bases/autels n'est pas évident à déterminer. VERMASEREN oscille entre deux (*CIMRM*) et trois (M. J. VERMASEREN, *Mithriaca IV. Le monument d'Ottavio Zeno et le culte de Mithra sur le Célius*, Leiden, E.J. Brill, 1978 [EPRO 16], p. 5) : le dessin superficiel ne permet pas de juger si *CIL* VI, 82a et b et les reliefs qui les accompagnent appartiennent, ou non, à un seul et même autel (ou base). Le contenu même des textes invite à y voir deux monuments différents. Il est invraisemblable et contraire aux pratiques observables ailleurs que le dédicant ait offert un même autel (ou base) à deux divinités différentes, à la suite de deux ordres indépendants l'un de l'autre. Il peut arriver en revanche que des dédicaces soient adressées à des divinités qui ont donné un ordre conjointement (on trouve alors des mentions du type *iussu eorum* ; voir par ex. *CIL* VI, 293, 413). Modius en était manifestement conscient puisque c'est sur l'ordre des divinités de la triade – un ordre manifestement conjoint – qu'il leur offre une dédicace.

relief, faites par M. Modius Agatho. Retrouvés au XVIᵉ siècle à proximité de Santa Maria in Domnica, sur le Caelius, ces monuments aujourd'hui perdus nous sont connus par des dessins réalisés par le Hollandais Pighius et G. Dosio[55].

L'un d'eux, réalisé à la suite d'un ordre du dieu, est dédié à Mithra invaincu, qualifié de *sanctus dominus*[56]. Cette séquence onomastique ne semble pas avoir été utilisée ailleurs pour qualifier Mithra[57]. L'épithète *sanctus* est en revanche appliquée au dieu à diverses reprises[58], tandis que le substantif *dominus* semble plus rare dans les formules onomastiques de Mithra[59]. Modius Agatho précise qu'il agit avec les siens, avec la permission d'un individu dont le nom manque ; les restitutions suggèrent *patris*, très vraisemblablement parce que l'inscription est mithriaque ; on relèvera toutefois qu'une telle formule – ou des équivalents – n'apparaît pas dans l'épigraphie mithriaque. Une autre piste mérite d'être envisagée, au vu des autres inscriptions laissées par le dédicant : cette permission pourrait avoir été accordée par son patron, qui apparaît dans les autres textes ici pris en considération, sous la formule *pro patrono*, soit en tant que bénéficiaire du geste posé soit comme celui à la place de qui agit Modius Agatho. Notons aussi que des formules du type *permissu patroni* apparaissent par ailleurs dans l'épigraphie, quand un affranchi pose

---

[55] VERMASEREN, *Mithriaca IV*, p. 3-5, 49-50. Dessins consultables à l'adresse suivante : https://www.tertullian.org/rpearse/mithras/display.php?page=cimrm327.

[56] *CIL* VI, 82a ; *CIMRM*, 333 ; EDR 161220 (A. Ferraro) : ⟨ :in corona et crepidine⟩ *Dedit M(arcus) Modius [Agatho] / permissu [patris ? patroni ?]*. ⟨ :in parte media⟩ *Sancto Domino / Inuicto Mithrae / iussu eius libens / dedit / [M(arcus)] M[od]/ius [Aga]/tho [cum] / suis*.

[57] Voir *CIMRM* et une recherche dans la base de données de Clauss-Slaby. J'emprunte au projet *ERC Mapping Ancient Polytheisms*, dirigé par C. Bonnet, la formule « séquence onomastique », comprise comme « combinaison[s] de noms divins ou éléments (noms, épithètes, titres, propositions, etc.), certains partagés par plusieurs dieux, d'autres spécifiques » (https://map-polytheisms.huma-num.fr/a-propos/).

[58] Voir *CIMRM*, 367 (Rome) ; 575 (Rome) ; 687 (reg. 6) ; 754 (reg. 10) ; 2183 (Dacie), 2238 (Mésie inf.). Une recherche rapide dans la base de données de Clauss-Slaby montre que l'épithète *sanctus* est surtout utilisée à Rome pour *Siluanus* et dans une moindre mesure pour Esculape et Apollon. Parmi les dieux dits orientaux, Sabazius peut être qualifié de *sanctus* à Rome (*CIL* VI, 30948 ; 30949 ; 37187 ; *AE*, 1950, 52).

[59] Voir *CIMRM*, 298 (Ostie) ; 563 (Rome) ; 767 (Bétique).

un geste nécessitant son autorisation[60]. Le dédicant a également spécifié qu'il a agi sur l'ordre du dieu – ce qui n'est pas fréquent dans l'épigraphie mithriaque[61]. Sous et à droite des premières lignes de l'inscription est figuré Sol, nu, la tête surmontée d'une couronne à rayons, les épaules couvertes d'une cape, un fouet à la main, debout sur un char tiré par quatre chevaux courant vers la droite. Sous l'inscription est représentée une figure féminine, identifiable à Luna, debout sur un char tiré par deux chevaux courant vers la gauche. Si la tête ou le buste de Sol et Luna apparaissent régulièrement sur des reliefs mithriaques, notamment au-dessus de la scène de la tauroctonie[62], ils sont moins souvent représentés sur leur char[63] et ne semblent pas apparaître seuls sur des dédicaces romaines à Mithra. Modius Agatho semble donc se singulariser, tant dans le choix d'une séquence onomastique inédite que dans la représentation qui accompagne son offrande.

M. Modius Agatho offre aussi, avec les siens, une dédicace à *Dominus Sanctus Optumus Maximus Salutaris* – que l'on peut identifier à Jupiter, étant donné les épithètes *Optimus Maximus* et le relief qui accompagne le texte (divinité debout sur une base, nue, tenant le sceptre dans la main gauche et le foudre dans la main droite, avec un aigle à ses pieds)[64]. Que le destinataire divin de l'offrande soit une seule divinité et non deux différentes m'apparaît assuré dans la mesure où Modius précise qu'il a agi *iussu eius* – autrement dit sur l'ordre de la divinité. Selon M. Vermaseren, les épithètes *dominus sanctus* montrent que ce Jupiter revêt les traits d'une divinité souveraine orientale, tel un Baal syrien[65]. Il faut toutefois relever que ces épithètes n'apparaissent que très rarement ensemble pour qualifier une divinité – pour Rome, je n'ai trouvé qu'une attestation, concernant Sil-

---

[60] Voir par ex. *CIL* VI, 7158, 12652 ; XI, 3990 ; XIV, 5090 : il s'agit d'inscriptions funéraires.

[61] Voir par exemple *CIMRM*, 704, 1252.

[62] En se limitant à Rome, voir *CIMRM*, 375, 334, 339, 350, 357, 366, 368, 372, 375, 390, 408, 417, 435, 437, 508, 529, 533, 542, 546, 556, 557, 585, 586, 588, 598, 606, 615, 617.

[63] Voir, à Rome, *CIMRM*, 335 ; 415 ; 532 ; 554.

[64] *CIL* VI, 82b ; *CIMRM*, 333 ; EDR 164507 (A. Ferraro) : [*Domi*]*no Sanct*[*o*] / [*O*]*ptumo Maxim*[*o*] / [*Sa*]*lutari iussu eius* / *libens dedit* / [*M*(*arcus*)] *Modius Aga*[*tho*] / *cum* [*suis*] / [*pro Faus*]*to* / [*p*]*at*[*rono*].

[65] Vermaseren, *Mithriaca IV*, p. 49-50.

vanus ; en Afrique, seul Saturne est régulièrement désigné comme *dominus sanctus*[66]. Il faut donc plutôt considérer que le dédicant a choisi d'appliquer les mêmes épithètes à Jupiter et à Mithra – rapprochant ainsi les deux divinités qu'il honore. Quant à l'épiclèse *Salutaris*, elle précise l'action attendue du dieu : il doit assurer la *salus* de ceux qui l'honorent, à savoir le bien-être physique et moral (point n'est besoin de chercher une visée eschatologique derrière l'épithète qui s'applique à une série de divinités, aussi bien traditionnelles qu'étrangères[67]). Le dédicant spécifie, à la fin de son texte, qu'il agit pour son patron Faustus[68].

Enfin, M. Modius Agatho offre une dédicace, en en ayant reçu l'ordre, à Jupiter, qualifié d'*optumus maximus, Caelus Aeternus*, à Junon reine et à Minerve[69]. Comme dans les textes précédents, Agatho agit, *cum suis*, mais cette fois, il le fait pour sa *salus* et pour celle de son patron Faustus, qui reçoit un qualificatif (très saint ?), et pour celle de sa femme Helpis[70]. La triade capitoline destinataire de l'offrande est figurée, de manière classique, au-dessus de l'inscription. En revanche la séquence onomastique *Caelus Aeternus* n'apparaît pas ailleurs, à ma connaissance, pour qualifier le dieu souverain des Romains. Selon M. Vermaseren, elle renverrait à une divinité souveraine syrienne. Il faut toutefois

---

[66] *CIL* VI, 669 : dédicace d'un vétéran à *dominus Siluanus sanctus deus*. En Afrique, Saturne peut être qualifié de *dominus sanctus* (voir par exemple *AE*, 1942/1943, 80 ; *CIL* VIII, 24036 ; *ILAfr*, 348). Sur les divinités qualifiées de *dominus*, voir le tableau dressé par R. Last, « The Silence of a God Fearer : Anonymous Dedication in *CIL* 6.390a = 30752 », *RRE* 6 (2020), p. 75-103, ici p. 79-88.

[67] Comme l'a justement relevé I. Campos Méndez, « Vinculos familiares en el contexto mitraico : las inscriptiones *pro salute* », *Klio* 97.2 (2015), p. 671-686 (ici p. 677).

[68] La restitution [*pro Faus*]*to* / [*p*]*at*[*rono*] apparaît comme très vraisemblable au vu de la dernière dédicace offerte par M. Modius Agatho.

[69] *CIL* VI, 81 ; *ILS*, 3949 ; *CIMRM*, 329 ; EDR 161219 (A. Ferraro) : *Optumus Maximus / Caelus Eternus Iup*[*pi*]*/ter Iunoni Reginae / Mineruae iussus liben*[*s*] */ dedit pro salute*{*m*} *sua*{*m*} */ M*(*arcus*) *Modius Agatho et pr*[*o*] */ Fausti patroni hominis s*(*anctissimi ?*) */ et Helpidis suaes cum s*[*uis*], avec, au-dessus de l'inscription, un relief de la triade capitoline.

[70] Alvar *et al.*, *Religiosidad*, p. 213-226 (ici p. 217-218) remarquent à juste titre que, même si le culte de Mithra semble exclusivement pratiqué par des hommes, ceux-ci peuvent intégrer leur femme dans leurs vœux ou dédicaces à ce dieu. Sur les dédicaces à Mithra, *pro salute* de membres de la famille, Campos, *Vinculos*, p. 672-678.

observer que cette séquence onomastique est très rare ; les trois attestations romaines que j'ai repérées ne permettent en rien d'appuyer l'affirmation du savant hollandais[71]. Quant à *Caelus* seul, il n'apparaît guère dans l'épigraphie et, quand c'est le cas, le plus souvent dans des 'litanies divines' où il forme une 'paire' avec *Terra*[72]. L'épithète *aeternus* peut, pour sa part, qualifier diverses divinités, dont, à Rome, *Caelus*, Mercure et Jupiter Optimus Maximus Dolichenus[73]. Il faut également noter que Victor Olympus, le sénateur fondateur du *mithraeum* tardif déjà évoqué ci-dessus, est qualifié par son petit-fils de *caelo deuotus et astris*, dévot du ciel et des astres[74].

Dans ces trois dédicaces, M. Modius Agatho agit avec les siens, pour son patron ou sous son contrôle – ce qui signifie qu'il s'agit d'un affranchi. La mention *cum suis* inclut vraisemblablement sa femme dans les deux textes qui ne la mentionnent pas, tout comme ses enfants et ses éventuels esclaves ou affranchis. Le contexte semble donc très familial, avec une présence forte du patron, dans la demeure duquel résidaient peut-être Agatho et les siens (qui n'avaient pas nécessairement été affranchis). Ces trois offrandes, retrouvées au même endroit, ont, selon toute vraisemblance, été posées dans un même espace. Il est tentant d'y reconnaître une chapelle située dans la demeure de la famille (même si on ne peut exclure d'autres possibilités, comme par exemple un *compitum* – une chapelle de carrefour). Différentes divinités y ont été honorées : la triade capitoline, dont Jupiter revêt certains traits très spécifiques, en étant qualifié de *Caelus Aeternus* ; Mithra qualifié de *sanctus dominus inuictus* ; une divinité qu'une partie de ses épithètes (*optumus maximus*) et sa représentation iconographique permettent d'identifier à Jupiter

---

[71] *CIL* VI, 83 (dédicace à *Caelus Aeternus*, par deux femmes) ; 84 : dédicace, par un fils et sa mère, à *Caelus Aeternus*, *Terra Mater* et Mercure *Menestrator* ; 85 : dédicace fragmentaire à *Caelus Aeternus*.

[72] *CIL* II, 2407 (Hisp. cit. ; dédicace à plusieurs divinités) ; *IMS*, 6, 7 (*ILJug* 2, 555 : à *IOM, Caelus, Terra* et *Pontus* (Moesia sup.) ; à Rome, dans une litanie d'un vétéran adressée entre autres à *Terra Caelus Mar Neptunus* (*CIL* VI, 31171).

[73] Pour *Caelus*, voir n. *supra*. *CIL* VI, 412 (*Jupiter Optimus Maximus A(eternus) Dolichenus* et *Sol Dignus Praestans*) ; 30975 (Mercure, suivi de la triade capitoline, Sol, Luna, Apollon, Diane et d'autres divinités).

[74] Voir *infra*.

– et qui, à l'instar de Mithra, est elle aussi qualifiée de *dominus sanctus*. On notera encore que, dans les trois dédicaces, Modius Agatho précise qu'il a agi sur ordre de la divinité – peut-être à la suite d'un rêve ou d'une 'vision'[75].

Reste à se poser la question de savoir si le lieu de culte où ont été posées ces dédicaces correspondait à un *mithraeum*. Avant de tenter d'y répondre, il faut d'abord rappeler que d'autres divinités que Mithra pouvaient être honorées dans une chapelle qui lui était dédiée, comme plusieurs exemples l'attestent, notamment à Rome et à Ostie[76]. Il convient ensuite d'attirer l'attention sur un fait peut-être moins connu : Mithra pouvait recevoir des dédicaces dans le sanctuaire d'un autre dieu, comme le montre l'exemple du *Dolichenum* de l'Aventin[77]. La grande majorité des dédicaces à Mithra semble cependant avoir été posée dans un lieu de culte qui lui était spécifiquement dédié, quel que soit d'ailleurs son contexte d'implantation (*domus*, *insula* ou autres).

---

[75] La formule *ex uisu* est attestée à quelques reprises dans les dédicaces à Mithra. Voir par exemple *CIMRM*, 214, 704, 1490, 1497, 1778, 1805. Je n'ai en revanche pas trouvé de dédicaces à Mithra du type *somno monitus*.

[76] Voir par exemple une représentation de Silvanus dans les *mithraea* d'Ostie suivants : Aldobrandini, « Palais impérial », Planta Pedis, (Van Haeperen, *Regio I : Ostia*, p. 150-153, 171-174, 179-182 (https://books.openedition.org/cdf/6522 ; https://books.openedition.org/cdf/6565; https://books.openedition.org/cdf/6582). À Rome, une représentation d'Isis a été retrouvée dans les *mithraea* des *castra peregrinorum* (E. Lissi-Caronna, *Il mitreo dei Castra Peregrinorum (S. Stefano Rotondo)*, Leiden, E. J. Brill, 1986 [EPRO 104], p. 38-40) et de S. Prisca (Vermaseren, *Nuove indagini*, p. 95, n. 23 et les remarques de Mahieu, *Les lieux de culte mithriaques*, p. 99-101) ; des représentations de Minerve et de Vénus dans le *mithraeum* du Grand Cirque (*CIMRM*, 441, 442).

[77] *CIMRM*, 467-471 ; C. Lega, *s.v.* « Mithra (s. Sabina ; Reg. XIII) », *LTVR*, III, 1996, p. 269-270 : Mithra avait-il en ce lieu une chapelle autonome ou son culte y a-t-il été associé à celui de Jupiter Dolichenus ? À moins qu'il ne s'agisse là d'offrandes faites, dans le sanctuaire de Jupiter Dolichenus, par un dévot qui aurait honoré et Mithra et le dieu de Commagène : d'après R. Gordon, il aurait ramené ces petits reliefs depuis la Mésie supérieure (« Small and miniature reproductions of the Mithraic icon : reliefs, pottery, ornaments and gems », in M. Martens, G. De Boe [éd.], *Roman Mithraism : the Evidence of the Small Finds*, Bruxelles, Institute for the archaeological heritage, 2004, p. 259-283 [part. p. 265]).

Il faut noter aussi que plusieurs divinités semblent avoir été honorées dans le *cosiddetto Sabazeo* à Ostie. S'agissait-il d'un *mithraeum*, comme le laissent penser ses caractéristiques planimétriques typiques d'un *mithraeum* ou d'une chapelle des travailleurs de ces *horrea* où plusieurs dieux étaient vénérés ? La question reste ouverte. Van Haeperen, *Regio I : Ostie*, p. 164-167 (https://books.openedition.org/cdf/6549).

Le contexte archéologique, tout comme les dimensions des autels/bases offerts par Modius Agatho, malheureusement inconnus, ne peuvent nous aider. Le fait que deux des autels soient dédiés à Jupiter ou à la triade, alors qu'un seul l'est à Mithra constituerait-il un indice ? Peut-être... mais on ne sait pas quelles étaient les autres offrandes posées dans le lieu de culte. D'autre part, le fait que Jupiter soit caractérisé dans ces dédicaces par des séquences onomastiques qui ne lui sont pas appliquées par ailleurs et que Modius Agatho utilise également pour Mithra (du moins pour l'une d'entre elles) pourrait-il signifier que Jupiter n'était pas la divinité principale de la chapelle ? Il m'est difficile de trancher dans l'état actuel des connaissances et de mes réflexions.

Le dernier dossier qui nous retiendra montre qu'un même *mithraeum* peut avoir été fréquenté et dirigé, sur plusieurs générations, par les membres d'une même famille.

Le *mithraeum* des *Olympii* est fondé, vers le milieu du IVe siècle, par le *uir clarissimus* Nonius Victor Olympius. Son petit-fils, Tamesius Augentius Olympus fait à son tour une grotte (*antra facit*), sans recourir à des fonds publics, comme il le précise dans une inscription métrique retrouvée au XIXe siècle, Piazza San Silvestro[78]. S'agit-il de la restauration de la chapelle érigée par son grand-père ou d'une nouvelle construction ? La question reste ouverte. Plusieurs autres inscriptions découvertes dans la même zone aux XVe et XVIIe siècles rappellent des cérémonies de type initiatique impliquant des membres de cette famille, entre

---

[78] *CIL* VI, 754 ; *ILS*, 4269 ; *CIMRM*, 406 ; EDR 167157 (S. Orlandi) : relief de marbre ; entre 371 et 400 : ⟨ :columna I, in ansa sinistra⟩ *Tamesii* // ⟨ :columna II, in tabula⟩ *Tamesii* // ⟨ :columna III, in margine superiore⟩ *Olympii* // ⟨ :columna III, in tabula⟩ *Olim Victor auus, caelo deuotus et astris,/ regali sumptu Phoebeia templa locauit. / Hunc superat pietate nepos, cui nomen auitum est,/ antra facit sumptusque tuos nec, Roma, requirit. / Damna piis meliora lucro ; quis ditior illo est,/ qui cum calicolis parcus bona diuidit heres ?* // ⟨ :columna IV, in tabula⟩ *Augentii* // ⟨ :columna V, in ansa dextra ⟩ //*Augentii*. Trad. V. Mahieu, *Recherches sur les coexistences religieuses à Rome au IVe siècle ap. J.-C. Païens et chrétiens dans un âge de transition identitaire*, Thèse de doctorat, Université catholique de Louvain-École pratique des hautes études, 2018, p. 554 : « Jadis, mon grand-père Victor, dévot du ciel et des astres, établit à frais royal un temple à Phoebus. Son petit-fils, dont le nom lui vient de son aïeul, le surpasse en piété : il a fait faire une grotte, et il n'a pas réclamé tes ressources, Rome. Les pieux préfèrent les pertes au lucre : qui est plus riche que cet héritier qui, sans excès, partage ses biens avec les habitants du ciel ? ».

357 et 376[79]. Celles-ci évoquent la transmission (*tradere*) de *sacra* qui sont désignés par « un substantif neutre pluriel forgé sur les différents grades », tels que *hierocoracica* pour le corbeau ou *leontica* pour le lion. Le verbe *tradere* « oriente vers la transmission d'un héritage » correspondant vraisemblablement à « un enseignement rituel avec transmission d'objets ou d'attributs symboliques liés à la charge » à laquelle accède le dévot[80]. Ces textes, gravés sur des bases imposantes de colonnes[81], rappellent le rôle joué dans ces cérémonies par les *Olympii*, qui transmettent ces *sacra* : Nonius Victor Olympus, *pater patrum*, et son fils Aurelius Victor Augentius, *pater* qui, à la mort de son père, devient à son tour *pater patrum* – plus haut responsable de la communauté mithriaque. En revanche, rien n'est dit des personnes qui en sont les réceptrices, sauf quand Aurelius Victor Augentius, désormais *pater patrum*, transmet, en 376, à son jeune fils Aemilianus Corfo Olympius les *hierocoracica*[82]. Il serait donc peu pertinent de voir dans ces inscriptions une sorte de compte-rendu des cérémonies qui se déroulaient dans le *mithraeum* : d'une part, parce qu'elles semblent limitées au rappel des célébrations qui impliquaient une *traditio* de *sacra*, d'autre part, parce qu'elles semblent particulièrement destinées à valoriser les fonctions remplies par les *Olympii*.

La question de la localisation précise du *mithraeum* fondé par Nonius Victor – voire de celui qu'aurait à son tour édifié son petit-fils – a déjà fait couler beaucoup d'encre. Était-il implanté au sein du *templum Solis* – dont la superficie devait s'étendre

---

[79] *CIL* VI, 749 (*ILS*, 4267a ; *CIMRM*, 400 ; EDR 167160 [S. Orlandi]), en 357 ; *CIL* VI, 750 (*ILS*, 4267b ; *CIMRM*, 401 ; EDR 167159 [S. Orlandi], en 358) ; *CIL* VI, 751 (*ILS*, 4267c ; *CIMRM*, 402 ; EDR 073473 [S. Orlandi], en 358) ; *CIMRM*, 403 (*ILS*, 4268 ; EDR 126724 [S. Orlandi], en 376) ; *CIL* VI, 752 (*ILS*, 4267d ; *CIMRM*, 404 ; EDR 167158 [S. Orlandi], en 358-359) ; *CIL* VI, 753 (*ILS*, 4267e ; *CIMRM*, 405 ; EDR 073474 [S. Meloni], en 362).

[80] BELAYCHE, *Dévots latinophones* et https://journals.openedition.org/asr/1879?lang=en#toctoln1.

[81] Du moins ceux pour lesquels on dispose d'informations : voir G. BASTIANELLI, « The last *cultores Mithrae* of late antique Rome and the *mithraea* of the Olympii », *Mediterraneo antico* 20.1-2 (2017), p. 201-224 (ici p. 206-207).

[82] Sur la participation de jeunes enfants aux rites mystériques, ALVAR *et al.*, *Religiosidad*, p. 220-221. *Confessio S. Cypriani* (*AA.SS.*, Sept. 26), cité par BASTIANELLI, *Last cultores*, p. 218 : Saint Cyprien d'Antioche (fin IIIe – début IVe s.) aurait été introduit aux mystères de Mithra à l'âge de sept ans.

jusqu'au lieu de découverte des inscriptions des *Olympii*[83] ? Faut-il supposer avec Giovanna Bastianelli[84] deux phases différentes, d'une part l'installation du *mithraeum* dans un espace du *templum Solis*, qu'elle propose de situer dans le secteur nord-est du portique du temple dédié par l'empereur Aurélien en 275, et d'autre part une construction *ex nouo*, peut-être dans un contexte domestique, par Tamesius Augentius Olympius ? La mention de l'absence de fonds publics pourrait-elle fournir un indice ? Celle-ci pourrait-elle signifier que le grand-père Nonius Victor avait, pour sa part, bénéficié de tels fonds – lui qui avait installé sa chapelle *regali sumptu*, littéralement à frais royal, signifiant sans doute dans ce texte poétique, aux frais de l'État ? Cela semblerait étonnant dans la mesure où le culte de Mithra n'appartenait pas aux *sacra publica* ; en revanche Nonius Victor aurait pu recevoir la permission d'installer son *mithraeum* au sein d'un édifice public ou sacré, tel que le temple du Soleil, sans devoir réellement édifier une chapelle mais en l'installant (*locauit*) dans une pièce ou une portion d'espace, dans un portique par exemple, qui lui aurait été concédée[85]. L'absence de fonds publics, dans le cas de Tamesius Augentius, permettrait-elle d'une part de supposer qu'il fit (re)construire l'antre, d'autre part que ceci eut lieu après les mesures prises par Gratien en 382, qui supprimaient les subsides dont bénéficiaient les cultes publics[86] ? Pas nécessairement puisque le culte de Mithra ne faisait pas partie des *sacra publica*[87]. Tamesius Augentius pourrait simplement avoir voulu insister de la sorte sur son évergétisme à l'égard de la communauté mithriaque qui fréquentait sa chapelle. Quoi qu'il en soit, il apparaît que les *Olympii* ont, durant trois générations, présidé une communauté mithriaque, dont la nature exacte nous

---

[83] En ce sens J. Calzini Gysens, *s.v.* « Mithra (M. degli Olympii, S. Silvestro in Capite ; Reg. VII) », *LTVR*, III, 1996, p. 264-265 ; S. Orlandi, « Per la storia edilizia di Roma nel IV secolo. Qualche contributo epigrafico », in G. Cecconi, R. Lizzi Testa, A. Marcone (éd.), *The Past as Present. Essays on Roman History in Honour of Guido Clemente*, Turnhout, Brepols, 2019, p. 507-523 (ici p. 517-518).

[84] Bastianelli, *Last cultores*, p. 204-215.

[85] *Ibid.*, p. 209.

[86] En ce sens Orlandi, *Per la storia*, p. 518.

[87] Comme le rappelle à juste titre Griffith, *Mithraism*, p. 13 à propos des sénateurs adeptes de Mithra au IVe siècle.

échappe : celle-ci était-elle uniquement composée de membres de la *familia* (incluant éventuellement aussi des membres d'un niveau plus modeste, esclaves ou affranchis –, ce qui expliquerait pourquoi leurs noms n'ont pas été gravés pour les siècles) ou recrutait-elle plus largement ses dévots et, dans ce cas, sur quelles bases ? Il n'est guère possible de répondre à la question. Le parallèle avec le *mithraeum* des *Nummii Albini* nous rappelle que des familles sénatoriales ont pu, à l'époque tardive, installer des chapelles dédiées à Mithra dans leur *domus*. Mais le constat, rappelé par G. Bastianelli, que les inscriptions ont été gravées sur des bases de colonnes imposantes va clairement dans le sens d'une implantation du *mithraeum* de Nonius Victor au sein du portique du temple du Soleil – ce qui pourrait signifier que les membres de la communauté qui s'y réunissait n'appartenaient pas nécessairement tous, ou pour la majorité d'entre eux, à la *familia* des *Olympii*.

Conclusion

Au terme de ce parcours, une comparaison entre les *mithraea* implantés dans des contextes résidentiels à Rome et Ostie révèle des situations contrastées. Ce constat tient-il à la nature de la documentation ou à des réalités de terrain diverses ? La seconde option semble s'imposer quand il s'agit des *mithraea* aménagés dans des *insulae* : si ceux-ci sont attestés à Ostie et non à Rome, c'est très vraisemblablement le cas parce que de tels complexes résidentiels restent peu connus dans la capitale. L'absence de *mithraeum* dans des *domus* à Ostie ne peut en revanche s'expliquer par la nature de la documentation, particulièrement abondante. On n'observe donc pas dans la ville portuaire l'évolution perceptible au IVe siècle à Rome, avec l'apparition de familles sénatoriales parmi les dévots du dieu. En revanche, tant dans la capitale que dans son port, Mithra a été honoré au sein de propriétés impériales : les *mithraea* qui y ont été installés par des affranchis n'étaient, selon toute vraisemblance, pas fréquentés par la famille impériale mais par les esclaves et affranchis qui œuvraient dans ces palais. Signalons aussi – même si je n'ai guère développé cet aspect ici – que des dédicaces familiales ont été retrouvées dans des *mithraea* implantés dans des contextes autres que résidentiels à Rome[88] mais non à Ostie. Ceci pourrait en partie s'expliquer par le fait que l'épigraphie mithriaque n'est guère abondante à Ostie – peut-être parce que la plupart des dévots du dieu n'avait pas les moyens de faire des offrandes onéreuses ou de graver sur la pierre le souvenir de leurs dons. Les quelques dossiers examinés ici permettent également de constater une variabilité certaine dans les séquences onomastiques appliquées au dieu tout comme dans la structuration de ces communautés implantées en contexte résidentiel (les grades que l'on considère généralement comme liés à l'initiation ne sont pas attestés dans chacune d'entre elles). Ce constat, tout aussi valable pour les communautés honorant Mithra hors contexte résidentiel[89], ne surprend pas : chacun de ces groupes fonctionnait de manière indépendante, s'appropriant, autour de référents partagés mais selon ses propres modalités, le culte de Mithra.

---

[88] Sur cet aspect, voir VAN HAEPEREN, *Honorer Mithra*.
[89] *Ibid.*

CARLA SFAMENI

DIVINE GUESTS: RELIGIOUS IDENTITIES AND GROUPS OF DEITIES IN ROMAN DOMESTIC SHRINES

Introduction

The Theodosius's Edict promulgated on 8th November 392 AD states: "No person at all, of any class or order whatsoever of men or dignities, whether he occupies a position of power or has completed such honors, whether he is powerful by the lot of birth or is humble in lineage, legal status and fortune, shall sacrifice an innocent victim to senseless images in any place at all or in any city. He shall not, by more secret wickedness, venerate his lar with fire, his genius with wine, his penates with fragrant odors; he shall not burn lights to them, place incense before them, or suspend wreaths for them."[1] The imperial decree attests the vitality of domestic cults in their traditional forms still at the end of the fourth c. AD and reaffirms the relation among the main household

---

[1] I wish to thank Alexandra Dardenay and Laurent Bricault for inviting me to contribute to this book. Many thanks also go to Giulia Giachetti for her help in translating my paper into English.
 Cod. Th. XVI, 10, 12: *Nullus omnino ex quolibet genere ordine hominum dignitatum vel in potestate positus vel honore perfunctus, sive potens sorte nascendi seu humilis genere condicione fortuna in nullo penitus loco, in nulla urbe sensu carentibus simulacris vel insontem victimam caedat vel secretiore piaculo larem igne, mero genium, penates odore veneratus accendat lumina, imponat tura, serta suspendat... is utpote violatae religionis reus ea domo seu possessione multabitur, in qua eum gentilicia constiterit superstitione famulatu* (J. ROUGÉ, R. DELMAIRE (eds.), *Les lois religieuses des Empereurs romains de Constantin à Théodose II (312-438)*, vol. I, *Code Théodosien Livre XVI*, Paris, Cerf, 2005 (Sources Chrétiennes 497), p. 442-443; for the translation see C. PHARR, *The Theodosian Cod and Novels and the Sirmondian Constitutions*, New York, Greenwood Press, 1952, p. 473).

gods, the Lares, the Genius and the Penates.[2] A person "guilty of the violation of religion shall be punished by the forfeiture of that house or landholding in which it is proved that he served a pagan superstition."[3] It is a clear sign that, as Cicero stated long time before, the house was a deeply sacred place, as the location of altars, hearths, cults, rites devoted to the household gods: "What is more sacred, what more inviolably hedged about by every kind of sanctity, than the home of every individual citizen? Within its circle are his altars, his hearths, his household gods, his religion, his observances, his rituals."[4]

In the long tradition of cults practiced within the Roman urban and rural residences from the Republican Age to Late Antiquity,[5] it is particularly interesting to analyse the evidence related to the groups and associations of gods and to reflect on their possible meanings. Nevertheless, such a survey has some limits, based on the available archaeological evidence. The mural paintings, well attested in Delos and especially in the Vesuvian cities,[6] have generally disappeared in most of the other contexts: we can therefore recognize spaces for worship in niches, shrines and other structures, but it is often impossible to know which

---

[2] Some Christian authors refer to and strongly condemn these practices: see for example Lact. *Epist.* 23.1-3; Hier. *In Is.* 16.57.7-8: Prud. *Contra Symm.* 199-211; August. *C.D.* 4.8.43. See C. SFAMENI, *Residenze e culti in età tardoantica*, Roma, Scienze e Lettere, 2014 (*Sacra publica et privata* 5), p. 40-46.

[3] *Cod. Th.* 16.10.12.2: *Is utpote violatae religionis reus ea domo seu possessione multabitur, in qua eum gentilicia constiterit superstitione famulatu* (ROUGÉ, DELMAIRE, *Les lois religieuses*, p. 442-443; PHARR, *The Theodosian Cod*, p. 474).

[4] Cic. *dom.* 109: *Quid est sanctius, quid omni religione munitius, quam domus unius cuiusque civium? Hic arae sunt, hic foci, hic di penates, hic sacra, religiones, caerimoniae continentur* (N. H. WATTS [ed.], *Cicero in twenty-eight volumes*, XI, Cambridge (Mass.) – London, The Loeb Classical Library, 1979, p. 263).

[5] The extensive bibliography on Roman domestic religion cannot be exhaustively cited. See M. BASSANI, Sacra privata *nell'Italia centrale: archeologia, fonti letterarie e documenti epigrafici*, Padova, Padova University Press, 2017 (Antenor quaderni 40), p. 19-22 and M. BASSANI, F. GHEDINI (eds.), Religionem significare. *Aspetti storico-religiosi, iconografici e materiali dei* sacra privata, *Atti dell'Incontro di Studi, Padova 8-9 giugno 2009*, Roma, Quasar, 2011 (Antenor Quaderni 19).

[6] Delos: M. BULARD, *La religion domestique dans la Colonie Italienne de Délos d'après les peintures murales et les autels histories*, Paris, de Boccard, 1926 (BEFAR 131); P. BRUNEAU, *Recherches sur les cultes de Délos à l'époque hellénistique et à l'époque impériale*, Paris, de Boccard, 1970 (BEFAR 217). Vesuvian cities: see *infra*.

gods were worshipped inside.[7] As attested in many Vesuvian *domus*, the painted "lararia" were associated with figurines in bronze or other materials,[8] which completed the range of deities worshiped in the house, but, according to Annemarie Kaufmann-Heinimann, also in Pompeii "par rapport à plus de 800 maisons d'habitation, une relation directe avec un laraire est attestée seulement pour environ trente ensembles de statuettes."[9]

Therefore, the location as well as the original composition of the groups of bronze statuettes that are displayed in many archaeological museums is often unknown, and yet, it is not possible to trace them back to specific places of domestic worship.[10] Moreover, some images could be made of more precious materials such as silver, or of perishable materials such as wood and so, for different and even opposite reasons, such objects may have been destroyed over time. Moreover, in the case of the myriad of statues and statuettes that belonged to the Roman households' furniture throughout the ages, it is often very difficult to recognize

---

[7] M. BASSANI, "Ambienti ed edifici di culto domestico nella Penisola Iberica," *Pyrenae* 36.1 (2005), p. 71-116; EAD., "Culti domestici nelle province occidentali: alcuni casi di ambienti e di edifici nella Gallia e nella Britannia romane," *Antenor* 6 (2007), p. 105-123; EAD., Sacraria, *Ambienti e piccoli edifici per il culto domestico in area vesuviana*, Roma, 2008 (*Antenor* Quaderni 9) and EAD. in this volume.

[8] M. Bassani in her studies has pointed out "how completely inappropriate is the use of the term *lararium* (even in its translation in modern languages) to refer to the *sacra privata*" (see in this volume, p. 174). However, in this contribution, I will use the term in a conventional way, referring to a long tradition of studies relating above all to the *aediculae* and niches of the residences of the Vesuvian cities connected to domestic worship, distinguishing them from *sacraria* (rooms dedicated to the *sacra privata*) and *sacella* (structures built in open spaces). For correct definitions and examples, see Bassani in this volume.

[9] A. KAUFMANN-HEINIMANN, "Statuettes de laraire et religion domestique à Pompéi," in L. BARNABEI (ed.), *Contributi di archeologia vesuviana*, Roma, L'Erma di Bretschneider, 2007 (Studi Soprintendenza archeologica Pompei 3), p. 151-157, part. p. 151. According to S. ADAMO MUSCETTOLA, "Osservazioni sulla composizione dei larari con statuette di bronzo in Pompei ed Ercolano," in U. GEHRIG (ed.), *Toreutik und figürliche Bronzen der römischer Zeit, Akten der 6 Tatung über antiken Bronzen, 13-17 Mai in Berlin*, Berlin, Staatliche Museen Preussischer Kulturbesitz, Antikenmuseum, 1984, p. 9-32, in part. p. 9, many houses were uninhabited due to the damage caused by the earthquake of 62 AD and the owners may have brought with them the statuettes of the household gods.

[10] ADAMO MUSCETTOLA, *Osservazioni sulla composizione*.

the specific religious value rather than a decorative or generally devotional character of the deities' images.[11]

Even with these premises, and without claiming to be exhaustive, it is nevertheless possible to develop research on these issues, with reference to precise and significant case studies in which the belonging of the divine figures to a domestic cult place is certain. An essential reference is obviously the documentation of the Vesuvian cities,[12] whose analysis may also provide useful elements for the interpretation of other contexts, in a diachronic perspective.

1. *The Vesuvian cities: Groups of deities in the domestic shrines*

Penates sunt omnes dii, qui domi coluntur.[13] This famous definition by Servius allows us to consider all the gods object of worship in the home as *Penates*. In fact, there is no specific iconography of the Penates, the deities of the "interior" of the house.[14] Due to the importance of the role played in domestic worship, however, it is necessary to distinguish at least the Lares and the Genius, to whom Vesta and the ancestors are associated.[15]

---

[11] L. M. STIRLING, *The Learned Collector. Mythological Statuettes and Classical Taste in Late Antique Gaul*, Ann Arbor, University of Michigan Press, 2005. See also, C. SFAMENI, *Tra culto e arredo. Ricerche sulle sculture mitologiche in età tardoantica*, Roma, Scienze e Lettere, 2020 (*Sacra publica et privata* 12).

[12] See A. KRZYSZOWSKA, *Les culte privés à Pompéi*, Wrocław, Uniwersytetu Wrocławskiego, 2002; W. VAN ANDRINGA, *Quotidiens des dieux et des hommes: la vie religieuse dans les cités du Vésuve à l'époque romaine*, Roma, EFR, 2009. For an anthropological approach to Roman domestic spaces, with particular reference to Pompeii, see the studies collected in A. DARDENAY, N. LAUBRY (eds.), *Anthropology of Roman Housing*, Turnhout, Brepols, 2020, and in particular M. MAUGER, "Sanctuaires et marges de l'habitat: perception et délimitation de l'espace domestique," p. 165-192.

[13] Serv. *Aen.* II, 514.

[14] P. BOYANCÉ, "Les pénates et l'ancienne religion romaine," *REA* 54 (1952), p. 109-115; D. G. ORR, "Roman Domestic Religion: The Evidence of the Household Shrines," *ANRW* II, 16.2, Berlin – New York, De Gruyter, 1978, p. 1557-1591, in part. 1562-1563; A. DUBOURDIEU, *Les origines et le développement du culte des Pénates à Rome*, Rome, École française de Rome, 1989 (Collection de l'École française de Rome 118).

[15] M.-O. CHARLES-LAFORGE, "*Imagines maiorum* et portraits d'ancêtres à Pompéi," in BARNABEI, *Contributi di archeologia vesuviana*, p. 158-171.

The richest archaeological documentation of the cult of Lares comes from Pompeii and other Vesuvian cities:[16] the first collection of lararia, mostly paintings but also with references of the statuettes that have been discovered, is the 1937 *Corpus of the lararia of Pompeii* by George Boyce. It is still a fundamental reference work, but it lacks a comparative analysis of the documentation as well as an interpretation with religious-historical lenses.[17] In 1978, David Orr, in a study on Roman domestic religion, provided a reinterpretation of the evidence of the Vesuvian cities and other contexts in a historical-religious perspective.[18] A systematic collection of the lararia paintings of the Vesuvian cities, analyzed both from the historical-artistic and historical-religious point of view, is therefore due to Thomas Fröhlich who in 1991 presented an accurate repertoire.[19]

In the Vesuvian cities there could be more than one household shrine in the same dwelling, to be distinguished on the basis of the location and the decoration. This is the case of painted shrines located in the kitchens and in the servants' quarters with images of the Lares and the Genius; more complex religious shrines – also architecturally – were located in the rooms used to receive the guests and presented painted representations and statuettes of deities. In the tradition of studies, this distinction has been attributed to a different social destination of the shrines. In particular, Th. Fröhlich argued that the Lares and the Genius were mostly connected to the servile quarters, where the Penates were rarely present.[20] According to A. Kaufmann-Heinimann,

---

[16] Macr. *Sat.* 1.10.10; Ov. *Fast.* 2.617-638. M. BORDA, *Lares: la vita familiare nei documenti archeologici e letterari*, Città del Vaticano, Pontificio Istituto di Archeologia Cristiana, 1947, p. 119-120; ORR, *Roman Domestic Religion*, p. 1563-1569; M. TORELLI, "La preistoria dei *Lares*," in BASSANI, GHEDINI, Religionem significare, p. 41-53; H. I. FLOWER, *The Dancing Lares and the Serpent in the Garden: Religion at the Roman Street Corner*, Princeton – Oxford, Princeton University Press, 2017.

[17] G. K. BOYCE, *Corpus of the Lararia of Pompeii*, Roma, American Academy in Rome, 1937 (MAAR 14).

[18] ORR, *Roman Domestic Religion*.

[19] T. FRÖHLICH, *Lararien- und Fassadenbilder in der Vesuvstädten, Untersuchungen zur "volkstümlichen" pompejanischen Malerei*, Mainz, Philipp von Zabern, 1991.

[20] FRÖHLICH, *Lararien- und Fassadenbilder*, p. 28-37; see also KAUFMANN-HEINIMANN, *Statuettes de laraire*, p. 152. M.-O. CHARLES-LAFORGE, *La reli-*

however, this division loses value taking into account that it was the *dominus* who decided the decoration and furnishing of the shrines in all parts of the house.[21]

Based on "una raccolta sistematica e ragionata il più completa possibile degli apprestamenti di culto dedicati ai Lari" in Pompeii,[22] Federica Giacobello re-opened the debate in a 2008 monograph, arguing that the real heart of the domestic cult was the shrine dedicated to the Lares. They were considered as the divinized ancestors that guaranteed the continuity of the *familia* and, as such, were linked to the hearth. This type of painted lararium was realized in the kitchen or immediately nearby. In other parts of the household, where more complex shrines from an architectural and decorative point of view were located, the Lares could be worshipped together with various other deities. However, in this case, the Lares could have been considered more in general as the guardians of the family.[23]

In the same year, Maddalena Bassani published a monograph dedicated to the analysis of the rooms and small buildings for domestic cult in the Vesuvian area, in which she also examined the paintings, statuettes, altars and other furnishing objects of the sacred spaces.[24]

The Lares were depicted as young people dressed in a short tunic, standing or, more frequently, in an attitude of dance and with the attributes of a rhyton or a cornucopia in one hand and, in the other, a patera or situla.[25] On the basis of the collected

---

gion privée a Pompei, Napoli, Centre Jean Bérard, 2009, p. 78-86. According to J. DRAYCOTT, "When lived ancient religion and lived ancient medicine meet: The household Gods, the household shrine and regimen," *Religion in the Roman Empire* 3.2 (2017), p. 164-180, lararia would be connected, as well as in general with the preparation of food, also with ancient medical practices to ensure the good health of the inhabitants of the house.

[21] KAUFMANN-HEINIMANN, *Statuettes de laraire*, p. 156.

[22] F. GIACOBELLO, *Larari pompeiani: iconografia e culto dei Lari in ambito domestico*, Milano, LED Edizioni Universitarie, 2008, p. 36.

[23] GIACOBELLO, *Larari pompeiani*, made a distinction between the household shrines devoted to the cult of the Lares, the only ones that in her opinion can be considered true "lararia", and other manifestations of domestic worship, in which the Lares could also appear "desemantizzati però del loro originario significato e venerati come semplici dèi tutelari della casa" (p. 59).

[24] BASSANI, Sacraria.

[25] V. TRAN TAM TINH, *s.v.* "Lar, Lares," in *LIMC* VI.1, 1992, p. 205-202;

data, F. Giacobello states that "l'espressione del culto dei Lari aveva, come forma privilegiata e quasi esclusiva, la raffigurazione dipinta della scena di sacrificio in cui partecipavano diversi personaggi," in particular the Genius, in the center, near an altar, in the act of making a libation, sometimes accompanied by a *camillus*, a *tibicen*, a *popa* or *victimarius* leading a pig for sacrifice, or by his female counterpart, Iuno. As indicated in its own linguistic root, the "*Genius*" represented the procreative force capable of ensuring the progeny.[26] Considered an *alter ego* of the *paterfamilias*, it was represented as a mature man, dressed in a toga and in the act of sacrifice or offering incense grains.[27] The sacrifice scene was generally completed by two snakes approaching an altar in the lower part of the sacred space (Fig. 1).[28] The snake, interpreted as a sort of guardian of the place, in its association with the Genius, could represent its procreative power.[29]

VI.2, p. 97-102; Giacobello, *Larari pompeiani*, p. 89-98; Flower, *Dancing Lares*, p. 46-52.

[26] Orr, *Roman Domestic Religion*, p. 1569-1573. H. Kunckel, *Der römische Genius*, Heidelberg, 1974 (MDAI(R) Erg.-Heft 20).

[27] Kunckel, *Der römische Genius*, p. 53-63. The statuettes of the Genius *togatus* can be dated mainly between the first century BC and the first century AD. After the Hadrian age, the iconography of the youthful Genius with a cloak (cape) and a cornucopia was established, similar to that of the Lares.

[28] See Giacobello, *Larari pompeiani*, p. 98-106. One of the most complete scenes is in the lararium of the kitchen of the *Casa di Iulius Polybius* (IX, 13, 1-3): see Frölich, *Lararien- und Fassadenbilder*, p. 298, L109, Taf. 14, 2; Kaufmann-Heinimann, *Statuettes de laraire*, p. 153-154. Giacobello, *Larari pompeiani*, p. 66. On the painted representations of the Genius, the Lares and the snakes, see Bassani, Sacraria, p. 82-84; for a definition of "sacred space" see p. 29, fn. 50.

[29] Orr, *Roman Domestic Religion*, p. 1573: "The Genius is closely linked to the serpent in the household shrines of Pompeii and is probably represented by that reptile in numerous contexts." J. M. C. Toynbee, *Animals in Roman Life and Art*, London, Thames and Hudson, 1973, p. 224, considers the snake an impersonal representation of the family's protector ancestors. Outside Pompeii and Herculaneum, snakes are only depicted in very few domestic religious contexts: in addition to the two paintings from the houses in Ostia for which see below, two snakes are depicted on an altar found in the peristyle of house 2 B of Ampurias: M. Pérez Ruiz, *Al amparo de los Lares: El culto doméstico en las provincias romanas Bética y Tarraconense*, Madrid, 2014 (Anejos de AEA 68), p. 233-235, fig. 34, acknowledges a form of domestic worship of Italic tradition.

FIG. 1.
Pompeii, the lararium of the *Casa di Iulius Polybius* (IX 13,3)
(from M. RANIERI PANETTA [ed.], *Pompeji. Geschichte, Kunst und Leben in der versunkenen Stadt*, Stuttgart, Belser, 2005, p. 108).

The second type of shrine, which found place above all in the *viridaria* and in the peristyles, but also in the atriums, cubicles, vestibules and on the facades, was characterized by the presence of many gods of the Roman pantheon, but also of Egyptian gods such as Isis and other deities of her circle,[30] both in painted

---

[30] V. TRAN TAM TINH, *Essai sur le culte d'Isis à Pompéi*, Paris, De Boccard, 1964. See also I. BRAGANTINI, "The Cult of Isis and Ancient Egyptomania in Campania," in D. BALCH, A. WEISSENRIEDER (eds.), *Contested Spaces: Houses and Temples in Roman Antiquity and the New Testament*, Tübingen, Mohr Siebeck, 2012 (Wissenschaftliche Untersuchungen zum Neuen Testament 285), p. 21-33.

representations[31] and with statuettes, generally in bronze[32] but sometimes also in marble, clay, wood or silver. Together with these deities, painted and plastic representations of the Lares and the Genius also appear, as in the atrium of the *Casa delle Pareti Rosse* (VIII 5, 37) where the Lares are painted at the bottom of an aedicule on either side of the Genius; they are also part of a group of bronze statuettes together with Apollo, Hercules and two statuettes of Mercury, one of which could be considered a divine assimilation of Augustus (Fig. 2).[33] According to Stefania Adamo Muscettola, the fact that the Genius is not represented among the bronze statuettes would demonstrate the complementarity of the two types of decoration; in general, however, according to other scholars, a precise correspondence could not be found between the statuettes and the paintings of the shrines.[34]

Of the 505 lararia that George K. Boyce analysed, only 27 contain statuettes.[35] Stefania Adamo Muscettola notes that those come from some of the richest houses, where they were placed in the niches of the atriums or peristyles, in cubicles and sometimes were stored inside cases.[36] The most represented gods are the Lares and the Genius associated with Mercury, Jupiter, Juno and Minerva (also as the Capitoline triad),[37] Fortuna, Venus, Hercules,[38] characters of Bacchus' inner circle and other Graeco-

---

[31] BASSANI, *Sacraria*, p. 84-86.
[32] A. KAUFMANN-HEINIMANN, *Götter und Lararien aus Augusta Raurica. Herstellung, Fundzusammenhänge und sakrale Funktion figürlicher Bronzen in einer römischen Stadt*, Augst, Römermuseum Augst, 1998 (Forschungen in Augst 26).
[33] BOYCE, *Corpus of the Lararia*, p. 77, n. 371, pl. 31, 1; KAUFMANN-HEINIMANN, *Statuettes de laraire*, p. 154; the assimilation to Augustus is proposed by ADAMO MUSCETTOLA, *Osservazioni*, p. 19, fig. 15-16; p. 20-23 and fig. 17-19; a reference to Livia could perhaps be found in a statuette of a seated divinity, interpreted as *Concordia Augusta* (Casa IX 7, 20). See also FLOWER, *The Dancing Lares*, p. 50-51 and Amoroso in this volume.
[34] ADAMO MUSCETTOLA, *Osservazioni*, p. 15; KAUFMANN-HEINIMANN, *Statuettes de laraire*, p. 153.
[35] BOYCE, *Corpus of the Lararia*, p. 17-18, and thematic index.
[36] ADAMO MUSCETTOLA, *Osservazioni*, p. 10.
[37] On the cult of the Capitoline triad in Pompeii, see ADAMO MUSCETTOLA, *Osservazioni*, p. 12-15.
[38] A. CORALINI, Hercules domesticus, *Immagini di Ercole nelle case della regione vesuviana (I sec. a.C.-79 d.C.)*, Napoli, Electa, 2001.

FIG. 2.
Pompeii, *Casa delle Pareti rosse* (VIII, 5, 37), the shrine in the atrium
with the statuettes as they were found
(from BOYCE, *Corpus of the Lararia*, pl. 31, 1).

Roman and Egyptian gods,[39] among which, first of all, Isis and Harpocrates.[40] Making a comparison between the deities represented in the paintings and the statuettes, some differences

---

[39] ORR, *Roman Domestic Religion*, p. 1581.
[40] KAUFMANN-HEINIMANN, *Statuettes de laraire*, p. 155. For Isis-Fortuna in the Vesuvian contexts, see N. AMOROSO, "The roles of Isis in Roman domestic cults: A study of the 'Isis-Fortuna' bronze statuettes from the Vesuvian area," *Archiv für Religionsgeschichte* 18-19 (2017), p. 37-74. Basing his analysis on the works by Kunckel and Boyce, CHARLES-LAFORGE, *La religion privée*, p. 82, pl. VII, reported 22 contexts, including one of Scafati, one of Herculaneum and one of Boscoreale, with very varied combinations of deities.

were noted: Fortuna is present more often in the paintings and Mercury in the statuettes.[41] Vesta is only painted in the aedicules in the kitchens, since she represented the sacralization of the hearth; the few anthropomorphic representations of the goddess give her a matronly and severe aspect.[42] Bacchus is more attested in the paintings of the reception rooms and in the *cauponae*.[43] Greco-Roman types are used for the statuettes of Venus but in the paintings the goddess is represented as the patron deity of the city of Pompeii.[44]

Some groups of deities are particularly interesting.

In the north wing of the peristyle of the *Casa degli Amorini Dorati* (VI 26, 7) there is a large aedicule where statuettes of the main gods of the Roman pantheon (Jupiter, Juno, Minerva, Mercury) accompanied by the two Lares were found; on the opposite side of the portico, the south-east corner is used as a sacellum, probably closed by a wooden gate.[45] On the south wall, at the top, Anubis, Harpocrates, Isis and Serapis are represented (Fig. 3). In the upper part of the east wall there are a sistrum, a patera and other symbols and cultic objects. The space under the panels is dedicated to the image of the two snakes in front of the altar.[46] An alabaster statuette of Horus, a marble statuette of a female goddess seated on a throne with a horn of plenty, interpreted as Isis-Fortuna[47] and a terracotta lamp with a repre-

---

[41] See also the group from the house IX 6, 5/7 with Mercury and the two Lares (ADAMO MUSCETTOLA, *Osservazioni*, p. 25, fig. 23).

[42] ORR, *Roman Domestic Religion*, p. 1560-1561.

[43] ADAMO MUSCETTOLA, *Osservazioni*, p. 10-11, observes that Bacchus, despite being together with Venus and Hercules among the most important gods of the city of Pompeii, is not represented in the lararia with bronze statuettes, except in one case, while he is present in the painted ones. In these lararia, there are also some "local" deities, such as the Pompeian Venus and the Sarno river: to understand these different choices, it is necessary to carry out historical and religious research, and also examine the evidence from other contexts.

[44] KAUFMANN-HEINIMANN, *Statuettes de laraire*, p. 156.

[45] F. DI CAPUA, "Sacrari pompeiani," in *Pompeiana, Raccolta di studi per il secondo centenario degli scavi di Pompei*, Napoli, Macchiaroli, 1950, p. 60-85, in part. p. 67-68.

[46] TRAN TAM TINH, *Essai sur le culte d'Isis*, p. 129, n. 17-18, pl. XVI, 1-2; FRÖHLICH, *Lararien- und Fassadenbilder*, p. 281, L74, Taf. 38, 1-2. CHARLES-LAFORGE, *La religion privée*, p. 37.

[47] TRAN TAM TINH, *Essai sur le culte d'Isis*, p. 155, n. 77 (generically from the *Casa degli amorini dorati*).

Fig. 3.
Pompeii, *Casa degli amorini dorati* (VI, 26, 7),
the south wall of the portico, detail (photo by the author).

sentation of Isis and Harpocrates[48] has also been found probably in connection with the chapel.[49]

In the *praedia di Iulia Felix* (II 4, 2) a traditional painted shrine is close to a chapel for Isis and Anubis (Fig. 4):[50] in both these contexts there are two distinct spaces of worship dedicated respectively to Graeco-Roman and Egyptian gods, but often the images of these gods are associated in the same shrine. In the atrium of the House of *Marcus Memmius Auctus* (VI 14, 27), for example, two bronze figurines of Isis and Anubis were found in a wooden box together with a pair of Lares and a seated old man; in the same place the discovery of a silver statuette of Harpocrates, a marble statue of Venus and an enigmatic figure on a *kline*[51] is also reported.

---

[48] *Ibid.*, p. 170, n. 132 (generically from the *Casa degli amorini dorati*).

[49] *Ibid.*, p. 162, n. 104, pl. XXI, 4 (southeast corner of the peristyle).

[50] CHARLES-LAFORGE, *La religion privée*, p. 39; DI CAPUA, *Sacrari pompeiani*, p. 67; FRÖHLICH, *Lararien*, p. 265-266, Taf. 30, 1, L40. On the decoration of this lararium, read also the remarks of E. Moormann in this volume, p. 157-162.

[51] BOYCE, *Corpus of the Lararia*, p. 53, no. 202, fn. 2; ADAMO MUSCETTOLA, *Osservazioni*, p. 23 and fig. 20.

Fig. 4.
Pompeii, *Praedia di Iulia Felix*, the shrine
(from F. Piranesi, *Antiquités de la Grande Grèce*, vol. I, Paris, 1807, pl. 1).

In one of the aedicule of the *Casa del Cenacolo* (V 2, h) the Genius and the Lares are missing, but Hercules is depicted in the act of sacrificing, accompanied by two bronze statuettes of Mercury, a kneeling woman perhaps part of a tool, a terracotta statuette of

Minerva, a large terracotta head, a small altar, a lamp, a dolphin-shaped amulet and two coins.[52] Around a pseudo-aedicule in the atrium of the *Casa di un Flamine* (V 4, 3) in via di Nola, eight gods are painted: in the side panels of the aedicule there are the Pompeian Venus with a cupid and Fortuna, while on the sides of the aedicule Jupiter and Mercury. The lower frieze depicts Mercury, Victoria, Hercules and Minerva.[53] In the cupboard of an adjacent room, the bronze statuettes of the Lares and the Genius were also found together with three amber statuettes (cupid, a seated woman and a hippo), pieces of silverware and coins.[54]

The very heterogeneous sets of religious figurines may have formed over time based on the preferences of the owners. The cult statuettes, in fact, could accompany the family for generations. It is not surprising, therefore, that some were brought with them by the fugitives as precious goods, but above all, probably in the hope of obtaining protection and salvation.[55] For example, a statuette of Fortuna found outside the Nola gate, near the body of a girl, is striking.[56] A study conducted on the materials found in relation to the victims, however, indicates the presence of only four statuettes, two in silver and two in bronze, in certain association with the corpse of a fugitive.[57]

Although the main record comes from Pompeii, there are also some interesting data from Herculaneum:[58] in this city some speci-

---

[52] Kaufmann-Heinimann, *Götter und Lararien*, p. 218, GFV21, fig. 162.

[53] Fröhlich, *Lararien- und Fassadenbilder*, 271-272, L52, Taf. 33, 1. See also Coralini, Hercules domesticus, P.054, p. 182-183.

[54] Kaufmann-Heinimann, *Götter und Lararien*, p. 218, GFV23, fig. 163.

[55] *Ibid.*, p. 216 and 223.

[56] See IV.268, p. 325 in A. d'Ambrosio, P. G. Guzzo, M. Mastroroberto (eds.), *Storie da un'eruzione. Pompei, Ercolano, Oplontis, Napoli, Museo Archeologico Nazionale, 20 marzo-31 agosto 2003*, Milano, Electa, 2003.

[57] A. d'Ambrosio, E. De Carolis, P. G. Guzzo, "I contesti di oggetti trovati presso le vittime," in d'Ambrosio *et al.*, *Storie da un'eruzione*, p. 73-83, in part. p. 75 observe that the statuettes must have been left to protect the house. However, it cannot be excluded that during the first excavations these materials were collected without considering their contexts.

[58] V. Catalano, *Case, abitanti e culti di Ercolano*, Roma, Bardi, 2002; C. M. Marchetti, "*Possidet domum*. Prime riflessioni a margine della religiosità domestica a Ercolano: fonti e dati archeologici," in F. Fontana, E. Murgia (eds.), Sacrum facere. *Lo spazio del 'sacro': ambienti e gesti del rito, Atti del III Seminario di Archeologia del Sacro, Trieste, 3-4 ottobre 2014*, Trieste, EUT Edizioni Università di Trieste, 2016, p. 405-427.

mens of completely carbonized wooden shrines have been preserved, for example that of the house III, 13-15, which contained bronze statuettes of Jupiter, Athena, Asclepius, Fortuna, Harpocrates and the Lares.[59]

A type of "cupboard" of this kind, with a shrine for the Lares, is described by Petronius in the *domus* of Trimalcione: "In a corner I saw a large cupboard containing a tiny shrine, wherein were silver house-gods, and a marble image of Venus, and a large golden box, where they told me Trimalchio's first beard was laid up ...".[60]

Among the few painted shrines in Herculaneum, that of the house V, 15 contains a particular representation of barefoot Lares together with the traditional snakes.[61] In the painted lararium in the kitchen of the *Casa di Nettuno e Anfitrite* two snakes are approaching an altar at the sides of which are the two Lares; traces remain of a pediment aedicule to be connected to examples of IVth style and a masonry altar: it could be a shrine belonging to an older phase of use of the room.[62]

Federica Giacobello believes that the analysis of some extra Pompeian sites confirms the religious model that can be reconstructed in Pompeii,[63] but according to Chiara Marchetti, in Herculaneum a clear distinction cannot be made between "primary" and "secondary" lararia such as the one proposed for Pompeii. This emerges not only from the analysis of the painted lararia, but also from the "mobile" documentation: the group of statuettes of the *Casa del Bicentenario* (depicting Jupiter, Mer-

---

[59] ORR, *Roman Domestic Religion*, p. 1585.

[60] Petr. 29.8 (G. P. GOOLD [ed.], *Petronius, Seneca Apocolocyntosis*, with an English translation by M. HESELTINE, Cambridge [Mass.] – London, The Loeb Classical Library, 1987, p. 50-51): *Praeterea grande armarium in angulo vidi, in cuius aedicula erant Lares argentei positi Venerisque signum marmoreum et pyxis aurea non pusilla, in qua barbam ipsius conditam esse dicebant.*

[61] ORR, *Roman Domestic Religion*, p. 1586.

[62] A. DARDENAY, J. N. ANDREWS, H. ERISTOV, M.-L. MARAVAL, N. MONTEIX, "Herculanum, architecture domestique et décor. Restitution graphique et virtuelle de la casa di Nettuno ed Anfitrite (V, 6-7). Campagne 2017 du programme ANR VESUVIA," *Chronique des activités archéologiques de l'École française de Rome* [Online], Les cités vésuviennes, Online since 14 February 2019, connexion on 1 May 2019. URL: https://journals.openedition.org/cefr/2119; DOI: 10.4000/cefr.2119, p. 16-18, figg. 9-10.

[63] GIACOBELLO, *Larari pompeiani*, p. 127.

cury and Minerva) comes from an area in front of a fresco of the Lares, inside a cubicle and not in a kitchen.[64]

Many statuettes depicting Isis and the deities of her circle, probably belonged to domestic shrines, have also been found in Herculaneum, but only in one case do we have a more precise association.[65] Other groups of lararia statuettes have been discovered in various locations in Campania:[66] the group of silver statuettes (Isis, Venus, snake, bull) from the villa of *Cn. Domitius Auctus* in Scafati,[67] and that of a villa in Boscoreale (Fondo d'Acunzo), which includes the Genius, Jupiter, two specimens of Isis Fortuna, Neptune, a faun and Helios are of particular interest.[68] In the *Ager Pompeianus* and exactly in the villa of the *Fondo Giovanni Imperiali*, two statuettes of Isis, two of Harpocrates, a Serapis, together with Diana, Mercury and the marble statuette of a seated goddess were found.[69] "Se la maggior parte dei manufatti sembra rientrare nella tipologia delle cosiddette statuette lararie di proporzioni ridottissime," in the rooms and domestic religious buildings of the Vesuvian area, examples of marble statuary were also found, mostly of modest size.[70]

---

[64] MARCHETTI, Possidet domum, p. 414 and 416-417.

[65] V. TRAN TAM TINH, *Le culte des divinités orientales à Herculanum*, Leiden, Brill, 1971 (ÉPRO 17), p. 13-16 (Isis Fortuna); 17-21 (Isis Panthea); 21-22 (Harpocrates); 22-23 (Bes). The Isis Panthea no. 3, fig. 13-14 and the Harpocrates no. 24, fig. 18 must have belonged to a domestic altar of the *Casa del Graticcio* (p. 12) together with two Lares, Jupiter, Minerva, Asclepius, Diana (KAUFMANN-HEINIMANN, *Götter und Lararien*, p. 210-211, GFV3, fig. 147). See also ORR, *Roman Domestic Religion*, p. 1586, and Amoroso in this volume.

[66] ORR, *Roman Domestic Religion*, p. 1586-1587. TRAN TAM TINH, *Le culte des divinités orientales*, pl. XIII-XVI.

[67] CHARLES-LAFORGE, *La religion privée*, p. 82, pl. VIII; A. KAUFMANN-HEINIMANN, "Les statuettes de Mâcon, un ensemble particulier," in F. BARATTE, M. JOLY, J.-C. BÉAL (eds.), *Autour du trésor de Mâcon. Luxe et quotidien en Gaule romaine*, Saint-Just-la-Pendue, Institut de recherche du Val de Saône Mâconnais, Mâcon, 2007, p. 30-31, fig. 20.

[68] BOYCE, *Corpus of the Lararia*, no. 500; KUNCKEL, *Der römische Genius*, p. 86, Z 2, pl. 46-47; BASSANI, Sacraria, p. 212-213, pl. 26. KAUFMANN-HEINIMANN, *Götter und Lararien*, p. 210 defines the statuette of Neptune as a standing Jupiter and the Helios and the Faun as the Dioscuri. See also AMOROSO, *The roles of Isis*, p. 65-68 and in this volume.

[69] KAUFMANN-HEINIMANN, *Götter und Lararien*, p. 201-211, GFV2, fig. 146. See also AMOROSO, *The roles of Isis*, p. 60-62 and in this volume.

[70] BASSANI, Sacraria, p. 125-132 (part. p. 127), p. 126, pl. 12.

2. *Beyond Pompeii and Herculaneum: Groups of deities in other contexts*

The context of origin for most of the little statues of deities that could have likely been used in places of domestic worship, stored over time in many different sites, and collected in museums, is generally unspecified.[71] Sometimes, when the location of their discovery is known, it consists in deposits of uncertain origin. In order to analyse the relationship among different deities in a single context, it is very important to be sure that the statuettes are a set of homogeneous elements and not items with different origin and function that were assembled afterwards without religious purposes, often simply to recycle their materials.

In some cases, the reference to a place of domestic worship is very likely: for example, the group of six bronzes found in Sibari-Copia in 1970 in a room of a residential building and depicting Hercules (Fig. 5), the Genius (Fig. 6), Athena/Minerva (two specimens), Apis and a cow nursing a calf may have constituted the furnishings of a domestic religious shrine to be dated in the first century AD.[72] The bronze statuettes depicting Apollo (two specimens), Venus (two specimens) and Fortuna, found in Rome, in a *domus* of the *Horti Domitiae*, dated to the second century AD, may have also belonged to a domestic shrine.[73]

Sometimes an attempt has been made to trace the contexts to which individual pieces belong.[74] Alternatively, some regional evidence has been collected, for example, in Emilia-Romagna, where there are representations of the Lares, Mercury, Minerva, *Copia* and Hercules of different quality and dating. In some cases, they can be traced back to a *domus* and be interpreted

---

[71] See, for example, the groups of Montorio Veronese, Schwarzenacker, Straubing and Avenches: ADAMO MUSCETTOLA, *Osservazioni*, p. 11-12.

[72] C. SFAMENI, "Il 'larario' di Copia (Sibari): una proposta di interpretazione," *Numismatica e antichità classiche* XXV (1996), p. 215-254.

[73] KAUFMANN-HEINIMANN, *Götter und Lararien*, p. 314, GF121, fig. 282. See Amoroso in this volume.

[74] E. PETTENÒ, "Sacra privata Concordiensium: *un percorso per* disiecta membra," in BASSANI, GHEDINI, Religionem significare, p. 135-156; E. DI FILIPPO BALESTRAZZI, "Piccola statuaria e rilievi nell'agro e negli spazi abitativi di *Iulia Concordia*," in BASSANI, GHEDINI, Religionem significare, p. 157-180.

FIG. 5.
Sibari-*Copia*, bronze statuette
of Hercules (from SFAMENI,
Il "larario" di Copia, p. 248, tav. II, 2 A).

FIG. 6.
Sibari-*Copia*, bronze statuette
of a Genius (from SFAMENI,
Il "larario" di Copia, p. 249, tav. III, 2 A).

very likely as items belonging to places of domestic worship.[75] Recently Maddalena Bassani surveyed all the statues and statuettes of gods attested in domestic contexts in central Italy (Tuscany, Umbria, Marche, Abruzzo, Molise), underlining that only in three cases it is possible "ricondurle a specifiche strutture cultuali."[76] A group of seven bronze statuettes depicting a Lar, Mercury, Jupiter, two dancers, an offerer and the Genius was found in a room of the *domus* of San Lorenzo in Arezzo, in the first half of the first century AD.[77] The scholar notes "una netta prevalenza dei culti tradizionali dedicati alle principali divinità

---

[75] V. CICALA, "Tradizione e culti domestici," in J. ORTALLI, D. NERI (eds.), *Immagini divine. Devozioni e divinità nella vita quotidiana dei Romani. Testimonianze archeologiche dell'Emilia Romagna*, Firenze, All'Insegna del Giglio, 2007, p. 43-56 and the catalogue p. 167-180. See also SANTORO, *Gli dei in casa*, p. 113-129.

[76] BASSANI, Sacra privata, p. 92.

[77] *Ibid.*, n. 32, p. 292-295: with the statuettes, a candlestick and other metal objects were found.

del pantheon romano rispetto alla documentazione relativa ai culti per le divinità orientali."[78]

In Ostia, many spaces for domestic worship, which dates from the second to the beginning of the fifth century AD but especially in the post-Severian period, are known, but Jan Theo Bakker points out that "hardly anything is known about the gods worshipped in the Ostian *domus*."[79] One domestic religious painting showing two serpents flanking a Genius and traces of another painting showing a large serpent are in the Museum: both of them were found in second century houses.[80]

Obviously, it is not possible to refer to all the statuettes connected to domestic contexts found in the various regions of the Roman empire, but there are some examples of particular interest. In Gaul, figures of Lares have rarely been found, while there are Mercury, Mars, Fortuna, Venus, Jupiter, Victoria, Apollo, Minerva, and other gods, made of different materials.[81] A very interesting group was found at Mâcon: eight silver statuettes depicting Jupiter, four different types of Mercury, Luna, Tutela Panthea and the Genius.[82] The group is exceptional for the stylistic homogeneity and high quality of the statuettes perhaps produced by a single workshop around the middle of the second century and belonging either to a private shrine or to a place of worship in a sanctuary.[83] Although there are some other interesting sets of statuettes, such as the one in Brèves, that displays five representations of Mercury, only for the group of Rezé (Loire-Atlantique)

---

[78] *Ibid.*, p. 220 (cults and gods, p. 220-230, pl. 21, 222-223).

[79] J. T. BAKKER, *Living and Working with the Gods: Studies of Evidence for Private Religion and its Material Environment in the City of Ostia (100-500 AD)*, Amsterdam, Gieben, 1994 (Dutch Monographs on Ancient History and Archaeology 12), p. 38. See also F. VAN HAEPEREN, *Regio I: Ostie, Porto* (Fana, templa, delubra. Corpus *dei luoghi di culto dell'Italia antica* (FTD) 6), Paris, Collège de France, 2019, p. 163-164 (domestic cults).

[80] ORR, *Roman Domestic Religion*, p. 1587.

[81] J. SANTROT, "Lares et laraires en Gaule romaine," in BARATTE *et al.*, *Autour du trésor de Mâcon*, p. 75-104, notes that a distinction can be made between owners, of more or less higher social classes, depending on the materials used. For example, the figurines of oriental gods, only in bronze, may have belonged to owners with an important social status (p. 92-93).

[82] KAUFMANN-HEINIMANN, *Les statuettes de Mâcon*.

[83] According to KAUFMANN-HEINIMANN, *Les statuettes de Mâcon*, p. 33, perhaps the Genius could be a later addition.

it is possible to connect with certainty some local statuettes to a domestic context.[84]

For what concerns Germany, the detailed study of A. Kaufmann-Heinimann on the Augusta Raurica's materials, which can be included in the broader context of the evidence coming from Italy as well as from other provinces, allows to acquire some interesting information: three quarters of the approximately 450 figured bronzes discovered in the colony was found in the inhabited area, especially in late antique buildings, where more ancient artifacts were kept and venerated. The bronzes depicting deities must have generally been placed in the domestic religious shrines; the composition of groups substantially corresponds to that found in Italy, although the figures of Lares are less frequent: the image of Mercury is particularly recurrent, in association with Minerva, Hercules, Juno, Victoria, Diana, but also Somnus, and Cupid.[85]

María Pérez Ruiz has dedicated careful studies to the domestic cults of *Hispania* but, apart from a painted lararium in the *Casa de la Fortuna* in Bilbilis-Zaragoza,[86] the only small-sized bronze sculptures that belong to a shrine are those of the villa in Vilauba (Camos, Gerona): Lar, Fortuna, Mercury and a figure in small fragments, Silvanus, Pan or a Faun.[87]

In Greece only three statuettes of Lari have been found, the first in a deposit found in Paramythia, the second in a well in the Agora of Athens, while the third, whose provenance is unknown, is kept in the National Archaeological Museum of Athens.[88] The bronze statuettes are quite rare, possibly because of the preference given to other types of materials.[89] Some groups of items linked to domestic contexts allow us to affirm that the deities

---

[84] J. SANTROT, "Le petit monde du 'laraire' gallo-romain de Rezé (Loire-Atlantique)," in *Hommage à Jean Marcadé, REA* 95 (1993), p. 265-294.

[85] KAUFMANN-HEINIMANN, *Götter und Lararien*; see also Amoroso in this volume.

[86] PÉREZ RUIZ, *Al amparo de los Lares,* p. 228.

[87] PÉREZ RUIZ, *Al amparo de los Lares,* p. 278, fig. 126; see also BASSANI, Sacra privata, p. 105-105 and fig. 73.

[88] H. F. SHARPE, "Bronze statuettes from Roman Greece," in E. DESCHLER-ERB, P. DELLA CASA (eds.), *New Research on Ancient Bronzes, Acts of the XVIII*[th] *International Congress on Ancient Bronzes*, Zürich, Chronos, 2015 (Zürich Studies in Archaeology 10), p. 157-160.

[89] SHARPE, *Bronze statuettes of Lares,* p. 159.

preferred by the inhabitants of Greece during the Roman imperial age were the same favorites in the classical and Hellenistic periods: Asclepius, Aphrodite, Cybele, Dionysus and Isis. For example, two deposits of bronze statuettes discovered in the agora of Athens with evidence related to the Sack of the Heruli (267-268 AD) were probably linked to some contexts of domestic worship. The previously mentioned Lar belonging to the first group, together with Aphrodite and Isis *lactans*.[90] The second group consists of five statuettes depicting Tyche (or Isis-Tyche), Aphrodite, Eros, Harpocrates and Telesphorus.[91]

In the residential area unearthed during the excavations at the new Acropolis Museum, small marble, metal and ivory sculptures were found, probably linked to places of domestic worship: salutary deities such as Asclepius, Hygieia, Isis and Cybele are the most represented.[92]

In the so-called House of the bronzes in Cos, statuettes of Mars, Isis-Aphrodite and Isis-Demeter were found together with a bronze corset of Caracalla or Geta: the emperor image testifies the adherence to the official religiosity, in line with a series of literary testimonies related to the use of venerating images of real characters and in particular of members of the imperial *domus* in domestic places of worship.[93] The bronze statuettes

---

[90] H. F. SHARPE, "Bronze Statuettes from the Athenian Agora: Evidence for Domestic Cults in Roman Greece," *Hesperia* 83.1 (2014), p. 143-187, part. p. 148-149 (Lares).

[91] *Ibid.*, p. 154-167.

[92] P. BONINI, "Le tracce del sacro. Presenze della religiosità privata nella Grecia romana," in BASSANI, GHEDINI, Religionem significare, p. 205-227, part. p. 211-212. See N. AMOROSO, "Objets isiaques en contexte domestique durant l'Antiquité tardive à Athènes et à Rome: le cas des images associant Isis à *Tychè/Fortuna*," in M. CAVALIERI, R. LEBRUN, N. L. J. MEUNIER (eds.), *De la crise naquirent les cultes. Approches croisées de la religion, de la philosophie et des représentations antiques, Actes du Colloque international organisé à Louvain-la-Neuve, 12-13 juin 2014*, Turnhout, Brepols, 2015, p. 207-232 (Homo Religiosus II, 15). See also Amoroso in this volume.

[93] F. SIRANO, "Immagini di divinità da contesto domestico a Cos. La documentazione dagli scavi italiani," *MEFRA* 116.2 (2004), p. 953-981 (*Casa dei bronzi*, p. 968-969). See also BASSANI, Sacra privata, p. 129, 101; Suetonius (*Aug.* 7) claims to have given the emperor (Hadrian) a statuette of a young Augustus which he placed among the Lares in his private chamber (*in cubiculo*). Ovid (*Pont.* 2.8.1) recalls that during his exile his friend Cotta Massimo had sent him the portraits of Augustus, Livia and Tiberius to decorate the household altar.

depicting Athena, Isis Panthea and Serapis found in Ephesus, in House 2 of Terrace House 2 and those of Mars, Hercules and a satyr found in Pergamum in the Peristyle House II also refer to the third century.[94]

3. *Late Antique contexts*

In Rome, the most famous case of a late antique shrine was identified inside a *domus* near the church of San Martino ai Monti on the Esquiline hill, in via G. Lanza (Fig. 7).[95] In the central apse of a large aedicule there was a statue of Isis-Fortuna in Pentelic marble; on the shelves in the side niches there were busts and statuettes depicting Egyptian gods (Serapis, Harpocrates,

Fig. 7.
Rome, *domus* of via G. Lanza, the "lararium" – lithography by L. Ronci
(from Ensoli Vittozzi, *Le sculture del "larario" di S. Martino ai Monti*,
p. 281, figg. 23-24).

The testimonies of the *Historia Augusta* on the lararium of Marcus Aurelius and especially on that of Severus Alexander are very controversial (C. Mondello, "Sui *lares* di Severo Alessandro (*HA Alex. Sev.* 29, 2; 31, 4-5): fra conservazione e trasformazione," *Ormos, Ricerche di Storia Antica* n.s. 9 (2017), p. 189-229).

[94] References in Sharpe, *Bronze Statuettes from the Athenian Agora*, p. 168, fn. 114-115.

[95] C. L. Visconti, "Del larario e del mitreo scoperti nell'Esquilino presso la Chiesa di San Martino ai Monti," *BCACR* 13 (1885), p. 27-36. See F. Van Haeperen in this volume.

stele of Horus on crocodiles) and Greco-Roman ones (Apollo, Dionysus, Aphrodite, Cybele, Hecate, Hercules, Lares). Behind the shrine there was access to an underground *mithraeum*, built in a cellar.[96] The shrine, interpreted as a "lararium", has been dated to the second century, but was rearranged in the Constantinian building phase of the *domus*.[97]

An inscription with a dedication to Mercury as *custos Larum Penatium* by two members of the *Aradii* family, Proculus and Rufinus, identified with L. Aradius Valerius Proculus Populonius and his son Aradius Rufinus,[98] dated between 340 and 360, allows us to recognize the religious function of a group of sculptures found in two rooms belonging to an aristocratic *domus* in the villa of Dino Grandi in via di Porta Latina 11.[99] A marble statue of Isis, 1.20 m high and dated between the second and third centuries AD (Fig. 8), was found together with a statuette of Dionysus, a headless female figure interpreted as Demeter, a naked child who is crowned, a naked child with a crocodile, the lower part of a draped statue with garlands of roses resting on a plinth, a statuette of a hunter putto, together with a fragment of a ribbed tub.[100] In an adjoining room, a headless statuette of Leda and the swan was found, a hoof on which feet wearing sandals, a crouching dog without a head, a statuette of Fortuna, a syringe held by a partially preserved hand were found. According to D. Candilio, the iconography of the sculptures refers to a unitary context in which a central role is played by Isis, with references to other cults and mystery rites.[101] The dedication to

---

[96] S. ENSOLI VITTOZZI, "Le sculture del 'larario' di S. Martino ai Monti. Un contesto recuperato," *BCAR* 95.1 (1993), p. 267-287. See also AMOROSO, *Objets isiaques*, p. 219-221.

[97] F. GUIDOBALDI, "L'edilizia abitativa unifamiliare nella Roma tardoantica," in A. GIARDINA (ed.), *Società romana e impero tardoantico*, Roma – Bari, Laterza, 2, 1996, p. 165-234, part. p. 197.

[98] S. PANCIERA, 1987, "Ancora sulla famiglia senatoria africana degli *Aradii*," in A. MASTINO (ed.), *Africa Romana, Atti IV Convegno di Studi (Sassari 1986)*, Sassari, 1987, p. 547-572.

[99] K. CAPRINO, "Notiziario, Via di Porta Latina n. 11," *BCAR* 72 (1946-1948), p. 182-183.

[100] See AMOROSO, *Objets isiaques*, p. 220.

[101] D. CANDILIO, *L'arredo scultoreo e decorativo della* domus *degli Aradii*, Roma, G. Bretschneider, 2005 (Accademia Nazionale dei Lincei, Monumenti Antichi, Serie Miscellanea X), part. p. 27-29.

Fig. 8.
Rome, the Aradii *domus*, statue of Isis – Museo Nazionale Romano
(from Sfameni, *Residenze e culti*, fig. 1).

Mercury demonstrates how the room was in use for cultural purposes around the middle of the fourth century, regardless of the dating of the sculptures and furnishings, all probably older.[102]

In Greece, a sculptural furniture of religious value was found in a room of the so-called house of Proclus in Athens (Fig. 9):[103] the base of a funerary monument of the fourth century BC reused as a pedestal or as an altar and two reliefs representing respectively the Cybele enthroned and Asclepius or Pankrates to which

---

[102] *Ibid.*, p. 33.
[103] Bonini, *Le tracce del sacro*, p. 213-214; Stirling, *The Learned Collector*, p. 200-203. For the *domus* called Building *chi*, see A. Karivieri, "The 'House of Proclus' on the Southern Slope of the Acropolis: A Contribution," in P. Castrén (ed.), *Post-Herulian Athens: Aspects of life and culture in Athens A.D. 267-529*, Helsinki, Foundation of the Finnish Institute at Athens, 1994, p. 115-139.

Fig. 9.
Athens, "House of Proclus" shrine
(from BALDINI, *Arredi scultorei*, p. 527, fig. 5).

three people offer a sheep. The room has an evident "pagan" character, attributed by Lorenz Baumer to the funerary cult of the philosophers,[104] or, rather, according to other scholars, to the cult of Cybele.[105] Many other late antique Athenian *domus* have been interpreted as residences of intellectuals and philosophers, thanks also to the presence of a rich sculptural furniture, which however cannot always be referred to specific places of worship.[106]

---

[104] L. BAUMER, "Klassische Bildwerke für tote Philosophen? Zu zwei spätklassischen Votivskulpturen aus Athen und ihrer Wiederverwendung in der späten Kaiserzeit," *AK* 44 (2001), p. 55-69, part. p. 66-68.

[105] BONINI, *Le tracce del sacro*, p. 214.

[106] I. BALDINI, "Arredi scultorei nelle case tardoantiche di Atene," in I. BALDINI, C. SFAMENI, (eds.), *Abitare nel Mediterraneo tardoantico, Atti del II Con-*

In Corinth, in the locality of Panaya, in a small room inside a dwelling, there were nine statuettes of deities, of different sizes, dated between the first and fourth centuries AD:[107] Artemis (two specimens), Asclepius (two specimens), Heracles, Dionysus, Pan, Europa / Sosandra and a particular representation of Rome armed on a throne that could represent the owner's adhesion to the imperial ideology or even his personal participation to the imperial administration.[108] The statuettes were probably placed in a shrine of which, however, no traces have been found.[109]

It cannot be excluded that some of the 20 statuettes found in the villa of Theseus in Nea Paphos (Cyprus) could also belong to a place of worship (Fig. 10).[110] Among the subjects represented there are Artemis, Hygieia, Asclepius, Hercules, Silvanus, Dionysus, Isis, Demeter and probably a satyr and a muse. The materials have been dated to the late second or early third century, although a dating to the fourth century cannot be excluded.[111]

Some marble and bronze statuettes were found in a basin in the peristyle of the so-called Theodosian Palace of Stobi. The bronze statuettes, dated between the first and second centuries, depicting a Lar, Apollo, Venus and a satyr could probably have been part of a domestic shrine.[112] According to Lea Stirling, even the marble statues would be from different periods, but

---

vegno Internazionale del Centro Interuniversitario di Studi sull'Edilizia abitativa tardoantica nel Mediterraneo (CISEM), Bologna 2-5 marzo 2016, Bari, Edipuglia, 2018 (Insulae Diomedeae 35), p. 523-534.

[107] L. M. STIRLING, "Pagan Statuettes in Late Antique Corinth, Sculpture from the *Panayia Domus*," *Hesperia* 77 (2008), p. 89-161.

[108] STIRLING, *The Learned Collector*, p. 208.

[109] STIRLING, *Pagan Statuettes*, p. 130.

[110] P. PANAYIDES, "Villa of Theseus, Nea Paphos. Reconsidering its sculptural Collection," in R. MAGUIRE, J. CHICK (eds.), *Approaching Cyprus: Proceedings of the Post-Graduate Conference of Cypriot Archaeology (PoCA) held at the University of East Anglia, Norwich, 1st-3rd November 2013*, Cambridge, Cambridge Scholars Publishing, 2016, p. 228-244.

[111] J. FEJFER, "Sculpture in Roman Cyprus," in L. W. SØRENSEN, K. W. JACOBSEN (eds.), *Panaya Ematousa II. Political, cultural, ethnic and social relations in Cyprus. Approaches to regional studies*, Athens, Danish Institute at Athens, 2006 (Monographs of the Danish Institute at Athens 6.2), p. 81-124, in part. p. 115.

[112] STIRLING, *The Learned Collector*, p. 117.

RELIGIOUS IDENTITIES AND GROUPS OF DEITIES IN ROMAN DOMESTIC SHRINES

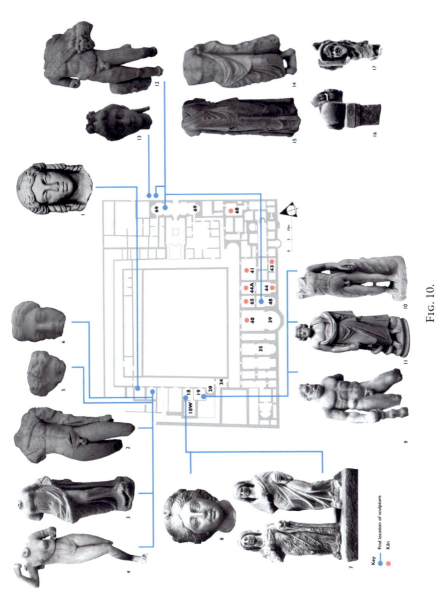

Fig. 10.
Cyprus, Nea Paphos, plan of the villa of Theseus in the third quarter of the fourth century with indication of the places where the sculptures were found (from PANAYIDES, *Villa of Theseus, Nea Paphos*, p. 244, pl. 5.1).

they could have been collected around the middle of the fourth century at the time of the construction of the building.[113]

Given the lack of precise indicators, such as inscriptions, the discovery in places devoted to the cult, particular religious features, as well as the relation to offers or sacrifices, it is often not possible to determine the religious or the ornamental function of the many statues and statuettes discovered in the domestic contexts of the Late Antiquity.[114]

4. *Some final remarks*

The contexts of the Vesuvian cities certainly remain the most interesting for our topic. Nevertheless, it is necessary to avoid generalizing and acquiring specific features of Roman domestic religion only from this rich evidence: as D. Orr notes, in fact, "there are notable differences between even the two principal Campanian towns where shrines are found in abundance, Herculaneum-Pompeii."[115] First of all, it must be observed how the traditional Genius-Lares association is typical of Pompeii; in Herculaneum the Lares are poorly represented and no image of the Genius is known. So "the typical role of Genius in making the libation to the twin Lares may not, in fact, be a universal feature, as far as we can tell."[116] Another peculiarity is the presence of snakes, very common in the domestic shrine iconography at Pompeii and attested also at Herculaneum. In other context outside Campania, snakes are rare[117] and we do not know whether they were associated with Lares elsewhere.[118] It is not easy to establish whether these differences are to be ascribed only to the state of the documentation, since in other contexts the mural paintings have not been preserved, or whether it was actually a local peculiarity. According to Harriet Flower "the snakes may perhaps be local gods of place in Campania who had learned to

---

[113] *Ibid.*, p. 198-199.
[114] *Ibid.*, p. 22-28.
[115] ORR, *Roman Domestic Religion*, p. 1585.
[116] FLOWER, *The Dancing Lares*, p. 74.
[117] e.g. Ostia, Ampurias (see *supra*).
[118] FLOWER, *The Dancing Lares*, p. 70.

live with the newer Roma Lares in largely separate but parallel religious worlds or they may have been more widely spread but the evidence has not survived."[119]

Regarding the composition of the Pompeian shrines with bronze statuettes, Stefania Adamo Muscettola states: "ciò che si mantenne invariato, pur nel diversificarsi dei livelli funzionali e sociali è il repertorio, che appare strettamente riflettere le forme della religione pubblica ufficiale: da ciò deriva da una parte l'estrema limitatezza di soggetti dai quali rimasero soprattutto assenti le immagini di Bacco, dall'altra l'importanza dei culti tipicamente romani – Triade capitolina – e imperiali – Mercurio Augusto e Concordia Augusta – che questa ricerca preliminare ha potuto evidenziare."[120] Scholars who have dealt with the analysis of domestic worship in the houses of the Vesuvian area have generally observed a difference between the painted lararia in the service quarters of the dwellings and those painted and/or with bronze statuettes in the residential zones, noting in the latter a closer link with the official cults. Isis and the deities of her circle, venerated in Pompeii in an important sanctuary, are very frequently included in this series. Therefore, it seems to be possible to deduce that the cult of the goddess had assumed a sort of official role in the city or at least it was perceived by some devoted people as a characteristic element of their own religious identity.

The other evidence does not naturally allow such a degree of in-depth analysis, due to the absence of contexts such as those of the Vesuvian cities. Nevertheless, it is possible to draw some general remarks. First of all, the bronze statuettes of deities in the best documented groups but also in the numerous museum collections are very different with regard to sizes, styles, and origins, suggesting "personal choice and availability, as well as collecting or inheriting over time."[121] The variety of gods, with multiple possible combinations, reveals that individual family members could embrace new deities among the "gods of the house" over time.

---

[119] *Ibid.*, p. 73.
[120] ADAMO MUSCETTOLA, *Osservazioni*, p. 26.
[121] FLOWER, *The Dancing Lares*, p. 523.

Examining the documentation of the different regions of the Roman empire, it can also be observed that the characteristics of the groups of domestic deities were also determined by geographical, cultural and social factors. For example, it is possible to recognize a greater similarity between the contents of the Italic domestic shrines and those of Gaul and Germany (also judging by the types of statuettes present in the museum collections, even without knowing their precise associations): Venus, Jupiter, the Genius, Minerva and Fortuna, Mars, Victoria are in fact among the most represented deities while the images of the Lares are rare.

In the Greek world, on the other hand, the bronze statuettes were not very popular; in comparison to the contexts of the western regions of the empire a certain difference can also be seen regarding the religious subjects, chosen also for marble statuettes: the gods venerated in the Greek houses are above all Aphrodite, Asclepius, Cybele, Heracles, Isis and Serapis, with a continuity from the Classical and Hellenistic period.

The groups of statues and statuettes of religious subjects from the late antique period, generally in marble rather than bronze, often refer to rooms and spaces of the house specifically intended for worship. These spaces are different from the "lararia" of the early imperial age, but the numerous niches that are in various rooms of the late antique residences could certainly house statuettes of a religious nature. Furthermore, even in the early imperial age, there were many spaces and structures (*sacraria* and *sacella*) specifically dedicated to domestic worship.[122] So, the theme of continuity and transformations in the forms of domestic worship during the imperial age should be further explored.

In the better known late antique contexts, which are often based on collections of older pieces, traditional gods of the Greco-Roman pantheon are attested together with some typical deities of domestic cult (Lares) and with many "oriental" gods. Laurent Bricault pointed out that "la composition des laraires révélés par l'archéologie offre un écho aux accumulations de prêtrises livrées par l'épigraphie."[123] The famous inscription of Praetexta-

---

[122] See Bassani in this volume.
[123] L. BRICAULT, "*Gens isiaca* et identité polythéiste à Rome à la fin du IVe s. apr. J.-C.," in L. BRICAULT, M. J. VERSLUYS (eds.), *Power, Politics and the Cult*

tus, where he is remembered as *augur, pontifex Vestae, pontifex Solis, quindecemvir curialis Herculis, sacratus Libero et Eleusiniis, hierofanta, neocorus, tauroboliatus, pater patrum*,[124] the numerous dedications to Cybele of the Vatican *Phrygianum*,[125] or texts as the *Carmen contra paganos*[126] offer interesting lists of the most popular cults up to the late fourth century which are also clearly attested in the archaeological documentation.

Regardless of the production date of the sculptures found in late antique domestic religious contexts, their use until the abandonment of the houses demonstrates a precise devotion to the deities they represented. The dedication of the *Aradii domus* to Mercury as *custos* of Lares and Penates, from the mid-fourth century, constitutes a particularly significant testimony: it demonstrates, together with other epigraphic, archaeological, literary, and legislative sources, that the cult of a plurality of divine figures maintained its centrality in the Roman houses despite the affirmation of Christianity, as a form of adherence to an uninterrupted cultural rather than strictly religious tradition.

---

*of Isis, V*th *International Conference of Isis Studies*, Leiden-Boston, E.J. Brill, 2014, p. 326-359, in part. p. 356.

[124] *CIL* VI, 1779.

[125] P. LIVERANI, "Il *Phrygianum* Vaticano," in B. PALMA VENETUCCI (ed.), *Culti orientali tra scavo e collezionismo*, Roma, Artemide Editoriale, 2008, p. 41-47; G. SFAMENI GASPARRO, "I culti orientali in Vaticano," in C. PARISE PRESICCE, L. PETACCO (eds.), *La Spina. Dall'agro Vaticano a via della Conciliazione*, Roma, Gangemi Editore, 2016, p. 47-51.

[126] L. CRACCO RUGGINI, "Un cinquantennio di polemica antipagana a Roma," in R. CANTALAMESSA, L. F. PIZZOLATO (eds.), Paradoxos politeia. *Studi patristici in onore di Giuseppe Lazzati*, Milano, Vita e Pensiero, 1979, p. 119-144; BRICAULT, Gens isiaca, p. 329-341; see also E. DAL COVOLO, G. SFAMENI GASPARRO (eds.), *Pagani e Cristiani: conflitto, confronto, dialogo. Le trasformazioni di un modello storiografico, Atti del Convegno Internazionale, Città del Vaticano 13-15 novembre 2019*, Città del Vaticano 2021.

II
GODS IN THE HOUSE

ERIC M. MOORMANN

SACRARIA OU 'CHAPELLES' RELIGIEUSES À POMPÉI : CULTE DOMESTIQUE OU VÉNÉRATION PUBLIQUE ?

*Ego Lar sum familiaris ex hac familia
unde exeuntem me aspexistis. Hanc domum
iam multos annos est cum possideo et colo
patri auoque iam huius qui nunc hic habet*

« Je suis le Lar de cette famille
dont vous me voyez sortir. Voici la maison
que je possède et habite depuis beaucoup d'années
pour le père et le grand-père de la personne qui habite ici maintenant. »

C'est ainsi que le *Lar familiaris* se présente dans le prologue de l'*Aulularia* de Plaute. Apparemment on s'imaginait, au moins à l'époque de Plaute, que le Lare ou les Lares habitaient dans la maison et désiraient l'attention et les offrandes de ses habitants[1]. Cela impliquerait donc qu'on eût une installation spécifique, voire un abri, chambre, chapelle ou autre forme d'espace, pour les Lares, les Pénates, les *Genii* et, également, pour les autres di-

---

[1] Plaute, *Aulularia* Prologue 2-5. V. B. CARDAUNS, *s.v.* « Lar (Lararium) », *RAC* 22 (2008), col. 980, qui souligne l'usage de la cohabitation. Sur ce passage P. W. FOSS, « Watchful Lares : Roman Household Organization and the Rituals of Cooking and Eating », in R. LAURENCE, A. WALLACE-HADRILL (éd.), *Domestic Space in the Roman World : Pompeii and Beyond*, Portsmouth, RI, JRA, 1997 (Journal Roman Archaeology Suppl. 22), p. 197-218, part. p. 197-198 ; A. DUBOURDIEU, « Les cultes domestiques dans le monde romain », *ThesCRA* VIII (2012), p. 32-43, part. p. 34-35 ; W. VAN ANDRINGA, *Quotidien des dieux et des hommes. La vie religieuse dans les cités du Vésuve à l'époque romaine*, Rome, École Française de Rome, 2009 (BEFAR 337), p. 226-227 ; A. HAUG, *Decor-Räume in pompejanischen Stadthäusern*, Berlin, De Gruyter, 2020, p. 44-46.

vinités qui protégeaient la maison[2]. Ces installations servaient au culte domestique, pratiqué à l'intérieur des maisons par tous les membres de la *familia* et cette pratique exigeait des espaces déterminés[3]. Il nous paraît donc pertinent, dans le cadre du présent volume, d'évoquer ces sanctuaires privés afin d'envisager les rapports entre espaces cultuels domestiques et sanctuaires publics. Cette approche nous permettra d'analyser plus spécifiquement la relation entre l'architecture sacrée monumentale et les installations religieuses à l'intérieur des habitations. Existait-il des liens entre eux, dans leurs concepts, leurs formes architectoniques et leur apparat décoratif ? Les Lares et autres divinités domestiques bénéficiaient-ils d'une 'maison' équivalant à un temple, telles les grandes divinités vénérées dans le domaine public ? Ces questions m'amèneront à explorer dans cette contribution des pièces particulières, dédiées à la vénération des dieux domestiques, en forme de 'chapelles' ou bien d'édicules de telles dimensions qu'on pouvait y entrer pour porter des offrandes, prier, communiquer des messages aux dieux. L'enquête s'attache à l'appareil ornemental de ces lieux de culte domestiques, mais j'ai dû exclure la question de la cohérence ou de la complémen-

---

[2] Pour la composition des populations des laraires, voir D. G. Orr, « Roman Domestic Religion. The Evidence of the Household Shrines », *ANRW* II, 16.2, Berlin-New York, 1978, p. 1557-1591, part. p. 1560-1575 ; S. Adamo Muscettola, « Osservazioni sulla composizione dei larari con statuette in bronzo di Pompei ed Ercolano », in U. Gehrig (éd.), *Toreutik und figürliche Bronzen römischer Zeit : Akten der 6. Tagung über antike Bronzen, 13.-17. Mai 1980 in Berlin : Madame G.-M. Faider-Feytmans zum Gedächtnis*, Berlin, Staatliche Museen Preussischer Kulturbesitz, Antikenmuseum, 1984, p. 9-32 ; A. Dubourdieu, *Les origines et le développement du culte des Pénates à Rome*, Rome, École Française de Rome, 1989 (Collection de l'EFR 118), p. 79-83 ; T. Fröhlich, *Lararien- und Fassadenbilder in den Vesuvstädten*, Mainz am Rhein, Von Zabern, 1991 (MDAI(R) Erg.H. 32), p. 21-61 ; A. M. Kaufmann-Heinimann, *Götter und Lararien aus Augusta Raurica : Herstellung, Fundzusammenhänge und sakrale Funktion figürlicher Bronzen in einer römischen Stadt*, Augst, Römermuseum, 1998 ; J. Bodel, « Cicero's Minerva, *Penates*, and the Mother of the *Lares* : An Outline of Roman Domestic Religion », in J. Bodel, S. Olyan (éd.), *Household and Family Religion in Antiquity*, Malden, Mass., Blackwell, 2008, p. 248-275, part. p. 255-264 ; Dubourdieu, *Cultes domestiques*.

[3] Pour une définition, voir Dubourdieu, *Cultes domestiques*, p. 32-34 ; Bodel, *Cicero's Minerva*, p. 248-275. J'utilise ici 'religion' ou 'culte domestique' et suis la terminologie acceptée généralement à côté du terme anglais 'household religion' (Bodel, Olyan, *Household*, p. 2-4 ; S. K. Stowers, « Theorizing Ancient Household Religion », in Bodel, Olyan, *Household*, 2008, p. 5-19).

tarité entre les statuettes et les peintures de laraires, parce qu'il n'existe que peu de cas pour lesquels le mobilier qui résidait *in situ* est attesté. Le contexte choisi pour mon étude est celui du site de Pompéi[4].

Commençons avec la terminologie des éventuels espaces. Nous sommes tous familiers avec le terme *lararium* / laraire[5] qui, cependant, ne se trouve que dans des sources tardives comme l'*Historia Augusta*. Le terme désigne des espaces assez grands, dans une ambiance impériale[6]. Aux époques antérieures, on emploie plutôt les mots *aedicula*[7] et *sacrarium*[8]. Le terme laraire

---

[4] Herculanum n'a pas été étudié autant que Pompéi. Voir toutefois M. MAUGER, « Sanctuaires et marges de l'habitat : perception et délimitation de l'espace domestique », in A. DARDENAY, N. LAUBRY (éd.), *Anthropology of Roman Housing*, Turnhout, Brepols, 2020 (Antiquités et sciences humaines. La traversée des frontières 5), p. 179-186. Ostie : *ibid.* p. 186-190.

[5] Première notation dans *CIL* IX, 2125. I. R. DANKA, « De Larum cultu rustico et familiari », *Eos* 71 (1983), p. 57-71, donne un récapitulatif des données : sources, places, surtout des maisons, offrandes. Voir aussi A. HUG, *s.v.* « Lararium », *RE* 12.1 (1924), col. 794-795 ; ORR, *Roman Domestic Religion* ; D. G. ORR, « Learning from Lararia : Notes on the Household Shrines of Pompeii », in R. I. CURTIS (éd.), *Studia pompeiana & classica in honor of Wilhelmina F. Jashemski*, New Rochelle, NY, A.D. Caratzas, 1988, p. 293-303 ; C. HÖCKER, *s.v.* « Lararium », *DNP* 6 (1999), col. 1145 ; A. COMELLA, *s.v.* « Lararium », *ThesCRA* IV (2005), col. 262 (l. étrusque) ; F. GIACOBELLO, *ibid.*, col. 262-264 (l. romain) ; CARDAUNS, *Lar (Lararium)* ; M.-O. LAFORGE, *La religion privée à Pompéi*, Naples, Centre Jean Bérard, 2009, p. 19-47. Pour la terminologie M. BASSANI, Sacraria. *Ambienti e piccoli edifici per il culto domestico in area vesuviana*, Padova, Libreria Universitaria, 2008 (Antenor Quaderni 9), p. 49-63 : 49-59 *sacrarium* ; p. 59-61 *aedes* et *aedicula* ; p. 61-62 *lararium* ; F. GIACOBELLO, « Testimonianze del culto dei Lari dall'area vesuviana : significato e nuove interpretazioni », in M. BASSANI, F. GHEDINI (éd.), Religionem significare. *Aspetti storico-religiosi, strutturali, iconografici e materiali dei sacra privata*, Rome, Quasar, 2011 (Antenor Quaderni 19), p. 79-89 ; C. W. KING, *The Ancient Roman Afterlife. Di Manes, Belief, and the Cult of the Death*, Austin, University of Austin Press, 2020, p. 76-79 ; MAUGER, *Sanctuaires et marges de l'habitat*, p. 166-169.

[6] *Historia Augusta* IV, 3, 5 : Marc Aurèle conserve des portraits dorés de ses précepteurs dans son laraire ; XVIII, 29, 2 : Alexandre Sévère aurait vénéré des *diui*, mais aussi Apollonius de Tyane, Jésus-Christ, Abraham, Orphée et Alexandre le Grand dans son *lararium maius* (voir BODEL, *Cicero's Minerva*, p. 263-264) ; XVIII, 31, 4-5 : second laraire avec des portraits de Virgile, Cicéron et Achille ; XXVII, 17, 4 : dans le laraire de l'empereur Tacite, des statuettes sont tombées, ce qui est vu comme un *omen* négatif.

[7] Juvénal VIII, 111 et Pétrone 29, 8. Voir M. MENICHETTI, *s.v.* « aedicula », *ThesCRA* IV (2005), col. 163 ; F. MARCATTILI, *ibid.*, col. 165 (à côté d'édicules publics).

[8] Cicéron, *Ver.* IV, 2, 4 et IV, 3, 7 ; *ad fam.* XIII, 2.

implique la vénération des Lares, les dieux protecteurs de la famille à côté des dieux de la maison, les Pénates[9]. En réalité nous connaissons aussi des laraires destinés aux dieux égyptiens, comme dans la Maison des Amours dorés à Pompéi, et les laraires, soit peints soit en trois dimensions, contenant des images d'autres dieux et déesses en même temps. Le terme *sacrarium* correspond bien aux exigences d'une installation point trop grande, mais spécifique, à l'intérieur de la demeure. Les sources mentionnent des petites 'chapelles domestiques' dans les chambres à coucher d'Auguste et Domitien[10]. Un des cas plus tardifs serait un *sacrarium* sur l'Esquilin, de l'époque constantinienne, où les archéologues ont trouvé, à la fin du XIXe siècle, des statuettes de « Fortuna-Isis » et des Lares dans une niche avec des compartiments[11]. Dès lors, les forces supra-humaines honorées pouvaient inclure les divinités mentionnées, qui, en lien avec les exigences de la *familia*, trouvaient place dans le culte domestique. Le choix de celles-ci semble avoir été dicté par le maître de maison.

Vitruve, dans le livre VI du *De Architectura*, n'évoque pas la question des *res sacrae* dans la maison. Il ne décrit pas non plus les lieux de culte ou le versant religieux de la maison. L'attention accordée aux *imagines maiorum* dans la partie sur l'atrium et les *alae* (VI, 3, 6) pourrait avoir une certaine pertinence à cet égard, mais ce chapitre ne contient pas de données assez concrètes qui puissent être confrontées à celles observées dans les villes vésuviennes : *imagines ita alte cum suis ornamentis ad latitudinem alarum sint constitutae* (« la hauteur des 'images' avec leurs ornements sera déterminée en fonction de la largeur des ailes »)[12].

---

[9] Sur les pénates en contexte privé, voir DUBOURDIEU, *Origines*, p. 57-120 ; R. A. TYBOUT, « Domestic Shrines and Popular Painting », *JRA* 9 (1996), p. 358-374, part. p. 359-361 ; DUBOURDIEU, *Cultes domestiques*, p. 35-36. Sur les laraires G. K. BOYCE, *Corpus of the lararia of Pompeii*, Rome, American Academy in Rome (Memoirs of the American Academy in Rome, 14), 1937 ; ORR, *Roman Domestic Religion* et ORR, *Learning from Lararia* ; DUBOURDIEU, *Origines*, p. 67-75 (avec une bibliographie souvent inadéquate et vieillie) ; FRÖHLICH, *Lararien- und Fassadenbilder* ; DUBOURDIEU, *Cultes domestiques*, p. 37-40.

[10] Suet., *Aug.* 7 et *Domit.* 17.

[11] HUG, *Lararium*, col. 795 ; DUBOURDIEU, *Origines*, p. 75 ; BODEL, *Cicero's Minerva*, p. 261, fig. 14.4 (avec bibliographie). Voir pour « Fortuna-Isis » la contribution de Nicolas Amoroso dans ce volume.

[12] Traduction de L. CALLEBAT, *Vitruve de l'architecture livre VI*, Paris, Les Belles Lettres, 2004 (CUF), p. 16, commentaire p. 129.

En revanche, il existe d'autres sources sur la position des *imagines maiorum* dans l'atrium, mais étant donné que nos *sacraria* ne contiennent guère d'objets du genre des *imagines*, nous pouvons clore ici ce point[13].

L'épicentre des cultes domestiques était localisé surtout dans l'atrium et la cuisine[14]. Il nous faut imaginer des pratiques régulières, voire quotidiennes, réalisées par les membres de la *familia* et comprenant des offrandes de produits agricoles comme du blé et des fleurs ou de l'encens. Il est probable qu'on ne sacrifiait pas souvent des animaux[15]. Des prières étaient par ailleurs formulées. Les offrandes exigeaient la présence de mobilier comme un autel ou une table ou un brûle-parfum. Dans le cas d'un sacrifice, il faut sans doute que le *sacrarium* dispose d'une cheminée ou d'une autre ouverture spécifique pour évacuer les fumées[16], et nous verrons que les *sacraria* présentaient bien une évacuation à cet effet.

Le dossier des laraires pompéiens est assez bien connu et compte environ cinq cents exemplaires. L'œuvre de base est le corpus compilé par George K. Boyce en 1937 suivi par des études de David Gerald Orr et la monographie, munie d'une interprétation plus profonde et comprenant des ajouts, de Thomas Fröhlich

---

[13] Voir H. FLOWER, *Ancestor Masks and Aristocratic Power in Roman Culture*, Oxford, Oxford University Press, 1996, p. 185-222. Pour notre discussion, l'observation d'Harriet Flower selon laquelle il n'existait pas un vrai culte des ancêtres (ou de leurs portraits) a une certaine pertinence (p. 210-211).

[14] Foss, *Watchful Lares* ; W. VAN ANDRINGA, « Dal sacrificio al banchetto : rituale topografia della casa romana », in M. BASSANI, F. GHEDINI (éd.), *Religionem significare. Aspetti storico-religiosi, strutturali, iconografici e materiali dei sacra privata*, Rome, Quasar, 2011 (Antenor Quaderni 19), p. 91-98 ; VAN ANDRINGA, *Quotidien des dieux et des hommes*, p. 220-225, 230-236, fig. 171-178 ; GIACOBELLO, *Testimonianze*, p. 87-89.

[15] VAN ANDRINGA, *Quotidien des dieux et des hommes*, p. 240 suggère l'existence de cette pratique.

[16] ORR, *Learning from Lararia*, p. 295 : « Although it must obviously be admitted that sacrifice can be accomplished without such architectural aids, the *lararium* must have played an important part in the domestic ritual. » Pour les offrandes, M. BASSANI, « Sacrifici in ambito domestico. Alcune esemplificazioni di età romana », *Scienze dell'Antichità* 23.3 (2017), p. 613-630. Elle mentionne (p. 622, fig. 7) un ensemble de fruits, os de porc et d'agneau dans le jardin de la Maison du bracelet d'or. Voir aussi LAFORGE, *La religion privée*, p. 97-133 ; VAN ANDRINGA, *Quotidien des dieux et des hommes*, p. 238-256 ; HAUG, *Decor*, p. 35. Le *sacrarium* des *Praedia* de Julia Felix (v. *infra*) avait un trou dans la voûte.

en 1991[17]. Ajoutons, pour citer seulement des monographies, les publications de Anna Krzyszowska en 2002, Maddalena Bassani en 2008 et 2017, de Federica Giacobello en 2008 et de Marie-Odile Laforge en 2009[18].

La forme la plus répandue des laraires est l'édicule en trois dimensions, soit en bois[19], soit maçonné, installé dans une position stable, comme dans un coin de l'atrium par exemple. Puis vient le laraire en deux dimensions, qui prend la forme d'une peinture murale, située le plus souvent dans la cuisine, près du foyer[20] ; mais il peut prendre également la forme du laraire peint dédié aux divinités égyptiennes du péristyle de la Maison des Amours dorés. Enfin, il existe des monuments construits qui se présentent soit comme des niches dans les murs, soit comme des 'chapelles' bâties[21]. C'est cette dernière catégorie qui nous occupera dans cette contribution, celle que David Gerald Orr désigna comme « the most uncommon shrine[22] ». On peut,

---

[17] ORR, *Roman Domestic Religion* et ORR, *Learning from Lararia* ; FRÖHLICH, *Lararien- und Fassadenbilder*. Il ne faut pas oublier le travail fondamental de Attilio De Marchi, *Il culto privato di Roma antica*, Milan, U. Hoepli, 1896 (fac-simile New York, Ares Press, 1975), part. 79-144. Voir le panorama donné dans F. GIACOBELLO, *Larari pompeiani. Iconografia e culto dei Lari in ambito domestico*, Milano, LED edizioni, 2008. Brèves mais bien conçues sont les synthèses de KING, *Ancient Roman Afterlife*, p. 171-174 et HAUG, *Decor*, p. 408-412.

[18] A. KRZYSZOWSKA, *Les cultes privés à Pompéi*, Wrocław, Wydawnictwo Uniwersytetu Wrocławskiego, 2002 (Acta Universitatis Wratislaviensis 2385) ; BASSANI, Sacraria ; BASSANI, *Sacrifici in ambito domestico* ; LAFORGE, *Religion privée*. GIACOBELLO, *Larari pompeiani*, se limite aux exemplaires avec des Lares seuls, ce qui explique un corpus de seulement 114 exemples dans la ville (dossier p. 132-209).

[19] Jusqu'à aujourd'hui seulement connu à Herculanum : ORR, *Roman Domestic Religion*, p. 1585-1589, pl. X.20 ; S. T. A. M. MOLS, *Wooden Furniture in Herculaneum. Form, Technique and Function*, Amsterdam, Gieben, 1999 (Circumvesuviana 2), p. 58-62 (*aediculae*). Je mentionne l'exemple dans la maison de Trimalchion : Pétrone 29, 8 : *praeterea grande armarium in angulo uidi in cuius aedicula erant Lares argentei positi Venerisque signum marmoreum et pyxis aurea non pusilla, in qua barbam ipsius conditam esse dicebant* (« en plus j'ai vu dans un coin une grande armoire, avec dans son édicule, des Lares d'argent et une statuette de marbre de Vénus et une boîte d'or, pas petite, dans laquelle on disait qu'il y avait sa barbe »).

[20] Plus récemment M. Mauger (*Sanctuaires et marges*, p. 170-178) a discuté de l'impact des laraires peints dans les maisons de Pompéi.

[21] BOYCE, *Corpus of the lararia*, p. 10-17 ; DUBOURDIEU, *Origines*, p. 73-74.

[22] ORR, *Roman Domestic Religion*, p. 1578. Il donne les exemples de la Maison de Caius Caesius Restitutus et de la Caupona VI 1, 1.

avec Maddalena Bassani, faire la distinction entre les espaces de cette catégorie situés à l'intérieur ou à l'extérieur de la maison[23]. Ces *sacraria* posent, évidemment, un problème en ce qui concerne la topographie de la maison : il va de soi que les 'chapelles' ne pouvaient pas être installées dans un atrium ou une cuisine, mais avaient besoin d'un espace plus vaste, comme le jardin, ou encore occuper une pièce spécifique dans la maison. On peut ainsi se demander si cette position n'eût pas des conséquences sur les pratiques cultuelles de la *familia*. Notons que les sanctuaires 'indépendants' ont été étudiés dans des contributions récentes pour ce qui est de leur architecture et de leur décor et nous nous y référerons le cas échéant[24].

Mais avant d'aborder l'analyse de quelques exemples, formulons quelques observations corollaires. Concernant l'iconographie des sanctuaires dans l'art romain, on constate que les représentations de temples monumentaux se concentrent essentiellement sur les reliefs commémoratifs ou historiques, tandis que ces images sont absentes du répertoire domestique, à l'exception d'un cas isolé à Pompéi, dans la Maison de Mars et Vénus ou des Noces d'Hercule (VII 9, 47), mais cette représentation ne faisait pas office de marqueur de lieu de culte comme c'était le cas pour les laraires[25]. Signalons, de plus, les deux temples figurés sur les façades de maisons de la Via dell'Abbondanza : le temple de la Fortune peint avec les *phalli* comme acrotères et le temple habité par Mercure[26].

---

[23] Bassani, Sacraria, p. 62-93 « ambienti interni » et p. 93-101 « ambienti esterni ».

[24] M. T. D'Alessio, *I culti a Pompei. Divinità, luoghi e frequentatori (VI secolo a.C. - 79 d.C.)*, Rome, Istituto Poligrafico e Zecca dello Stato, 2009 ; E. M. Moormann, *Divine Interiors. Mural Paintings in Greek and Roman Sanctuaries*, Amsterdam, Amsterdam University Press, 2011 (Amsterdam Archaeological Studies 16) ; Van Andringa, *Quotidien des dieux et des hommes*.

[25] Dernièrement E. M. Moormann, « Ministers of Isiac Cults in Roman Wall Painting », in V. Gasparini, R. Veymiers (éd.), *Individuals and Materials in the Greco-Roman Cults of Isis*, Leiden – Boston, Brill, 2018 (Religions in the Graeco-Roman World 187), p. 366-383, part. 378-379. Je ne discute pas les deux scènes rituelles isiaques d'Herculanum, pour lesquelles voir aussi cette étude, p. 367-372 et p. 1039-1040, fig. 12.1-2.

[26] IX 7, 1-2 = Fröhlich, *Lararien- und Fassadenbilder*, p. 332-333, pl. 59,1-2 ; PPM IX, p. 773 (Fortuna). IX 7, 7 = Fröhlich, *Lararien- und Fassadenbilder*, p. 333-335, pl. 61,3 ; PPM IX, p. 775 (Mercure). Les deux pein-

Ajoutons un point qui nous paraît significatif, mais nous échappe quasiment totalement faute de documentation conservée dans les 'chapelles' : la question de la présence et donc de la visibilité des dieux qui habitent l'édicule. Dans les temples majeurs, on le sait, la statue de culte est visible à travers les portes ouvertes durant la journée[27]. Les laraires peints ou construits ne disposent pas de *ualuae* ou de battants et ne peuvent donc pas être clos et on ne connaît pas non plus de voiles à soulever. Conséquemment, les dieux dans les laraires peints ou les statuettes dans les exemplaires en trois dimensions sont toujours visibles. La petitesse des statuettes et des représentations est proportionnée au format du laraire, mais aussi aux dimensions de la *domus*.

En ce qui concerne les 'chapelles', on observe immédiatement qu'elles constituent un petit groupe. Les *sacraria* ont la forme de pièces ou de grandes niches et sont accessibles à partir d'un jardin, *viridarium*, portique ou espace plus grand aux membres de la *familia*. Pour August Hug, ce sont des « Hauskapellen[28] ». George K. Boyce utilise le terme de *sacellum* et le définit comme « a room set apart for the service of the cult and especially equipped for that purpose[29] ». Le mot *sacellum*, cependant, signifie dans la plupart des cas un espace hypèthre, même si on utilise également le terme pour de petites pièces de culte public et semi-public[30]. Marcel Van Doren définit le terme *sacrarium* dans le sens technique et dans le cadre du droit romain. L'attestation la plus ancienne concernerait le *sacrarium* de la *Regia* de Numa Pompilius sur le Forum romain, suivi par des *sacraria* destinés à Janus et Vesta[31]. Plus tard, on trouve la mention de *sacraria*

---

tures ont été portées à l'Antiquaire de Pompéi, où elles se trouvent dans l'exposition permanente (vues en Avril 2022).

[27] A. Dubourdieu, « Voir les dieux à Rome », in P. Borgeaud, D. Fabiano (éd.), *Perception et construction du divin dans l'Antiquité*, Genève, Droz, 2003, p. 19-34 : bonne analyse de la question de la visibilité.

[28] Hug, *Lararium*, col. 795.

[29] Boyce, *Corpus of the lararia*, p. 18. Il donne 11 « exemples sûrs » (Laforge, *La religion privée*, p. 32, note 67).

[30] M. Menichetti, *ThesCRA* V (2005), col. 314, avec des exemples comme le *Sacellum* des Augustales à Herculanum et le *Sacellum* de Silvanus à Ostie. Voir aussi Laforge, *La religion privée*, p. 10-11.

[31] M. Van Doren, « Les *Sacraria* : une catégorie méconnue d'édifices sa-

dans le culte de Bona Mens et des mystères[32]. Pour Marie-Odile Laforge, ce type concerne une « pièce à l'écart, destinée au culte et spécialement équipée dans ce but[33] ». Annie Dubourdieu voit le *sacrarium* comme une « pièce qui semble exclusivement réservée au culte privé[34] », ce qui a été confirmé par un corpus d'exemples – peu nombreux – compilé par Mario Torelli qui les définit comme « tutte le strutture di ambito privato, diverse dai lararia [...], sede di culti prestati a personaggi storici[35] ». Annie Dubourdieu conclut ainsi : « Les *sacraria* sont distingués des simples 'laraires' par le fait qu'ils ont un pavement, des murs, un toit[36] ».

On doit à Maddalena Bassani l'étude la plus aboutie à ce jour sur les *sacraria* campaniens, dont elle relève trente-neuf attestations[37]. La plupart des espaces situés à l'intérieur des demeures sont des pièces rectangulaires ; quelquefois un *sacrarium* est muni d'une abside ou d'une ou plusieurs exèdres, avec des dimensions limitées d'environ 5 m²[38]. Les composants habituels de ces espaces sont : autel, niche, *aedicula*, base, colonnes, bancs, et décorations des sols, des murs et des voûtes[39]. Les *sacraria* situés à l'extérieur se présentent également comme des pièces rectangulaires de diverses dimensions, situées dans des cours, péristyles

---

crées chez les Romains », *AntCl* 27 (1958), p. 31-75, 42-46. Champs militaires : p. 46.

[32] VAN DOREN, Sacraria, p. 46-49.

[33] LAFORGE, *La religion privée*, p. 31. Catégorie « Les chapelles privées » (p. 31-47).

[34] DUBOURDIEU, *Cultes domestiques*, p. 39.

[35] M. TORELLI, *ThesCRA* V (2005), col. 316-317. Il se réfère à F. DI CAPUA, « Sacrari pompeiani », in *Pompeiana. Raccolta di studi per il secondo centenario degli scavi di Pompei*, Napoli, Gaetano Macchiaroli editore, 1950, p. 60-85, et VAN DOREN, Sacraria. Voir aussi LAFORGE, *La religion privée*, p. 31 note 56.

[36] DUBOURDIEU, *Origines*, p. 71. Aussi DUBOURDIEU, *Cultes domestiques*, p. 39, se basant sur BASSANI, Sacraria, p. 163. Voir aussi dans ce volume la contribution d'A. Durand, 333-357.

[37] BASSANI, Sacraria, p. 65-93. Voir F. PESANDO, « *Sacraria pompeiana*. Alcune note », in M. BASSANI, F. GHEDINI (éd.), Religionem significare. *Aspetti storico-religiosi, strutturali, iconografici e materiali dei sacra privata*, Roma, Quasar, 2011 (Antenor Quaderni 19), p. 11-27 pour un compte-rendu et quelques observations supplémentaires.

[38] BASSANI, Sacraria, p. 68 tableau 4 : 17 × de 5 m², 8 jusqu'à 12 m². La Villa des Mystères dispose d'une installation (n. 25) extrêmement grande.

[39] *Ibid.*, p. 73 tableau 5 ; p. 81-93 sur les décorations.

ou jardins[40]. Trente-quatre pièces ont des peintures murales, dont l'étude iconographique a été réalisée par Maddalena Bassani, qui identifie les occupants habituels comme les *Genii* et les Lares, les serpents *agathodaimones* (moins fréquents), ainsi que d'autres divinités, dans quelques cas. En revanche, on n'y trouve pas les 'personnages historiques' mentionnés par Mario Torelli, figures vénérées plutôt dans des sanctuaires publics[41].

Tandis que les petits lieux de culte (peintures, niches, édicules) faisaient partie de pièces utilisées dans la vie quotidienne, au long de la journée, sous des formes diverses – ce qui impliquait le changement de mobilier et d'occupants d'heure en heure – les *sacraria* consistaient en des pièces de dimensions modestes, avec des exigences architecturales simples et occupant une place plus ou moins remarquable dans le plan d'une maison. Ces pièces, semble-t-il, n'avaient pas d'autre fonction et étaient spécifiées par les activités qu'elles abritaient, leur décor, leur aménagement et leur position. En tant que catégorie, il est donc pertinent de les étudier spécifiquement. Toutefois, comme pour beaucoup d'aspects de l'archéologie pompéienne, nous devons prendre en compte le biais du temps : la majeure partie du dossier se limite aux dernières décennies avant 79, et même si les pièces à étudier ont des origines plus anciennes, il est souvent difficile de distinguer des changements d'affectation[42]. Pour Fabrizio Pesando, cette présence tardive s'expliquerait peut-être par un degré de religiosité plus forte après le tremblement de terre de 62 ap. J.-C. Il fait ainsi référence aux reliefs ornant le laraire de l'atrium de la Maison de Caecilius Iucundus et à la présence de tablettes apotropaïques comme signes de l'expression d'une « inevitabile superstizione[43] ». Il est difficile de prouver cette séduisante hypothèse, parce que nous n'observons pas simultanément un supplément d'intérêt spécifique pour les grands sanctuaires publics. Le biais observé pourrait avoir influencé Fabrizio Pesando en formulant sa conclusion positiviste.

---

[40] *Ibid.*, p. 93-101. 5 pièces rectangulaires entre 3 et 11.15 m^2.

[41] M. Torelli, *ThesCRA* V (2005), col. 316-317.

[42] De plus, en raison de la crise sanitaire de 2020-2021, je n'ai pas eu l'opportunité de faire des observations sur le terrain.

[43] Pesando, Sacraria pompeiana, p. 23-24, avec fig. 14 ; p. 26 (citation).

Dans cette contribution, je voudrais discuter quelques exemples et étudier les aspects de l'architecture et du décor qui donnent le caractère de sacralité et qui sont (ou non) comparables à l'apparat des sanctuaires publics. Parmi les maisons identifiées par Maddalena Bassani, j'ai choisi la Maison du Ménandre comme exemple datable, probablement, d'époque républicaine, mais refaite à un moment plus récent, tandis que les autres exemples datent des dernières décennies de l'histoire pompéienne. Ainsi, les études de cas choisies couvrent potentiellement une grande partie l'histoire pompéienne, du Ier siècle av. au Ier siècle ap. J.-C.

La Maison du Ménandre (Figg. 1-2)

Ce *sacrarium* – dont les deux phases chronologiques sont nettement distinctes – est un espace ouvert vers un portique dans l'angle sud-ouest du péristyle de la Maison du Ménandre (I 10, 4,

Fig. 1.
Maison du Ménandre, niche 25, décor du deuxième style
(cliché Domenico Esposito).

Fig. 2.
Maison du Ménandre, niche 25, autel avec des figures
(cliché Domenico Esposito).

niche 25)[44]. La pièce est dépourvue de mobilier à l'exception d'une niche occupant la paroi ouest, dans laquelle se dressent cinq petites figures.

La décoration s'articule en deux phases. Les parois montrent un décor de deuxième style, phase IIa, donc autour de 40-30 av.

---

[44] Boyce, *Corpus of the lararia*, n. 49 ; Di Capua, *Sacrari pompeiani*, p. 82 ; Foss, *Watchful Lares*, p. 214-215 ; PPM II, p. 371-375 ; Krzyszowska, *Les cultes privés à Pompéi*, p. 24-27, 161-163, 175 ; R. Ling, L. Ling, *The Insula of the Menander at Pompeii* II. *The Decorations*, Oxford, Oxford University Press, 2005, p. 19-20, fig. 76-78, pl. 39 ; M.-O. Charles-Laforge, « 'Imagines maiorum' et portraits d'ancêtres à Pompéi », in *Contributi di archeologia vesuviana* III. *I culti di Pompei*, Roma, L'Erma di Bretschneider, 2007 (Studi della SAP 21), p. 158-171 ; Bassani, *Sacraria*, p. 172-173 scheda 2 ; Giacobello, *Larari pompeiani*, p. 256-257 cat. V12 ; G. Stefani, *Menander. La Casa del Menandro di Pompei*, Milano, Electa, 2013 ; King, *Ancient Roman Afterlife*, 56.

J.-C.[45] : on distingue une colonnade devant une arcade avec des rideaux ; trois sections sur la paroi sud, une section sur les deux autres parois, est et ouest. Dans les perspectives ainsi constituées, on observe un ensemble d'arbres que Roger Ling appelle « the magic forest motif ». Des oiseaux fantastiques peuplent cette forêt d'arbres anciens, dépourvus de feuilles[46]. Par ailleurs, des objets dionysiaques sont posés dans l'entrecolonnement, devant les tentures : syrinx, nébride, tympan et *pedum*[47]. Les objets suggèrent une relation très claire avec Dionysos, mais il n'est pas possible d'identifier des divinités en particulier. Les divinités qui habitent les niches voisines dans l'aile sud du péristyle, Diane et Vénus, pourraient former avec Dionysos – symbolisé qui plus est, dans la niche, par Euripide et Ménandre[48] – une triade spécifique. Grâce au décor du deuxième style, ce *sacrarium* semble constituer le plus ancien exemple du groupe. Il se trouve dans une partie ouverte et bien accessible de la maison et montre une certaine richesse en accord avec le prestige du complexe dans sa totalité.

Le soubassement des trois parois, ainsi que la voûte de la pièce, ont été restaurés après 62[49]. À cette époque, on a construit le petit autel et la niche dans le mur ouest. Cette intervention secondaire se reconnaît du fait qu'on a procédé à une découpe dans la paroi du mur ouest pour ouvrir cette niche, ornée avec un décor imitant du marbre de Chemtou ; un petit podium fut installé

---

[45] H. G. BEYEN, *Die pompejanische Wanddekoration vom zweiten bis zum vierten Stil* II.1, La Haye, Staatsuitgeverij, 1960, p. 170-172, suivi par R. LING, *The Insula of the Menander at Pompeii* I. *The Structures*, Oxford, Oxford University Press, 1997, p. 79.

[46] R. A. TYBOUT, *Aedificiorum figurae. Untersuchungen zu den Architekturdarstellungen des frühen zweiten Stils*, Amsterdam, Gieben, 1989, p. 41 : « monströsen vogelartigen Geschöpfen ». Autres caractéristiques citées par TYBOUT, *ibid*. n. 152. Description plus exhaustive chez BEYEN, *Die pompejanische Wanddekoration*, p. 162-172, pl. coul. II p. 161 (d'après l'*editio princeps* d'A. Maiuri) ; fig. 69-70.

[47] Cette atmosphère a été soulignée par Roger LING dans STEFANI, *Menander*, p. 23, 25. Le dieu se trouverait dans la niche 23 à côté d'Euripide et Ménandre. Les rinceaux dans la calotte de la niche de Dionysos sont pareils au feuillage dans le *sacrarium*, comme l'a observé Domenico Esposito (communication personnelle).

[48] À ce sujet, voir note précédente.

[49] BEYEN, *Die pompejanische Wanddekoration*, p. 172 suggère une décoration de la voûte du troisième style. Si c'est correct, il y aurait trois phases décoratives de cette niche.

pour poser les statuettes et, devant le mur même, un autel en *opus caementicium* fut érigé, lui aussi décoré avec un enduit à imitation de marbre de Chemtou. Autour de la niche, on distingue une partie du décor végétal, ainsi qu'une façade partiellement moulée et peinte en jaune au-dessus de l'ancienne décoration. Sur la paroi sud, le précédent décor d'enduit peint a été découpé à la hauteur des bases de colonnes du portique.

La fonction religieuse se déduit des figures abritées dans la niche. Il y avait une statuette d'un homme nu assis, interprété comme le *Lar praestes*, et quatre têtes, dont deux se dressent sur des hermès sans indication d'anatomie humaine. Alors que la statuette a été transportée dans les réserves de Pompéi, les figures encore en place sont des moulages de plâtre réalisés à partir des cavités laissées par le bois ou la cire des effigies originelles, détruites après 79[50]. Harriet Flower hésite sur leur fonction et pense à des représentations des « originators of the *gens Poppaea* or distant but famous ancestors of the owner of the house[51] ». Son hésitation pourrait avoir comme origine la position de ce *sacrarium*, mais elle souligne aussi la taille très modeste des quatre bustes[52]. En ce qui concerne la position, il est vrai que le *sacrarium* se trouve loin de l'atrium, emplacement ordinaire pour la conservation et l'exposition des *imagines maiorum*. L'hypothèse proposée est séduisante, mais ne peut pas être prouvée, car on ne peut pas non plus donner des preuves plus décisives pour une identification en tant qu'images de cire. Il semble plus pertinent d'interpréter ces bustes comme des objets précieux, éventuellement des portraits d'ancêtres, mais pas installés ici en tant qu'objets de culte. Malheureusement, nous ne sommes pas assurés de l'identification des propriétaires de cet édifice – majestueux dans

---

[50] A. DE FRANCISCIS, *Il ritratto romano a Pompei*, Naples, Gaetano Macchiaroli editore, 1951 (Accademia di Archeologia, Lettere e Belle Arti di Napoli, Memorie 1), p. 19-21, fig. 1 ; KRZYSZOWSKA, *Les cultes privés à Pompéi*, p. 162-163 ; CHARLES – LAFORGE, Imagines maiorum, p. 164-165.

[51] FLOWER, *Ancestor Masks*, p. 42-46, citation p. 44.

[52] Pour les bustes en détail, voir DE FRANCISCIS, *Il ritratto romano*, p. 19-21. Deux bustes presque identiques ont été trouvés dans un *lararium* dans la cuisine de la maison I 8, 18, dite de Balbus ou de l'atrium dorique (FRÖHLICH, *Lararien- und Fassadenbilder*, p. 254, pl. 25,3 ; FOSS, *Watchful Lares*, p. 199-201, fig. 2-4).

ses formes, dimensions et décor –, l'attribution traditionnelle à la *gens Poppaea*, ici évoquée par Harriet Flower, ne se basant pas sur des données fiables[53].

La niche avec les hermès appartient à la dernière phase du site et pourrait constituer une intervention propre du *dominus* de cette ultime période, afin d'installer des portraits d'ancêtres plus dignement, plus efficacement ou, en tant que nouveau propriétaire, de créer un aménagement à son goût pour ces figures 'historiques'. Certes, les figures en question n'étaient pas les images mêmes des ancêtres et, il faut tenir compte de l'absence d'un vrai culte fondé sur un droit de classe. Harriet Flower a mis fin à l'idée de l'existence d'un droit aux *imagines maiorum* comme un privilège basé sur une loi spécifique, le *ius imaginum*[54], mais ces figures avaient, pour les derniers habitants de la maison, une valeur qui nous échappe. Apparemment, l'installation du culte des ancêtres avait transité vers une atmosphère plus riche. On a aussi voulu constater un changement dans l'utilisation de l'atrium, moins important aux époques plus récentes, et une transition vers d'autres quartiers de la maison, dont le péristyle formait un élément plus central à l'époque impériale. En tout cas, nous devons tenir compte également de la présence de l'édicule construit dans l'angle nord-ouest de l'atrium, en tant que lieu de culte traditionnel, et toujours présent en cette phase finale de l'édifice[55].

Reste la question de savoir si cet espace était déjà un *sacrarium* avant les dernières modifications mentionnées plus haut. Avec sa forêt représentée au fond de la perspective en trompe-l'œil, la pièce pouvait évoquer un bois sacré, mais il est impossible de le déduire sur la seule base des données iconographiques. Les représentations de forêts et d'objets dionysiaques ne se limitaient pas à l'ornementation d'espaces spécifiquement cultuels,

---

[53] Sur le propriétaire LING, LING, *Menander* I, 142-144 (pas certain) ; R. LING dans STEFANI, *Menander*, p. 11 ; A. VARONE, *ibid.*, 47-52. FLOWER, *Ancestor Masks*, p. 45-46, KRZYSZOWSKA, *Les cultes privés à Pompéi*, p. 162 et CHARLES-LAFORGE, Imagines maiorum, p. 161 et 168 suivent Amedeo Maiuri et d'autres dans l'attribution de la maison aux *Poppaei*.

[54] FLOWER, *Ancestor Masks*. Charles-Laforge (Imagines maiorum) admet toujours cette existence.

[55] C. CICIRELLI dans STEFANI, *Menander*, p. 184-187.

mais étaient devenues, à la fin de l'époque républicaine, une forme de décoration très appréciée. Pensons à la pièce souterraine de la villa de Livie à Prima Porta, avec ses jardins idylliques, de même date, qui offrait un agréable séjour souterrain et un abri dans les périodes de chaleur.

Quoi qu'il en soit, rien ne suggère l'atmosphère sacrale d'un sanctuaire public dans aucune des deux phases d'aménagement architectural et de décoration de cet espace. On n'observe pas non plus de traces de gonds de portes ni d'une courtine pour isoler la pièce. Il n'y a pas non plus d'éléments architectoniques marquant l'espace sacral et seul le décor de la première phase pourrait avoir un caractère évoquant une telle atmosphère. Nous nous trouvons dans un pavillon ou un portique à l'intérieur d'une forêt. L'espace est domestique, pourvu de pans de textile pour fermer les colonnades. En même temps, ce mince portique se trouve dans la nature faunique, où les compagnons de Dionysos ont laissé leurs attributs et cessé de jouer. Enfin, dans la phase finale, prédominent les statuettes d'ancêtres et du *Lar*. Elles nous invitent à développer des activités de révérence vers les membres défunts de la famille sans plus prendre en compte le décor dionysiaque.

La Maison de Sabazios (Figg. 3-4)

Dans la maison II 1, 12 – où on a trouvé des objets de culte en lien avec Sabazios – se trouvait un *sacrarium* spécifique (pièce 5), appartenant à une association d'initiés[56]. Le complexe date de l'époque médio-républicaine et a subi des interventions assez radicales après 62, dont l'installation du *sacrarium*. Le plan du complexe, quasiment carré dans cette phase, montre une pièce

---

[56] W. F. JASHEMSKI, *The Gardens of Pompeii* I, New Rochelle, NY, A.D. Caratzas, 1979, p. 135-137, fig. 213-215 ; W. F. JASHEMSKI, *The Gardens of Pompeii* II, New Rochelle, NY, A.D. Caratzas, 1993, p. 76 ; *PPM*, III, p. 19-41 ; R. PACE, « Il 'Complesso dei Riti Magici' a Pompei II, 1,11-12 », *Rivista di Studi Pompeiani* 8 (1997), p. 73-97 ; M.-O. CHARLES-LAFORGE, « Le 'Complexe des rites magiques' et le culte de Sabazios à Pompéi », in *Contributi di archeologia vesuviana* II, Rome, L'Erma di Bretschneider, 2006 (Studi della SAP 18), p. 161-184 ; VAN ANDRINGA, *Quotidien des dieux et des hommes*, p. 331-336 ; MOORMANN, *Divine Interiors*, p. 183-184.

Fig. 3.
Maison de Sabazios, pièce 5, vue générale
(cliché Domenico Esposito).

Fig. 4.
Maison de Sabazios, pièce 5, décor
(cliché Domenico Esposito).

particulière (5), juste en face de l'entrée (1) et de la pièce (2) du côté nord du péristyle-*viridarium*. Cette pièce de 4,6 × 4,6 m environ est pourvue d'un podium et présente des peintures sobres de quatrième style : socle rouge et panneaux rouges et jaunes. Il y aurait eu, sur le mur nord, des traces de feuillages suggérant l'image d'un jardin, mais il n'existe pas d'illustrations de cette partie perdue[57]. Le podium portait au moment des fouilles, en 1954, des offrandes, comme des mains en bronze de Sabazios et des ustensiles pour servir les repas. En général, on suit Robert Turcan qui a suggéré que la pièce 5 était utilisée pour des réunions des 'Sabaziastes' qui y tenaient des repas préparés dans une des deux cuisines de l'édifice. Des graffiti à l'entrée mentionnent le terme *antru[m]* qui désigne probablement ce *sacrarium*[58].

En ce qui concerne les décors, à l'extérieur étaient représentés sur le jambage de la porte le couple Mercure et Bacchus et une Vénus du type *anadyomène*. Leur compagnon Priape se trouvait dans le vestibule[59]. Selon William Van Andringa, ces dieux servent d'intermédiaires entre les dieux 'normaux' et la divinité 'étrange'[60]. En revanche, à l'intérieur de la pièce, le décor peint de quatrième style, réalisé autour de 62, ne présente rien de particulier et ne détermine pas non plus sa fonction comme *sacrarium*.

On peut observer que la maison (ou les trois petites maisons antérieures[61]) a subi autour de 62 des modifications de plan et d'usage. C'est aussi la raison pour laquelle on peut se demander si la pièce 5 est un bien un *sacrarium* du type discuté dans cet essai – c'est-à-dire une installation dans une maison privée – ou bien un vrai sanctuaire, comme le suggèrent Rossella Pace et Marie-Odile Charles-Laforge ; par conséquent le nom ordinaire

---

[57] VAN ANDRINGA, *Quotidien des dieux et des hommes*, p. 331-336 ; PACE, *Riti Magici*, p. 82-83. Seule photo dans *PPM*, III, p. 39 (angle sud-ouest avec des panneaux rouge et jaune).

[58] *CIL* IV, 10104d ; PACE, *Riti Magici*, p. 87 et 89 (qui donne un panorama des recherches, incluant Turcan), p. 90. Plus détaillée est la discussion du culte par CHARLES-LAFORGE, *Complexe des rites magiques*.

[59] Les peintures ont été portées dans les réserves (PACE, *Riti Magici*, p. 80-81). Pour des images, voir *PPM*, III, p. 20-21.

[60] Cf. CHARLES-LAFORGE, *Complexe des rites magiques*, p. 165.

[61] L'histoire du bâtiment est bien expliquée par PACE, *Riti Magici*, p. 83-87.

de la maison « Complesso dei riti magici » serait justifié[62]. Bien que quelques pièces (3, 9, 11) n'aient pas subies de modification, ni dans leur structure, ni dans leur aménagement et décor, la prépondérance de la pièce 5, avec les pièces secondaires 6, 6a, 7 et 8, suggère une fonction assez centrée sur des rites, dans un complexe resté privé, mais accessible aux membres du culte qui doivent avoir été des amis ou des relations du propriétaire[63]. Si cette hypothèse se confirmait, nous pourrions écarter cet exemple de notre liste mais, quoi qu'il en soit, il offre un beau parallèle aux *sacraria* installés dans les jardins. Il ne présente rien de particulier, ni dans son décor, ni dans son architecture, tout comme les autres cas discutés ici. Le commanditaire, suppose-t-on, n'a pas eu de projet concret concernant l'aménagement de ce sanctuaire, même si le culte de Sabazios doit avoir eu des particularités méconnues de la majorité des habitants de Pompéi. Mais il est probable que le propriétaire ne voulait pas susciter un rejet du culte et a choisi un format familier dans la cité.

Le sanctuaire isiaque dans les Praedia de Julia Felix (Figg. 5-7)

Explorés en 1755 et puis fouillés par Amedeo Maiuri en 1950, les *Praedia* de Julia Felix (II 4, 3) ont, entre autres, livré une pièce (55) appelée '*sacrarium*' qui se situait dans le jardin 50 mais a été démantelée à l'époque des Bourbons pour être remontée au Museo Borbonico. Des fragments se trouvent au MANN et ont été étudiés par Christopher Parslow, qui a aussi restitué l'histoire de la découverte. Récemment, en 2016, la niche a été restaurée et présentée de nouveau au public du Museo Archeologico Nazionale de Naples, et nous pouvons mieux l'analyser grâce à des études de Valeria Sampaolo[64]. Sont conservées les parois latérales

---

[62] PACE, *Riti Magici*, p. 87 : « luogo, ormai divenuto un santuario. » Nom utilisé à partir de 1958 (*ibid.* p. 87). Elle développe cette hypothèse p. 91-92. Voir aussi CHARLES-LAFORGE, *Complexe des rites magiques*, p. 179 et 181.

[63] Propriétaire : l'affranchi Lesbianus ou Sextilus Pyrricus ? Voir PACE, *Riti Magici*, p. 92 ; CHARLES-LAFORGE, *Complexe des rites magiques*, p. 179.

[64] MANN inv. Romano 837, 838, 829. Voir V. SAMPAOLO, « Nuove acquisizioni per i *praedia Iuliae Felicis* », in I. BRAGANTINI, E. MORLICCHIO (éd.),

Fig. 5.
Praedia de Julia Felix, *sacrarium* 555, reconstruit au Museo Archeologico Nazionale di Napoli, paroi gauche (photo Musée).

et la voûte, tandis que la paroi arrière est perdue. C'est dans cette pièce qu'on trouva le fameux trépied aux satyres ithyphalliques (inv. 27847) et beaucoup d'autres objets, ce qui devait conférer à cet espace l'atmosphère d'un dépôt plutôt qu'une chambre sacrée[65].

Winckelmann e l'archeologia a Napoli, Napoli, Università degli Studi di Napoli L'Orientale, 2019 (AION Series Minor 1), p. 195-210, part. p. 195-201 ; V. SAMPAOLO, « Per una ricomposizione degli apparati pittorici dei Praedia Iuliae Felicis di Pompei », in P. GIULIERINI, A. CORALINI, V. SAMPAOLO (éd.), *Picta Fragmenta. La pittura vesuviana. Una rilettura*, Milano, Silvana editore, 2020, p. 21-37, part. p. 31-36, fig. 7.1-3. Je remercie Valeria Sampaolo pour les clichés du *sacrarium* restauré.

[65] C. PARSLOW, « The Sacrarium of Isis in the Praedia of Julia Felix in Pompeii », in C. MATTUSCH (éd.), *Rediscovering the ancient world on the Bay of Naples*, New Haven – London, Yale University Press, 2013, p. 47-72, part. p. 55-57, fig. 7-10. Les objets n'étaient pas conservés ensemble au musée et la composition a été reconstruite par Parslow.

Fig. 6.
Praedia de Julia Felix, *sacrarium* 555, reconstruit au Museo Archeologico Nazionale di Napoli, paroi arrière (photo Musée).

La pièce mesurait 1,34 par 1,53 m, avec une hauteur de 2,44 m, et était complètement décorée de thèmes égyptiens[66]. La décora-

---

[66] W. Helbig, *Die Wandgemälde der vom Vesuv verschütteten Städte Campaniens*, Leipzig, Breitkopf & Hartel, 1868, n. 79 ; Boyce, *Corpus of the lararia*, p. 95, n° 471 ; Di Capua, Sacrari pompeiani ; Fröhlich, *Lararien- und Fassadenbilder*, p. 265-266, pl. 30.1 ; M. Pagano, R. Prisciandaro, *Studio sulle provenienze degli oggetti rinvenuti negli scavi borbonici del regno di Napoli : una lettura integrata, coordinata e commentata della documentazione*, Roma, Bardi, 2006, p. 17, n. 47 ; Bassani, Sacraria, p. 218-219 scheda 29 ; Laforge, *La religion privée*, p. 39-40, fig. 23-24 ; Bassani, Ghedini, Religionem significare, p. 105 ; Parslow, *Sacrarium of Isis* ; R. Ciardiello, « Donne imprenditrici a Pompei. Eumachia e Giulia Felice », in R. Berg, *The Material Side of Marriage. Women and Domestic Economies in Antiquity*, Roma, Institutum Romanum Finlandiae, 2016 (Acta Instituti Romani Finlandiae 43), p. 223-234, part. p. 232, fig. 5 ; C. E. Basset, *Domestic Empire. Egyptian Landscapes in Pompeian Gardens*, Oxford, Oxford University Press, 2019, p. 119 note 208. Sur Julia Felix, voir Ciardiello, *Donne imprenditrici*, p. 229-234. Sur le décor de ce sanctuaire, lire également les remarques de C. Sfameni dans ce volume, p. 116-117.

Fig. 7.
Praedia de Julia Felix, *sacrarium* 555, reconstruit au Museo Archeologico Nazionale di Napoli, paroi droite (photo Musée).

tion est connue, entre autres, par une gravure parue dans l'ouvrage monumental de Francesco Piranesi ; toutefois, quand on étudie cette gravure, il faut rester prudent, car comme l'a montré Christopher Parslow et l'a souligné Valeria Sampaolo, il existe des différences considérables entre dessin et réalité[67]. De plus, en raison du caractère égyptisant du décor, Piranesi l'a attribué par erreur au Temple d'Isis : « Niche dans le temple d'Isis à Pompéia. Les peintures représentent différentes divinités, et deux grands serpents symboles du bon génie[68] ».

---

[67] F. Piranesi, *Antiquités de la Grande Grèce, aujourd'hui royaume de Naples*, Paris, Firmin Didot, 1807, III, pl. 1. Critiques de ce dessin déjà chez Helbig, *Wandgemälde*, n. 79. Voir Sampaolo, *Nuove acquisizioni*, p. 199 ; Sampaolo, *Ricomposizione*, p. 36.

[68] Piranesi, *Antiquités*, III, planche 1, titre.

En bas, on voit le socle décoré avec des arbres et buissons sur un fond de couleur blanche ; dans la gravure, sa hauteur est trop importante. Au-dessus, dans le registre médian de la paroi du fond, l'autel est figuré au centre, flanqué par deux grands serpents dont les corps se déploient sur les parois latérales, et qui se meuvent vers l'autel sur lequel se trouve un cône de pin. Dans la zone supérieure se dressent des divinités. Les personnages sont placés sur un terrain semé de petits buissons contre un fond neutre. Au centre de la paroi arrière, au sud, se dressent à gauche Anubis en robe longue et tenant une palme, au centre une Isis couronnée de laurier, avec un sistre et un plat dans les mains, et à droite la figure couronnée de Sérapis avec un bâton dans la main gauche et une branche dans la droite. Sur la paroi gauche, on voit une femme qui tient une branche de palmier sur un globe à ses pieds, et une corne dans la main gauche, peut-être Isis, et l'enfant Harpocrate[69]. La paroi de droite présentait des serpents flanquant une figure non identifiée, qui pourrait être une prêtresse selon Valeria Sampaolo[70]. Le fond est rempli d'autres buissons, apparemment des lauriers. Finalement, la voûte semble représenter une pergola, avec des pièces de bois en trompe-l'œil, figurées en noir sur un fond blanc[71].

Le *sacrarium* ne semble pas avoir eu le caractère d'un laraire traditionnel, sauf en ce qui concerne les *agathodaimones*, et abrite des divinités égyptiennes, comme le laraire peint dans la Maison des Amours dorés, qui contient les mêmes serpents ainsi que des divinités égyptiennes. Même si on ne peut plus considérer Isis et son entourage comme des étrangers dans le panthéon romain au Ier siècle ap. J.-C., l'atmosphère créée par les décorateurs voulait souligner la beauté du pays du Nil et évoquer un certain exotisme. La position dans le jardin se prête bien pour suggérer la richesse donnée par Isis, Sérapis et leurs acolytes[72]. La prêtresse sur

---

[69] Sampaolo, *Nuove acquisizioni*, p. 199, fig. 3 ; Sampaolo, *Ricomposizione*, fig. 7.3.

[70] Sampaolo, *Nuove acquisizioni*, p. 199, fig. 2 ; Sampaolo, *Ricomposizione*, fig. 7.2. Pour l'iconographie de prêtresses dans la peinture Moormann, *Ministers of Isiac Cults* (hormis cet exemple).

[71] Sampaolo, *Nuove acquisizioni*, p. 200. Elle les confronte avec de vrais treillis de bois dans le jardin.

[72] Sur les motifs égyptisants dans les jardins, voir Basset, *Domestic Empire*.

la paroi droite pourrait en même temps servir d'intermédiaire entre les divinités et les visiteurs du *sacrarium*. Elle est aussi une sorte de 'Zuschauerfigur', un spectateur à l'intérieur de l'image, qui stimule nos activités vers les dieux installés ici. Mais, le 'public' de cet espace reste difficile à déterminer, d'autant que les *Praedia* furent mises en location par Julia Felix. L'idée d'un groupe cultuel égyptien n'a pas de fondement sûr et doit être vérifiée sur la base d'autres données, jusqu'ici manquantes[73]. Valeria Sampaolo a fait une observation très importante sur le style et la qualité des peintures brièvement discutées ici. Selon elle, leur qualité est assez raffinée, en dépit des altérations de la couche picturale, et on peut observer des correspondances avec les autres peintures détachées et rassemblées au Musée de Naples. Cela pourrait avoir une certaine importance, s'agissant d'établir le commanditaire et les occupants de l'édifice. Le *sacrarium* faisait partie intégrante du programme ornemental du complexe et ne formait pas une exception exotique isolée des autres décorations.

Maison de Optatio (Figg. 8-9)

Il y a, dans cette demeure quasi totalement perdue et connue sous le nom de Optatio (VII 2, 13-15), un petit espace (l) appelé *viridarium* et interprété comme *sacrarium*, qui adopte la forme d'un couloir voûté, mesurant 4,35 × 1,85-82,10 m environ. Sa position était assez isolée, avec l'entrée donnant dans le couloir k[74]. Dans l'angle nord-ouest se trouvait un autel très bas et orné, peint à l'imitation de *giallo antico*. Dans le mur ouest s'ouvrait une niche pour placer des offrandes ou des statuettes. Les restes du décor sont très mal conservés, mais grâce à un dessin de 1880

---

[73] CIARDIELLO, *Donne imprenditrici*, p. 232-233. Sur le problème de l'interprétation du complexe, voir SAMPAOLO, *Nuove acquisizioni*, p. 209-210 ; SAMPAOLO, *Ricomposizione*, p. 21-22.

[74] HELBIG, *Wandgemälde*, n° 60b ; BOYCE, *Corpus of the lararia*, n° 249A (« tiny garden ») ; JASHEMSKI, *Gardens* I, p. 62, fig. 100 ; A. VARONE et al., in *Italienische Reise. Pompejanische Bilder in den deutschen archäologischen Sammlungen*, Napoli, Bibliopolis, 1989, p. 189-190 et 291 n. 45 ; FRÖHLICH, *Lararien- und Fassadenbilder*, p. 283, pl. 40,1.3 ; JASHEMSKI, *Gardens* II, p. 173 ; PPM VI, p. 520-525 ; BASSANI, Sacraria, p. 182-183 scheda 8 ; GIACOBELLO, *Larari pompeiani*, p. 278 cat. V60.

Fig. 8.
Maison de Optatio, *sacrarium*, aquarelle de 1881
(après *Italienische Reise*, p. 291).

conservé à l'Institut archéologique allemand de Rome, nous connaissons la décoration peinte des parois nord et ouest. Le fond du mur ouest présente un jardin peint, couronné en haut par une guirlande à laquelle sont pendus des *oscilla* de marbre et un masque théâtral. En bas se dresse une statue de Vénus au milieu des plantes à côté d'un bassin de marbre avec des colombes. La lunette montre un autre bassin et un oiseau, probablement une colombe. Le jardin se prolonge dans la moitié supérieure du mur nord. La moitié inférieure contient deux registres à fond blanc. En bas est figuré le serpent familier orienté vers l'autel. Dans une frise séparée, on distingue Jupiter, deux Lares auprès d'un autel et une Minerve. À droite de l'ensemble se dresse une figure masculine très altérée, de taille plus grande, peut-être un offrant. Il pourrait avoir la même fonction que la figure isolée dans le *sacrarium* des *Praedia* de Julia Felix brièvement men-

Fig. 9.
Maison de Optatio, *sacrarium*, état actuel
(cliché Domenico Esposito).

tionnée plus haut. Nous pouvons imaginer un décor végétal sur l'autre long mur du côté sud, qui ne fut pas documenté ni photographié autrefois.

Le décor connaît deux phases, la plus ancienne étant une peinture de jardin de quatrième style, ornant un *viridarium* sans toit. La phase la plus récente est la niche insérée dans le mur ouest, avec une frise blanche qui endommage l'ancien décor, et toute la moitié inférieure de la paroi nord. La voûte, elle aussi, semble une addition à l'espace hypèthre d'origine, et conçue pour le transformer en *sacrarium*[75]. Tout le premier décor semble associé

---

[75] Il ne m'a pas été possible de contrôler cette suggestion. Avec ou sans toit, l'argument de M. Bassani, Sacraria, p. 182, que la pièce ne fût pas un *viridarium* à cause du décor n'est pas valide. Il existe de nombreux jardins ouverts ornés de peintures !

à Vénus et le jardin, qui contient plusieurs oiseaux, est un *locus amoenus*. Évidemment, Vénus trouve place dans d'autres jardins, dont celui, fameux, de la Maison de la Vénus à la coquille. Les éléments du *sacrarium* sont tous postérieurs et on peut se demander si le changement tenait compte du décor végétal qui existait déjà et, dès lors, si ce décor jouait un rôle spécifique dans ce nouvel ensemble. La niche du premier état n'était pas nécessairement un *sacrarium*, mais aurait pu servir comme alcôve ouvrant sur le jardin.

La Villa des colonnes en mosaïque (Figg. 10-11)

Directement à la sortie de la Porte du Vésuve, du côté est de la rue qui mène vers le nord, se trouve la *Villa delle colonne a mosaico*, fouillée en 1837. Un *sacrarium* est situé dans la pièce du côté ouest de la « cour no. 2 du sacellum »[76]. Grâce à Heinrich Wilhelm Schulz, nous en avons une description approfondie[77] : « un gran larario ornato di pitture eleganti, intieramente corrispondente alla forma di quello della casa detta di Felice che attualmente vedesi collocato nel Museo borbonico. » Heinrich Wilhelm Schulz voit une correspondance avec le *sacrarium* des *Praedia* de Julia Felix, qui se limite, sans doute, à l'architecture et à l'emplacement. L'intérieur de la pièce de 3 × 2 m environ présente un décor du quatrième style sur les parois et la voûte : socle noir, champ rouge central avec candélabre, champs latéraux jaunes avec des petites images au centre (perdues), cadres rouges, bordures ajourées blanches. Sur la voûte : fond blanc avec une composition centralisée, bandes noir et vert, bandeau feuillu et couronne verte. Il y a un autel à l'arrière[78]. Sur la paroi du fond,

---

[76] Étude principale : V. KOCKEL, B. WEBER, « Die Villa delle colonne a mosaico in Pompeji », *MDAI(R)* 90 (1983), p. 51-90. Voir Fig. 14 (plan) et pl. 35.2. Voir aussi BOYCE, *Corpus of the lararia*, n° 479 ; JASHEMSKI, *Gardens* I, p. 151-153 ; FRÖHLICH, *Lararien- und Fassadenbilder*, cat. L 112 ; JASHEMSKI, *Gardens* II, p. 277-278 ; BASSANI, Sacraria, p. 232-233 scheda 36 ; GIACOBELLO, *Larari pompeiani*, p. 221, cat. 2 ; LAFORGE, *La religion privée*, p. 44, fig. 28.

[77] E. G. SCHULZ, « Rapporto intorno gli scavi pompeiani negli ultimi quattro anni », *Annali dell'Instituto di corrispondenza archeologica* 10 (1838), p. 148-201, part. p. 195. Heinrich Wilhelm Schulz a signé ses textes des prénoms italianisés Enrico Guglielmo.

[78] KOCKEL, WEBER, *Villa delle colonne*, p. 86-88, avec fig. 13.

Fig. 10.
Villa des colonnes en mosaïque, *sacrarium*, dessin
(après E. Breton, Pompéia, p. 233).

Fig. 11.
Villa des colonnes en mosaïque, *sacrarium*, état actuel
(cliché Domenico Esposito).

dans la niche, Wolfgang Helbig a vu une massue et un *skyphos* de grand format. Valentin Kockel en a noté encore des traces[79]. La façade du *sacrarium* est ainsi décrite par Heinrich Wilhelm Schulz[80] : sur le fronton, un Bacchus reçoit un porcelet en sacrifice d'un ministre du culte et dans les écoinçons se trouvent des génies ailés avec une couronne. Le décor de la pièce ne présente rien de spécifiquement religieux, mais est une simple composition de 'Nebenzimmer'. L'aspect religieux doit être dérivé des éléments figuratifs sur l'autel et sur le fronton, et que l'on connaît grâce à Heinrich Wilhelm Schulz et Wolfgang Helbig[81].

On se demande s'il y a une connexion entre la représentation du Bacchus sur la façade et les attributs d'Hercule sur l'autel à l'intérieur du *sacrarium*. Heinrich Wilhelm Schulz n'osa pas se prononcer fermement sur la divinité vénérée[82] ; Bacchus est fréquemment représenté sur les façades, mais à l'intérieur on attendrait plutôt la vénération des Lares et du Génie du lieu, en plus d'Hercule. Intéressante est la comparaison entre ce *sacrarium* et celui des *Praedia* de Julia Felix (*supra*) qu'on retrouve également chez Ernest Breton et chez George K. Boyce qui attribue le *sacrarium* à la fois à Bacchus et Hercule, ainsi que chez Valentin Kockel et Berthold F. Weber[83].

Un autre autel de tuf se dresse dans la cour, devant la niche même[84]. L'extérieur se présente comme une *aedicula*, à ouverture incurvée et couronnée par un fronton à orle de terre-cuite avancé.

---

[79] *Ibidem*, p. 84.

[80] Mentionné par HELBIG, *Wandgemälde*, p. 25, n. 77 « nach älterem Berichte » et cité par KOCKEL, WEBER, *Villa delle colonne*. Voir aussi A. CORALINI, *Hercules domesticus*, Napoli, Electa, 2001 (Studi della SAP 4), p. 234 cat. P143. Elle met en lien cet Hercule avec le *symposion* (p. 91-92).

[81] HELBIG, *Wandgemälde*, p. 25, n. 77.

[82] SCHULZ, *Rapporto intorno gli scavi pompeiani*, p. 196.

[83] E. BRETON, *Pompéia décrite et dessinée*, Paris, Gide et J. Baudry, 1855, 2ᵉ édition, p. 232-234 (avec un dessin à la p. 233) ; BOYCE, *Corpus of the lararia*, p. 97 note 4 ; KOCKEL, WEBER, *Villa delle colonne*, p. 57.

[84] KOCKEL, WEBER, *Villa delle colonne*, p. 82 : autel décoré : « Vorderseite Opferdiener und Schwein mit Bauchbinde, Rückseite Hahn, Nebenseiten Skyphos und an Basis gelehnte Keule ». Cf. HELBIG, *Wandgemälde*, p. 25, n. 77 pour une description presque identique. Voir aussi I. FIORELLI (éd.), *Pompeianarum Antiquitatum Historia*, Napoli, 1860-1863, vol. II.5, p. 305 ; vol. III.1, p. 134 : « nicchia ove vedesi la piccola aretta, che resta di fronte dell'ingresso della stanza sinistra del giardino » (= KOCKEL, WEBER, *Villa delle colonne*, p. 70).

La construction se situe probablement dans la dernière phase de Pompéi, après 62[85]. Les premiers observateurs ont vu l'image d'un ministre du culte, le *popa*, peint sur l'autel[86].

Conclusion

Ces quelques exemples ont montré que les édifices de culte 'publics' n'avaient pas de correspondances très claires avec les *sacraria* privés en ce qui concerne leur apparat architectonique et décoratif. Dans les maisons, on ne retrouve pas d'éléments monumentaux comme des colonnes, des frontons, des corniches sculptées, des statues de taille considérable ... Les petites pièces destinées aux divinités domestiques ne ressemblaient guère à des temples et n'invitaient pas non plus à chercher des mises en scène extraordinaires des dieux abrités dedans. Elles ne sont que des pièces, modestes qui plus est, à l'intérieur des maisons et des jardins, et revêtaient un apparat architectonique et décoratif en accord avec l'atmosphère de la *domus*. Seul leur usage demeurait fixé sur des pratiques cultuelles et ne pouvait pas changer au cours du jour, comme c'était le cas avec les autres pièces de la maison[87]. Leur modestie se montre aussi dans les décors peints, très proches des ensembles peints dans les *lararia*, au moins en ce qui concerne l'iconographie, tandis que les schémas décoratifs ne diffèrent pas non plus de ceux de la maison. Cependant nous avons eu lieu de faire le même constat pour les peintures de temples, qui étaient proches des décors privés, sauf dans le cas de quelques cultes plus ou moins 'étrangers'. Ce qui prédomine, c'est le décor 'normal' des édifices privés, avec des panneaux, des petites vignettes, des peintures de jardins, et rien de particulier. Seul le *sacrarium* des *Praedia* de Julia Felix présente un décor spécifique, que l'on retrouve dans les décors de sanctuaires dédiés à des divinités 'non olympiennes'. Pour l'exemple de la Maison du Ménandre, on pourrait le penser également – en postulant un décor évoquant spécifiquement Dionysos – mais l'insertion de la niche avec les

---

[85] Kockel, Weber, *Villa delle colonne*, p. 84.
[86] Coralini, *Hercules domesticus*, p. 234.
[87] Dernièrement, avec résumé des débats, Haug, *Decor*.

petits bustes a changé le décor originel ainsi que la fonction de l'exèdre, laquelle n'avait pas nécessairement un usage cultuel au moment de sa construction autour de 40-30 av. J.-C. La conclusion peu spectaculaire que l'on peut donc avancer est que les *sacraria* jouaient, certes, un rôle important dans la vie domestique et occupaient une place spécifique à l'intérieur des *domus* pompéiennes, mais qu'ils ne présentaient pas de lien avec les grands sanctuaires urbains. En tant que partie intégrante d'un édifice privé, les *sacraria* ne se distinguaient pas forcément, mais étaient une des nombreuses pièces du puzzle qui constituait la maison.

MADDALENA BASSANI

MORPHOLOGIES OF *SACRA PRIVATA* IN THE ROMAN HOUSE: ARCHITECTURE, FURNISHINGS, CULTS

The study and analysis of domestic cults within ancient houses, especially in the Roman age, is particularly relevant, and it is thanks to the efforts of the editors of this volume that it has been possible to publish essays that approach the theme from the historical-religious, architectural, structural and anthropologic points of view.[1] The investigation of *sacra privata* is indeed a complex matter: only in recent years they have been given due attention, as previously they had been investigated only marginally and without the rigorous research methodology reserved for the *sacra publica*.[2]

The approach devised for the study of architectural structures dedicated to the celebration of domestic rituals involves two opposite, yet converging, actions: on the one hand it invokes conceptual freedom from the so-called *lararium* category, which appears too simplistic and not attentive enough to the underlying chronological, morphologic, ideal and social differentiations pertaining to the manifestation of the private sacred. On the other hand, the *sacra privata*, by virtue of their complexity and variability, need to be examined with 'taxonomic' criteria and interpreted not

---

[1] A thought goes to professor Mario Torelli, with whom I had the privilege to study and work on the topic of the *sacra privata*.

[2] For a history of the studies on domestic sacred I refer to my recent work that traces the *status quaestionis* up to 2017: M. Bassani, Sacra privata nell'Italia centrale. Archeologia, fonti letterarie e documenti epigrafici, Padova, Padova University Press, 2017, p. 19-22. For previous studies, see also A. Maiuri, Sacra privata. Rituali domestici e istituti giuridici in Roma antica, Roma, L'Erma di Bretschneider, 2013.

only as singular entities but always as part of a dynamic 'organism': from the moment it was built to its abandonment, the house could be conceived as space of relevant 'cultural semantics' in the self-representation strategies of its owners.[3]

1. *On the* sacra privata *concept*

Archaeological literature still employs the so-called *lararium* category to broadly include artifacts pertaining the *sacra privata*: painted images, statues or statuettes, altars/bases, pseudo niches and aedicules (as defined by G. K. Boyce)[4] in addition to rooms and *sacella*. This habit appears to me as misleading in relation to a precise understanding through description and interpretation of ancient domestic religious practices, as the *Lares* were only two of many deities that were worshipped in the ancient house. Thus, many were the rites and the spaces, instruments, ceremonies and, probably, people involved.

An exemplary case is the cult of Hercules in the *Villa dei Galloni* in Setteville (Rome), on the *Via Tiburtina*: there was not only a (probable) small temple dedicated to the god in the open-air part of the dwelling, with a statue of the god in the likeness of a child, but, as an inscription makes it explicit, he was considered as protector of the *domus*: [Her]culi Sospitali, Custodi / [d]omus Gallonianae, / [---]atius Sabinus, procurator / [Gall]oniorum Nigri et Frontonis, / [vot]o suscepto, fecit.[5] Hercules was thus the primary referent for the Galloni *domus*, intended not only as a family but also as architectural structure and patrimonial entity: in fact, the god protected, as *sospitalis*, the family members and

---

[3] I put forward a methodological proposition in my first research in 2008 on the Vesuvian area: M. BASSANI, Sacraria. *Ambienti e piccoli edifici per il culto domestico in area vesuviana*, Roma, Quasar, 2008, in part. p. 25-43 and later in the 2017 volume (Bassani, Sacra privata *nell'Italia centrale*, p. 35-45), as well as the very recent contributions published in A. DARDENAY, N. LAUBRY (eds.), *Anthropology of Roman Housing*, Turnhout, Brepols, 2020.

[4] G. K. BOYCE, *Corpus of Lararia of Pompeii*, Rome, American Academy, 1937 (*Memoirs of the American Academy in Rome* 14).

[5] BASSANI, Sacra privata, p. 317-320, with specific bibliography. For the Vesuvian cases, see A. CORALINI, Hercules domesticus. *Immagini di Ercole nelle case della regione vesuviana (I secolo a.C. – 79 d.C.)*, Napoli, L'Erma di Bretschneider, 2001.

he was considered, more than other deities in that geographic context, as the *custos* of the *domus*' property. As custodian, Hercules indeed could keep vigil over the family's economic activities, probably related to breeding livestock, in the Tiburtine area; the particular preference accorded to him was all the more understandable, as there he was worshipped in a famous temple connected to livestock commerce.[6]

I have recently analysed Greek and Latin literary sources and some epigraphic examples related to domestic contexts in order to understand the role of written testimonies for the definition of a correct research methodology. The information I gained was not only extremely interesting *per se*, and from a legal standpoint as well, but it provided important elements on which to establish the conceptual and semantic limits of the analysis of archaeological data.[7] In short, ancient texts mention *aedes* and/or *aediculae*, *sacella* or *sacraria* as domestic sacred spaces, whose association to the *Lares* is extremely rare: the small temples (*aedes, sacella*) and the inner spaces (*sacraria*) were normally furnished with at least one altar and with images of the chosen deities, among which the *Lares* were only two of the many present. In this regard, it is to be noted that within Latin and Greek vocabulary the word *lararium* is never used to indicate private sacred spaces: the term appears just once in the late Latin, with a very specific meaning. The passage is found in Elius Lampridius' (fourth century AD) biography of Severus Alexander (who reigned between 222 and 235 AD); in the *Historia Augusta*, describing the private habits of the emperor, the term *lararium* is employed to indicate the places where he worshipped his gods.[8] Among those mentioned there are the divinised emperors (*divos principes*), but also

---

[6] For this interpretative method, see BASSANI, Sacra privata, p. 228; on the Tiburtine temple and on economic activities related to livestock, see J. BONETTO, "Ercole e le vie della transumanza: il santuario di Tivoli," *Ostraka* VIII.2 (1999), p. 291-307.

[7] BASSANI, Sacraria, p. 49-63 and p. 153-161; BASSANI, Sacra privata, p. 145-162 and p. 199-220.

[8] S. Settis' study on the text is still valid (S. SETTIS, "Severo Alessandro e i suoi Lari," *Athenaeum* n.s. 50, fasc. I-II (1972), p. 237-251); see also C. MONDELLO, "Sui Lares di Severo Alessandro (HA Alex. Sev. 29, 2; 31, 4-5): fra conservazione e trasformazione," Ὅρμος. *Ricerche di Storia antica* n.s. 9 (2017), p. 189-229.

Orpheus, Christ, Abraham, Vergil, Cicero and Alexander the Great.

It is thus plain to understand how completely inappropriate is the use of the term *lararium* (even in its translation in modern languages) to refer to the *sacra privata*: not only the *paterfamilias* could have many 'private' deities other than the *Lares*, but it was Roman custom for *clientes* to transfer their own *Lares* to the *patronus*, in turn worshipping them. An exemplary study in this regard is Mario Torelli's work on the C. Manlius altar from Cerveteri:[9] on the main side of the structure the *clientes* are represented as bringing their deities to the patron, who is seated on a high-backed seat on an upper level, in order for him to perform the *imposition manus*, the act of protection towards *filiifamilias*.

On their own part, the servants could have 'personal' gods, not necessarily coinciding with those of the family housing them. Tacitus explains this clearly in a passage from the *Annales* dedicated to social changes happening at the time: while in the past the *patroni* controlled slaves, considering them strangers but at the same time 'familiars' who deserved affection and with whom one shared the cults, in recent times the servants' different nationalities were perceived as dangerous because each, with his/her own rites and *externa sacra*, could be ready to rebel against *patronus*, since they shared nothing but the same roof. The master was thus forced to maintain a climate of terror in his own house in order to guarantee constant control on the servants living there.[10]

Once the inadequacy of the use of *lararium* is made clear in respect to the *sacra privata*, at what time one could trace back the beginning of the use of the term in contemporary archaeological

---

[9] M. TORELLI, *Typology and Structure of Roman Historical Reliefs*, Ann Arbor, University of Michigan Press, 1992, p. 16-20.

[10] Tac. *ann.* 14 44: *Sane consilium occul[ta]vit, telum inter ignaros paravit: num excubias transire, cubiculi fores recludere, lumen inferre, caedem patrare [poterat] omnibus nesciis? multa sceleri indicia praeveniunt: servi si prodant, possumus singuli inter plures, tuti inter anxios, postremo, si pereundum sit, non inulti inter nocentes agere. Suspecta maioribus nostris fuerunt ingenia servorum, etiam cum in agris aut domibus i[s]dem nascerentur caritatemque dominorum statim acciperent. Postquam vero nationes in familiis habemus, quibus diversi ritus, externa sacra aut nulla sunt, culluviem instam non nisi metu coercueris.*

literature? The question bears asking, as it can help understand the historical process of an interpretative and conceptual category that has proven itself completely wrong.

According to the "Dizionario etimologico della lingua italiana" (M. Cortelazzo, P. Zolli, Zanichelli 1983, *s.v.* p. 652) *lararium* is used by Francesco Baldelli in 1587, as he states that 'thus is called the sacred place that can be found in the house:' the authors deem that he takes the term from *Lampridius*, that is to say the *Historia Augusta*, as we saw above.

However, in Charles du Cange's *Glossarium mediae et infimae latinitatis*, concerning Medieval Latin, appear only the terms *Lar*, either meaning the given name of a commander or the domestic hearth, and the phrase *Larem fovere, Larem tenere* to indicate those who lived in any sort of residence: the term was thus not in use with the meaning we're concerned with. In the *Vocabolario degli Accademici della Crusca*, which includes Greek, Latin and Italian vocabulary, *lararium* appears in the Latin section and it is translated as 'tabernacle' (as in 'niche/aedicula'), while it is absent from the Italian section: the edition consulted is dated 1612, demonstrating that at least up until the seventeenth century the word was not known, or at least not in use, in Italian.[11]

Later, Vincenzo Monti in his work "Proposta di alcune correzioni ed aggiunte al vocabolario della Crusca" (Milano 1817-1824) acquires the term from the current archaeological vocabulary. This lends plausibility to the hypothesis that the modern use of lararium originates in the eighteenth century. One could wonder if that usage could be connected with the extraordinary discoveries of Ercolano (1738) and later Pompeii (1748). The term served to designate and somehow 'codify' the numerous and well-preserved painted images and statuettes depicting the *Lares* that were found in houses and shops. The discoveries sparked a renewed interest for ancient texts, among which the *Historia Augusta* could serve as an effective guide for the newly

---

[11] The edition was printed in Venice in 1612 by Giovanni Alberti. The research could interestingly be extended to modern lexicons for the main European languages, in order to verify if the term is absent up until the same period and if it gains prominence from the seventeenth century onwards.

discovered settlements. While it is of course impossible to trace the use of the term to a single author, it still can be supposed that the practice was introduced in the European and Italian neo-classical intellectual milieus, where one of the most prominent figures was, as it is well known, Johann Joachim Winkelmann. Reading the first Italian edition of *History of Ancient Art* it can be noted that the term *lararium* is used to describe a sculpture mentioned by Cicero in relation to the statues present in the Eius from Messina's private *sacrarium*.[12] Despite Cicero's use of a completely different word, deliberately chosen – *sacrarium* is in fact used to describe a particular space for private worship – Winckelmann proposes a term that might have appeared perhaps more generic – 'lararium' – but that could be associated in the readers' memory more immediately with the *Lares* and the other deities that protected the house. Thence, it is believed, the term was diffused in the archaeological vocabulary, with a general misunderstanding of its meaning and its correspondence to historic and archaeological reality: the more surprising aspect to this is that Cicero's passage describes numerous *simulacra* of deities present in Eius' *sacrarium*, none of them being the *Lares*!

2. *For a research methodology of the* sacra privata

Once the reasons are clear for freeing the archaeological analysis and vocabulary from the *lararia* category, with reference to the abovementioned terminological study on the Latin terms used in antiquity for describing the *sacra privata*, it is worth giving due attention to the methodology of their recognition, description, and interpretation.

Given the multiplicity of situations, artefacts, deities, rituals that pertain to domestic cult, it is necessary to employ a 'taxonomical' method: the term, which I referenced in the introduction to this essay, does not have a pedantic, classificatory over-

---

[12] Widely discussed in BASSANI, Sacraria, p. 52-56. The cited passage from J. J. Winckelmann can be read in the first Italian edition of his work, published in Prato in 1930-1934 for the Fratelli Giachetti, vol. IV, p. 225 and fn 243. See also a recent study on the translations into various languages of Winckelmann's work: S. FERRARI, "Tradurre Winckelmann nel secondo Settecento: i casi di Francia, Inghilterra e Italia," *Diciottesimo Sec.* 5 (2020), p. 81-88.

tone; rather, it serves to highlight the rigorous methodological focus, composed of precise analytical and interpretative frames in order to describe (and subsequently attempt to interpret) the multifaceted structural and material reality of the phenomenon. I have thus attempted to propose a classification system that can be applied to different Italian peninsula and provincial geographic contexts, with specific common elements:[13] I termed 'cult indicators' all those structural, decorative and mobile elements that contribute to the identification (certain or probable) of the spaces and instruments for the sacred in the ancient house. Among those, naturally, are included fixed and portable altars, *aediculae* (and *pseudo-aediculae*), niches (and pseudo-niches), the bases for *simulacra* and ritual objects, paintings or mosaics, reliefs, statues and statuettes, herms, inscriptions, perfume burners: these elements are *primary* indicators because they indicate, through multiple morphologies and iconographies, the traces of domestic cults.

There are, however, also *secondary* indicators of the sacred, that is to say elements that contribute to emphasize the recognition and the importance of sacred spaces in the ancient house by means of refined architectural and decorative elements, which were not only for the owner but mainly for visitors. Columns, steps, tables and seats used for ritual and ceremonial purposes, as well as lamps, candelabra, safes and money boxes, if found in conjunction to primary indicators can be eloquent on *sacra privata*, i.e. on the self-promotion strategies enacted by the *dominus* towards the visitors.[14]

The definition of primary and secondary indicators guarantees a solid enough knowledge process on 'what' constituted the

---

[13] On cult indicators and their appearance in the ancient house, see BASSANI, Sacraria, p. 22-43; BASSANI, Sacra privata, p. 35-45. Partially different approaches in the essay of E.M. Moorman in this volume.

[14] This aspect, which I have developed in some essays, had been justly brought to attention by A. Wallace Hadrill in a valuable study on the Roman house (A. WALLACE HADRILL, *Houses and Society in Pompei and Herculaneum*, Princeton, NJ, Princeton University Press, 1994) and, later, was approached by other authors, among whom P. W. FOSS, "Watchful Lares: Roman household organization and the rituals of cooking and eating," in R. LAURENCE, A. WALLACE HADRILL (eds.), *Domestic Space in the Roman World: Pompeii and beyond*, Portsmouth, RI, JRA, 1997 (JRA Suppl. 22), p. 196-218; DARDENAY, LAUBRY, *Anthropology of Roman Housing*.

domestic sacred, however, it does not mean a thorough understanding of the fruition modes, the transformations and the relationship with the other spaces of the houses: the 'how', the 'when', the 'why'.

The horizon should be broadened in order to understand sacred spaces in their relation to multiple other aspects: the construction /reconstruction /abandonment phases, the pathways from the entrance to the more private spaces, the possible ownership changes and successions, the different strategies enacted by the owners throughout years or centuries. It is necessary as well to attempt to appraise the role of these 'sacred' spaces in the self-celebratory dynamics put in place by the *dominus* towards the other household members, as well as (and perhaps mainly) towards illustrious or prominent guests, clients and sporadic visitors.

Finally, moving towards a more general approach, we can attempt to consider the individual material and structural evidences pertaining to the *sacra privata* in a wider perspective, beyond the single *domus/villa*: we can analyse the instances relative to communities, beliefs and ritual practices enacted at a public level, or instances relative to political and cultural transformations that originated at a central level. As an example, a small temple dedicated to Diana was discovered in the house of M. Spurius Saturninus at Pompeii (Fig. 1): it was located in the *domus*' small peristyle, as well as its worship statue, with smaller than actual dimensions and archaic features, that could be dated to the Augustan era. It is not sufficient to state that the owner was a follower of the hunter goddess in order to understand the value of the worship context: it is necessary to question if the small *sacellum* with its peculiar *simulacrum* was rather an explicit reference not only to the religious *pietas*, but also to the stigmatized fashion of Augustus' politics, which reintroduced archaizing iconographies on the side of institutionalised classicism. This was related to the promotion of some cults in favor of others, aiming to reference practices and rituals of Rome's early period.[15]

---

[15] P. ZANKER, *Pompei. Società immagini urbane e forme dell'abitare*, Torino, Einaudi, 1993; BASSANI, Sacraria, p. 128-132. Ample discussion can be found in

Fig. 1.
Pompei, *Domus* of *M. Spurius Saturninus*, VII 6, 3.
The outdoor shrine in a photo of 1910 (BASSANI 2008, p. 227 e p. 128, fig. 38).

In other words, by means of a rigorous and analytic study, the domestic sacred emerges as a fundamental piece in the reconstruction of a broader general 'history', where the individual *domus*, intended as a household, a building, a set of material and economic possessions (*sacra privata* included), represented one of the main elements of the historical and social transformations of a particular context.

3. *Three main categories of private cults*

Before considering the architectural, structural and decorative morphologies belonging to the sphere of the *sacra privata* it is

---

E. LA ROCCA, C. PARISE PRESICCE, A. LO MONACO, C. GIROIRE, D. ROGER (eds.), *Augusto, Exhibition catalogue (Rome, 18 October - 9 February 2014)*, Milano, Electa, 2013.

necessary to clarify which cults are referred to here and to which subjects the manifestations of the sacred pertain in the Roman house. Naturally, it is not a catalogue of divine subjects, but rather of macro-categories, to which I have reserved specific detailed studies, mainly regarding central Italy.[16]

Ancestor cult constitutes, as we'll see, the most ancient form of private worship, surviving well into late Antiquity. The ancestors, sometimes chosen for their exemplary conduct, constituted in fact a set of divine entities: they were the *dei parentes* or *divi parentum*, invoked to uphold the family code of conduct within the domestic spaces. It was forbidden, for example, for younger family members to perform acts of arrogance or abuse on those older or weaker: a son hitting a parent became hostile to the *divi parentum* and for this reason *sacer*, in the negative sense, hostile to men and alienated from *ius*, abominable and cursed; the same happened if a daughter-in-law hit her husband's parents, or in case of incest or murder between blood relatives.[17] These behaviours were completely unacceptable for the Roman mentality and should not soil the *sacra iura parentum*. The *dei parentes* were thus always present and always worshipped in order to guarantee respect for the norms in case of parricide, violence or sexual transgression: they lived in the same spaces of the *domus* and their images served as warning for the inhabitants. As it is made clear in the famous passage from Polybius for the second century BC and in Vergil's verses on the primordial history of Rome,[18] the exhibition of *imagines maiorum* (wax masks or veritable head portraits) had a double value: within the house they admonished the residents and displayed the dynasty's high rank, during funeral processions they recalled to mind the public roles and the deeds done in favour of Rome by the main *maiores* of the family.

The cult of traditional and 'foreign' gods was equally important. As we have seen in the introduction to this essay, archaeology manuals still mainly connect domestic cult and its manu-

---

[16] BASSANI, Sacra privata, p. 221-239 and related bibliography.

[17] See M. MORANI, "Lat. 'sacer' e il rapporto uomo-dio nel lessico religioso latino," *Aevum* LV (1981), p. 30-46, part. fn. 43-48.

[18] Polyb. 6.53.

facts to the cult of the *Lares* who, as protectors of the domestic hearth, that is to say of the house intended as a geographically and topographically definite space, were certainly central in the private sphere. But they were not the sole ones, and indeed, as the aforementioned improper usage of the term *lararium* shows, in research conducted in various areas of the Roman Empire evidence emerges of worship of numerous other deities. The choice depended on the household, on its tradition, its members, the professional activities of the house owner: this latter point constitutes an important fact, which I believe is innovative in the attempt to reconstruct the dynamics of the worship choices of each house.

Finally, recent research has brought to light new and unexpected documentation on the imperial cult as practiced at the domestic level. Starting from theories proposed in the 1970s, the worship of the divinised emperors has been studied in its public projection: the monuments that could be interpreted as *Augustea* have always been magniloquent, as well as the wealth of inscriptions and literary sources mentioning public figures, rites and ceremonies dedicated to the emperors and their *genius*. There was, on the other hand, a distinctive lack of a perspective going beyond the almost obvious 'official' sphere, exploring the traces of this phenomenon in the private dimension: this was generated by the prevalent tendency to consider as peculiar to private residences only the traces of the *Lares* and the *Penates*. It is not possible to state for certain that the spaces in the house dedicated to the worship of the emperors were 'physically' coincident with the spaces dedicated to the *Lares*: in some instance this was decidedly not the case, as if the worship of the emperors was ideally more associated with the worship of the ancestors rather than that of the *Lares-Penates*. It is a problem for which the analysis of many contexts will be needed and that at the moment cannot be fully resolved, but I deem it important to bring it to attention in the light of the documentation that will be exposed in the following pages. The aim is to produce a reflection on the transformation of the forms of the domestic sacred in the Italic and Roman house, and to attempt an interpretation of its characters within the context of the sociopolitical dynamics of imperial Rome.

4. The space of the sacred in the archaic and Republican house

To what time can the first traces of private worship in ancient Italy be traced back? M. Torelli, in a ground-breaking work published in 2011, has rightly recognised in Etruscan archaism the first material and structural traces of the *sacra privata*, from which Roman ones have taken shape; more recently, other studies have confirmed their importance.[19] The second phase of the palace of Murlo, near Siena, can be dated to 580 BC: it is articulated as a series of spaces around a central, open-air court (Fig. 2):

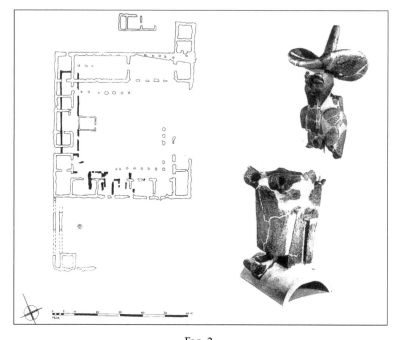

FIG. 2.
Murlo, Siena. The map of the archaic palace with the cult shrine and a statue of ancestor (M. MENICHETTI, *Archeologia del potere: re, immagini e miti a Roma e in Etruria arcaica*, Milano, Longanesi, 1994, fig. 21).

---

[19] M. TORELLI, "La preistoria dei *Lares*," in M. BASSANI, F. GHEDINI (eds.), Religionem significare. *Aspetti storico-religiosi, strutturali, iconografici e materiali dei* sacra privata, *Atti dell'Incontro di studi (Padova, 8-9 giugno 2009)*, Padova, Quasar, 2011, p. 41-55. A more recent study is F. RONCALLI, "Abitare il palazzo, abitare il tempio: riflessioni su un rapporto antico," in G. M. DELLA FINA (ed.), *Dalla capanna al palazzo. Edilizia abitativa nell'Italia preromana, Atti del XXIII Convegno Internazionale di Studi sulla Storia e l'Archeologia dell'Etruria*, Roma, Quasar, 2016, p. 21-42. Finally, see the volume of A. PICCIONI, *Culti domestici in Italia meridionale ed Etruria*, Regensburg, Schnell und Steiner, 2020.

here, just in front of the main receiving room of the *tyrannos*, was built a quadrilateral *sacellum* (or rather an *oikos*, that is to say an *aedes*) with a complex decorative system of acroteria statues placed on the roof. They depicted the ancestors and were accompanied by other statues of fantastic animals (sphinxes, griffons) as symbols of the ideal and religious sphere within which the household found its identity.

The divinised ancestors ensured not only a special kind of tutelage for the residents due to their role of super-human entities that validated the superiority of the dynasty's ancestry and thus its function of command; but also they guaranteed, by virtue of their liminal position between the human and celestial worlds, the inhabitants of the *domus* with a constant and longstanding intercession with the divine. The sacred rituals were carried out in the *sacellum*, thus defining the close relationship between the cult of the god and that of the divinised ancestors. Around 540 BC, in Etruria at Acquarossa, there is a further definition of the *sacra privata*: in the zone B of the excavated area were found four residential units, constituted mostly by three rooms facing an entrance, organised around a court with a central water-well. This represented not only a common open space, but the place where rituals involving a group of peers who shared the same gods and ancestors were performed. The court can be interpreted as the *compitum* related to the *Lares Compitales* cult, who were worshipped by multiple families all residing in the same area: aedicules, niches, or painted images placed at crossroads were, in Roman times, cult manifestations and are conceptually not so different from the modest, modern structures at the crossing of urban or rural paths.

The transformations that took place between the regal and the imperial period are not easily traceable due to the lack of archaeological evidence available.[20] For this reason, Stefania Quilici

---

[20] M. FIORENTINI, "Culti gentilizi, culti degli antenati," in G. BARTOLONI, M. G. BENEDETTINI (eds.), *Sepolti tra i vivi. Evidenza e interpretazione di contesti funerari in ambito privato, Atti del Convegno Internazionale (Roma, 26-29 aprile 2006), ScAnt* 14.2 (2007-2008), p. 987-1046; A. DE FRANZONI, *Culti gentilizi a Roma tra III e II sec. a.C.*, Doctoral dissertation, Università di Trieste, 2011-2013, with specific bibliography.

Gigli's studies of the city of Norba[21] appear particularly relevant, as they refer to evidence of the middle Republican era. In some of the small, simple houses were found fixed altars and/or portable *arulae*, of quadrangular or cylindrical shape, made of stone or ceramic: in some case they were found in rooms near the entrance, in some others in spaces around the *atrium*, without a specific dedicated space for the *sacra*.

In this period, characterized mostly by isonomic configurations, the phenomenon of domestic cult has a material manifestation in mobile objects, in most residences[22] without a specific room dedicated to the family rituals: in fact, only in individual cases in aristocratic residences, such as the cult room in the Villa of the Auditorium[23] or the small temple in the court of the Serra di Vaglio[24] residence, there are spaces or buildings reserved exclusively to worship; in most houses, which were constituted by few rooms, the sacred was 'punctual' – an arula, a *thymiaterion*, a small niche in the wall.

Evidence recorded from the second century BC onwards is instead much more complex and needs to be analysed and inter-

---

[21] S. Quilici Gigli, "Arule nei culti domestici: testimonianze da Norba," *Orizzonti* XII (2011), p. 53-68. In 2015 and 2018 were published two complete volumes on the building history of the city: S. Quilici Gigli, P. Carfora, S. Ferrante, *Norba: strade e domus*, Roma, L'Erma di Bretschneider, 2015; S. Quilici Gigli et al., *Norba: scavi e ricerche*, Roma, L'Erma di Bretschneider, 2018.

[22] They could be compared to the Greek houses: F. Pesando, *Oikos e ktesis: la casa greca in età classica*, Roma, Quasar, 2006; M. M. Sicca, "Eusèbeia domestica: Attestazioni di culto nelle case di Olinto," *Siris* 3 (2003), p. 107-177. Other cases have been found in Southern Italy and Sicily: A. Ruga, "Espressioni di eusèbeia domestica a Crotone," in L. Lepore, P. Turi (eds.), *Caulonia tra Crotone e Locri, Atti del Convegno Internazionale (Firenze, 30 maggio - 1 giugno 2007)*, 2 vols, Firenze, Firenze University Press, 2010, p. 209-226; G. F. La Torre, "Urbanistica e architettura ellenistica a Tindari, Eraclea Minoa e Finziade: dati nuovi e prospettive di ricerca," in M. Osanna, M. Torelli (eds.), *Sicilia ellenistica, Consuetudo italica. Alle origini dell'architettura ellenistica d'Occidente, Atti del Convegno (Spoleto, 5-7 novembre 2004)*, Roma, Edizioni dell'Ateneo, 2006, p. 83-95.

[23] A. Carandini, M. T. D'Alessio, H. Di Giuseppe (eds.), *La fattoria e la villa dell'Auditorium nel quartiere Flaminio di Roma*, Roma, L'Erma di Bretschneider, 2004, p. 147-148.

[24] Serra di Vaglio: E. Greco, "Per una definizione dell'architettura domestica di Serra di Vaglio," in F. D'Andria, K. Mannino (eds.), *Ricerche sulla casa in Magna Grecia e in Sicilia, Atti del Colloquio (Lecce, 23-24 giugno 1992)*, Galatina, Congedo Editore, 1996, p. 255-299, part. p. 294.

preted in the light of the new social and economic system and a much more widespread dialogue with hellenistic culture, where the role of *sacra privata* was already emphasized by Philip II and Alexander's successors.[25] Residential buildings in many cases are designed according to a precise plan, or they are subject to general processes of expansion[26] in which domestic cult seem to play a prominent role. If we observe some cases in the vesuvian area and we imagine to enter a residence from the road, we meet a first, important trace, halfway between private and 'public': the vestiges of peculiar *sacelli* built near the façades of some residences, which have been analysed some years ago by Lara Anniboletti.[27]

On the entrance door frame, which was visible from the road, small niches could be carved under which originally an altar was placed and small votive pits could be excavated: offerings, such as coins or other objects that served the function of purifying the space, had to be dedicated to the cult of the *Lares Compitales* and were part of rituals that were celebrated by the owners of the houses together with their neighbours. They were the *compitum* rites, related to the common shared space, such as the aforementioned one performed at Acquarossa.

Another exemplary case is that of Caesius Blandus' *domus* in Insula VII (VII 1, 42: Fig. 3) where, near the entrance there was a niche with an altar underneath (of which the base is preserved) and a now lost painted panel, which depicted in the upper portion the *Lares* accompanied by the *magistri* during a sacrificial act, in the lower portion the usual serpent moving towards the altar. Anniboletti's research has brought attention to the fact that these niches were not exclusive to the worship of the *Lares* but also to

---

[25] On the first manifestations of an 'imperial' cult see the works of A. M. PRESTIANNI among which in particular "Τεμενη Φιλιππου α Φηιλιππι: ai prodromi del culto del sovrano?," in *Ancient Macedonia* VI, *Papers read at the sixth International Symposium held in Thessaloniki (October 15-19, 1996)*, 2 vols, Idryma Meletōn Chersonēsu tu Haimu, Thessalonikē, 1996, p. 921-943. See also F. PESANDO, "Sacraria pompeiana. Alcune note," in BASSANI, GHEDINI, Religionem significare, p. 11-27, part. p. 14-15.

[26] A. ZACCARIA RUGGIU, *Spazio privato e spazio pubblico nella città romana*, Roma, École Française de Rome, 1995 (Collection de l'EFR 210).

[27] L. ANNIBOLETTI, "*Compita vicinalia* a Pompei. Testimonianze archeologiche del culto domestico di *theoi propylaioi*," in BASSANI, GHEDINI, Religionem significare, p. 57-78. Further data in the essay of Marin Mauge in this volume.

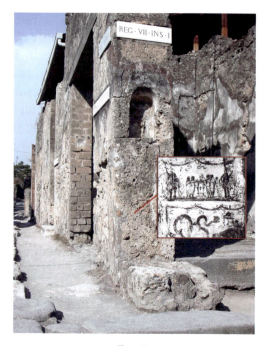

Fig. 3.
Pompei, *Domus* di *Caesius Blandus*, VII 1, 42.
The niche and the outdoor cult painting (ANNIBOLETTI 2011, p. 62 e fig. 5).

the cult of Mercurius and Hercules, protectors of places of transit and passage: they are depicted in a panel near the door frame of House I 12, 11, over an altar, or on the entrance door frame of House II 1, 1, often accompanied by their respective symbolic animals – a pig for Hercules, a rooster for Mercurius.

That it was not a phenomenon specific to Pompeii but rather a Roman praxis is made evident by the fact that similar configurations and worship scenes have been documented in Delos, a free port since the late Republican period. The documentation collected by Marcel Bulard[28] has made it possible to confirm that on the side of the entrances of some houses there could be, as in Pompeii, altars (sometimes richly decorated) but also niches and panels with painted images: it is the case of the "Maison dite des Dauphins", where Mercurius was evoked by means of a *cadu-*

---

[28] M. BULARD, *Description des revêtements peints à sujet religieux*, Paris, Académie des Inscriptions et Belles-Lettres, 1926 (*Exploration archéologique de Délos* IX).

ceus painted on the wall on either side of the entrance, in addition to an *aedicula* with Hercules on the left side of the building. Moreover, in the "Maison I C du Quartier du Stade", an image of Hercules[29] with the club lying on the ground is preserved near the entrance, along with the rooster, sacred to Mercurius.[30] The two deities were indeed the *theoi propylaioi*, the tutelary deities of entrances: if we ideally continue our path through the interior spaces of the house, other deities and other more specific spaces for familiar devotion can be found.

In this context, we will not consider the individual niches or *aediculae* catalogued by Boyce in 1937 and recently studied in their depicting apparatus by Federica Giacobello;[31] rather, we will analyse the spaces proper to domestic ceremonies (the *sacraria*): it can be noted how they often occupy a prominent position on a wing of the *atrium*, that is to say in the most representative space of the *domus*. In the *Casa del Torello* (V 1, 7), already in the first phase (second century BC) there was one (Fig. 4):[32] it was small (1,75 × 0,90 m) but with an entrance of the same height as the

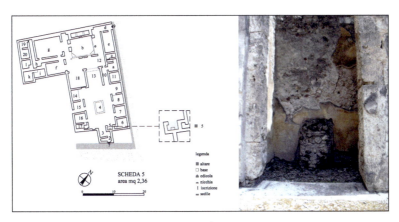

Fig. 4.
Pompei, *Domus* del Torello, V 1, 7. The map and the indoor cult room opened on the *atrium*, close to the entrance, with an altar (BASSANI 2008, p. 178).

---

[29] *Ibid.*, p. 117-121, ensemble n° 22.
[30] *Ibid.*, p. 133-149, ensemble n° 25.
[31] F. GIACOBELLO, *Larari pompeiani. Iconografia e culto dei Lari in ambito domestico*, Milano, Il Filarete, 2008.
[32] BASSANI, Sacraria, p. 178.

other nearby rooms, it was adjacent to the vestibule on the southeastern side of the *atrium* and to other rooms (*cubicula*), drawing a visual axis with the dominus' *tablinum*. On its far side there was a quadrangular masonry altar (0,60 × 0,40 m; H. 0,90 m), originally painted in vibrant colours, as a fragment of red plaster on its right side suggests (probably a faux-marble decoration?). The *sacrarium* walls were painted as well: on a yellow background, on either side of the altar, two *agathodaimon* serpents slithered towards the altar, a well-studied iconographic theme widely diffused in the vesuvian area.[33]

The location of the *sacrarium* on a side of the *atrium*, as well as the fixed worship structures (altar and painted images) and its small dimensions are elements that allow a confident interpretation as for the function of the space, that evidently was used exclusively for ceremonial purposes, and for its symbolic value. That sector of the house was in fact often populated with *clientes* and visitors, and just by transiting by one could perceive the relevant role that the *sacra privata* had within the domestic walls.

These elements – location, relationship with other domestic spaces, visibility within inner paths – are extremely important for the analysis of private cult spaces: they will prove strategic also in later times and constitute the indication of a specific building choice on the owner's part that emphasized both social status and cultural horizon. It is evident in another example at Pompeii, the house of M. Pupius Rufus (VI 15, 5) that again included a *sacrarium* in its first building phase: as for the *Casa del Torello*, the sacred space was adjacent to the entrance, on the same axis as the *tablinum* and near other spaces that faced the *atrium*.[34] It is a small space (1,40 × 1,10 m) that featured a high masonry niche (1,27 × 0,14 m; H. 1,75 m) hosting numerous worship indicators (Fig. 5): on the back side three smaller, arched niches had been carved and painted red, in front of which two quadrangular altars were placed, with masonry elements. The room's painted decoration is very fragmentary but nonetheless traces of yellow

---

[33] Other than the already mentioned work by F. Giacobello, in which an extensive bibliography can be found, see W. Van Andringa, *Quotidien des dieux et des hommes: la vie religieuse dans les cités du Vésuve à l'époque romaine*, Rome, École Française de Rome, 2009 (BEFAR 337).

[34] Bassani, Sacraria, p. 178 and 182-183.

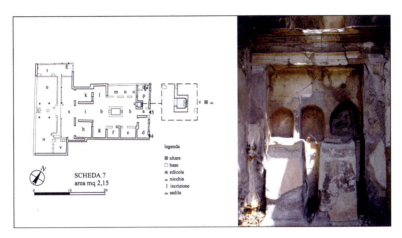

Fig. 5.
Pompei, *Domus* of *M. Pupius Rufus*, VI 15, 5. The map and the indoor cult room opened on the *atrium* close to the entrance, with niches and altars
(BASSANI 2008, p. 180-181).

paint (to imitate marble) and white plaster on the surfaces of the main niche can be recognised; the floor was made of concrete and is preserved only on the south side. The deities worshipped there are not known. August Mau's hypothesis postulated that the small niches were dedicated one to the *Genius*, one to the *Lares* and the last to the *Penates*,[35] but it has no material validation. They could, in fact, have hosted images of other deities such as the *imagines maiorum*, as it was found in the well-known *sacrarium* 25 of the *Casa del Menandro* (I 10, 4),[36] or in the *Casa del Citarista*, where by the left side of the *tablinum* and in the north wing were located on pedestals the portraits of two ancestors of the *gens Poppea*: the ceremonial value of these images is confirmed by the finding, in the same excavation campaign, of a bronze altar.[37]

Similar situations, for the same period, can be found again in Delos but also in Southern Italy and in Sicily, where significative

---

[35] A. MAU, "Ausgrabungen von Pompeji, Insula VI, 15," *Bullettino dell'Istituto Archeologico Germanico* 7 (1898), p. 3-59, part. p. 11-14.

[36] BASSANI, Sacraria, p. 172-173, with specific bibliography. The context can be dated to the first century AD.

[37] BASSANI, Sacra privata, p. 112-113 and fn 103, with specific bibliography. The context can be dated to the first century AD.

traces abound: in the Delos island, rooms opening on the peristyle could host altars, statues, statuettes and niches with an evident worship function.[38] In Finziade and Eraclea Minoa houses could host an altar and a niche in the courts or near the entrances; nonetheless in some cases they also featured a specific space for domestic rituals.[39] Although nothing seems to exclude the presence of *sacraria* also in the most private and less visited portions of the house, the prevalence of the choice of the *atrium* / peristyle location constitutes, in my view, a 'semantic paradigm' that is of extreme importance even in later phases.

5. Sacraria *and* sacella *between the first century* BC *and the first century* AD

During the first century BC there is a marked increment of formalised sacred spaces, and it is indeed at this time that the term *sacrarium* appears to be used specifically to indicate a private room dedicated to the *sacra*: Cicero, always careful to use a refined yet 'meaningful' language, employs it to refer to a room in Eius' House in Messina.[40] Here, as it is well known, the owner worshipped his deities depicted in precious *signa* that were stolen by Verres: in their honour Eius practiced rituals through *arulae* that Cicero aptly mentions as the main cult indicators for that venerable room (… *Ante hos deos erant arulae, quae cuivis religionem sacrarii significare possent*).

Sacraria

From a morphologic point of view, in this period a more precise interpretation of architectural form and sacred furnishings can be found. Interior worship spaces can maintain their small dimensions (for example in the *Casa del Gallo* VIII 5, 2.5,

---

[38] PESANDO, *Sacraria pompeiana*, p. 15-20.

[39] For comparison with Southern Italy and Sicily see BASSANI, Sacra privata, p. 175-183, with specific bibliography; S. GUIDONE, *L'architettura privata in Italia meridionale e in Sicilia fra IV e I secolo a.C. Modelli abitativi, strutture sociali e forme culturali*, Padova, Padova University Press, 2022.

[40] Cic. *Verr.* II, 4.1.2-4: widely discussed in BASSANI, Sacraria, p. 52-56; see also the introduction to this essay.

room 4)[41] but often they are wider and with a more complex layout. In the Agro Vesuviano the *Villa in Contrada Giuliana* (Fondo Zurlo) was furnished from the first century BC with the worship space A, 3 × 3,5 m wide and opening into a *porticus*.[42] It was functionally recognised by virtue of primary and secondary indicators: a niche with a shelf, a base and a cylindrical altar on which, during the excavation, was found a quite large ceramic basin (diameter 0,52 m) containing ashes, the probable trace of a sacrifice. There were also found common objects such as five glass perfume vases, five small ceramic dishes, a small covering, two lamps and a lock, that could have been used during ceremonies.[43]

In the city of Pompeii another example can be found in the Casa della Venere in Conchiglia (II 3, 3) where, on the far side of the *peristylium* with the well-known fresco of the goddess, a room was created with a masonry altar and two inner bases, probably used as supports for sacred images and ritual instruments.[44] A painted image of Mars at the entrance and a red-painted inscription in the interior, dedicated by Decimus Lucretius Valens to his wife and sons, owner of the house, confirm the central role of the space. In this case, despite being open towards the garden on one side, the *sacrarium* is located in a more private portion of the house, on the far side of the open court, a choice that is mirrored elsewhere.

Yet again, at *Lucus Feroniae* in the *Volusii Saturnini* Villa there is a well-known, relevant and very monumental example of domestic *sacrarium*, built during the Augustan period and then restored: it is rectangular and accessible from the peristyle, it featured a floor mosaic with geometric-floral decoration and was

---

[41] *Ibid.*, p. 193.

[42] *Ibid.*, p. 211, with bibliography; see also a website that collects excavation data for the Pompeii suburbium: https://pompeiiinpictures.com/pompeiiinpictures/VF/Villa_014.htm.

[43] On the possible relation between common objects found in *sacraria* and *sacella* and domestic rites, see M. BASSANI, "Gods and Cult Objects in Roman Houses. Notes for a Methodological Research," in R. BERG, A. CORALINI, A. KOPONEN, R. VÄLIMÄKI (eds.), *Tangible Religion. Materiality of Domestic Cult Practices from Antiquity to Early Modern Era*, Roma, Institutum Romanum Finlandiae, 2021 (Acta Instituti Romani Finlandiae 49), p. 101-118.

[44] BASSANI, Sacraria, p. 176-178, with bibliography: the space is 2.10 × 1.60 m, the altar 0.80 × 0.80 m, H. 0.70 m; the other, interior, bases were smaller (0.45 × 0.40 m; H. 0.35 m).

provided with an extremely rich array of fixed and mobile sacred furnishings (Fig. 6).[45] Among those is worth noting an altar, a *trapeza* and a bench in solid marble, but also a large inscription dedicated to L. Volusius Saturninus, dated to 63 and 70 AD, whose text and typography seem to allude to a public context. From this same space come statues and portraits of ancestors of the *Volusii*, as well as a portrait head of Sabina (or Marciana): there are no traces of *Lares* worship but tangible evidence of a cult dedicated to the *maiores* to which was probably later associated the cult of the members of the *domus Augusta*.

These three aforementioned cases belong to different contexts: they pertain to families with different ranks and that expressed their own *sacra privata* in distinct ways and configurations, appropriate to their respective social status.

In the Ercolano suburb, the famous *Villa dei Papiri* attributed to the *Pisoni* where recent excavations have improved the existing knowledge about its chronology,[46] had a space that during

FIG. 6.
Lucus Feroniae, Villa of the *Volusii Saturnini*. The map and the indoor cult room opened on the *peristylium* (BASSANI 2008, p. 180-181).

---

[45] BASSANI, Sacra privata, p. 307-312, with bibliography and description of all worship and ceremonial elements; the room is 6.50 × 5 m wide.
[46] M. P. GUIDOBALDI, "La Villa dei Papiri di Ercolano: inquadramento architettonico e decorativo alla luce delle recenti indagini archeologiche," in G. F. LA TORRE, M. TORELLI (eds.), *Pittura ellenistica in Italia e in Sicilia. Linguaggi e tradizioni, Atti del Convegno (Messina, 24-25 settembre 2009)*, Roma, G. Bretschneider, 2011, p. 519-529. The villa is dated to 40-30 BC on building technique and floor and painted decoration analysis.

the Bourbonic excavations was interpreted as a '*lararium*'. It is room A (*c.* 4 × 4,5 m) located in the north-eastern sector of the square peristyle: it has an apse where a base was placed, probably to hold a statue whose feet's remains were recorded but it does not figure among those recovered from the campaign. Even in the case that excavations confirm the proposed interpretation, it is interesting to note how the richness of the space is characterized both by the presence of the apse with the *simulacrum* base and the antechamber.

In fact, the association between *sacrarium* and antechamber is a feature that can be found in many contexts and I believe it should be treated with due attention: a similar example, if slightly later, is found in Pompeii, in the *Villa dei Misteri*, where the rather large *sacrarium* 25 (4,80 × 5,50 m) not only had an apse with side *exedrae*, but it was connected to room 26, that evidently functioned as connection between the peristyle and the sacred space (Fig. 7).[47] At the moment of the eruption the room (25) was undergoing renovations, dated to the Augustan period: the floor was being reconstructed (in 79 AD it was 15 cm lower

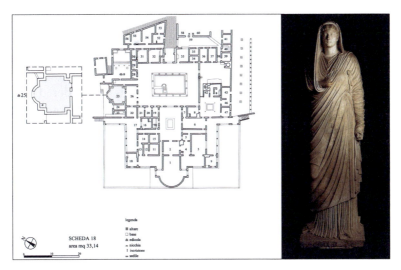

Fig. 7.
Pompei, Villa dei Misteri. The map with the indoor cult room and the cult statue of *Istacidia Rufilla* (BASSANI 2008, p. 200-201).

---

[47] BASSANI, Sacraria, p. 200-201, on *sacraria* antechambers p. 111-112.

than in room 26 and was simply paved) and in the antechamber were stored numerous marble elements such as small balusters, columns, slabs, fragments of cornices and lesenes, that were originally placed on the walls and on a probable aedicule. To this 'work in progress' it is also attributed the small shelf near the apse, defined as a "rustic kitchen", perhaps used by the workers. The confirmation that these works were indeed aimed at improving the appearance of room 25 can be traced to the finding of the probable worship statue of Istacidia Rufilla (according to some, identifiable as Livia), placed by the entrance to room 26: it is she that the residents and visitors of the villa worshipped, and it is possible that room 26 served as a sort of 'waiting room' for the clients that tributed homage to the *matrona*, and perhaps even for servants, for whom she served as *domina*.

This interpretation is also valid for the context of the *Villa di Oplontis*, where the *sacrarium* A together with the antechamber 27 is accessible from the peristyle.[48] It lacks the apse, a feature that, instead, as M. Torelli[49] proposed recently, could constitute a specific cult marker for the *sacraria*. These spaces, designed in the public and private sphere to preserve 'sacred things', as it is made clear in the *Digesta*,[50] could have been chosen as buildings for the imperial cult around 2 BC, the year when Augustus became *pater patriae* and, notably, the institution of the *sacerdotes Caesaris Augustis*, chosen amongst the *nobiles* of the urban élite, was founded. At the *princeps*' death, his will ordered that Livia was to be his daughter and as such obliged to tribute him a specific worship; the Augusta chose to build the *sacrarium divi Augusti* within the birth home of her husband, in the area of the *Curiae Veteres*: despite the original structure being destroyed and substituted by Claudius' temple, the other examples of imperial cult *sacraria* proposed by the Author appear indeed as a 'public' transposition of the domestic *sacraria* built in the most prestigious houses.

---

[48] BASSANI, Sacraria, p. 209-210.

[49] M. TORELLI, "Per un lessico degli edifici del culto imperiale," *Ostraka* XXVII (2017), p. 193-209, with further bibliography.

[50] *Dig.* 1.9.2.

Sacella

Sacella are another building type that appears to have developed specifically for the *sacra privata* during the first century BC and that will be maintained, despite transformations and adaptation, throughout the imperial period. They are exclusively built in open spaces such as small courtyards, gardens or inner areas of the peristyles and are initially small and with a small altar in front. From a terminological point of view, it is appropriate to use the term, as it is the same employed by ancient sources to describe this kind of structure (*sacella*): small temples or *aedes* built either in the city or in the country.[51]

Despite some instances of *sacella* in the Magna Graecia area dated to the fourth and second century BC, the findings are more numerous from the first half of the first century BC[52] onwards: in this case, as it happens with *sacraria*, they could either be modest structures or more elaborate and complex both from the architectural and decorative point. One of the earlier, most interesting and notable examples is the building discovered in the *Villa di Palombara Sabina* (Roma), at Formello (Fig. 8), recently studied and published by Zaccaria Mari and Massimiliano Papini.[53] A temple (7,5 × 10 m) was built within a large garden enclosed in a peristyle, rectilinear on three sides and with an apse on the fourth. The building is placed on a podium with probable columns on the front, with an altar testified by a rectangular base found in front of the entrance. The architectural appearance, the location on the scenic side of the peristyle and the finding of statues nearby (*Eirene* and *Hephaestus*, and the portrait of a poet) have correctly suggested that this building was dedicated to the performing of the house owner's private ceremonies: I believe that the comparison with a very similar case found in Montegrotto Terme, in a lav-

---

[51] For a lexical discussion, see BASSANI, Sacraria, p. 56-61.

[52] See the small building interpreted as *naiskos* in the court of the residential complex A in Roccagloriosa (BASSANI, Sacraria, p. 115-117 with specific bibliography), or the *aedicula* in the villa di Banzi (*ibid.*, fn 9, with bibliography).

[53] Z. MARI, M. PAPINI, *Un nuovo Efesto per il IV sec. a.C. e la villa romana di Palombara Sabina*, Roma, Scienze e Lettere, 2015.

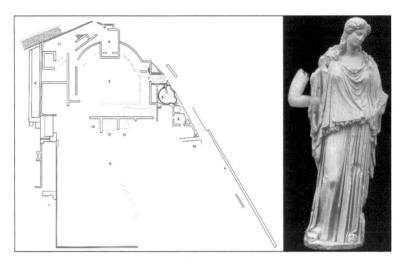

Fig. 8.
Palombara Sabina (Roma), Villa in the venue Formello.
The map with the outdoor shrine 6 and the cult statue of *Eirene*
(Bassani 2017, p. 313 and p. 315).

ish villa from the Tiberian period, can only confirm this interpretation.[54]

Other examples from the Augustan era or the first decades of the first century AD can be found in the Vesuvian areas and in other parts of the Empire: they are similar in dimension (or smaller) and feature a refined decorative and architectural system. In addition to the *sacellum* mentioned in the first paragraph, in the House of M. Spurius Saturninus, a similar one can be found in Pompeii in the garden of the *Casa della Regina Carolina*. The two buildings have many common elements: they were both located in open areas (the extremely small peristyle 18 in VII 6, 3 and the large garden in VIII 3, 14), they were built with a modest masonry foundation base (1,80 × 1,50 m; 2,20 × 2,30 m) with steps imitating the temple *podia*, and a roof sustained by columns (only two in the *Casa della Regina Carolina* as the small temple was adjacent to the border wall, so that the north side was placed on the far side of the garden). If in the case of Spurius Saturninus there was a facing altar, in VIII 3, 14

---

[54] Bassani, Sacra privata, p. 62-63 and p. 312-315.

there were instead two herms on the temple's front; but on the podium of both a base held a smaller than actual statue of Diana.

Other, slightly later, examples traceable to Diana can be found in Pompeii and elsewhere:[55] but it is worth noting that the well-studied[56] *Casa di Augusto* on the *Palatinus* is an extremely interesting context that might even be considered the prime *exemplum* that served as inspiration for the others. A small building there could have served as a domestic *sacellum*. Within the private portion of the residence, built on terraced landscape, the open space extended southward: a square base 6 × 6 m wide was intercepted near the rear containment wall. No specific worship element was found there, partly because the remains pertain only to the foundations; but the comparison with both the above mentioned cases and ancient sources that remark the care and attention given by Ottavianus Augustus to the sacred, both public and private, might confirm the hypothesis of the scholars.

If it is indeed so, we can imagine that here sacrifices were performed in honor of the *Lares*, but also of the main protectors of Augustus and the *gens Iulia*, mainly Venus, Apollo, Diana, Latona, whose vibrant image is found on the famous Sorrento base. *Simulacra* dedicated to Diana were also found in small temples in Pompeii, in Cosa and in other private contexts, where, one can rightfully wonder, the deities favored by Augustan propaganda could be evoked, thus demonstrating a good adherence to regime policies.[57]

On the one hand, this could confirm how Augustus, through his own private example of *sacra privata*, promoted the elaboration and the definition of a specific building typology for *sacella*

---

[55] For further study see BASSANI, Sacraria, p. 128-132.

[56] After G. CARETTONI ("Roma (Palatino). Saggi per uno studio topografico della casa di Livia," *NSc* 7 (1953), p. 126-147), recent excavations led by A. Carandini have produced numerous publications: A. CARANDINI, D. BRUNO, *La casa di Augusto: dai Lupercalia al Natale*, Roma-Bari, Laterza, 2008, *contra* T. P. WISEMAN, "The House of Augustus and the Lupercal," *JRA* 22 (2009), p. 527-545; A. CARANDINI, D. BRUNO, F. FRAIOLI, *Le case del potere nell'antica Roma*, Roma-Bari, Laterza, 2010, *contra* F. COARELLI, *Palatium. Il Palatino dalle origini all'impero*, Roma, Quasar, 2012. The data discussed here are based on this work by F. Coarelli and widely discussed in BASSANI, Sacra privata, p. 186-191.

[57] ZANKER, *Pompei*, p. 176-184.

placed in exterior spaces; on the other hand, this fact could demonstrate the centrality of the domestic cults for the construction of a new shared mentality for the empire.

In fact, as M. Torelli has remarked in his work on the vocabulary of the imperial cult, "if Augustus had, with the civic crown, brought every citizen into a life-debt towards him, with the title of *pater patriae* he reduced them to *filiifamilias*, a status of complete subordination."[58] His house on the Palatine, with his domestic *sacellum*, was thus the *domus* of the *pater*, inspiring the *filii-cives* to reproduce in their own *domus* the echoes of a shared ideology.

6. *The* sacra privata *throughout the imperial period*

During the imperial age there are numerous evidences of domestic cults manifested through *sacraria* and *sacella*, in many different contexts: despite the rise of Christianity, archeological, epigraphic and literary traces all concur to confirm the permanence of customs, practices and rituals within the domestic environment up until the fifth century AD.[59]

It is not possible here to describe in details a plethora of examples and situations that have been elsewhere described and analysed;[60] instead, it is useful to consider some elements of interest in order to attempt to describe recurrent and specific aspects of the *sacra privata* during the imperial period: among those, the morphologic development, the location within the house, the information on cults gleaned by the analysis of inscriptions and statues. The morphology of the quadrangular interior spaces stays essentially the same, with a possible improvement on fixed and moveable decorative furnishings: some small recesses have been found, such as the space discovered in one *domus* of Carthago Nova, located on a side of the *tablinum* and with

---

[58] Torelli, *Edifici del culto imperiale*, p. 199.

[59] G. Binazzi, *Il radicamento dei culti tradizionali in Italia fra tarda antichità e alto medioevo: fonti letterarie e testimonianze archeologiche*, Roma, L'Erma di Bretschneider, 2012. For further data, see the essays of Nicolas Amoroso and G. Sfameni Gasparro in this volume, with bibliography.

[60] For all my research accessible online I refer to https://iuav.academia.edu/MaddalenaBassani.

a floor inscription dedicated to Fortuna.[61] Or, in another case, the small room discovered in Pola in the S. Teodoro district, and carved into the far side of the main hall (Fig. 9):[62] it was decorated with a bichrome floor mosaic featuring geometric and figured motifs, among which a notable *tabula ansata* with the name of *Salus*, probably the goddess protecting the family, and a stylised small altar on the center of the upper portion of the mosaic. A connection between the cult of *Salus* and a nearby spring feeding the city aqueduct cannot be excluded, as well as a related cult of Hercules attested by an inscription: this was a common practice in the Roman world, where multiple deities could be

FIG. 9.
Pola, *Domus* in the S. Teodorus area. View of the indoor cult room with the mosaic (STARAC 2008, p. 305, fig. 3).

---

[61] E. RUIZ VALDERAS (ed.), *La casa romana en Carthago Nova. Arquitectura privada y programas decorativos*, Murcia, Editorial Tabularium, 2001.

[62] A. STARAC, "Salus, Hercul i izvor vode. Primjer Pule," *Archaeologia Adriatica* 11 (2008), p. 301-313.

protectors of the same *fontes*.⁶³ The latter were considered bringers of good health and as such always worshipped: *nullus fons non sacer*, as expressed by Servius (*ad Aen.* 7 84).

In other cases the spaces are bigger and there the religious function is made manifest by fixed furnishings such as altars, bases or niches, as well as herms and statues. Disregarding here the many cases of domestic *mithraea* (which I have nonetheless examined),⁶⁴ we can see for example the *Casa di Tito Vareno* at *Augusta Praetoria*, which in a renovation phase (second century AD) featured the rather large *sacrarium* 7 (3 × 3,20 m) adjacent to the main living room: the floor was in *opus sectile* with red and white tiles, and was furnished with an herm (or a base?) dedicated, by a freedman named Symphoros,⁶⁵ to the *Genius* of Titus Varenus and to his daughter Severilla's *Iuno*.

This kind of inscriptions, made by lower-ranked people and dedicated to the *patronus*' deities, are quite recurrent. In the *Casa di M. Epidius Rufus* at Pompeii (IX 1, 20) the room *g*, opening into the *atrium*, was transformed from *exedra* to domestic *sacrarium* in the latest phase of the city: it contained an *aedicula* in the back, with a marble inscription dedicated from two freedmen to the *Genius* of the master of the house. These were homage practices but probably also a veiled form of worship of M. Epidius Rufus, who in the meantime had died.⁶⁶ In Acholla a limestone cippus found in the entrance of the large house of M. Asinius Rufinus Sabinianus, who was one of the most prominent *gentiles* of the Proconsular African city, featured a dedication from the

---

⁶³ M. BASSANI, "La schedatura dei contesti cultuali presso sorgenti termominerali. Osservazioni preliminari su aspetti strutturali e materiali," in M. BASSANI, M. BRESSAN, F. GHEDINI (eds.), Aquae Patavinae. *Montegrotto Terme e il termalismo in Italia. Aggiornamenti e nuove prospettive di valorizzazione*, Atti del II Convegno Nazionale (Padova, 14-15 giugno 2011), Padova, Padova University Press, 2012, p. 391-410.

⁶⁴ M. BASSANI, "I vani cultuali," in P. BASSO, F. GHEDINI (eds.), Subterraneae domus. *Ambienti residenziali e di servizio nell'edilizia residenziale romana*, Caselle di Sommacampagna, Cierre, 2003, p. 399-442.

⁶⁵ S. FINOCCHI, "Resti di abitazioni urbane ad Aosta," *Rivista di Studi Liguri* XXIV.1-2 (1958), p. 144-157, on which more recently see M. BASSANI, "Strutture architettoniche a uso religioso nelle *domus* e nelle *villae* della Cisalpina," in BASSANI, GHEDINI, Religionem significare, p. 99-134, part. p. 112-113.

⁶⁶ BASSANI, Sacraria, p. 194-195 with bibliography.

cultores domus:[67] but who were they? Probably lower-middle rank people that paid homage to (worshipped?) some of the most distinguished members of the *Asinia* dynasty, following the example of the *domus Augusta* cults. A recent study has investigated the *cultores domus Augustae* at Volubilis in the second century AD: in an inscription dedicated to Antoninus Pius they declared to practice the imperial cult through the act of building a temple in a private area.[68]

In fact, during the imperial era domestic space appears to acquire a close connection with the private cults that is made explicit through both built architecture and non-structural indicators such as statues and inscriptions. A notable example of complex religious building are the three identical temples built in the Brioni bay in Histria, located within the estate of the Villa of the *Laecani* (Fig. 10). In the Julio-Claudian era three prostyle, tetrastyle large buildings (11,83 × 5,90 m = 20 × 40 *pedes*) were built on a high pedestal and accessible through a flight of steps. The central building featured two recesses and a facing rectangular base that can be interpreted as an altar similar to the one found at Palombara Sabina. The three edifices were located in a scenic *exedra*, more magnificent than the ones framing the small temples at Palombara Sabina and Montegrotto Terme (see above) but with the same emphatic function. These structures contributed to highlight the family's rank and the protection accorded to its members by the deities worshipped there (Neptune, Venus or maybe Hercules or Mercurius):[69] it is possible that all these kept vigil over the economic and commercial activities of the family, who had after all built the entire villa facing the sea.

---

[67] V. BLANC-BIJON, "Le propriétaire: M. Asinius Rufinus Sabinianus," in S. GOZLAN, N. JEDDI, V. BLANC-BIJON, A. BOURGEOIS (eds.), *Recherches archéologiques franco-tunisiennes à Acholla. Les mosaïques des maisons du quartier central et les mosaïques éparses*, Rome, École Française de Rome, 2001 (Collection de l'EFR 277), p. 13-18; see also BASSANI, Sacra privata, p. 162-163.

[68] N. BRAHMI, "Les *cultores domus Augustae* et le temple du culte impérial à *Volubilis*," in M. MILANESI, P. RUGGERI, C. VISMARA (eds.), *L'Africa Romana, I luoghi e le forme dei mestieri e della produzione nelle province africane, Atti del XVIII convegno di studio (Olbia, 11-14 dicembre 2008)*, Roma, Carocci, 2010, p. 1529-1541.

[69] BASSANI, GHEDINI, Religionem significare, p. 116-122, with bibliography.

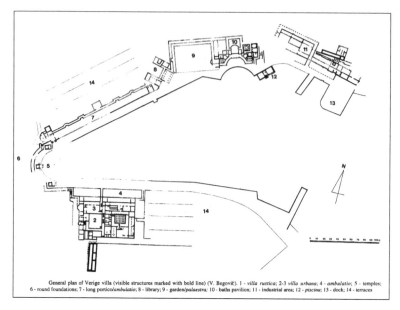

Fig. 10.
Brioni Island, Villa of the *Laecanii*. The map of the villa opened on the sea with the three shrines n. 5 (I. SCHRUNK, V. BEGOVIC, "Roman estates on the island of Brioni, Istria," *JRA* 13.1 (2000), p. 252-276, part. p. 260, fig. 10).

Regarding statues and epigraphs, a recent volume edited by Rebecca Benefiel and Peter Keegan presents numerous examples, the most notable of which are the ones analysed by Elisabeth Rathmayr in Ephesus.[70] The Dwelling Unit 6 in Terrace House 2 is a most interesting case. It belonged to G. Flavius Furius Aptus, member of the *ordo equester* and a Dionysus Oreios Bacchios priest and probably also a *neokoros*, a position closely linked to the imperial cult. Thanks to a brilliant public career he began rebuilding his own house during the second century AD, which naturally included a lavish and very interesting celebratory and decorative system (Fig. 11). Near the peristyle 31 a first inscription was found, located on the south side adjacent to the parapet, in which G. Flavius Furius Aptus was remembered as a priest of Dionysus: the traces on the wall show that there were two

---

[70] E. RATHMAYR, "The Significance of Sculptures with Associated Inscriptions in Private Houses in Ephesos, Pergamon and Beyond," in R. BENEFIEL, P. KEEGAN (eds.), *Inscriptions in the Private Sphere in the Greco-Roman World*, Leiden – Boston, E.J. Brill, 2016, p. 146-178.

Fig. 11.
Ephesus, Dwelling Unit 6, Terrace House 2.
The map of the *Domus* of *G. Flavius Furius Aptus* with the places
of the inscriptions and statues, and a view of the bases with inscriptions
at the entrance of room 8 (RATHMAYR 2020, p. 149, fig. 8.3 and p. 154, fig. 8.5).

associated sculptures, which should have depicted him together with the god. Other inscriptions were found at the entrance of room 8, on two pedestals near the steps: they mention Aphrodite (of which a sculpted fragment was found), who, together with Dionysus, was clearly the *dominus*' personal deity.

The aforementioned examples refer to *sacraria* built mostly at the heart of the *domus*, adjacent to the main receiving rooms, following a widespread and well-documented location criteria.

There are however also numerous cases of *sacraria* built near the entrance: this choice, mentioned above in reference to the republican period, continued to be adopted in the following centuries. Indeed, sacred spaces at the entrance of the *domus* or of the villa can assume strong religious values that translate to a self-celebration of the family intended towards guests and visitors, as evidenced by the votive cippus at Acholla. In addition to instances from the first imperial period, the case of the renowned *Villa Filosofiana* at Piazza Armerina (fourth century AD) is particularly notable: there, adjacent to the entrance, a room with an apse was built between two columns of the main peristyle.[71]

---

[71] C. AMPOLO, A. CARANDINI, G. PUCCI, P. PENSABENE, "La villa del Casale a Piazza Armerina," *MEFRA* 83.1 (1971), p. 141-281, part. p. 163-164, fig. G.

The ceremonial function is proved by the base in the curved portion of the wall, where perhaps the statue was located (they are less likely the remains of an altar, which generally was in the centre of the room or on one side); other, secondary, indicators contribute to define its function. They are the four corner columns and the rich floral-geometric mosaic, with racemes and vine or ivy leaves in a band near the base and a larger leaf at the centre of the room, enclosed within a crown of oak leaves. The reference to the Dionysus-Liber cult can be only hypothetical, as the vine can signify a general concept of the wealth, health and prosperity ensured by the correct performance of the rituals.

In fact, the iconography of the fixed (walls and floors, cult furnishings) and moveable (statues and statuettes) elements can contribute to the definition of the religious function of a *sacrarium* or *sacellum*. In this sense the House of Dionysus at Dion, in ancient Macedonia, is particularly eloquent: the house built in the second century AD featured a room (3 × 6 m) with depictions of Dionysus both on the polychrome floor mosaic (with scepter and ivy crown) and on a smaller statue (without the head).[72]

In recent studies I have highlighted how the domestic sacred could permeate other, less apparent rooms of the house, as it was something that did not involve just the master of the house but also the servants, who often employed less precious materials such as the *instrumentum domesticus* in order to dedicate offerings to the gods.[73] I refer to that study for a more in-depth analysis on the topic, and I would like to conclude this essay with a focus on the imperial cult at a domestic level, which I deem extremely interesting and on which I brought forward literary and archaeological sources in the 2017 volume.[74]

In the survey conducted in the central Italy area, as well as in other areas of the Empire, many relevant traces of worship of the members of the *domus Augusta* have emerged: not only the emperors, but also the *Augustae* and other members of the impe-

---

[72] P. Bonini, "Le tracce del sacro. Presenze della religiosità domestica privata nella Grecia romana," in Bassani, Ghedini, Religionem significare, p. 205-227, with specific bibliography.

[73] Bassani, Sacra privata, p. 131-143.

[74] *Ibid.*, p. 232-239.

rial family. Busts and portraits of Augustus, Marcellus, Agrippa, Livia, Drusus, Tiberius Gemellus, Caligula, Traianus, Sabina up to Marcus Aurelius and Caracalla (Fig. 12)[75] come in fact from domestic contexts. The problem cannot be solved by simplistically considering them as forms of homage and loyalty to the *domus Augusta*, as by reading ancient text many domestic devotion practices emerge that involve both divinised figures and still-living members of the imperial family.

Ovid, for example, sends letters from the exile in Ponto where he asks for statuettes of the Julio-Claudian *gens* in order to worship them at home, almost as if he found comfort in praying to these new deities for a chance to return to Rome: among

FIG. 12.
Kos, *Domus* of the Bronzes. View of the cult statuettes in which a bust of Caracalla was found (A. KAUFMANN-HEINIMANN, *Götter und Lararien aus Augusta Raurica: Herstellung, Fundzusammenhägen und sakrale Funktion figürlicher Bronzen in einer römischen Stadt*, Augst, Römermuseum, 1998, p. 308, Abb. 275).

[75] *Ibid.*, p. 120-130.

which he not only mentions Augustus, who had already died, but also the still-alive Livia and Tiberius.[76] Moreover, Suetonius recalls having gifted to Hadrian a statuette of the young Octavianus in order for him to worship it in his private rooms, as it happened with other images of deities.[77] This tells us that there was a quite widely diffused commerce of *imagines Augustorum* and aimed not only to the public but also to the private sphere. From a re-reading of a *scholium* to Juvenal the existence of *sigilla* emerges, that is to say clay statuettes of the *Agrippinae* sold on stalls (*casas*) in the area of the Trajan *Thermae* and at the *porticus* of Agrippa:[78] as if there were areas in the city specialised in selling *imagines* of the dynasts, not unlike what still happens today with the stalls selling holy cards and statuettes of Saint Anthony near the Basilica del Santo in Padua (this did not exclude, naturally, that they could also be found elsewhere).

On this particular point Tacitus' testimony appears crucial: he relates the case of a Falanius, who lived during Tiberius' times, who was accused of various crimes among which "that he had admitted a certain Cassius, mime and catamite, among the '*cultores* of Augustus' who were maintained, after the fashion of fraternities, in all the great houses: also, that when selling his gardens, he had parted with a statue of Augustus as well."[79] The accusation, on which Tiberius will later gloss over, is twofold: to have admitted into his house during the religious meetings for the cult of Augustus an execrable person such as Cassius, and mainly to have relinquished a statue of the *princeps* in the selling of the gardens. This information appears extremely interesting as it testifies how it was praxis for private individuals to host in their own houses the *cultores Augusti* as if it was a public gathering (*in modum collegiorum*); this means that, at least in that occasion, a dedicated room was furnished in which the image of the *divus*, perhaps along some of his relatives, was

---

[76] Ov. *ex Pont.* 2.8.1 and 4.9.105.

[77] Svet. *Hadr.* 2.7.

[78] In BASSANI, Sacra privata, p. 236-239, part. fn. 97. In this volume, see the essay of Aude Durand.

[79] Tac. *ann.* 1.73. Transl: https://penelope.uchicago.edu/Thayer/E/Roman/Texts/Tacitus/home.html.

necessarily exhibited. On the other hand, Tacitus' passage demonstrates how the religious value of these *imagines* was perceived as extremely important, so much that it appeared sacrilegious to dispose of them as if they were common objects: they were an integral part of the *sacra* and as such they had to be preserved with the utmost care.

Nonetheless, Tiberius' reaction was soft: he maintained that it was not "an act of sacrilege, if the effigies of that sovereign, like other images of other gods, went with the property, whenever a house or garden was sold."[80] But the information is still valuable, as it reiterates that the value of the *simulacra* of emperors or members of the *domus Augusta* was perceived as equal as those of the gods. This proves that the imperial cult had seeped into the private sphere, and it was there that it could be practiced with more freedom than in the public sphere: this is a new perspective for further research that will lead, in the near future, to many important documental discoveries.

Conclusion

What do the *sacra privata* tell us in the Roman house? As we have seen, much more information than what it was deemed possible to desume from the study of the so-called *lararia*. We have attempted here to trace, in a first, cursory and still not comprehensive way, the main elements that have emerged from the latest research: the necessity to adopt a rigorous research method, with specific vocabulary and tools, the possibility to ascertain different structural and decorative morphologies within Roman houses.

Moreover, these elements speak of the multiplicity of divine entities that were referred to in the private sphere, with numerous different influences, just as it happened in the public sphere. To these entities were reserved religious spaces within or outside the residence, of variable dimensions and richness of decorations. They indicate, ultimately, their highly representative function in

---

[80] *Ibid.*: *nec contra religiones fieri, quod effigies eius (scil. Augusti), ut alia numinum simulacra, venditionibus hortorum et domuum accedant.*

the dynamics of social self-promotion brought forward by the residents of each *domus/villa*.

Each of these elements deserves further investigation, as it is through them that an attempt can be made to reconstruct new and interesting pieces of the Roman house through the centuries and its inhabitants, who made it a living and paradigmatic organism.

ALEXANDRA DARDENAY

HERCULANEUM'S *INSULA* V DOMESTIC CULT PLACES: REFLECTIONS ON TYPOLOGY, LOCATIONS AND FIELDS OF ACTION

Since deities were essential figures of the domestic space, they populated the house and supervised the household's activities, as reported in so many Latin sources.[1] At the center of this system, the Lares (*Lares familiares*), the home's protective deities,[2] also had a topical function[3] and circumscribed both the physical space of the dwelling that they protected and the Penates'[4] field of ac-

---

[1] These texts are commented on and compared with the material remains in W. VAN ANDRINGA, *Quotidien des dieux et des hommes : la vie religieuse dans les cités du Vésuve à l'époque romaine*, Rome, École française de Rome, 2009 (Bibliothèque des Écoles françaises d'Athènes et de Rome 337), p. 217-269.

[2] A passage from Plautus directly evokes this protective dimension: "Do not ask me who I am: in two words I will tell you. I am the Lare, the 'domestic god' of this house you saw me come out of. This house has been my establishment and residence for many years: I was already there at the time of its present occupant's father and grandfather. Now, the grandfather once secretly entrusted me with a treasure: he locked it up in the middle of the house, begging me to watch over it for him" (Pl., *Aulul.*, prol.).

[3] The frequent association, in *lararia* paintings, of the snake image, the *genius loci*, with the figure of the Lares, reinforces this spatial anchoring. 191 representations of pairs of snakes are attested in Campanian *lararia* (T. FRÖHLICH, *Lararien- und Fassadenbilder in den Vesuvstädten: Untersuchungen zur ,volkstümlichen' pompejanischen Malerei*, Mainz, Philipp von Zabern, 1991, p. 165-169). A painting from Herculaneum (MANN 8848) associates the image of the snake wrapped around an altar with the inscription *"genius huius loci montis"*. In Latin legal sources, the Lares define the *domicilium* (Y. THOMAS, *Origine et commune patrie. Étude de droit public romain : 89 av. J.-C. - 212 ap. J.-C.*, Rome, École française de Rome, 1996, p. 44). On the Lares figure, associated with the snake figure, let us cite a recent synthesis that takes up the whole historiography of the subject and in particular the academic disagreements on their origin, nature and function: H. I. FLOWER, *The dancing Lares and the Serpent in the Garden. Religion at the Roman Street Corner*, Princeton, Princeton University Press, 2017.

[4] T. Fröhlich, the author of a monograph on Campanian *lararia*'s decorations, says the Lares (*familiares, domestici*) protect and symbolize the *domus*.

tion. While, in theory, Lares and Penates resided everywhere in the residence,[5] their worship is generally considered to have taken place in small domestic sanctuaries. These shrines varied in typology, from the simple niche for the humblest, to the most luxurious masonry sanctuaries, besides a whole range of wooden sanctuaries, whose size and mobility varied very much as well.[6]

For a long time, these sanctuaries have been referred to as *"lararia"* in modern and contemporary historiography, although this term was hardly ever used in Roman times, as the Latins generally called them *sacrarium* or *aedicula*.[7] Since the last century, several *lararia* corpora have been published,[8] followed by synthe-

---

The *Genius* (from *pater familias*, who protects the *familia*) and the Lares are not generally included among the *Dei Penati*, who for their part represent all the household's other gods: FRÖHLICH, *Lararien- und Fassadenbilder*, p. 21; R. A. TYBOUT, "Domestic Shrines and 'Popular Painting'. Style and Social Context," *Journal of Roman Archaeology* 9 (1996), p. 358-374. In addition, T. Fröhlich deduces from a series of 31 inscriptions that the Lares and *Genius* worships concerned freedmen and slaves (p. 28-29), just as they did for the *compita*. In fact, the iconographic corpus reveals that 54 of the 78 paintings depicting the *Genius* flanked by the Lares are found in kitchens or service areas (the other 23 come from small dwellings).

[5] Servius, *Ad Aen.* 2.514: *"penates sunt omnes dii qui domi coluntur"*. On the cult of the penates, see A. DUBOURDIEU, *Les origines et le développement du culte des Pénates à Rome*, Rome, École française de Rome, 1989, in particular the second part on "the private penates" (p. 63-101). On the matter of painted images of the penates in the house: V. HUET, S. WYLER, "Associations de dieux en images dans les laraires de Pompéi," in F. LISSARAGUE, S. ESTIENNE, F. PROST (eds.), *Figures de dieux. Construire le divin en images*, Rennes, PUR, 2015, p. 195-221.

[6] On typology: M. BASSANI, Sacraria: *ambienti e piccoli edifici per il culto domestico in area vesuviana*, Rome, Quasar, 2008 (Antenor Quaderni 9), p. 23-34. Regarding the wooden *lararia*: S. T. A. M. MOLS, *Wooden furniture in Herculaneum. Form, Technique and Function*, Amsterdam, J.C. Gieben, 1999 (Circumvesuviana).

[7] The oldest occurrences, dating from late antiquity, are found in these authors' works: SHA *Aur.* 3, 5 and SHA Sev. *Alex.* 29.2-3, 31, 4, 5; also *CIL* IX, 2125. On this subject, please consult Giacobello's article in *ThesCRA* (4, 2005, 262-264), as well as BASSANI, Sacraria, p. 49-63 and p. 200, and M.-O. LAFORGE, *La religion privée à Pompéi*, Naples, Centre Jean Bérard, 2009 (Études), p. 19-21.

[8] G. K. BOYCE, *Corpus of the Lararia of Pompeii*, Rome, American Academy in Rome 1937 (*Memoirs of the American Academy in Rome* 14); FRÖHLICH, *Lararien- und Fassadenbilder*; F. GIACOBELLO, *Larari pompeiani: iconografia e culto dei Lari in ambito domestico*, Milan, LED, Ed. universitarie di lettere, economia, diritto, 2008; D. G. ORR, "Roman Domestic Religion: The Evidence of the Household Shrines," ANRW II, 16.2, Berlin – New York, De Gruyter, 1978, p. 1557-1591".

sis studies[9] that shed light on this phenomenon and its importance in Romans' everyday lives, on the place they occupied in the home, as well as on their role in the family unit's cohesion.

1. *Location of domestic sanctuaries and the issue of "multiple* lararia*"*

Among the most debated issues, a particularly delicate and sometimes divisive one revolves around the distribution and possible duplication of places of worship within the house, since the boundaries of the housing units within a building are not always easy to define. Moreover, the structuring of domestic worship rituals and their intra-family and generational organization are not always clear (between theoretical principles and effective practices), not to mention the fact that they were not necessarily permanent fixtures. In his 1991 work, Thomas Fröhlich underlined the polymorphous character of domestic worship in Vesuvian cities, which, he believed, manifested a separation between, on the one hand, worship concerning the household's humble community (slaves and freedmen) and, on the other hand, the cult orchestrated by the *dominus*. Painted *lararia* (with representations of the Lares surrounding the *Genius*), often laid out in the dwelling's service areas, would gather the humblest members of the *familia*, while the *dominus* and his close relatives would honor the Penates, in one of the *familia*'s representation areas, around a niche, a masonry *lararium* (or a wooden piece of furniture). Taken up by other researchers, this distinction is said to have made it possible to underline status differences, while ensuring the slaves and freedmen's loyalty – in charge of serving the Lares and *Genius* – to the *dominus* and his house.[10] However,

---

[9] BASSANI, Sacraria; GIACOBELLO, *Larari pompeiani*; LAFORGE, *La religion privée à Pompéi*; VAN ANDRINGA, *Quotidien des dieux et des hommes*; FLOWER, *The dancing Lares*. To this list of monographs, I add two very stimulating articles: A. KAUFMANN-HEINIMANN, "Statuettes de laraire et religion domestique à Pompéi," in *Contributi di archeologia vesuviana III : I culti di Pompei*, Roma, 2007, p. 151-157; HUET, WYLER, *Associations de dieux en images*.

[10] T. Fröhlich identified a series of inscriptions showing that the *Genius* and the Lares worship was taken care of, in the house, by freedmen and slaves, thus granting them a valorizing role within the *familia* (FRÖHLICH, *Lararien- und Fassadenbilder*, p. 30). For example *CIL* X, 861: "To our master's genius and to

in more recent works, this dichotomous organization of domestic cults within a household is being challenged to a considerable extent.[11] Thus, the analysis of material vestiges highlights the absence of a generalized pattern and the organization of domestic cults must have been as varied as the number of households.[12] Moreover, the multiplication of sanctuaries in the house may have met purely functional needs. Indeed, W. Van Andringa, quoting Cato, recalls that, in accordance with the custom, the master of the house presided over domestic sacrifices, with the exception of cults rendered in *compito*, at the crossroads, and above all *in foco*, on the hearth, in other words, to the Lares.[13]

the Lares, both *Diadumeni*, freedmen." P. W. FOSS, "Watchful Lares. Roman Household Organization and the Rituals of Cooking and Eating," in R. LAURENCE, A. WALLACE-HADRILL (eds.), *Domestic Space in the Roman World. Pompeii and Beyond*, Portsmouth, RI, JRA, 1997 (JRA Suppl. 22), p. 196-218, will support and extend this hypothesis, arguing around the doubling of the sanctuaries and couples of Lares in a number of residences, with a main sanctuary in the *atrium* (often) and a secondary one in the kitchen, reserved for slaves. M.-O. Laforge seems to support the hypothesis of a separation between the cults performed by the slaves and those performed by the *dominus* (LAFORGE, *La religion privée à Pompéi*, p. 81-84).

[11] "It seems excessive to see the kitchen as a place of worship for slaves, while the main sanctuary, in the *atrium* or peristyle, would be dedicated to the master. This would be at odds with the characteristics of Roman domestic religion, which was entirely subject to the authority of the father of the family," says Van Andringa (W. VAN ANDRINGA, "Dal sacrificio al banchetto: rituali e topografia della casa romana," in M. BASSANI, F. GHEDINI (eds.), Religionem significare. *Aspetti storico-religiosi, strutturali, iconografici e materiali dei sacra privata, Atti dell'Incontro di studi (Padova, 8-9 giugno 2009)*, Padova, Quasar, 2011, p. 238-239). For him, the location of the various religious facilities in the house are rather a marking of the different sacrificial stages. Read also F. Giacobello's remarks in his study on the cult of the Lares in Campania: it confirms the link between the Lares and the home and therefore the kitchen, but emphasizes the "high religious value" of these worship places and the existence of a link with the self-representation of the *dominus*. She also disputes that the lares could have been intended for different groups of users depending on the room they were located in: F. GIACOBELLO, "Testimonianze del culto dei Lari dall'area vesuviana: significato e nuove interpretazioni," in BASSANI, GHEDINI, Religionem significare, 2011, p. 88: "l'allestimento di due o più sacelli all'interno della casa pompeiana non corrisponde a una diversità dei fruitori, ma a una non identità dell'espressione religiosa."

[12] Thus Van Andringa notes that: "in terms of location, there is no rigid model, but very clear principles have guided the installation of places of worship" (VAN ANDRINGA, *Quotidien des dieux et des hommes*, p. 227-228).

[13] Cato *De Agr.* 5.3. VAN ANDRINGA, *Quotidien des dieux et des hommes*, p. 238. Van Andringa also highlights the very convincing hypothesis of the exist-

This is undoubtedly why several sanctuaries can be found in the house, and why *lararium* paintings – like the one in the *Casa di Nettuno ed Anfitrite*'s upstairs apartment of the (V, 6-7) – can be found above some fireplaces.[14]

In Herculaneum, the presence of multiple places of worship within the same house is difficult to demonstrate.[15] It is however a phenomenon attested in several houses in Pompeii, geographically variable,[16] one of the two *lararia* may be in the kitchen, but not necessarily. In Pompeii, in the *Casa degli Amorini Dorati*

---

ence, in the house, of a "geography of the sacred", the multiple *lararia* marking the different stages in the accomplishment of the rituals that justified moving around inside the the house: "the different religious arrangements located in the house actually constituted as many markings of the main stages of the sacrifice". VAN ANDRINGA, *Quotidien des dieux et des hommes*, p. 239-240.

[14] On the cult of the Penates localization in the house, DUBOURDIEU, *Culte des Pénates à Rome*, p. 63-71.

[15] There are two university dissertations on Herculaneum's domestic sanctuaries (C. M. MARCHETTI, *Il culto domestico ad Ercolano. Le evidenze archeologiche*, Tesi di Specializzazione in Archeologia e Storia dell'Arte Romana, Università del Salento, 2009 and E. MUNOS, *Les laraires à Herculanum*, Master 1, Université de Toulouse II – Jean Jaurès, 2017). Marchetti's dissertation included almost all niches indiscriminately as places of domestic worship. While it would have been appropriate to keep only those with an architectural typology (*aedicula* type framing, presence of an overhanging altar) or ornamental (presence of religious paintings or in situ deity statuettes) that attests to this function, or at least makes it likely. This is, moreover, what Munos attempted to do in his Master's thesis on Herculaneum *lararia*. We note the same reservation in the characterization of niches in most of the authors who have worked on the subject (e.g., LAFORGE, *La religion privée à Pompéi*, p. 23 "niches are numerous in houses and their use is varied. Two elements enable us to identify the *lararia* in an unquestionable way: the presence of deities in the form of paintings or statuettes and the presence of an altar"; also, among others, BASSANI, Sacraria, p. 74-75. About the sanctuaries in the workplaces, which in Herculaneum are closely linked to the dwellings: A. DURAND, "Pratiques religieuses des artisans et marchands de la *Civitas Herculanensis*: un reflet des statuts de travail?", *Vesuviana*, XI, 2019, p. 11-90.

It should also be noted that some large houses, such as the *Casa dei Cervi*, have yielded few or no *lararia* remains. In the latter's case, only a block of tuft placed near the cooking bench could possibly be assigned to a religious function, but no specific architectural or decorative elements confirm this. This absence of material remains is only an indication that the domestic sanctuary or sanctuaries have not been preserved.

[16] I borrow the expression from Van Andringa (VAN ANDRINGA, *Quotidien des dieux et des hommes*, p. 218). He specifies further that three criteria could intervene in the installation of the *lararia*: religious, functional and social (*ibid.*, p. 244).

(VI 16.7) for example, the two sanctuaries are in the peristyle, and in the *Casa del Menandro* (I 10, 4), one is in the *atrium* and the other in the peristyle.[17]

In Herculaneum, however, some large residences suggest the material coexistence of several domestic sanctuaries. Thus, in the *Casa del Rilievo di Telefo* (Ins. Or. I, 2-3), the remains of three structures – positioned in different spaces – could possibly be interpreted as domestic sanctuaries, with an unequal degree of probability: the remains of a masonry mass against the southern wall of the *atrium* (H. 70 cm; W. 50 cm; Th. 43 cm); those of a massif positioned in the north-western corner of the circulation space between the peristyle and the garden (H. 96 cm; W. 110 cm; Th. 70 cm); the third is an *aedicula* with a pediment placed on two colonnettes and situated against the northern wall of the garden. Of these three structures, the last is the most convincing, from the architectural and typological point of view, in its function as a place of domestic worship; as for the first two, on the other hand, the remains strike me as insufficient to decide. A more significant example could be that of the *Casa del Salone Nero* (VI, 11), which has yielded two *aediculae*. One, made of masonry and composed of a high podium topped with a pedimented structure (H. 226 cm; W. 103 cm; D. 60 cm) was located in a small courtyard (space 6), along the southern wall. The second is a piece of wooden furniture, whose upper part took the form of a shrine with a pediment, which was discovered in fragments between *oecus* 7 and the peristyle.[18] Perhaps it was located in the western wing of the peristyle (10) that opens onto the large *oecus* (7)?

This is one of the four wooden *aediculae* found at Herculaneum, the other three coming from the *Casa del Sacello di Legno*

---

[17] On these two examples read the analysis in HUET, WYLER, *Associations de dieux en images*.

[18] Antiquarium di Ercolano (inv. 198-2020). Dimensions: H. 100 cm; W. 100 cm; D. 40 cm. T. BUDETTA, M. PAGANO, *Ercolano, legni e piccoli bronzi : testimonianze dell'arredo e delle suppellettili della casa romana : Roma, Castel S. Angelo, 23 marzo - 26 aprile 1988*, Rome, C.E.T.S.S., 1988 (Le Mostre (Soprintendenza archeologica di Pompei) 3), no. 9, p. 36-37. MOLS, *Wooden furniture in Herculaneum*, p. 60, cat. 30. A. MAIURI, *Ercolano. I nuovi scavi, 1927-1958*, Roma, Libreria dello Stato, 1958, p. 239, fig. 187.

(V, 31, room 2),[19] another from the *cenaculum* V, 18 (room 53) (Fig. 1)[20] and the last one from the *cenaculum* located on the floor of the *Casa a Graticcio* (III, 13), which contained several divinity statuettes, including two Lares.[21]

The survey will be limited to a single residential area – the *insula* V of Herculaneum – in order to propose observations considering all the available data, in a limited but coherent urban space (Fig. 2).

Other cases of "multiple *lararia*" inside a house are subject to a very particular interpretation, linked to the architectural history of the place. We will examine the example of the "two *lararia*" of the *Casa di Nettuno ed Anfitrite* (V, 6-7) and those of the *Casa*

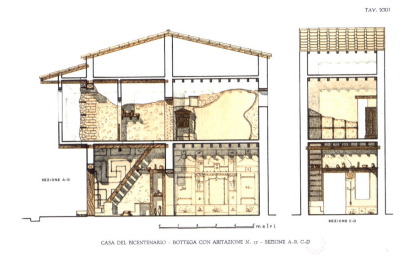

FIG. 1.
Cenaculum V, 18. Indication of the place of discovery of the wood *aedicula* in A. MAIURI, *Ercolano. I nuovi scavi, 1927-1958*, 1958, pl. XXII.

[19] MOLS, *Wooden furniture in Herculaneum*, cat. 29, p. 58-60.
[20] *Ibid.*, cat. 28, p. 58. FRÖHLICH, *Lararien- und Fassadenbilder*, p. 30. MAIURI, *Ercolano*, vol. II, pl. XXII. Another piece of wooden furniture, a cupboard, was found in the adjoining room, which could have served as a kitchen (MOLS, *Wooden furniture in Herculaneum*, cat. 37).
[21] MOLS, *Wooden furniture in Herculaneum*, cat. 27, p. 58 and 243-244; MAIURI, *Ercolano*, p. 416-419. The statuettes uncovered in this piece of furniture-sanctuary represent, in addition to the Lares, Mars, Jupiter, Isis, Aesculapius, Diana, Isis / Fortuna, Harpocrates and an unidentified figure, probably female.

Fig. 2.
Ground floor (left) and upper floors (right) of *insula* V in 79, with the location of potential sanctuaries. Positioning of the staircases and the stairways. Plan: ANR Vesuvia.

del Bicentenario (V, 15-16). In these two cases, in fact, one of the *lararia* is in an apartment fitted out inside the *domus*.[22]

When it was built at the end of the Augustan period, the *Casa di Nettuno ed Anfitrite* was provided with a floor composed of a series of residential rooms accessible from a staircase located south of the *atrium*, in space 5. After the earthquake in 62, the western part of the floor was restructured so as to be independent and accessible from the store (V, 13), thanks to the opening of a door for direct access to the staircase that remained in room 5.

---

[22] On the subject of multi-storey houses and housing units, see also LAFORGE, *La religion privée à Pompéi*, p. 116-119.

One of the reception rooms was partitioned and the spaces thus created were assigned to service functions: a latrine (18), an access corridor from the landing (19) and a kitchen (20)[23] (Fig. 3).

In this last space, a heater table is identified as being built against the southern wall. The old Fourth Style painting articulated around a pedimented *aedicula* in *trompe l'oeil* is preserved and is therefore a residual vestige of the old decoration of this room. However, when the room was redesigned as a kitchen, a *lararium* painting partially covered this Fourth Style decoration, in the western part of the wall, above a very eroded masonry mass, which could correspond to the remains of an altar or low fireplace[24] (Fig. 4a-b). The performance of domestic rituals above this masonry structure located between the heating table and the latrine is deduced from the presence of a painted picture with an unequivocal iconographic pattern. In the preserved part of the painting, executed on a white background, two Lares can be seen standing symmetrically on either sides of the central element,

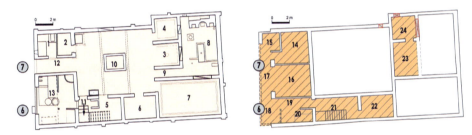

Fig. 3.
Casa di Nettuno ed Anfitrite. Plans of the ground floor (left) and of the upper floor (right).
Plan: ANR Vesuvia.

---

[23] For details on these restructurings since the construction of the building, see A. Dardenay, *L'insula V d'Herculanum. Transformations spatiales et diachroniques de l'architecture et du décor des habitations*, Leuven, Peeters, 2022 (Babesch Supplements, 45), p. 208-210.

[24] It is most likely an altar with a heating surface delimited on at least three sides by a concrete bead. On this point see A. Dardenay, J. N. Andrews, H. Eristov, M.-L. Maraval, N. Monteix, "Herculanum, architecture domestique et décor. Restitution graphique et virtuelle de la casa di Nettuno ed Anfitrite (V, 6-7). Campagne 2017 du programme ANR VESUVIA," *Chronique des activités archéologiques de l'École française de Rome* (2018) (https://journals.openedition.org/cefr/2119).

Fig. 4a-b.
Casa di Nettuno ed Anfitrite – room 20, masonry "altar" to the right of the firing bench *lararium* painting above the masonry "altar".

but the poor state of preservation of the pictorial surface makes it impossible to distinguish the details of their clothing; the one on the left holds a rhyton in his left hand and a situla in his right hand, while the Lare on the right holds a rhyton in his right hand and a situla in his left. Two snakes approaching an altar on which offerings were displayed have been almost erased by the sun and the weather. This is therefore one of the few kitchen sanctuaries in Herculaneum that have left convincing[25] archaeological traces.

According to the *domus* planimetry, the apartment rearranged on the first floor after the year 62 could either function as an independent dwelling unit (accessible from the store), or as an annex of the ground floor (to accommodate relatives, or to settle in during the winter?). In any case, insofar as this apartment could be used in a completely autonomous way with respect to the ground floor, and could be rented to third parties, it can be considered as an independent housing unit. The ground floor of the *domus* was also provided with facilities that could be considered redundant to those of the *cenaculum* on the upper floor. A kitchen, combined with a latrine, was thus arranged immediately to the left of the entrance door (space 1) and a domestic sanctuary of the *aedicula* type, masoned and covered with marble, was located in the *atrium*. As such, this duplication, combined with the relative

---

[25] In fact, in Herculaneum, the list of clearly identifiable kitchen sanctuaries is very short: three are associated with a religious painting: *Casa del Colonnato Tuscanico*, *Casa di Nettuno ed Anfitrite* (*cenaculum* in the first floor) and *Casa del Bicentenario* (*cenaculum* in the first floor, under reservation that this space was indeed used as a kitchen). Others are kitchen niches, more questionable in the function of *lararium*: Casa III, 18, *Casa dei Cervi*, *Casa del Bicentenario*.

autonomy of the two levels of the house, suggests that the *Casa di Nettuno ed Anfitrite* should not necessarily be classified as a multiple *lararia* house.

The heuristic difficulties arise in equivalent terms in the case of the domestic worship places of the *Casa del Bicentenario* (V, 13-16). The ground floor did not have a masonry *aedicula*, of the type that is found in some large residences, especially in Pompeii.[26] However, we must qualify this absence by underlining that the masonry sanctuaries are of rather sporadic attestation in Herculaneum.[27] On the *domus* ground floor, the only trace – a debatable one – of *sacellum* would be at the bottom of the peristyle, in space 13 interpreted as a kitchen and where there are two niches, sometimes interpreted as possible domestic sanctuaries,[28] but which do not present any material trace (architectural or ornamental) of such an assignment (Fig. 5).

It is on the first floor, in room 44 of the *cenaculum* (V, 13-14) that vestiges there can be unquestionably interpreted as the traces of an arrangement devoted to the *sacra privata*. The "lararium painting", which adorns a large part of the south wall of room 44 (Fig. 6), is particularly interesting, because this type of religious decoration is rare in Herculaneum. As in the attested[29] Pompeiian examples, the scene is structured in two superimposed registers: in the upper part, the symmetrical Lares dance under a canopy festooned with garlands; in the lower register, two "agathoi daimones" serpents emerge from the chthonian world and undulate symmetrically on either side of an altar bearing a pine cone. In the small niche on the right was discovered a charred wooden

---

[26] Often, but not only, in the *atrium*, the peristyle or the garden. On this subject FRÖHLICH, *Lararien- und Fassadenbilder*, p. 28 and *passim*, who speaks of "representation spaces"; BASSANI, Sacraria, p. 103, and LAFORGE, *La religion privée à Pompéi*, p. 84.

[27] In *insula* V, which we are interested in here, only two examples are attested, in two adjoining houses: one in the *Casa di Nettuno ed Anfitrite*'s *atrium* (V, 6-7) and one in the *Casa del Mobilio Carbonizzato*'s garden (V, 5). We will come back to this point in due course.

[28] M. MAUGER, "Sanctuaires et marges de l'habitat : perception et délimitation de l'espace domestique," in A. DARDENAY, N. LAUBRY (eds.), *Anthropology of Roman Housing*, Turnhout, Brepols, 2020 (Antiquité et sciences humaines 5), p. 165-192, part. p. 185 and MARCHETTI, *Il culto domestico ad Ercolano*, p. 69-71.

[29] BOYCE, *Corpus of the Lararia of Pompeii*; VAN ANDRINGA, *Quotidien des dieux et des hommes*.

Fig. 5.
Casa del Bicentenario, ground floor, kitchen (13), view towards the southeast corner with two niches, one of which is above the cooking bench.

Fig. 6.
Casa del Bicentenario, upper floor room 44, south wall, *lararium* painting.
Photo N. Monteix.

statuette representing a female figure, perhaps Venus.[30] In the same room, a wooden chest, 1.43 m high and 0.35 m wide, was discovered, containing a bronze lamp and 2 kg of charred barley.[31] Was this space used as a kitchen? Despite the absence of a fireplace or preserved masonry plan, one can assume so, as this type of scene is frequently found in kitchens.[32] Moreover, the storage of 2 kg of barley in this room indicates a function related to food. What do we know about the status of this room and the apartment in which it is located in relation to the ground floor? When the *Casa del Bicentenario* was built, in the Augustan period, the ground floor belonged to the same housing unit as the ground floor, the whole forming a large *domus*. However, in a phase subsequent to the 62 earthquake, the north floor of the *Casa del Bicentenario*, a vast 114 m² apartment, was detached from the main dwelling by the destruction of the staircase in room 2 and attached to store V, 13-14. A staircase was then built in room 24, which transformed the north floor into an autonomous apartment with access to V, 14 (see plan Fig. 7).

The staircase rests against a wall of *opus craticium* that divides the space of the room into two (delineating room 24 to the north from room 1 to the south) (see plan Fig. 7). The staircase that leads to this *cenaculum* is no longer accessible from inside the house. It is therefore not a "spare apartment", but a totally independent *cenaculum*. The articulation with the *domus* ground floor is reminiscent of that observed in the *Casa di Nettuno ed Anfitrite*, but with an autonomy reinforced by the absence of a communication passage between the two dwelling levels, since the *cenaculum* was only accessible from room 24 of store V, 13-14. This arrangement seals the discontinuity with the dwelling unit on the *domus* ground floor and makes it unlikely that it would have been used, even seasonally or occasionally, by the family that resided there. The domestic sanctuary in the upstairs apartment (room 44) was therefore probably used by another family than

---

[30] *GSE*, 15 mars 1938. About this *sacrarium* see also DURAND, *Pratiques religieuses des artisans et marchands de la* Civitas Herculanensis, p. 14-15.

[31] Wooden chest: *GSE*, 16 March 1938; bronze lamp: inv. E 1955; 2.1 kg of barley: inv. E 1895, GSE, 17 March 1938.

[32] VAN ANDRINGA, *Quotidien des dieux et des hommes*, p. 230-244. VAN ANDRINGA, *Dal sacrificio al banchetto*.

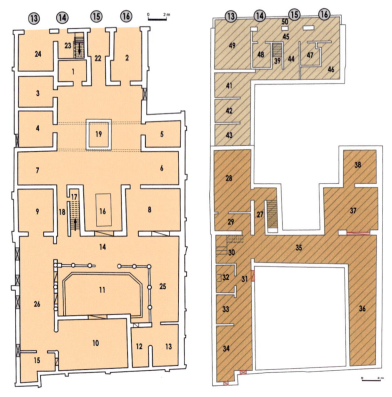

Fig. 7.
Casa del Bicentenario during the last phase of occupation of the site.
Plan of the ground floor (left) and the upper floor (right).

the one on the ground floor, the latter gathering for the celebration of its *sacra privata* around a cult arrangement that has now disappeared.

These two examples show that caution must be exercised in interpreting cases of multiple sanctuaries within the same *domus*. Some examples can thus be explained by the development of several housing units in the same building.

2. *Typology of the* insula *V sanctuaries*

It is extremely difficult to determine the exact number of domestic sanctuaries attested at Herculaneum. In fact, while some are easily identifiable (masonry or wooden *aediculae*, sanctuaries identifiable by the presence of paintings or characteristic statuettes), many of them could be presented as niches, whose identification is very problematic. Indeed, while some, unfortunately all too rare, present characteristics specific to domestic sanctuaries, most cannot be distinguished from simple niches used to store or place domestic furniture (lamps, crockery, etc.).[33] The elements that allow us to identify a niche as a domestic sanctuary are the following:

1. the discovery *in situ* of statuettes of Lares and or Penates,
2. the discovery *in situ* of characteristic paintings (Lares, *Genius*, snakes).

More uncertain and fragile are the following criteria:

3. stucco dressing of the niche to represent an *aedicula* or a shell vault,
4. insertion of a *tegula* to enlarge the support.

Depending on whether or not the last two criteria are taken into account, we get an estimate varying between 54 *lararia* (all types taken together) over the whole city for the high estimate and about 30 for the low one.[34]

In fact, the ornamental apparatus discovered *in situ* does not make it easy to find Herculaneum's domestic sanctuaries. On the scale of the entire site, only five *lararia* paintings could be identified.[35]

---

[33] The problem is well known as noted, in particular, by P. Allison in his work on the *instrumentum domesticum* in Pompeii: P. M. ALLISON, *Pompeian Households. An Analysis of Material Culture*, Los Angeles, Cotsen Institute of Archaeology, University of California Press, 2004 (Monograph Cotsen Institute of Archaeology), p. 48-51. On these niches intended to accommodate the penates, read also Dubourdieu's remarks (DUBOURDIEU, *Culte des Pénates à Rome*, p. 71-72).

[34] Marchetti counts about fifty of them, therefore many niches whose cultic interpretation is questionable: C. M. MARCHETTI, "Possidet domum. Prime riflessioni a margine della religiosità domestica a Ercolano: fonti e dati archeologici," in F. FONTANA, E. MURGIA (eds.), Sacrum facere: *atti del III Seminario di archeologia del sacro : lo spazio del « sacro »: ambienti e gesti del rito, Trieste, 3-4 ottobre 2014*, Trieste, Editrice Università di Trieste, 2016, p. 405-427. The Herculaneum *lararia* have been of little interest to researchers who have produced syntheses and corpora concerning the places of domestic worship in Campania: neither BOYCE, *Corpus of the Lararia of Pompeii*, nor FRÖHLICH, *Lararien- und Fassadenbilder*, nor GIACOBELLO, *Larari pompeiani*, have produced a catalog on Herculaneum.

[35] Three of them in *insula* V: V, 6 (floor); V, 13-14 (floor); V, 24 (*atrium*). Another is in a store in I.O. II.9, around a shell niche, and one last one in house VI, 17, southern wall of the space identified as kitchen. The same observation

Moreover, few of the Lares and Penates statuettes found in situ are mentioned in the *GSE* (*Giornale degli Scavi di Ercolano*). Given the state of the documentation, it is therefore neither prudent nor serious to venture providing statistical data.

TABLE 1.
The domestic *insula* V sanctuaries

Dwelling unit	Sanctuary in niche	Masonic edifice	Wooden edifice	Paintings of worship	Statuettes of worship
V, 1 *Casa Sannitica*					
V, 2 *Cenaculum*					
V, 3-4 *Casa del Telaio*					
V, 5 *Casa del Mobilio Carbonizzato*		Garden			
V, 6-7 *Casa di Nettuno ed Anfitrite*		*Atrium*			*Atrium*
V, 6 *Cenaculum or winter apartment*				Kitchen floor Above fireplace: Lares	
V, 8 *Casa del Bel Cortile*					
V, 9-12 *Casa dell'Apollo Citaredo*					
V, 13-14 *Cenaculum*	Room 44			Room 44 Lares and snake	Wooden statuette in the niche
V, 15-16 *Casa del Bicentenario*	Two niches in the kitchen (13)				

is made by FRÖHLICH, *Lararien- und Fassadenbilder*, p. 301-303. There is also a sixth *lararia* painting, detached in the eighteenth century, whose provenance we have not been able to identify to date (MANN, inv. 8848).

HERCULANEUM'S *INSULA* V DOMESTIC CULT PLACES

Dwelling unit	Sanctuary in niche	Masonic edifice	Wooden edifice	Paintings of worship	Statuettes of worship
V, 17 *Cenac. en rdc*					
V, 18 *Cenaculum*	Room 52		Room 53		Female statuette red marble niche room 52
V, 19-20					
V, 21					
V, 22 *Cenaculum*					
V, 23					
V, 24 *Casa della Colonna Laterizia*	*Atrium* (espace 7)			*Atrium* (area 7)	
V, 25					
V, 26					
V, 27					
V, 28					
V, 29					Lare statuette
V, 30 *Casa dell'Atrio Corinzio*					
V, 31 *Casa del Sacello di Legno*			Room 2		Room 2 in furniture: Hercules, goddess, patera
V, 32					
V, 33 *Casa con Giardino*					
V, 33a *Cenaculum*					
V, 34					
V, 35 *Casa del Gran Portale*					

The inventory of facilities and objects related to domestic worship, attested in *insula* V, is presented in the table above and reflects their sporadic character: out of twenty-nine dwelling units identified in this *insula*, nineteen have not yielded any trace of domestic sanctuary, i.e., almost two thirds ... It is difficult, on the basis of such elements, to propose a synthesis on the domestic cults at Herculaneum. In any case, these data extracted from *insula* V are in conformity with what one observes at site scale. First of all, we note the rarity of masonry sanctuaries (five in all, two of which are in *insula* V) or that of the wooden sanctuaries (four on the site, two of which are in *insula* V).[36] For the humbler arrangements, the observation is identical: only five paintings of "*lararia*" are attested on the site[37] (three of which are in *insula* V). This is why it is so difficult to distinguish, among the niches, those that were intended for domestic cults. Concerning statuettes, the inventories of the Museum of Naples and of the Deposit of the *Ufficio Scavi d'Ercolano* offer numerous examples of divinities that could have been counted among the Penates, but the defects of localization make any analysis perilous. As for Lares statuettes, properly speaking, they are very rare (four specimens).[38]

As for statuettes, the situation is not particularly specific to Herculaneum and, all things considered, the observation is almost identical in Pompeii, with only thirty statuary sets attached to domestic sanctuaries, out of about eight hundred houses.[39] Thus, one can say at most that the archaeological attestations of domes-

---

[36] Read above the mention of all the preserved copies, *supra* p. 214-215.

[37] On this subject see *supra* note 35, p. 223.

[38] At the Antiquarium di Ercolano: Inv. 75623 / 347 and 75624 / 348 (I, in a wooden *aedicula*); Inv. 76410 / 1133 (*cenaculum* V, 28); Inv. 76756 / 1478 ("*palestra*"); Inv. 76721 / 1443 ("*Insula Orientalis* II, casa 8"). It is possible, moreover, that a certain number of Lares (and Penates) statuettes were removed in the eighteenth century and are preserved today in the MANN. On this subject see the (uncertain) attempts to relocate the small statuary in M. PAGANO, R. PRISCIANDARO, *Studio sulle provenienze degli oggetti rinvenuti negli scavi borbonici del Regno di Napoli: una lettura integrata, coordinata e commentata della documentazione*, 2 vol., Castellammare di Stabia, Nicola Longobardi Editore, 2006. For statistics on the representation of deities in the Pompeii *lararia*: KAUFMANN-HEINIMANN, *Statuettes de laraire*, fig. 5. It can be seen there that the Lares and Egyptian deity figures predominate.

[39] KAUFMANN-HEINIMANN, *Statuettes de laraire*, p. 151.

tic cults in Herculaneum confirm and supplement those observed in Pompeii.[40]

For the rest, as often, it is wealthy people's cults that have left the most traces, confirming the privileged status of the inhabitants of the houses at the center of *insula* V: *Casa di Nettuno ed Anfitrite*, *Casa del Mobilio Carbonizzato* and *Casa del Sacello di Legno*.[41] Thanks to the quality of the decoration and furniture, we also knew we could place the *cenaculum* V, 18[42] inhabitants in this category. On the other hand, the absence of traces of masonry or wood *aediculae* should not be interpreted as a sign of low status: what with the furniture removed by the inhabitants during their escape, and the furnishings destroyed during the cataclysm and later, during the excavations of the Bourbons, losses and lacks are enormous. Hence, the domestic sanctuaries of the *Casa Sannitica*, of the *Casa del Bicentenario*, of the *Casa dell'Atrio Corinzio*, and of so many other Herculaneum houses must be considered as lost.

3. *The case of the masonry sanctuary of the* Casa di Nettuno ed Anfitrite *atrium*

Let us dwell for a moment on the case, interesting though poorly preserved, of the masonry sanctuary that was built, in the Flavian

---

[40] Let us formulate an observation that, albeit not definitive, deserves to be pointed out, in view of the current state of the corpus. To my knowledge, no representation of the *paterfamilias*' *Genius* exists in Herculaneum, whereas it is so often associated with the Lares in Pompeii, to the point of forming an almost canonical triad: thus they are all three mentioned and associated in the 392 Theodosius edict officially abolishing the polytheistic cults and explicitly aiming at the domestic cults: "secretiore piaculo Larem igne, mero Genium, Penates odore" (*Cod. Theod.* 16.10.12) on the association Lares/*genius* of the *paterfamilias* in Pompeii read FRÖHLICH, *Lararien- und Fassadenbilder*, p. 111-128. A. DUBOURDIEU, "Les cultes domestiques dans le monde romain," in *ThesCRA*, Los Angeles, 2012, vol. VIII, p. 37. VAN ANDRINGA, *Quotidien des dieux et des hommes*, p. 219 and 245.

[41] On that subject, see DARDENAY, *L'insula V d'Herculanum*, p. 103-136.

[42] A. DARDENAY, "Decoration in Context. Decorative Programs in Light of the Archaeology of Buildings from the *Insula* V of Herculaneum," in E. M. MOORMANN, S. T. A. M. MOLS (eds.), *Context and Meaning, Proceedings of the Twelfth International Conference of the Association Internationale pour la Peinture Murale Antique, Athens, September 16-20, 2013*, Leuven, Peeters, 2017 (Babesch Supplements 31), p. 283-290.

period, in the northwest corner of the *Casa di Nettuno ed Anfitrite atrium* (Fig. 3a). In fact, few remains have been preserved, except for the in situ massive, and we have no elements pertaining to the architecture of the upper part of the small monument.

This imposing masonry and marble veneer *lararium* was discovered in a very altered state during the A. Maiuri excavations in 1933. The most likely hypothesis for its sorry state of preservation is that the *lararium*, leaning against the north wall, was badly damaged by the excavations commissioned by the Bourbons in the eighteenth century. The investigation conducted by A. Allroggen-Bedel revealed that the excavators were in this house in the spring of 1746[43] and that at least two cunicoli ran across the house, one of which ran through the north wall at the *lararium* site: in the excavation journals (*GSE*), on April 19, 1933, the discovery of the *lararium*'s mass is mentioned, the upper part of which was allegedly destroyed by the boring of a tunnel under the Bourbons.[44] On that same date, the discovery was reported, very close to this massif, of two bronze statuettes, one representing a camel (no. 1059) and the other a small hermes (no. 1060).[45] Both statuettes may have been part of the *lararium instrumentum*.

After consulting the published Campanian *lararia* corpus,[46] we opted for a fairly generic architecture:[47] the thickness and width of the base are indicated by the remains of in situ masonry; as for the height, we assume the altar plane should have been

---

[43] On 21 March 1746, they were in the *triclinium* 7, next to the *atrium*. See A. DARDENAY, A. ALLROGGEN-BEDEL, H. ERISTOV, M.-L. MARAVAL, N. MONTEIX, "Habitat et société à Herculanum," *Chronique des activités archéologiques de l'École française de Rome* (2015), http://cefr.revues.org/1339, part. § 17-30.

[44] A. DARDENAY, A. ALLROGGEN-BEDEL, H. ERISTOV, A. GRAND-CLÉMENT, M.-L. MARAVAL, C. MAROTTA, N. MONTEIX, E. ROSSO, "*Herculanum*. Des archives aux restitutions architecturales et décoratives," *Chronique des activités archéologiques de l'École française de Rome* (2016), § 36, https://journals.openedition.org/cefr/1588.

[45] *Ibid.*: furniture inventory.

[46] FRÖHLICH, *Lararien- und Fassadenbilder*; BOYCE, *Corpus of the Lararia of Pompeii*.

[47] Within the framework of the ANR VESUVIA program, which proposes a computer graphics and 3D restitution of the *Casa di Nettuno ed Anfitrite*. http://vesuvia.hypotheses.org.

about 1.20 or 1.30 m from the ground, to allow a man standing to carry out his rituals. As a crowning feature, we can envision a pedimented roof supported by four colonnettes, examples of which abound in Campanian[48] masonry *lararia*. Since the *lararium* is not stuck against the north wall, the part above the base will have a symmetrical composition, as if it stood in the middle of a room. Finally, the altar could have been enclosed by small wooden shutters, like the one in the Pompeii *Casa del Menandro* (I 10, 4).[49]

Concerning the decoration of the *lararium*, the *GSE* reports, on April 20, 1933, the presence of numerous marble fragments that littered the floor in the *atrium* northwest corner, which are straight away attributed to the domestic altar decoration. We have retained this hypothesis, because the base of the massif itself has marble veneer elements. Thus, the depiction of the *lararium* represents it entirely covered with marble, although the parallels are rare[50] and it offers a somewhat extravagant luxury, especially when considering the pavement coarseness. However, the *atrium* painted decoration was in the process of being repaired,[51] so it may well be that a brand-new marble *lararium*, too, was to show a revival of the dominus's fortunes.

The two marble *pinakes* discovered in the *atrium* in 1933, also constitute a luxurious decorative element in this space.[52] In the

---

[48] BOYCE, *Corpus of the Lararia of Pompeii*, no. 67 (*Casa di Obellio Firmo*); no. 176 (*Casa dei Dioscuri*); no. 386 (*Casa di Epidio Sabino*).

[49] R. LING, P. ARTHUR, *The insula of the Menander at Pompeii*. Vol. I, *The structures*, Oxford, Clarendon Press, 1997.

[50] Such as the lares in the *Casa di Caecilius Iucundus* (V 1, 26) in Pompeii.

[51] See A. DARDENAY, H. ERISTOV, A. GRAND-CLÉMENT, M.-L. MARAVAL, N. MONTEIX, P. MORA, M. MULLIEZ, "*Herculanum*. Conception du modèle 3D de restitution et restauration virtuelle de la Casa di Nettuno ed Anfitrite. Campagne 2016 du projet ANR VESUVIA," *Chronique des activités archéologiques de l'École française de Rome* (2017), https://journals.openedition.org/cefr/1739.

[52] In the excavation journals of the *Casa di Nettuno ed Anfitrite*, on April 20, 1933 was mentioned the discovery of marble slabs painted with figured subjects, near the laraire: "20 aprile. Si è ripigliato il lavoro sul vuoto che trovasi nell'ambiente 3, della casa N° 6, sul 4 cardine, lato est. Molti frammenti di marmi colorati sono stati raccolti, marmi che potevano adornare l'ara votiva ieri accennata. Due lastre di marmo, una della lunghezza di m. 0.39 e l'altra m. 0.50, l'altezza manca perché la parte superiore è spezzata, si sono anche raccolte e sopra esse vi sono delle figure fatte con colori vari." These reliefs were taken directly to

GSE, they were reported on April 20 as having been discovered near the altar; besides, A. Maiuri, in his 1958 work, proposed to restore them as an ornament of the *lararium*. Now, in the absence of an archaeological parallel – and of a satisfactory answer to the question of where the two marble *pinakes* could be restored in the architecture of the *lararium* – we have given up on inserting them.

Despite these uncertainties and its poor state of preservation, this masonry sanctuary – the most luxurious of those discovered at Herculaneum owing to its marble veneers[53] – is an exceptional monument. Its presence harmonizes perfectly with the overall design of this house, which is relatively modest in size, but was entirely redecorated with a measure of pomp in the 70s.[54] The same taste for a somewhat flashy luxury was expressed in the summer *triclinium*, arranged in the ancient *hortus*, and whose ground and benches were also covered with marble plates.[55]

---

the National Museum of Naples where they were inventoried under the numbers 150210 and 150211. On these marble *pinakes* I. BRAGANTINI, V. SAMPAOLO, *La pittura pompeiana*, Milano, Electa, 2013, p. 119, no. 14 (with previous bibliography) and more recently: A. DARDENAY et al., *Des archives aux restitutions architecturales et décoratives*; S. LENZI, *La policromia dei monochromata: la ricerca del colore su dipinti su lastre di marmo di età romana*, Firenze, Firenze University Press, 2016, p. 245-246 and fig. 72-79.

[53] There are few parallels, even in Pompeii. Let us point out in particular the one found in the house known as "Caecilius Iucundus" (V 1-26) that Boyce qualifies as unique: BOYCE, *Corpus of the Lararia of Pompeii*, p. 14: "The shrine in the *atrium* of the house of Caecilius Iucundus is unique in having its base covered with slabs of greyish marble."

[54] *Atrium* 10 (8.87 × 7.20 m) has been described, by A. Maiuri, as "the most sumptuous and scenographic decoration of the *atrium* (...) due to an artist of great coloristic richness, of sure skill, of daring and inventive imagination, of an artist, finally specialized, we could also say, in the genre of the baroque architectural painting, and not alien, as it happens instead in the current decorators of the Herculaneum house, from inserting figured subjects and isolated figures and animalistic motifs in the field of the architectural decoration." (MAIURI, *Ercolano*, p. 397). The enthusiasm of this description can only cause regret not only for the near disappearance of the decoration, but also for the absence of graphic or photographic documentation. In its present state, only fragments of the decoration remain, most of which are located in the lower zone, with a few in the middle zone on the north and south walls.

[55] According to the archaeological and architectural study of this area, carried out by D. Camardo and M. Notomista during a restoration campaign, the fountain and benches were installed after 62. The marble veneers were installed

4. *The issue of the position of the sanctuary in the house*

The position of the domestic sanctuary(s) in the house was supposed to enable the deities to watch over almost all the rooms, as well as the front door. It was therefore one of the *Lares familiares*' key attributions, who were attached to the protection of the territory covered by the house, up to the entrance door.[56] Several studies have highlighted the effects of a "field of visual protection" the *lararium* was the nerve center of, though this type of device was not systematic.[57] The masonry sanctuary situated in the *Casa di Nettuno ed Anfitrite atrium* did not let the Penates "look" towards the *fauces* and the entrance door of the house (Fig. 8a-b). On the other hand, this *lararium*, located in the north-western corner of the *atrium*, was turned towards the interior of the

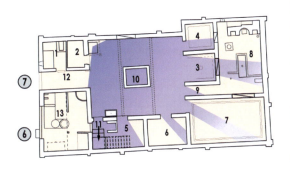 

FIG. 8a.
Casa di Nettuno ed Anfitrite, ground floor with simulation of the visual protection field of the *lararium* deities. (plan M.-L. Maraval).

FIG. 8b.
Casa di Nettuno ed Anfitrite, view from the threshold.

only in a last phase, which we suppose was contemporary to the house restoration and systematic redecoration campaign, in the 70s.

[56] I am referring here to a verse by Ovid: "Every door has two sides, one looks at the passers-by, the other at the Lare" (Ov. *Fast.* 1.89-144).

[57] See on this subject the diagram by M. Sohn reproduced in *PPM*, V, "*Casa del Principe di Napoli* (VI 15, 7-8)," p. 677 and HUET, WYLER, *Associations de dieux en images*, fig. 3. See also Van Andringa's remarks on the positioning of the *lararia*, between theoretical rules, uses and topographical constraints (VAN ANDRINGA, *Quotidien des dieux et des hommes*, p. 225-229).

house, from which it "protected" all the ground floor spaces.[58] The same observation could be made about the *Casa del Sacello di Legno* wooden sanctuary, located in room 2. On the other hand, the masonry sanctuary at the bottom of the *Casa del Mobilio Carbonizzato* garden was definitely turned towards the entrance of the house[59] and was even visible from the street (Fig. 9a-b), in accordance with the implantation principle observed in several Pompeii houses, such as the *Casa del Sarno* (I 14, 7), or the *Casa del Principe di Napoli* (VI 15, 7-8).

The implantation chosen in the *Casa del Mobilio Carbonizzato* can be deemed the most judicious, when it came to extend the scope of the visual protection field, which covers the whole ground floor and is aligned with the entrance door. In contrast, in the *Casa di Nettuno ed Anfitrite*, the entrance door is completely outside the protective field.

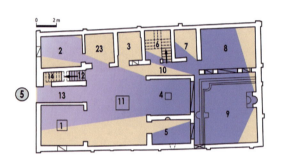

Fig. 9a.
Ground floor of V, 5 with a simulation of the *lararium* deities' visual protection field.

Fig. 9b.
Casa del Mobilio Carbonizzato, view of the domestic sanctuary through the house from the street.

[58] The position of the masoned *lararium* of the *atrium* of the house of L. Caecilius Iucundus in Pompeii is identical (see M. Mauger in this volume, p. 252-253 and Fig. 6).

[59] Sanctuary built in the Julio-Claudian period (T. Ganschow, *Untersuchungen zur Baugeschichte in Herculaneum*, Bonn, R. Habelt, 1989 (Antiquitas), p. 280).

This result is undoubtedly the upshot of a well-considered decision on the part of the owner, who wanted to completely restructure his *hortus* into a luxurious summer *triclinium* with marble-covered benches. The focal point of this "*triclinium nymphaeum*" was the mosaic known as "Neptune and Amphitrite",[60] inserted in the eastern wall, and visible from the street thanks to the alignment and opening of the walls. Thus, it was not the masonry *lararium* that was framed in the axis of the entrance door – as is the case, for example, in the *Casa del Mobilio Carbonizzato*, next door to it – but an aquatic type of scenography. As for the domestic sanctuary, which must have been the house owner's pride, it was visible to guests in the summer *triclinium* and, more generally, to all those who circulated in the house living areas. It is towards these rooms, and towards those who occupied them, that this *lararium*'s "field of visual protection" was oriented.

This type of configuration is not isolated. Thus, the internal organization of the *Casa di Nettuno ed Anfritrite* and the planning of points of view and fields of vision are very comparable to those in Marcus Lucretius' *domus* in Pompeii (IX 3, 5-24)[61] (Fig. 10). In the axis of the entry door was built a fountain with staircase in cascade feeding a circular basin placed just in front, in a *viridarium* populated with numerous statues.[62] The masonry

---

[60] Or then again Neptune and Venus according to C. LOCHIN, "Mosaïque et statue de culte. Neptune et Amphitrite à Herculanum," in H. MORLIER (ed.), *La mosaïque gréco-romaine, Actes du IXe Colloque international pour l'étude de la mosaïque antique et médiévale, Rome 5-10 novembre 2001*, Rome, École française de Rome, 2005 (Collection de l'EFR 352), p. 35-49.

[61] *PPM*, IX, p. 249-251; R. BERG, I. KUIVALAINEN (eds.), *Domus Pompeiana M. Lucretii IX 3, 5.24: The inscriptions, works of art and finds from the old and new excavations*, Helsinki, Societas Scientiarum Fennica, 2019 (Commentationes humanarum litterarum) (monograph on the findings of this *domus*, with mention of the previous bibliography).

[62] On the statuary ornamentation of this *domus* and of the *viridarium* in particular (mid first century AD realization): E. J. DWYER, *Pompeian domestic sculpture: A study of five Pompeian houses and their contents*, Roma, G. Bretschneider, 1982, p. 22-52; BERG, KUIVALAINEN, *Domus Pompeiana M. Lucretii*. About this fountain, read also in particular N. NEUERBURG, *L'Architettura delle Fontane e dei Ninfei nell'Italia Antica*, Napoli, Gaetano Macchiaroli, 1965, p. 62 and 131-132 and H. DESSALES, *Le partage de l'eau: fontaines et distribution hydraulique dans l'habitat urbain de l'Italie romaine*, Rome, École française de Rome, 2013, cat. 107, p. 485-486, and p. 140-141). Parallels are numerous and it would not

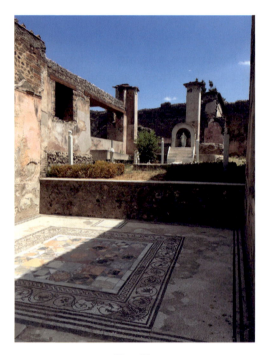

Fig. 10.
Pompeii, House of *Marcus Lucretius* (IX 3, 5), axial view from the street towards the fountain built at the back of the *viridarium*.

lintel was erected in the southwest corner of the *atrium*, where the field of visual protection extended towards the ground floor living rooms, the garden and the reception rooms, but without covering the entrance door. As in the *Casa di Nettuno ed Anfitrite*, the domestic sanctuary was invisible from the street, but the passer-by could admire the splendid water features, thanks to a visual perspective crossing the *atrium* and the *tablinum* all the way to the bottom of the garden.[63] In both houses, pictorial

---

be possible to list them all here. A statistical study has revealed that in Pompeii fountains are almost always visible from the street (Dessales, *Le partage de l'eau*, p. 367 and fig. 182).

[63] Several studies have focused on analyzing the staging of the fountain as a focal point of visual perspective from the street. See J. R. Clarke, *The Houses of Roman Italy: 100 B.C. – A.D. 250. Ritual, Space, and Decoration*, Berkeley – Los Angeles – Oxford, University of California Press, 1991, p. 16-21; S. Hales, *The Roman House and Social Identity*, Cambridge, Cambridge University Press, 2003, p. 107-122; Dessales, *Le partage de l'eau*, p. 366-367.

decorations include a choice of figurative themes related to water (nymphs, the myth of Narcissus) which accentuate this specific atmosphere. With this type of arrangement, the premises owner wished to give an ostentatious image of himself, in a setting conducive to *otium*, closer to the canons of Hellenistic domestic architecture than the Roman *mos maiorum*.

In any case, it is possible that the formal and architectural porosity between the "fountain *aedicula*" and the "*lararium aedicula*"[64] has led, in some houses, to a substitution of the *lararium* by a fountain, in the position of field of vision focal point from the outside.

Conclusion

What can we conclude from the scarcity of archaeological traces that could be associated with domestic worship places in Herculaneum? Beyond these observations, we can essentially formulate two hypotheses. The first is that we cannot stop at the only preserved remains, and that a large part of the objects and structures consecrated to the *sacra privata* at Herculaneum have certainly disappeared, whether they were taken away by their owners, destroyed as a result of the eruption or despoiled afterwards. However, we can still make some observations and draw up a number of *scenarii*.

A second hypothesis would be to suppose that the *sacra privata* were closely merged with domestic practices and that rituals had to be performed on ordinary, multipurpose furniture. Insofar

---

[64] On this subject in particular, H. LAVAGNE, Operosa antra. *Recherches sur la grotte à Rome de Sylla à Hadrien*, Rome, École Française de Rome, 1988, p. 639. Let us mention the example of the *Casa del Principe di Napoli* (VI 15, 7-8), whose *aedicula* located in the axis of the entrance door looks as much like a fountain as a *lararium* (on this subject DESSALES, *Le partage de l'eau*, p. 366). In Herculaneum, the *aedicula* covered with mosaic, shells and rockeries of the *Casa dello Scheletro* is interpreted alternately as a *lararium* or fountain (A. Maiuri refers to it as "sacello-ninfeo" (MAIURI, *Ercolano*, p. 272). The matter of its function is not completely clear-cut, so the ambiguity. H. Dessales designates it as a potential *lararium* and not as a fountain (DESSALES, *Le partage de l'eau*, p. 498). Regardless, in the last years of the site, the "basin" (a remnant of an ancient aquatic arrangement) at the foot of the *aedicula* was filled in and laid out as a garden.

as most of the furniture that decorated Herculaneum's houses has not reached us, it is difficult to make further use of this hypothesis ...[65] In any case we can assume an exclusive (or specific) masonry place of worship was not indispensable to carry out the *sacra privata*: a brazier, a table, possibly statuettes representing the penates and domestic divinities were probably sufficient.[66]

Finally, beyond the theoretical arrangement, between permanent and temporary devices, the places of domestic worship may not have always been assigned to an immutable place inside the house.[67] Nevertheless, we need to keep in mind it is quite possible that the protection strategies underlying the establishment of a number of sanctuaries elude us completely today. However, the examples developed in this contribution testify to the fact that, in at least some of the houses, the positioning of the domestic shrine(s) had been the subject of in-depth reflection. In this case, two implementation scenarios are preferred. The first must allow optimal surveillance (by the deities of the *lararium*) of the spaces located in the center and at the back of the house; the second allows surveillance of the entrance door and the rooms located in the front part of the house. However, when choosing the second option, the concern of the owner was perhaps not limited to questions of protection of the front area of his house. Indeed, we have highlighted architectural and ornamental similarities between "larary aedicules" and "fountain aedicules." These can then be placed in the axis of the entrance door and visible

---

[65] As many archaeologists and historians have pointed out. On the absence and/or disappearance of the furniture, see remarks and bibliography in A. DARDENAY, "Restituer l'espace domestique à Herculanum grâce aux outils informatiques de reconstruction virtuelle : enjeux et problèmes," *Anabases. Traditions et réceptions de l'Antiquité* 27 (2018), p. 41-51, part. p. 45-47.

[66] DUBOURDIEU, *Les cultes domestiques dans le monde romain*, p. 42: "these objects are undoubtedly often borrowed from the daily use and rather coarse dishes." Van Andringa postulates, for example, that in the kitchen the ritual was performed directly over the flame of the cooking device. I daresay this assumption can be extended to other spaces and circumstances. VAN ANDRINGA, *Quotidien des dieux et des hommes*, p. 232.

[67] Some devices are indeed "portable", for example the small portable tuft altar taken from the floor of the *Casa del Mobilio Carbonizzato* (inv. 76103/826). As for the statues of the Lares, several sources say they could be moved and even sit at the table: Petr. *Sat.* 60-61; Virg. *Aen.* 5.62; Hor. *Od.* 4.3. On this subject FRÖHLICH, *Lararien- und Fassadenbilder*, p. 30.

from the street, in a successful search for perspective effect. This parallelism – which as we have seen could sometimes lead to confusion – probably resulted from a desire to "show off" ornamental elements enhancing the *pietas* or the owner's fortune, or even both at the same time.

III
TOWARDS AN ANTHROPOLOGICAL ANALYSIS OF SPACES AND RITUALS

MARIN MAUGER

DOMESTIC RELIGION AND THE ANTHROPOLOGY OF SPACE IN THE ENTRANCE TO THE ROMAN HOUSE

This paper is an extension of thoughts, first presented in the previous volume of the collection *Anthropology of Roman Housing*, focusing on the contribution of domestic cults to our understanding of Roman houses.[1] The aim of this methodology is to turn on its head the initial investigation based on the organisation of the domestic space as a means of explaining the distribution of shrines within the house.[2] While this latter approach clearly offers a better understanding of domestic cults and their place in family life,[3] it is often based on a static image of the Roman house. By contrast, approaching the topic from the opposite angle provides an opportunity to use our knowledge about family religion in order to gain an alternative insight into the perception

---

[1] M. MAUGER, "Sanctuaires et marges de l'habitat: perception et délimitation de l'espace domestique," in A. DARDENAY, N. LAUBRY (eds.), *Anthropology of Roman Housing*, Turnhout, Brepols, 2020, p. 165-192.

[2] This rationale is obviously derived from the distribution of the *lararia* in the main corpuses: G. K. BOYCE, *Corpus of the Lararia of Pompeii*, Roma, American Academy in Rome, 1937 (Memoirs of the American Academy in Rome 14); D. G. ORR, "Roman Domestic Religion: The Evidence of the Household Shrines," *ANRW* 2.16.2, Berlin-New York, 1978, p. 1557-1591; T. FRÖHLICH, *Lararien- und Fassadenbilder in den Vesuvstädten. Untersuchungen zur 'volkstümlichen' pompejanischen Malerei*, Mainz, Philipp von Zabern, 1991.

[3] Cf. inter alia: A. KRZYSZOWSKA, *Les cultes privés à Pompéi*, Wroclaw, Uniwersytetu Wrocławskiego, 2002; M. BASSANI, *Sacraria, ambienti e piccoli edifici per il culto domestico in area vesuviana*, Padova, Quasar, 2008; F. GIACOBELLO, *Larari Pompeiani: iconografia e culto dei Lari in ambito domestico*, Milano, LED, 2008; M.-O. CHARLES-LAFORGE, *La religion privée à Pompéi*, Naples, Centre Jean Bérard, 2009; W. VAN ANDRINGA, *Quotidien des dieux et des hommes: la vie religieuse dans les cités du Vésuve à l'époque romaine*, Rome, EFR, 2009 (BEFAR 337).

of domestic space. However, as a prerequisite for this method, we must accept that lifestyle determines the form in which cult activity is expressed. The position of domestic shrines, the composition of the pantheon, and the spatialisation of rituals in the house are partially determined by architectural constraints and the individual head of the household's perception of their living space. Consequently, the transformation of the domestic space is necessarily reflected in a reformulation of strategies around cult practices within the dwelling with the aim of adapting divine protection to new domestic realities.

The argument put forward in the previous article tested the effectiveness of the method by exploring the perception of the boundaries of the home based on spatial positioning intrinsic to certain deities, such as the Lares. I would now like to pursue this exploration of liminarity using a more specific case study – the house entrance – which is the focal point for religious and social issues associated with crossing the threshold.

The door of a Roman house is an obvious locus of tension around security, notably due to the risk of break-ins. In literary sources, while a door may prove impassable to a tearful lover, it offers little or no resistance to enemy incursion.[4] But in addition to this primary concern, opening the entrance makes the domestic space porous. The house is exposed to the scrutiny of the senses of the curious,[5] and to prying ears[6] and eyes.[7] Families therefore introduced a set of architectural, symbolic and religious features to protect the house and household.

Certain protective rituals associated with doors are mentioned by ancient authors in compendia of remedies and various prescriptions. This formulation was swiftly seized upon by modern

---

[4] The number of doors which are battered down in the *Metamorphoses* of Apuleius provides compelling evidence.

[5] Plut. *On Curiosity* 12.

[6] The idea that doors are porous to sound occurs in the elegies, where doors speak and reveal the household's secrets.

[7] There are a number of studies on prying eyes in connection with envy (Φθόνος and *inuidia*) and the depiction of the evil eye (Βασκανία). See notably K. DUNBABIN, "*Individa rumpantur pectora*. The iconography of Phthonos/Invidia in Graeco-Roman Art," *Jahrbuch für Antike und Christentum* 26 (1983), p. 7-37.

folklore scholars who have played a role in establishing the sacred nature of the door as a religious cult space in its own right. Thus, rituals carried out at the entrance to a house have been the focus of several studies ranging from the inventory of folklore superstitions compiled by Marbury B. Ogle,[8] to the psychosociological approach favoured by Ardle Mac Mahon,[9] or the more recent analysis of shrines at the doors of houses by Lara Anniboletti in the context of research on the wayside *compita* of Pompeii.[10] The development of thoughts in these studies only serves to highlight the growing need for openness to spatial analysis. The aim of this paper is, therefore, to consider the topography of the sacred (rituals and shrines) within the context of the construction of the domestic space in order to move beyond the idea that entering a house merely involves crossing the threshold. The evidence provided by domestic cults would appear to suggest a more complex process. By going beyond a basic folklore compilation of magico-religious rituals and other anecdotes associated with doors, we can gain a clearer understanding of the main entrance and its social role.

1. *Doors, thresholds and folklore*

Crossing the threshold of a house is a social, symbolic or magico-religious ritual in all human cultures.[11] Different traditions established around the same space – the entrance to a house – have attracted the attention of folklore scholars. Arnold Van Gennep posited a theory of thresholds in his work on rites of passage.[12] The quality of his thoughts for this era, which extended beyond

---

[8] M. B. OGLE, "The House-Door in Greek and Roman Religion and Folk-Lore," *The American Journal of Philology* 32.3 (1911), p. 251-271.

[9] A. MAC MAHON, "The Realm of Janus: Doorways in the Roman World," in G. CARR, E. V. SWIFT, J. WEEKES (eds.), *Proceedings of the Twelfth Annual Theoretical Roman Archaeology Conference, Canterbury 2002*, Oxbow Books, Oxford, 2003, p. 58-73.

[10] L. ANNIBOLETTI, "*Compita vicinalia* a Pompei: testimonianze del culto," *Vesuviana* 2 (2010), p. 77-138.

[11] M. Ségaud confirms the existence of thresholds in all human societies. They are virtually a universal concept: see M. SÉGAUD, *Anthropologie de l'espace. Habiter, fonder, distribuer, transformer*, Paris, Armand Colin, (2007) 2010, p. 130.

[12] A. VAN GENNEP, *Les rites de passage*, Paris, E. Nourry, 1909.

a mere compilation of rituals and proposed an overall system of interpretation, brought historiographic depth to the paradigm of rites of passage which shaped subsequent research. Yet it is apparent that Van Gennep's theory, aside from his three-part ritual, raises several problematic areas in his thinking around the threshold. The author devotes a chapter to the physical act of crossing the threshold which attempts to provide a spatial basis for the ritual. However, he overlooks the spatial issue in favour of a physical boundary which only symbolises a social margin. Consequently, crossing a threshold is merely an aggregative act, devoid of everyday significance, during community-focused rites of passage marking life stages. This approach features heavily in subsequent scholarship influenced in part by sources which do not mention everyday acts, but only exceptional rituals. This tendency is still apparent in current work such as the folklore inventory of household geniuses by Claude Lecouteux[13] and, more recently, Pascal Dibie's ethnology of the door, which devotes a chapter to folk beliefs.[14]

Studies focusing on Antiquity have been heavily influenced by this folklore approach especially as ancient sources explicitly connect passing through the domestic door with rites of passage punctuating family life (birth, marriage, death). Furthermore, the abundance of different anecdotes relating to the door or to rituals for warding off evil reinforces this cumulative rather than cross-sectional analysis. Georges Dumézil points out: "Dans cette vie domestique, l'imprévu se réduisait aux souillures et à leur nettoyage mystique, dont les recettes devaient être aussi variées que dans tous les folklores."[15] Since then, inquiry has been limited to explaining the nature of the taint or the potential danger. In this respect, the conclusion to Ogle's folklore-focused analysis of Greek and Roman domestic house doors is fairly symptomatic of this trend. For Ogle, tensions around the domestic entrance are associated with the spirits of the deceased who were

---

[13] C. LECOUTEUX, *La maison et ses génies*, Paris, Imago, 2000.

[14] P. DIBIE, *Ethnologie de la porte, des passages et des seuils*, Paris, Métailié, 2012.

[15] "In this domestic life, the unforeseen was reduced to taints and their mystical cleansing, for which recipes were probably as varied as in all folklores." G. DUMÉZIL, *La religion romaine archaïque*, Paris, Payot, (1974) 2000, p. 601.

originally buried under the threshold to the house. But although some sources confirm this practice in the early Hellenistic period, there is no such evidence in Roman sources, with the exception of the borderline case of infant burial outside the entrance space. In addition to problematic references to a fantasy version of "Greco-Roman" culture, this conclusion illustrates a frequent drift towards explaining dangers, taints and taboos relating to the domestic space by the presence of spirits of the deceased. In short, this takes us back to the original debate about the nature of the *Lares*, deities representing either an ancient god of place or the soul of the deceased who have been heroized. While the former explanation is favoured by current historiography on the basis of evidence advanced by Georg Wissowa,[16] the latter still has a strong afterlife.[17] This second aetiology, which has existed since Antiquity,[18] is transmitted mainly by folklore scholars and was adopted by the tentative comparativism of early anthropology to explain the existence of domestic cult of ancestor worship in the republican and imperial periods. Although the universality of ancestor worship has now been challenged and there is no evidence to prove the existence of funerary honours observed in the Roman house, the issue remains topical in historiographic debate, notably in discussions around ancestor portraits – *imagines maiorum*.[19]

In more general terms, the folklore vision has constructed an image, which is still very current, of the family and home as the special repository of traditions.[20] Thus, the persistence of this static idea refutes not only the adaptation of the family in a changing society, but also its capacity for innovation. The development of architecture is certainly one of the most significant examples.

---

[16] G. Wissowa, *Religion und Kultus der Römer*, München, C.H. Beck, 1902, p. 148-153.

[17] For a historiographical survey, see H. Flower, *The Dancing Lares and the Serpent in the Garden*, Princeton-Oxford, Princeton University Press, 2017, p. 6-17.

[18] *Ibid*.

[19] M.-O. Charles-Laforge, "*Imagines maiorum* et portraits d'ancêtres à Pompéi", *Studi della soprintendenza archeologica di Pompei* 21 (2007), p. 158-171.

[20] This image is still very much alive in current publications, including history textbooks for the French *Agrégation* examination topic 'Family and Society in the Greek World and Italy from the 5th century to the 2nd century BC'.

We therefore need to shift the focus away from the folklore debate constructed around tradition and immutability, in which gods, spirits and geniuses are placed at the centre of the dialectic. The aim here is not to compile superstitions around the door of the Roman house, but rather to understand the socio-cultural role of the door through the ritualisation of domestic interactions.

As a starting point for this thinking, the many remedies handed down by Pliny the Elder provide a cohesive corpus of perceptions of the domestic entrance. The author presents over a dozen rituals associated with the main door of the house. The different recipes are classified in terms of their effectiveness. Although the majority belong to common lore, other rituals mentioned are specifically attributed to an authoritative author. Another category features dubious or even deceptive remedies communicated by mages and presented in the book as embodying false knowledge.

Rituals performed at the door fall into these three categories but share common characteristics despite their diversity. The encyclopaedic format of Pliny's work, which attempts to compile knowledge about plant and animal products, precludes any precise detail about the ritual recorded and focuses on the anticipated effect of the gift. Although Pliny specifies that when burying the head of a snake under the threshold of the door it is necessary to visit propitious deities beforehand,[21] other recipes do not pin down the framework of the ritual to specify whether it has its origins in the practice of magic or religion. However, the intended result is always prophylactic or apotropaic. The aim is to fight evil spells and those who cast them.

With the exception of certain plants, such as scilla which offers protection against mages, according to Pythagoras, or laurel which guards the doors of pontiffs and emperors,[22] offerings made at the entrance to the house take the form of animal substances. The dominant forms are blood[23] and fat[24] or the body

---

[21] Plin. *Nat.* 29.67.
[22] *Ibid.*, 20.101; 15.127.
[23] *Ibid.*, 28.104; 30.82; 32.44.
[24] *Ibid.*, 28.135; 28.142.

part of an animal,[25] often a dog or one of its wild counterparts such as a fox, wolf or hyena.[26]

The form of this work leads to a focus on the substance offered or the intended effect, but the place in which the ritual is performed should not be overlooked. The remedies used at the entrance to the domestic space consider the door and the threshold together as a metonymic representation of the house. Performing a ritual at the main entrance of the house can be explained by the need to prevent mages and evil spells from gaining access. However, if prophylaxis does not have the desired effect, purification rituals can also be performed at the entrance. Purification carried out at the door is valid for the house as a whole.[27]

But the door is more than just a spatial synecdoche, with the part representing the whole. Returning to the example of the snake's head, placing it under the threshold after visiting the propitious deities is intended to bring good luck (*fortuna*) to the house (*domus*). In this instance the propitiatory rituals are aimed at the *domus*, understood as the household, the inhabitants of the dwelling. This reading is even more powerful for magic rituals performed against an enemy. Tainting the animal offering, for example by soaking a chameleon's intestines in monkey urine, has a negative effect and, in this instance, application to the door of a house will make the owner universally reviled.[28] In another recipe for treating fever, known to mages and challenged by Pliny, it is recommended to stir the patient's nail clippings into wax and to apply the mixture to the door of a house before sunrise.[29] The fever is then transmitted to a member of an enemy family, according to the principle of the transfer of illness to animals.[30] These various examples not only confirm the porosity of the door to evil spells, but also reveal its metonymic value as the representation of the house and household.

---

[25] *Ibid.*, 28.57; 28.117; 29.67; 30.82.

[26] Hyenas are not canines and were not considered as such in Antiquity. However, several texts present an opposition between hyenas and dogs. See T. GALOPPIN, *Animaux et pouvoir rituel dans les pratiques « magiques » du monde romain*, Doctoral thesis, Paris, EPHE, 2015, p. 483.

[27] Plin. *Nat.* 28.85.

[28] *Ibid.*, 28.117.

[29] *Ibid.*, 28.86.

[30] *Ibid.*, 30.42-43.

Pliny's remedies therefore offer an insight into a familiar concept in the psychology and anthropology of space, namely the physical extension of the individual to the boundaries of their dwelling. Philippe Bonnin identified this phenomenon in his study of practices and rituals associated with thresholds in Japan through the type of deposits found at house doors.[31] He identifies two types of deposit; on the one hand there are "symbolic deposits" related in part to the magico-religious protection of the dwelling, and on the other, "dépôts identitaires" or "dépôts de soi" representing the family and its interaction with the world. This line of thinking offers a fruitful way of interpreting the nature of permanent and temporary features at the entrance to the Roman house.

Although symbolic objects and representations are mentioned most frequently in literature, it is clear on studying Pliny's remedies that the issue of identity associated with deposits at the door had significance for Romans. The variant mentioned by Macrobius of suspending *effigies* of the family on the door[32] rather than at the wayside chapel[33] during the festival of *Compitalia*, is a very apt illustration of the phrase "deposit of self." The door acts as the interface between the family and the district. Denys of Halicarnassus mentions that the *Compitalia* offer an opportunity for *vicomagistri* to record the number of people living in each house.[34] Unlike the symbolic deposit, which is a conscious act designed to protect the domestic space, the identity deposit is generally associated with a social practice in which the value of the object is not necessarily considered.

The practice of hanging greenery at the entrance to the house is one such use of the door as a tool (whether consciously or not) for communicating with the outside world. For example, Pliny and Servius mention the custom of attaching a cypress or pine bough[35] to the door of a house in mourning to alert people to the

---

[31] P. BONNIN, "Dispositifs et rituels du seuil: une topologie sociale. Détour japonais," in P. BONNIN, J. PEZEU-MASSABUAU, *Façons d'habiter au Japon. Maisons, villes et seuils*, Paris, CNRS éditions, (2000) 2017, p. 377-410.

[32] Macr. *Sat.* 1.7.34.

[33] See Paul. ex Fest. p. 158 Müll (*pilae* and *effigies*), for *maniae* see Paul. ex Fest. p. 144 Müll.

[34] D.H. *Ant. Rom.* 4.14.

[35] Plin. *Nat.* 16.40; 16.139; Serv. *Ad Aen.* 3.64. For the role of cypress in

family's situation and the tainting of the domestic space. In more general terms, the group of fronds, wreaths and garlands decorating an entrance demonstrated to the district that the house was celebrating and the type of vegetation could indicate the nature of the celebration. While the door announced the major stages of family life, identified by Van Gennep as rites of passage, it also signalled the calendar of domestic events to all, demonstrating to the outside world that the household was celebrating a special day.

The full meaning of Ovid's phrase "every door has two faces"[36] therefore becomes apparent. The inner face sealed off the domestic space under the protection of the *Lar*, and the outer face, by contrast, exposed the family to the public sphere.[37] However, this connection with the outside world was more logically expressed on a district scale. The proximity of the neighbourhood to the door of the house was often reiterated in ancient literature. In the comedies of Plautus, the sound of a neighbour's door offers an excuse for a character to escape and for a change of scene,[38] whereas in the novel by Apuleius, neighbours are security guards ready to fight fires, outlaws or wild beasts seen at the entrance to a house in the district.[39] Lastly, looking beyond the folklore aspects of anecdotes, the various rituals mentioned define the specific role of the door as a tool for social control and a vehicle for integration into the local community.[40] Although the entrance to a house was perceived as a metonymic representation of the

---

funeral rites, see J. Scheid, "*Contraria facere*: renversements et déplacements dans les rites funéraires," *Annali dell'Istituto Universitario Orientale di Napoli* 6 (1984), p. 119.

[36] Ov. *Fast.* 1.135.

[37] *Ibid.*, 1.136.

[38] Pl. *Mil.* 2.4.410.

[39] The misadventures of Thrasyleon offer a good compilation: Apul. *Met.* 4.13.1-22.5.

[40] M. Bettini highlights the connection between the *Lar* and the neighbourhood (M. Bettini, "Entre 'émique' et 'étique'. Un exercice sur le *Lar familiaris*," in P. Payen, E. Scheid-Tissinier (eds.), *Anthropologie de l'Antiquité. Anciens objets, nouvelles approches*, Turnhout, Brepols, 2012, p. 196-198). Although the Lar represents control over the domestic space, it has no qualms about leaving the house in *Aulularia* (Pl. *Aulul.* 0.3) to present the storyline of the play and to appeal to a neighbouring uncle to resolve the plot. This connection is also expressed in the study by L. Anniboletti through the organic relationship between the worship associated with Compitalia, the door, and domestic religion (Anniboletti, Compita, p. 110-120).

family and the domestic space, crossing the threshold implied not only entry into a private space, but also integration into the heart of a community.

2. *The door and the monumentalisation of the sacred space*

The identity aspect of deposits of greenery should not cause us to overlook the fact that this ritual is essentially polysemic and that these objects were viewed in different ways by different observers. Although a garland indicated to the neighbourhood that a family was celebrating, its position on the outside edge of the dwelling also performed a function as a space marker. On the painted *lararia* of Pompeii, garlands framed the composition and reinforced the sacred nature of the scene.[41] Archaeological evidence has been found of small hooks [42] for hanging a real garland on paintings. The interplay between the figurative representation and the real object therefore helped to update the divine image during family celebrations. However, the garland in these compositions was also a space marker and circumscribed the extent of the shrine.[43] The garland served a dual purpose when it was attached to the door of a house: on the one hand, it announced that the family was celebrating; on the other, it marked the boundaries of the sacred domestic space. This natural green marker likened the entrance to the house to the entrance of a shrine.

Like Cicero, whose famous argument in *De domo sua* recalls the highly sacred nature of the domestic space,[44] other authors

---

[41] F. Gury, "Du décor éphémère au décor pérenne en Campanie. Une sacralisation de l'espace domestique?," in F. Fontana, E. Murgia (eds.), Sacrum facere. *Lo spazio del 'sacro': ambienti e gesti del rito*, Trieste, Edizioni Università di Trieste, 2016, p. 59-97.

[42] Examples include the recent discovery of the *lararia* of house V 3, 12, where one of the two hooks is still embedded in the corner of the painted garland framing the snakes. For a more detailed account, see also D. Rogers, "The Hanging Garlands of Pompeii: Mimetic Acts of Ancient Lived Religion," *Arts* 9.2, 65 (2020). (https://doi.org/10.3390/arts9020065).

[43] This function of painted garlands can also be seen in sacro-idyllic paintings, or when they are attached to torches to mark the boundaries of the primitive sanctuary. See notably: G. Sauron, *L'histoire végétalisée. Ornement et politique à Rome*, Paris, Picard, 2000, p. 32.

[44] Cic. *Dom.* 41.109.

compare the house door to a temple. Livy makes the connection on several occasions between opening domestic doors and public festivals.[45] Ovid, in the *Tristia*, compares the house of Augustus to the dwelling of Jupiter as the door is decorated with an oak wreath and laurel,[46] just like the houses of pontiffs,[47] according to Pliny. Imitation of the prince and the elite senatorial class probably democratised this representation of the door if we are to believe authors who repeatedly mention the decoration of domestic doors with laurel,[48] or archaeological examples such as house II 2, 4 in Pompeii whose door is topped with a wreath in relief framed by two painted laurel trees (Fig. 1).

FIG. 1.
Entrance to house II 2, 4. Photograph: author.

---

[45] Liv. 5.13.7; 25.12.15.
[46] Ov. *Tr.* 3.1.30-40.
[47] Plin. *Nat.* 15.127.
[48] Juv. *Sat.* 6.50; Tert. *Idol.* 15; *Cor.* 13.9.

Fig. 2.
Perspective of the house of L. Caecilius Iucundus from the entrance.
Photograph: V. Huet.

In more general terms, doors in Pompeii define the entrance to the house as the boundary of the sacred domestic space. Several dwellings demonstrate a sacred spatial arrangement through the use of views. At least a dozen houses have a sight line from the door to an edicule.[49] The view of a miniature temple recreates the illusion of a public shrine through intercolumniation, with key topographic reference points: a portico, a space set aside for worshippers, the altar which mediates between man and god, and the temple which houses the deity. The example of house VII 6, 3 is particularly significant as the view culminates in a *sa-*

---

[49] I 14.7; II 1.9; V 1.26; V 3.4; V 4.b; VI 8.3; VI 9.6; VI 13.13; VII 2.14; VII 6.3.

cellum, which reproduces the form of a podium temple with a stone pedestal at the front for the altar. In the house of L. Caecilius Iucundus (V I, 26), the sight line culminates in an exedra to the rear of the garden (Fig. 2). The south wall features a niche which was originally decorated with stucco. The area was given a monumental appearance with two series of columns: the first pair frames the room and serves as *antae*, and the second pair extends the exedra by encroaching on the garden. The latter two columns were the only ones in the peristyle to be fully coated with red paint, which in this use of perspective would certainly have drawn the eye.[50] Thus, staging the sacred through a built sight line reinforces the assimilation of the house with a shrine. The door helps to create this sacred ambiance and focuses attention at the same time on transitions: from public to private and from profane to sacred.

Yet although its layout presents the house as a shrine populated by deities, the multiplicity of niches or edicules within the dwelling disrupts the perception of a unitary sacred space. It is customary to avoid considering different domestic religious spaces as a coherent whole, but instead to relate them to the profane function of the room in which they are located. On this basis, the rituals performed at the door have given rise to the interpretation of the domestic entrance as one of these specific shrines.

Thinking of doors as shrines can be explained by the belief that Janus is present in every door of the empire.[51] Although this interpretation may have made sense to an inhabitant of Rome, it is more difficult to contextualise in time and space. While Janus may have been very popular throughout the empire, it is not known whether his role as doorkeeper was as widespread. For example, there are no mentions of the god in epigraphs or iconography in the Vesuvian cities. The fact that religious ceremonies began with his name suggests that the god was known and revered, but his presence at the door is purely conjectural. It is

---

[50] A persuasive argument for the role of colour in reinforcing the perspective effect can be found in the 3D reconstruction of the house of Caecilius Iucundus developed by Swedish universities within the framework of the Swedish Pompeii Project (http://www.pompejiprojektet.se).

[51] MAC MAHON, *The Realm of Janus*, p. 58-60.

implied on the basis of a shared Romanity. The issue with respect to domestic religion is all the more significant as it highlights the frequent recourse to aniconism, embodying gods in objects or elements, to justify the absence of archaeological evidence. Thus, the absence of images of Vesta is explained by her embodiment in the primal flame of the hearth, Neptune or nymphs by the water in fountains, and Janus by every door in a house, and the entrance door in particular. This quasi-animist formulation of domestic religion raises the question of whether research has attempted to create primitive family religion in response to tradition, as we have observed in the case of folklore, or if the lack of representations made sense to Romans for whom the door was inseparable from deities. The case of Vesta in Pompeii is certainly more convincing than that of Janus. This deity is never depicted in kitchens or in a domestic role, but she is represented as the patron of bakeries and in a painted series of the twelve gods. Does the absence of a depiction in the domestic sphere necessarily translate into her absence from the pantheon? Unfortunately, this question cannot be answered in the case of Vesta or Janus.

Lastly, even if Janus were to belong to the shared imaginary of the door, more specific study of his functional involvement is complex. However, it would be interesting, in the context of a fresh approach to the study of the domestic space, to compare the deep roots of the god of the door and his role as the deity of beginnings. These two facets of the god could provide the starting point for wider thinking on the chronotopology not just of the door, but also of the domestic space as a whole.[52]

The absence of a divine image to equate the door to a shrine is all the more complex in the case of *indigitamenta*, who by their very nature were not represented in any way.[53] Several of these

---

[52] In 2010, Philippe Bonnin was already suggesting that developments in chronotopology of cities could be applied more specifically to houses (P. BONNIN, "Pour une topologie sociale," *Communications* 87 (2010), p. 54). This would add a temporal framework to purely spatial thinking about the rooms of a house. The approach is particularly relevant to the Roman period when the variation in function of the rooms meant that they could be used for different purposes depending on the time of day, day or season.

[53] M. PERFIGLI, *Indigitamenta. Divinità funzionali e Funzionalità divina nella Religione Romana*, Pisa, Edizioni ETS, 2004. Doorway deities are not mentioned in detail, but see p. 40-46.

"specialised" gods had the role of watching over a specific part of the door. As with Janus, the absence of representations means that we cannot confirm if they were present outside Rome or if other deities took over their specific role. In reality, these gods are mainly cited by Christian writers who used them to formulate a fundamental critique of polytheism and the multitude of pointless gods.[54] Thus, Augustine reminds us that for Christians, a doorkeeper was sufficient to guard the house, whereas pagans required at least three gods to perform the same function.[55] These criticisms, whose similarities suggest that they have their origins in a shared literature, provide an insight into specific thinking around the door. Although the lists are many and varied, three deities recur systematically: Forculus for the door panels, Limentinus for the threshold, and Cardea for the hinges. These are more important components of the door than the lintel, jambs, lock or key.[56] Thus, Forculus represents the visible and most imposing part of the door. Augustine actually asked why Forculus could not be solely responsible for the door. Yet in Roman thought, Cardea embodied the main element of the door, namely the hinges which bring it to life through motion. This deity presents similarities with Carna, the goddess of hinges mentioned by Ovid.[57] Thus, the door manifests itself in the world by the movement and sound of its hinges.[58] Moreover, in consecration rituals, hinges represent both the door, and by extension, the building as a whole. Lastly, Limentinus has a tangible and

---

[54] Arnob. *Adv. Nat.* 1.28; 4.9.3; 4.11.1; August. *C.D.* 4.8; 6.7; Cypr. *Idol.*, 4; Tert. *Idol.* 15; *Cor.* 13.9; *Nat.* 2.15; *Scorpiace* 10.

[55] August. *C.D.* 4.8.

[56] L. Anniboletti lists the many specific gods which guard the door (ANNIBOLETTI, Compita, p. 117-118).

[57] Ov. *Fast.* 6.101-182. M. Perfigli makes a distinction between Cardea and Carna: the former belongs to the *ianitores* group, and the latter to the deities of infancy (PERFIGLI, *Indigitamenta*, p. 41).

[58] The sound of the door seems to be a key aspect which merits in-depth study. Texts mention the screech of doors and the sound of hinges in the context of the urban soundscape. There is also a contrast between doors which talk and doors which are dumb. In certain elegies, the door comes to life and chatters about domestic life, or by contrast, remains frustratingly silent in the presence of a tearful lover. In rituals, the worship of Tacita Muta at the door or the anointing of hinges (doubtless to stop them creaking) form part of thinking around doors. Lastly, one could consider sound effects at the threshold (birds greeting visitors, *tintinnabula* or the doorkeeper's voice).

fundamental role – to guard the threshold which is the boundary between the interior and the exterior, between the domestic and the undomesticated.

The presentation of the threshold as the boundary of the domestic space is particularly apparent during major family celebrations. The most important example, mentioned by Augustine and cited in the writings of Varro, refers to the protection of the house following a birth.[59] To ward off attacks by Silvanus, who could torment the mother or newborn infant, three men would strike the threshold with an axe, pestle, and broom, representing the deities Intercidona, Pilumnus and Deverra respectively.[60] Once again, the entrance to the house, with its liminal and metonymic characteristics, expresses tensions relating to the household. However, in this instance, the boundary was not marked by the threshold and its guardian Limentinus. It was embodied by the external frontier represented by Silvanus. The liminal nature of the god offers a deeper insight into the often restricted vision of the threshold and the act of crossing it. While the threshold does indeed mark the visual boundary of the space, this raises the question of whether the dividing line between inside and outside can be reduced to a simple piece of stone from a social point of view.

In this respect, the example of Silvanus is thought-provoking. Surveyors report that each estate had three Silvani; the first, known as *domesticus*, was in close proximity, the second, *agrestis*, was located on the fringes and the third, *orientalis*, was at the outer periphery.[61] This spatial reading of the deity reveals an alternative reading of the boundary which is not reduced to a simple line, to a duality between the domestic and the uncivilised. The three Silvani reflect different degrees of boundary and give it mental depth, without any specific connection with territorial marking. In short, they represent the owner's perception of their space, from near to distant and from the known to the unknown.[62]

---

[59] August. *C.D.* 6.9.

[60] D. Briquel, "Le pilon de Pilumnus, la hache d'Intercidona, le balai de Deverra," *Latomus* 42.2 (1983), p. 265-276.

[61] *Ex libris Dolabellae*, 13-19. ("*Ex libris dolabellae*", in *Texte und Zeichnungen*, Berlin-Boston, De Gruyter, 2018, p. 302-304).

[62] This fluid perception of the boundary can be compared to the significant example of the Gurunsi people in Upper Volta who view their environment as

3. *The topography of the sacred and the depth of the threshold*

As we have seen, anecdotal folklore has reduced crossing the threshold to a ritualised act of stepping over the entrance stone to mark admission to the family community in a metaphorical way. Yet this specific vision of crossing the threshold is stripped of any connection with everyday experience. It overlooks the multitude of entrances into the house and exits from it over the course of a day and the different ways in which these are carried out depending on the family member or guest. Is the transition between the street and the house restricted to this inside/outside duality represented by the threshold, or is there a gradual transition from the public to the private sphere? In short, how do we analyse the depth of the boundary?

Several passages mention superstitions associated with crossing a threshold, such as avoiding stumbling, and entering with one's right foot first.[63] These anecdotes are evidence of concrete thinking about boundaries. However, from a social point of view, integration into the house was undoubtedly a far more complex process.[64] An individual's relationship to Roman society was not altered simply by passing through the entrance door. The gradual transition was intended to redefine the status of the person arriving in relation to the community they were entering. As they shifted from citizen, magistrate or member of an association, they could resume the role of *paterfamilias*, for example, on entering the house, and this called for a change in their social interactions.[65]

In order to experience this depth of threshold, we must consider a site for study that is contextualised in time and space. Pompeii is the most fruitful example for this thinking. However,

---

a series of spaces moving from the known to the unknown. The village is *sago* (the bush); cultivated land outside the village is *gabio* (open bushland); the bush further afield is *goa*; dangerous bushland is *oalon gaoe*; and *bago* is distant, unfamiliar bushland (SÉGAUD, *Anthropologie*, p. 128).

[63] Plut. *Quest. Rom.* 29; Petr. *Sat.* 30.

[64] J. BERRY, "Boundaries and control in the Roman house," *Journal of Roman Archaeology* 29 (2016), p. 125-141.

[65] Even a slave, whose status could be considered absolute, was perceived differently for example in the house, in work spaces within the ambit of the head of the family, and outside the home.

specific data relating to the domestic layout is not applicable to all Roman cultures and only the social process aspect can be transposed outside the Pompeiian context.

The *Casa dei Dioscuri* (VI 9, 6-7) is a stimulating case study for beginning to think about the depth of the boundary (Fig. 3). Although features which were temporary or made from perishable materials have disappeared, the distribution of paintings and shrines in the house allows us to evaluate specific thinking about space.

The entrance to the house (VI 9, 6) was monumentalised by two pillars with square capitals framing the main double-leaf door (Fig. 4). It was topped by an imposing cornice. On the south pillar, a painting of Mercury and Fortuna helped to integrate the family into local religious activities.[66] The boundary of the domestic space was marked at a physical level by a white marble

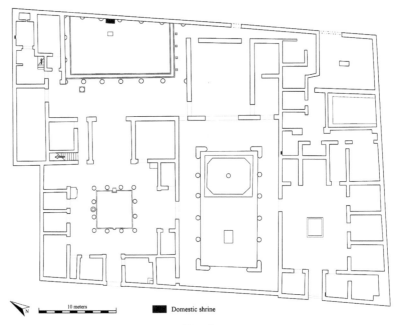

Fig. 3.
Plan of Casa dei Dioscuri (after L. Richardson Jr, drawing: author).

[66] Frölich, *Lararien- und Fassadenbilder*, p. 483.

Fig. 4.
Entrance to the Casa dei Dioscuri (Licence creative commons).

threshold slightly raised above the street. This change in level forced the person arriving to lift their foot to cross the threshold. This action was the first indicator of a change of space.

Arrival in the entrance corridor was not the end of the process of integrating the domestic space. In fact, despite the cleverly constructed sight line, a second door at the end of the entrance hall sealed off the view.[67] Creating this corridor as a sealed space invites questions about the boundary space in the dwelling. This corridor was a checking and transition zone, as is evidenced by the door in the south wall leading to the porter's lodge. In addition to a human check, the arrival was subjected to divine surveillance. On either side of the corridor was a painted panel in the centre of the wall depicting a Dioscorus and his horse. These two guards placed in the middle of the corridor, where they were not concealed when the doors were open, helped to theatricalise the entrance to the house. Attention has been paid to the gaze

---

[67] E. Proudfoot, "Secondary Doors in Entranceways at Pompeii: Reconsidering Access and the 'View from the Street'," in Carr et al., *Twelfth Annual Theoretical Roman Archaeology Conference*, 2013, p. 91-115.

of the twin gods. Their wide-open, almost staring eyes give the impression that they are following the visitor (Fig. 5). This sentinel role was reinforced when the secondary doors were open and the incomer could see the view. In fact, the sight line which begins with the Dioscorus paintings and ends with the edicule is not dissimilar to the layout of the temple in the forum. On the *lararium* of L. Caecilius Iucundus, access to the temple, just like in the Capitol of Pompeii,[68] was framed by statues of Dioscorus. Thus, in the context of the corridor, they amplify the sacred staging, while watching the person who is passing through.

Once permission to enter had been granted, and the secondary doors had been opened, the incomer entered the *atrium*, whose

Fig. 5.
Detail of the painting of a Dioscurus (after *PPM*, VI, p. 879).

[68] V. Huet, "Le laraire de L. Caecilius Iucundus: un relief hors norme?", *Studi della soprintendenza archeologica di Pompei* 21 (2007), p. 144. Van Andringa, *Le quotidien des dieux et des hommes*, p. 40-43 and p. 177-179.

walls were adorned with a dozen panels depicting gods.[69] Arriving in the *compluuium deorum Penatium*, to quote Suetonius,[70] implicitly suggests that integration into the domestic space goes hand in glove with entry into the family shrine. The visitor is warned that their time in the dwelling will be spent under the gaze of the gods.

This house therefore offers an interesting perspective on the controlled progression of the incomer. The cohesive iconographic scheme between the entrance corridor and the *atrium* suggests that the domestic space begins at the boundary of the threshold. However, the integration of the individual into this space is not automatic as soon as they step through the main door. The social process is gradual and subjects the incomer to a succession of thresholds and multiple checks (divine, human and physical).

A second example, which has architectural similarities with the *Casa dei Dioscuri*, offers scope for further thinking about the depth of the boundary. The entrance to the house of L. Caecilius Iucundus (V 1, 26) was framed by two shops, both of which had a door leading to the *atrium* (Fig. 6).[71] The main two-leaf door was monumentalised with two pillars topped by square capitals and an imposing cornice crowned the entire structure. The pillars were covered with municipal *tituli picti*, which situated the façade outside the domestic space and simultaneously integrated the owner into civic life. The white limestone threshold was raised above those of the adjoining shops. An incomer therefore had to step up to the threshold, thus marking a change of space. In this house, the corridor also operated as a closed reception area, sealed by secondary doors.[72] The space was divided into two parts:

---

[69] L. RICHARDSON JR., *The casa dei Dioscuri and its Painters*, Roma, American Academy, 1955 (Memoirs of the American Academy in Rome 23).

[70] Suet. *Aug.* 2.92.

[71] These secondary doors offered additional means of accessing the house. They create a hierarchy of spaces and also of individuals through the access points designated for them. Within the scope of this study, I have chosen to focus on the scenography of the main door, reserved primarily for free family members and their guests. However, these secondary doors would merit specific attention to define the arrangements associated with using them.

[72] PROUDFOOT, *Secondary Doors*, p. 91-115.

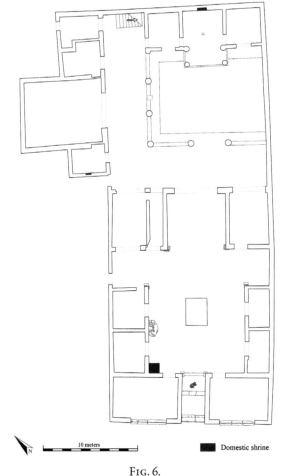

Fig. 6.
Plan of house of L. Caecilius Iucundus
(after E. Pinto Guillaume, The Swedish Pompeii Project, drawing: author).

first a *cocciopesto* floor extending from the threshold to a limestone step, and then a second section of floor with a dog mosaic spanning the area from the step on the threshold to the secondary doors.

Once the visitor had crossed the first threshold, which controlled the right to enter the *atrium*, and the secondary doors had been opened for them, they could see the sacred sight line. The view, as mentioned above, culminated in an exedra with a niche in the wall, monumentalised by two red-painted columns. In the same alignment, two hermaic pillars, each topped with a bronze portrait, framed the entrance to the *tablinum*. These sculptures, or at least one of them, represented the *genius* of the *pater familias*. Thus, the entrance to the house was once again subjected to the gaze of the deities, combining on this occasion the image of the god and of the homeowner.

The visitor then continued their progress into the house by climbing the step in the centre of the corridor. The change of level naturally caused them to shift their gaze away from the view in order to focus on the placement of their foot. As they lowered their eyes, they would see the mosaic of a black dog on a white background. This depiction of a dog was one of the symbolic features placed at the entrance to the house.[73] The image was effective and polysemic. It alerted the visitor to the danger of a real dog,[74] acted as a deterrent to thieves or other arrivals with sinister motives[75] and, lastly, served as a space marker since the liminal nature of the dog marked the transition from the undomesticated world to the domestic world, from outside to inside.[76] At the end of the corridor, the incomer entered the *atrium*, where they were subject to even greater scrutiny by the gods. While they remained within the line of sight of the niche and herms, this surveillance was amplified by the edicule placed in the north-west corner of the *atrium* (Fig. 7). Generally, the special position of edicules against the wall at the entrance to the *atrium* could partly be explained by the desire to monitor the opening to the *fauces*.

Lastly, the house of L. Caecilius Iucundus offers a further illustration of the proliferation of checks on exiting the entrance corridor, and the incomer's progress under the watchful eye of the gods. But the process is reinforced by symbolic features such as an image of a dog or architectural features including negotiating a series of levels (thresholds and steps).

---

[73] Four houses in Pompeii have dog mosaics at their entrance: I 7, 1; V 1, 26; VI 8, 5; VI 14, 20. A painted depiction is also mentioned for house IX 2, 26.

[74] In the *Satyricon*, the painted dog (Petr. *Sat.* 29) serves as a warning that there is a real dog, which appears when the protagonists leave (Petr. *Sat.* 72).

[75] This is the subtext of the *caue canem* message of the mosaic in the House of the Tragic Poet (VI 8, 5).

[76] An illustration of this opposition is provided by the mosaic at the entrance to the House of the Boar (VIII 3, 8) which depicts a hunting scene pitting two dogs against a boar, a quintessential depiction of the fight between the wild and the domesticated.

Fig. 7.
View of the entrance of the house of L. Caecilius Iucundus from the *atrium*
(after H. Thorwid, The Swedish Pompeii Project).

A final example deepens our exploration of the depth of boundaries by looking at features for which there is no surviving archaeological record. A passage from the *Satyricon*, describes the protagonists entering Trimalchio's home.[77] The plot takes place in the Bay of Naples during the reign of Nero. The place and time are similar to the previous examples and it is therefore still relevant. The narrator's first comment on arriving at the house refers to the inscription at the door. It is a warning to enslaved people who do not follow the orders of the head of the family. This warning on the boundary of the domestic space is both an identity deposit extending the homeowner's authority to the boundary of his home and a space marker for a slave preparing to leave the house. The protagonists enter under the gaze of a slave whose duty is to guard the door (*ostiarius*). When they cross the threshold, the visitors are greeted by a magpie in a cage attached

[77] Petr. *Sat*. 28-29.

to the lintel. The bird's call is associated with a transition between spaces. However, the narrator's focus on the bird distracts him. He is brought back into line by a *trompe-l'œil* dog painted on the wall. The layout is actually similar to the house of L. Caecilius Iucundus, where the architecture compels the person arriving to look at the dog positioned in the transitional space. Once the narrator has crossed the threshold, he looks at a mural portraying the life of Trimalchio (an identity deposit). Lastly, when he turns away from the painting, he mentions the household shrine and the statuettes in it. Once again, the gods play a role in the process of integration into a house. The guests continue to move forward into the domestic space until they reach the *triclinium*. This description, which focuses exclusively on contextual details, nevertheless allows us to observe the number of control markers. While these features reinforce the surveillance of the domestic space, they also encourage the person arriving to focus on what they are doing. Symbolic and identity-related features, as well as divine, human and animal guards all play a role in extending the depth of the boundary via a series of thresholds.

Conclusion

The gradual reduction in the number of threshold spaces and the trend towards the de-ritualisation of social interactions goes some way towards explaining the revival of folklore approaches in contemporary research. In this dynamic, the rite of passage is considered in terms of community density, often taking a primitivist approach, but its topographic roots are limited to a specific space. Passing through is no longer a process but a stage. This limited influence of ritual is translated into a reduction in the boundary to be crossed. The threshold of a house is considered in terms of the stone which separates the interior from the exterior, and the door as its visual expression.

The aim of the approach which we have attempted to develop by cross-referencing spatial data intrinsic to domestic cults with concepts of the archaeology of space, is to rethink the depth of the threshold and the Roman perception of the domestic entrance. In conclusion, it is possible to present a new assessment of the domestic boundary. Symbolic and identity deposits which proliferated at house doors mean that we can be more specific about their functions. In addition to its role as sealing the house, the door is associated with the family's social interactions. It is a display area for communicating with the neighbourhood and plays a role in making the domestic space sacred. The threshold is more than just the physical presence of the entrance stone and defines a transitional space, in which an incomer is gradually integrated into the domestic space and the family community.

The examples from Pompeii illustrate this succession of levels of threshold and allow us to observe the depth of the boundary. However, the case studies presented are restricted to *atrium* houses which demonstrate clearly-staged transitional spaces. Joanne Berry has already highlighted the various boundaries and control mechanisms in this type of house.[78] Further investigation would involve extending this approach to a wide variety of dwellings. Although more modest houses certainly did not boast such cohesively organised arrangements for welcoming visitors, other houses, without an *atrium*, were certainly designed in such a way as to control people arriving in the domestic space. It would be interesting to explore the reception arrangements in houses where the entrance opened onto the peristyle. This significant architectural change reflects not just a different view of the domestic space but, more particularly, of a way of living. Although doors retained similar functions to those observed above, mechanisms for controlling the space undoubtedly changed to adapt to the new organisation of the home.

---

[78] J. BERRY, *Boundaries and control*, p. 125-141.

ANNA-KATHARINA RIEGER

FROM ROUTINES TO RITUALS IN POMPEIAN HOUSES – HOW LAYOUT AND IMAGE-OBJECTS OF HOUSEHOLD SHRINES SHAPE RELIGIOUS KNOWLEDGE

1. *Household religion, religious practices, and routines*

The worship of deities "at home" can be studied particularly well in Pompeii and Herculaneum as these cities preserve many images, objects, and spatial contexts in houses, dwellings, villas and workshops reflecting religious practices. On the day of the eruption in 79 CE, altars in front of images of the gods, decorated with real or painted garlands, were filled with grain seeds and pieces of chicken, carbonised in the sacrificial process. These are remains of a (daily) routine of communicating with the *Lares* and other deities, asking them for protection and support in personal, family-related, and economic regards. The evidence informs us about the socio-religious environment of households in which people lived with the gods. "At home" in *domus*, *tabernae*, or *villae*, as the core activity areas of the many Pompeians, religion was embedded in and part of daily routines of individuals from childhood on, where dynamic processes of social bonding and habitualisation, production and transmission of (religious) knowledge took place.[1] In the socio-spatial frame of dwellings and houses,

---

[1] Note: If *sacraria* have images, they are quoted according to the catalogue by T. Fröhlich, *Lararien- und Fassadenbilder in den Vesuvstädten: Untersuchungen zur ‚volkstümlichen' pompejanischen Malerei*, Mainz, Philipp von Zabern, 1991 (Mitteilungen des Deutschen Archäologischen Instituts, Römische Abteilung, Ergänzungsheft 32) with "L*". I thank the Faculty of Humanities of the University of Graz, that offered the proof-reading service for this article. The International Graduate School "Resonant Self-World-Relations in Ancient and Modern Socio-Religious Practices" – a cooperation of the University of Graz

people inscribed and embodied many of their routines, when their activities began, took place or ended, observed by the gods over the day.[2] Material remains in Pompeian houses mirror habitual actions, and routinized practices, from which we can infer their potential to engage in ritualised religious actions and to establish knowledge.[3]

1.1. How Pompeians connected to the deities

To archaeologically analyse household religion as a core religious practice in Pompeian society, we need to look for the entanglements of image-objects and human agents in the living areas that reflect communication with the gods. Religious acts could take

---

and the Max Weber Centre for Advanced Cultural and Social Studies, University of Erfurt, with its spokesperson Wolfgang Spickermann and Jörg Rüpke, gave opportunity and time to do the research on religion in Pompeii.

M. B. McGuire, "Embodied Practices: Negotiation and Resistance," in N. T. Ammerman (ed.), *Everyday Religion: Observing Modern Religious Lives*, Oxford-New York, Oxford University Press, 2007, p. 192 claims that habitual and routinised embodied practices shape children's experience of "their material and spiritual worlds thus sacralizing and making those religious worlds real, tangible, and accessible", generating religious knowledge.

[2] Daily-life practices gained attention in socio-cultural studies by the application of phenomenological approaches of M. Merleau-Ponty, *Phénoménologie de la perception*, Paris, Gallimard 1945 (Bibliothèque des idées) and Bourdieu's praxeological approaches to human action; P. Bourdieu, *Le sens pratique*, Paris, Éditions de Minuit, 1980 (Le sens commun); P. Bourdieu, *Esquisse d'une théorie de la pratique. Précédé de Trois études d'ethnologie kabyle*, Genève, Librairie Droz, 1972 (Travaux de Sciences Sociales). On "dwelling" in comparison to "household" and the implications for the entanglement of material objects and human agents see T. Ingold, *The perception of the environment: Essays on livelihood, dwelling and skill*, London, Routledge, 2000; see A. Dardenay, "From Insula to Dwelling: Architectural Transformations and Principles of Decor in Insula V at Herculaneum," in A. Haug, M. T. Lauritsen (eds.), *Principles of Decoration in the Roman World*, Berlin, De Gruyter, 2021, p. 107-122 for an application on an *insula* in Herculaneum.

[3] See above n. 1, and D. Morgan, *The embodied eye: Religious visual culture and the social life of feeling*, Berkeley, University of California Press, 2012; on ancient embodied religious practices E.-J. Graham, *Reassembling Roman Religion*, London, Routledge, 2020; A.-K. Rieger, "The Spectrum of Religiousness, or What Makes an Object Religious. Habits, Patterned Evidence and Religious Meanings of Image-Objects in Pompeii," *ARYS. Antigüedad: Religiones y Sociedades* 18 (2020), p. 51-94, esp. p. 76 on habits as "repeated, embodied, learned, and taught in the frame of a social habitus of how and when to communicate with the gods" and as "seeds for ritualized practices" in religious communication that are "discursively negotiated evaluations of common imagery".

place almost anywhere, employing mundane objects by sacralising the setting – i.e. marked-off spaces, marked-off persons by dress, behaviour or attributes, or marking time by sound, and area/air by smell. Whether or not we can speak of a sacralised place in a house depends on the elements such as recognisable deities, fixed or portable, objects such as altars or incense burners, or archaeological remains of sacrificial goods. Yet, many markers are indiscernible for us: whether a lamp in a niche was a religious object in the moment of its excavation, whether a niche temporarily contained statuettes of deities, or seeds were an offering.[4] There are many greyscales between sacred and non-sacred.[5] However, in need of continuous support by the deities, Pompeians imagined permanent installations and iconographies to be suitable. To better understand the material evidence of the Pompeian "gods at home", we need to examine how patterned assemblages and (spatial) arrangements of image-objects, such as a niche in the wall

---

[4] See M.-O. LAFORGE, *La religion privée à Pompéi*, Naples, Centre Jean Bérard, 2009 (Études / Centre Jean Bérard 7), p. 26-31 on the problem of identification. Numbers of shrines, statuettes or paintings (e.g. H. I. FLOWER, *The Dancing Lares and the Serpent in the Garden: Religion at the Roman Street Corner*, Princeton, Princeton University Press, 2017, p. 53 with n. 3) are misleading, since niches could be temporarily used for religious purposes. For my argument I do not differentiate forms and terminology (on differentiation, see Bassani this volume, p. 176-178), but speak of *sacraria* with the only distinction of with or without mobile items (i.e. painting) allowing for mobile parts to be stored away (see A. VAN OYEN, *The socio-economics of Roman storage: Agriculture, trade, and family*, Cambridge, Cambridge University Press, 2020, p. 113). On forms see J. R. BRANDT, "Sacra privata in the Roman domus Private or Public? A Study of Household Shrines in an Architectural Context at Pompeii and Ostia," *Acta ad archaeologiam et artium historiam pertinentia* 23 (2017), p. 57-117. My basic understanding of ancient material religion bases on the Lived Ancient Religion paradigm, see J. ALBRECHT, C. DEGELMANN, V. GASPARINI, R. GORDON, M. PATZELT, G. PETRIDOU, R. RAJA, A.-K. RIEGER, J. RÜPKE, B. SIPPEL, E. R. URCIUOLI, L. WEISS, "Religion in the making: The Lived Ancient Religion approach," *Religion* 48 (2018), p. 568-593; see also M. BASSANI, F. GHEDINI (eds.), Religionem significare. *Aspetti storico-religiosi, strutturali, iconografici e materiali di Sacra Privata: Atti dell'Incontro di Studi, Padova, 8-9 giugno 2009*, Roma, Quasar, 2011 (Antenor quaderni 19).

[5] See DARDENAY, this volume, p. 209-237. On the situational meaning of objects R. RAJA, L. WEISS, "The Significance of Objects: Considerations on Agency and Context," *Religion in the Roman Empire* 2 (2016), p. 297-306; esp. on niches in house contexts L. WEISS, "The consumption of religion in Roman Karanis," *Religion in the Roman Empire* 1 (2015), p. 71-94; RIEGER, *Spectrum of religiousness*, p. 76 on image-objects that receive their "'degree of religiousness'" only through the habitual knowledge and social agreement".

of a courtyard showing the stereotyped figure of a deity framed by garlands, reveal religious meanings people ascribed to them.[6]

To tackle the problem of religious materials and rituals, we need to open our perspective methodologically and take a look at patterned motifs, i.e. iconographies, arrangements of objects and their position in the spatial fabric of dwellings, workshops and houses to carve out rituals in the archaeological material.[7] A past routinized practice was, for example, to decorate a niche and put a statuette there on specific days (implying the gesture of raising the head in front of the image). Routines and rituals rested both on repetition, as did patterned arrangements. Whereas routines can be defined as a standard procedure, rituals require an additional symbolic investment. Routines are conceived of as sociomaterial practices in the houses over the time of the day, season(s), and year(s) that involve various constellations of participants.[8]

---

[6] Individuals of a household have varying roles apart from being a family member: worker, female, mother, neighbour, market vendor, defined by gender, age, sex, profession, legal status, etc. linked by co-sanguinal, legal, social, and economic bonds. They form changing groups in household activities, and are highly structured through individual shares of knowledge about its material and human agents, see VAN OYEN, *Storage*, esp. p. 93-96 approaching the archaeology of household organisation based on objectual knowledge beyond social and gendered categories; K. COOPER, "Closely Watched Households: Visibility, Exposure and Private Power in the Roman *Domus*," *Past & Present* 197 (2007), p. 3-33. J. BODEL, "Cicero's Minerva, Penates, and the mother of the Lares: an outline of Roman domestic religion," in J. P. BODEL, S. M. OLYAN (eds.), *Household and family religion in antiquity*, Malden, MA, Wiley Blackwell, 2008, p. 265 assumes different *familiae* in one household (i.e. nested households), that allow for a fluid social grouping of members (cf. N. ANDERSON, "Finding the Space between Spatial Boundaries and Social Dynamics: The Archaeology of Nested Households," in K. S. BARILE, J. C. BRANDON (eds.), *Household Chores and Household Choices: Theorizing the Domestic Sphere in Historical Archaeology*, Tuscaloosa, The University of Alabama Press, 2004, p. 109-120). On time as structuring the functions of (social) space, see J.-A. DICKMANN, "Space and Social Relations in the Roman West," in B. RAWSON (ed.), *A companion to families in the Greek and Roman worlds*, Malden, MA, Wiley-Blackwell, 2011, p. 65. On social distinction in the use of *sacraria*, see M. LIPKA, "Notes on Pompeian Domestic Cults," *Numen* 53 (2006), p. 344; LAFORGE, *Religion privée*, p. 95-217, esp. p. 118-121.

[7] RIEGER, *Spectrum of religiousness*, p. 74-78 on "patterned arrangements" as reflections of "habitual practices and routinized behavior".

[8] In contrast to routine, habit is a rather unconsciously pursued series of regular actions. The more formalised a practice is, the more it becomes a ritual. For a definition of rituals in Graeco-Roman contexts, see E. KYRIAKIDIS, "Archaeologies of Ritual," in E. KYRIAKIDIS (ed.), *The Archaeology of Ritual*, Los Angeles, Cotsen Institute of Archaeology University of California Los Angeles,

Although they could turn into rituals by way of symbolic investment and formalisation, they were primarily repeated practices involving counterintuitive addressees.

I depart from the assumption that repeated embodied practices (routines as the basis of rituals) in spaces and with image-objects, installations, commodities and resources allow to negotiate the socio-material connectedness to and in the household, and of human agents to their – divine – environment. Based on a notion of religion as an arena of social negotiation and a communicational and reciprocal practice, I comprehend religious practices as social practices involving both human and divine agents bound in space and time, including the material environment.[9] Acknowledging the multimodality of interaction and communication in the socio-spatial context of a house(hold),[10] the following questions arise: How may the image-objects, paraphernalia, and installations for the deities have affected people, where was the imagery located in the houses, how did people engage with them, and what does this tell us about the embeddedness of the gods in daily practices

---

2007 (Cotsen advanced seminars 3), p. 289-308 relating ritual to gradually differentiated institutionalised practice; J. ELSNER, "Material Culture and Ritual: State of the Question," in B. D. WESCOAT (ed.), *Architecture of the Sacred: Space, Ritual, and Experience from Classical Greece to Byzantium*, Cambridge, Cambridge University Press, 2012, p. 1-26 clarifies the relation of ritual to material culture. For the influential (structuralist) theories of ritual and ritualisation in anthropology, see C. M. BELL, *Ritual theory, ritual practice*, Oxford, Oxford University Press, 1992 and R. A. RAPPAPORT, *Ritual and religion in the making of humanity*, Cambridge, Cambridge University Press, 1999; L. FOGELIN, "The archaeology of religious ritual," *Annual review of anthropology* 36 (2007), p. 55-71, with a practice-oriented approach. B. STOLLBERG-RILINGER, *Rituale*, Frankfurt am Main, Campus Verlag, 2013 (Historische Einführungen 16), p. 9 has the criteria of "Standardisierung der äußeren Form, Wiederholung, Aufführungscharakter, Performativität und Symbolizität ... und eine elementare sozial strukturbildende Wirkung".

[9] Cf. J. RÜPKE, "Religious agency, identity, and communication: reflections on history and theory of religion," *Religion* 45 (2015), p. 344-366; on fluid religious groupings see P. LICHTERMANN, R. RAJA, A.-K. RIEGER, J. RÜPKE, "Grouping together in lived ancient religion: Individual interacting and the formation of groups," *Religion and Society* 3 (2017), p. 3-10.

[10] On multimodal relations of communication L. ELLESTRÖM, "A medium-centered model of communication," *Semiotica* 224 (2018), p. 269-293 and for archaeology, recently J. BRACKER (ed.), *Homo pictor: Image Studies and Archaeology in Dialogue*, Heidelberg, Propylaeum, 2020 (Freiburger Studien zur Archäologie und visuellen Kultur 2).

and routines? Foregrounding image-objects of deities on walls, statuettes in niches or shelves, painted offerings on altars, framing garlands, etc., and spatial relations rather than human agents, unravels the potentials of image-objects for enabling religious communication. To unpack the affordances and effectiveness of imagery, I use the heuristic tools of "image-act" and "viewing-act", whereas analysing the spatial relations, embracing visibility and embeddedness in practices and routines of the household and of the capacities of social bonding are based on practice-theoretical approaches. This offers insights into the pictorial-spatial strategies and habitualisation pertaining to practices that, in total, constitute "household religion". For gods and goddesses are not only in the houses, they are enmeshed in the household, construct it, and are "at home" like and with their human counterparts.

1.2. *Lares* and other deities in the Pompeian dwellings: marking places and sharing spaces

Lares, whose iconography was fully-fledged around the mid-first cent. BCE, were the most typical of Roman domestic gods.[11] It is common knowledge that the *Lares* protected supplies, food, tools, instruments, and containers, and helped to keep the household and/or workshop running.[12] They were locative and genealogical deities of the *familia*. Pompeians also favoured other deities such as Minerva, Mercury or Venus that received veneration in

---

[11] See BASSANI, this volume, p. 171-176. On statuettes of *Lares* as an invention of late Republican times, see C. HALLETT, "'Corinthian Bronzes': Miniature Masterpieces—Flagrant Forgeries," in J. HOPKINS and S. MCGILL (ed.), *Beyond Deceit: Valuing Forgery in Ancient Rome*, Oxford, forthcoming, 2023. However, we must assume their earlier presence in different material and shape (puppets, appliques, etc.); on terminology and background, F. GIACOBELLO, *Larari pompeiani: Iconografia e culto dei Lari in ambito domestico*, Milano, LED, 2008; J. RÜPKE, *Pantheon. A new history of Roman religion*, Princeton, NJ, Princeton University Press, 2018, p. 253-254 (not entirely convincing on the interchangeability of *Lares* and *penates*); based on literary sources is FLOWER, *Dancing Lares*.

[12] P. W. FOSS, "Watchful Lares: Roman Household Organisation and the Rituals of Cooking and Dining," in R. LAURENCE, A. WALLACE-HADRILL (eds.), *Domestic space in the Roman world: Pompeii and beyond*, Portsmouth, RI, Journal of Roman Archaeology, 1997 (Supplementary series 22), p. 197-218 and P. KASTENMEIER, *I luoghi del lavoro domestico nella casa pompeiana*, Roma, L'Erma di Bretschneider, 2007 (Studi della Soprintendenza Archeologica di Pompei 23), p. 76 on *sacraria* at service facilities.

the dwellings in the form of imagery, niches, altars, and *aediculae*. We can grasp such a materialised form of household religion in Pompeii in the first cent. CE. Enmeshed in the economic, social and material world of the household's production and consumption, the deities marked places in the houses, but how did they connect to other agents, and how did religious communication work at home? To this end, we have to scrutinise what areas gods and humans shared in a dwelling, and what the layout, design and location tells us about the routines in which they were embedded. Based on pivotal studies on household religion and their remains in urban dwellings,[13] this approach touches upon debates of lived material religion and embodiment as well as socio-spatial and -material organisation of the Roman house.[14] On the one hand, meth-

---

[13] G. K. BOYCE, *Corpus of the lararia of Pompeii*, Rome, American Academy, 1937 (Memoirs of the American Academy in Rome 14); FRÖHLICH, *Lararien- und Fassadenbilder*; A. KAUFMANN-HEINIMANN, *Götter und Lararien aus Augusta Raurica: Herstellung, Fundzusammenhänge und sakrale Funktion figürlicher Bronzen in einer römischen Stadt*, Augst, Römermuseum Augst, 1998 (Forschungen in Augst); GIACOBELLO, *Larari*; W. VAN ANDRINGA, *Quotidien des dieux et des hommes: la vie religieuse dans les cités du Vésuve à l'époque romaine*. Rome, École Française de Rome, 2009 (BEFAR 337), p. 217-269; L. ANNIBOLETTI, "Compita vicinalia a Pompei: testimonianze del culto," *Vesuviana* 2 (2010), p. 77-138; L. ANNIBOLETTI, "Testimonianze preromane del culto domestico a Pompei: i compita vicinalia sulla facciata di abitazioni," *FastiOnLine documents & research* (2007); M. BASSANI, *Sacraria: Ambienti e piccoli edifici per il culto domestico in area vesuviana*, Roma, Quasar, 2008 (Antenor quaderni 9); M.-O. CHARLES-LAFORGE, "Les cultes privés chez les Romains (IIIe s. avant – IIIe s. après J.-C.)," *Pallas* 111 (2019), p. 171-197 with a broad temporal and topographical span; M. MAUGER, "Sanctuaires et marges de l'habitat: perception et délimitation de l'espace domestique," in A. DARDENAY, N. LAUBRY (eds.), *Anthropology of Roman housing*, Turnhout, Brepols, 2020 (Antiquité et sciences humaines 5), p. 165-192; J. R. CLARKE, *Art in the lives of ordinary Romans: Visual representation and non-elite viewers in Italy, 100 B.C.-A.D. 315*, Berkeley, University of California Press, 2003, p. 75-81. See this volume, BASSANI, p. 182-184, SFAMENI, p. 121-126, AMOROSO, p. 63-73 for non-Pompeian evidence. The most recent contributions to this topic in the *Open Arts Journal* 10 (2021) by A. HAUG, P.-A. KREUZ, "The diversity of Pompeii's domestic cult activity," p. 13-32 on chronological changes and heterogenity of the cult of the *Lares* and by E.-J. GRAHAM, "At home with the Lares: Lived religion rematerialised at Pompeii," p. 33-50 on the motif of *Lares* and serpents in houses and the streets as materialised and localised religious knowledge could not be considered for my argument.

[14] P. ZANKER, *Pompeji: Stadtbild und Wohngeschmack*, Mainz, Philipp von Zabern, 1995 (Kulturgeschichte der antiken Welt); A. WALLACE-HADRILL, *Houses and society in Pompeii and Herculaneum*, Princeton, Princeton University Press, 1994, differentiated by J.-A. DICKMANN, *Domus frequentata: Anspruchsvolles Wohnen im pompejanischen Stadthaus*, München, Pfeil, 1999 (Studien

odological limits are given by the relation of material object, find spot and function, that cannot only be interpreted space-bound, but also as mobile, multifunctional and changing relation.[15] On the other hand, short-term temporal aspects of activities (not only) in a Pompeian dwelling – when making food, processing goods, repairing, storing, idling, weaving, cleaning, washing, eating, sleeping, heating, etc. – make spaces themselves dynamic and flexible. The activity defined the human agents involved, so that people would form different groups according to the activity. Moreover, the long-term changes of property relations and architectural connections in the *insulae* are difficult to determine.[16] This approach foregrounding dynamic space and the role of image-objects shifts away from a too static and hierarchically fixed view on roles of actors and opens the perspective of shared practices.[17]

Another methodological challenge of this perspective on sociomaterial routines and practices is the oscillating relation of appropriateness (*decor*) and meaningfulness of image-objects in the Roman living space, of aesthetic effects, mimetic illusions and symbolic meanings of images, which has been the subject of recent

---

zur antiken Stadt 4); DICKMANN, *Space and Social Relations*; A. HAUG, *Decor-Räume in pompejanischen Stadthäusern*, Berlin-Boston, De Gruyter, 2020 (Decor 1); K. LORENZ, *Bilder machen Räume: Mythenbilder in pompeianischen Häusern*, Berlin-Boston, De Gruyter, 2008 (Image & context 5); see recently the contributions to A. DARDENAY, N. LAUBRY, *Anthropology of Roman housing*, 2020 and the introduction to this volume by BRICAULT, DARDENAY, p. 7-18.

[15] Cf. the seminal work of P. M. ALLISON, *Pompeian households: An analysis of the material culture*, Los Angeles, Cotsen Institute of Archaeology, University of California, 2004 (Monograph 42) and J. BERRY, "Household artefacts: Towards a re-interpretation of Roman domestic space," in R. LAURENCE, A. WALLACE-HADRILL, *Domestic space in the Roman world*, 1997, p. 183-195 continued, e.g. in B. SIGGES, Vita cognita. *Die Ausstattung pompejanischer Wohnhäuser mit Gefäßen und Geräten*, Dissertation, Universität Köln, 2002; see also VAN OYEN, *Storage*, p. 112-115 with n. 165.

[16] See e.g. the Casa del Cenacolo V.2.h below, p. 296-298.

[17] See VAN OYEN, *Storage*, 94 on multifunctional, temporally structured spaces in houses. The hierarchical order of a Roman *familia* is not doubted here (cf. M.-O. CHARLES-LAFORGE, "*Pater familias* et culte domestique à Rome du IIIe s. av. au IIIe s. n. è.," in C. HUSQUIN, C. LANDREA (eds.), *Religion et pouvoir dans le monde romain de 218 avant J.-C. à 250 ap. J.-C.*, Paris, Ellipses, 2020, p. 159-172). However, in daily life, roles and responsibilites changed according to people's activity in the household. See also COOPER, *Households*, scheme fig. 2 and n. 73 on socioeconomic relations of Roman families.

exhaustive discussion in relation to architecture:[18] Approaches guided by perception and reception aesthetics open up routes to the spatial and bodily dimensions of aesthetics as a basis for individuals to create meaning and connectedness to their material (and visual) environment, other people and the divine.[19] The concepts of affordances and effects are crucial for deciphering the imagery.[20] Applied to the field of religious meanings, the question arises as to what role composition, configurations, shapes,

---

[18] Cf. HAUG, *Decor-Räume*, 17: "...die Architektur und ihr Decor" unterliegen "Wahrnehmungsprinzipien, die sich an Größe, Material (Oberflächentextur), Farbe, Kontrast ..., Komplexität, Redundanz / Überraschung (Regel / Abweichung), Ordnung / Unordnung ..., Balance / Instabilität, Ruhe / Bewegung sowie Qualität und Quantität des Decors orientieren. Diese Prinzipien wirken in die Wahrnehmung inhaltlicher Qualitäten hinein, sie organisieren das visuelle Feld".

[19] Connectedness embraces the material-spatial aspects of "belonging", "identity", "closeness", see R. BRUBAKER, F. COOPER, "Beyond 'identity'," *Theory and Society* 29 (2000), p. 1-47, esp. p. 19-21; VAN OYEN, *Storage*, esp. p. 94 privileges "knowledge" which can be an element of how connectedness is established; on aesthetic perception and the imagery/imaginary-environment HAUG, *Decor-Räume*; LORENZ, *Bilder*.

[20] "Bildakt" after H. BREDEKAMP, *Theorie des Bildakts: Frankfurter Adorno-Vorlesungen 2007*, Berlin, Suhrkamp, 2010 is further developed to "Blickakt", viewing act, by S. KRÄMER, "Gibt es eine Performanz des Bildlichen? Reflexionen über ‚Blickakte'," in L. SCHWARTE (ed.), *Bild-Performanz*, München, Fink, 2011 (Eikones), p. 7: "(i) Das Anschauen von Bildern kann ... als ein ‚Blicken' spezifiziert werden ... was zugleich ein Angeblicktwerden durch das Bild impliziert ...; (ii) Dieses Angeblicktwerden wird als ein Geschehen erfahren, bei dem das Bild ‚zum Akteur' wird, während dem Betrachter etwas widerfährt, das seiner Kontrolle nicht einfach unterliegt...; (iii) Das Blicken vollzieht sich in einem somatischen Milieu ..., das mit unserer Körperlichkeit ebenso verknüpft ist, wie mit der Materialität des Bildes; (iv) Das Blicken / Angeblicktwerden ist jenseits ikonologischer Identifikationsleistungen .... Die Blickbeziehung zum Bild ist ... dem Fühlen mehr verwandt als dem Denken; (v) Die Distanziertheit, die dem Sehen von Objekten (und Bildern) eigen ist, wird im Augenblick des Angeblicktwerdens durch das Bild annulliert, zugunsten einer distanzlosen Anwesenheit, in welcher gerade die Medialität des Bildes, die für das ‚Sehen in' grundlegend ist, in Form der Unterscheidung zwischen ... Bild und nichtbildlicher Realität, ein Stück weit außer Kraft gesetzt wird." Recent image-studies in archaeology in J. BRACKER, *Homo pictor*; on sacred gaze, see below n. 27. On affordances of image-objects, see C. KNAPPETT, "The Affordances of Things: a Post-Gibsonian Perspective on the Relationality of Mind and Matter," in E. DEMARRAIS, C. GOSDEN, C. RENFREW (eds.), *Rethinking Materiality: The Engagement of Mind with the Material World*, Cambridge, McDonald Institute for Archaeological Research, 2004, p. 43-51; E. GÜNTHER, J. FABRICIUS (eds.), *Mehrdeutigkeiten: Rahmentheorien und Affordanzkonzepte in der archäologischen Bildwissenschaft*, Wiesbaden, Harrassowitz, 2021 (Philippika 147); J. J. GIBSON, *The theory of affordances*, Hillsdale, N.J., Lawrence Erlbaum Associates, 1977.

materials, colours, surfaces, and locations play in the formation of religion and in the transmission of religious knowledge.[21] What do the choices tell us about notions of and relations to the counterintuitive agents, the gods, as, for example, the small size of the deities or the painted altars under niches favoured in late Republican and early Imperial times?

The hermeneutical tools of the image- and viewing-act as well as that of "practice-arrangement-bundle" help to analyse the entangled mesh of human, material and divine agents in a built space.[22] Daily, often unconsciously conducted practices, such as greeting the *Lares* by raising the gaze, re-arranging items in and around the niche, altar, or image, or touching the statuette when passing, are embodied viewing acts and habitual practices with material objects that are likely to be ritualised by households members.[23]

2. *Image(-objects) and routines, motifs and recognisability as elements of religious communication and meaning*

All features and non-human agents in a dwelling's environment – architecture, surfaces, colours, material (image-)objects and their iconographies, as well as light, accessibility, and visibility – structure the habitual practices and routines of its inhabitants. In Pompeian houses, patterned installations for communication with the deities appear immobile or mobile: figurative paintings are stationary, while objects such as altars, figurines, offerings

---

[21] See the paradigm of Lived Ancient Religion emphasising situational meanings and embodiment, ALBRECHT *et al.*, *Religion in the making*.

[22] On "practice-arrangement bundle" in praxeological sociology accounting for the material determinants and embodiment as relating individual action and experience to social structure: T. R. SCHATZKI, *The site of the social: A philosophical account of the constitution of social life and change*, University Park, Pennsylvania State University Press, 2002; K. KNORR CETINA, "Objectual practice," in T. R. SCHATZKI, K. KNORR-CETINA, E. V. SAVIGNY (eds.), *The practice turn in contemporary theory*, London, Routledge, 2000, p. 175-188; A. RECKWITZ, "The Status of the 'Material' in Theories of Culture: From 'Social Structure' to 'Artefacts'," *Journal for the Theory of Social Behaviour* 32.2 (2002), p. 195-217; see also E. SHOVE, "Matters of Practice," in A. HUI, T. SCHATZKI, E. SHOVE (eds.), *The Nexus of Practices. Connections, Constellations, Practitioners*, London-New York, Routledge, 2016, p. 155-168.

[23] Cf. E. SHOVE, "Habits and their creatures," in A. WARDE, D. SOUTHERTON (eds.), *The habits of consumption*, Helsinki, Collegium, 2012, p. 100-113.

and lighting could be used situationally. As such, they have a dynamic aspect. Iconographies make representations in household *sacraria* recognisable – especially the *Lares*, *Genii* and serpents, which obtained their look in late Republican and early Imperial times; adaptations to particular spaces make them individual, as do the combinations with other deities, such as Hercules, Mercury, Jupiter, Venus, Fortuna, Minerva, etc., depicted in well-known iconographical schemes.[24] These figures were often painted by specialised painters ("Figurenmaler").[25]

With the help of some examples of imagery and installations of the households' *sacraria*, I show how they foster social bonding, give order to the environment, and create and support routines and tacit (religious) knowledge and routines, that can be family-based (or small-group-based) and transmitted intergenerationally. It is possible to disentangle these multimodal elements of religious practices by analysing the affordances and effects of the imagery of household shrines as described above, and then identify their spatial relations, i.e. their position in the dwellings that enabled humans and deities to connect and interact.[26]

2.1. Seeing as religious practice, viewing as ritual act – how image(-objects) interact

The following pictorial strategies can be subsumed as affordances which make images effective for the beholders:

i) composition, style, and size
ii) explicitness, detailed depiction and recognisability
iii) mimetic illusions and overlaps to a real environment

---

[24] See above n. 11. For reasons of simplification I use only *sacrarium* for the household shrines mentioned here, and do not apply the conclusive differentiation between *sacrarium* and *sacellum* as outlined by BASSANI, this volume, p. 171-176, going also beyond the Pompeian evidence.

[25] FRÖHLICH, *Lararien- und Fassadenbilder*, p. 95-104, speaks of the specialised craftsmanship (*pictores imaginarii*), distinguishing two major workshops. However, there are examples of painters of decorative systems (*pictores parietarii*) among *sacraria* (L105 and L111).

[26] See above n. 10 on the multimodality of (religious) communication; on practice theory n. 22. We can look for the "use of objects or the modification of an environment that instantiates religion either directly or by physically commemorating religious experiences and practices, thus creating the infrastructure for further religious action by others" (ALBRECHT et al., *Religion in the making*, p. 580).

These features offer perceptive, receptive and mnemonic anchors that support, generate, and accompany religious practices and experiences.[27] They create an immediateness of the depicted figures and scenes.

i) Composition, style and size

Instead of assessing style and quality of the *sacraria* paintings as markers of social status of commissioners and viewers, which could pose methodological pitfalls, since often modern criteria applied on artworks are applied, they should be seen as social practice and be analysed as carrying a social, religious and communicational meaning.[28] Beyond the label for images of *sacraria* and street facades as vernacular art, their formal-technical, pictorial and compositional characteristics need to be scrutinised for their iconographical, aesthetic and mimetic (and further, symbolic) effectiveness that has an impact on their perception and meaning(s).[29]

---

[27] On "sacred gaze" see D. MORGAN, *The sacred gaze: Religious visual culture in theory and practice*, Berkeley, University of California Press, 2011, p. 1-21 and 48-52. P. 21: one should refuse "to see it as a fixed, aesthetically permanent entity, but seeing it instead as a social phenomenon…" and D. MORGAN, *Images at work: The material culture of enchantment*, New York-Oxford, Oxford University Press, 2018, p. 20, 50-51, 98, 109 and 129. On the gaze as ritual in Indian religious practices, e.g. B. LUCHESI, "Darśan-Bilder: Hinduistische Verehrungspraxis und populäre Poster in Nordindien," in B. BEINHAUER-KÖHLER, D. PEZZOLI-OLGIATI, J. VALENTIN (eds.), *Religiöse Blicke – Blicke auf das Religiöse: Visualität und Religion*, Zürich, Theologischer Verlag Zürich, 2010, p. 201-225; in Classical antiquity see J. ELSNER, "Between Mimesis and Divine Power," in R. S. NELSON (ed.), *Visuality before and beyond the Renaissance: Seeing as Others Saw*, Cambridge, Cambridge University Press, 2000 (Cambridge studies in new art history and criticism), p. 45-69; J. ELSNER, *Roman eyes: Visuality & subjectivity in art & text*, Princeton, Princeton University Press, 2007 and recently the contributions in A.-F. JACCOTTET (ed.), *Rituels en image – Images de rituel. Iconographie – histoire des religions – archéologie*, Bern-Wien-Berlin, Peter Lang, 2021 (Études genevoises sur l'Antiquité 9). HAUG, *Decor-Räume*, p. 40 claims a different "Aufmerksamkeitslage (und Rezeptionsbedingungen)" for imagery on facades and in domestic shrines in contrast to the wall systems in *triclinia* without further specification of what an "Aufmerksamkeitslage" is, or how archaeology can know about it. My approach tries to fill this void.

[28] Cf. MORGAN, *Images at work*, who understands image as social practice, of course, also based on *aisthesis*, freed of modern qualitative evaluations such as "beautiful" or "artwork". Comparable imagery in the street shrines links the two realms where Pompeians act on a daily base, FRÖHLICH, *Lararien- und Fassadenbilder*, e.g. L105 and L109 linked to F7; L5 linked to F71.

[29] FRÖHLICH, *Lararien- und Fassadenbilder*, p. 189-210 inquires into elements of "Gattungsstil".

Sacraria paintings are characterised by immediateness and salient simplicity of the style, as, for example, the imagery of the *aedicula* in the Casa del Larario del Sarno (I.14.6/7, Fig. 1) shows, with its scenes of activities on the river below the niche, in which the *Genius* sacrifices.

A qualitative evaluation is evoked by Fröhlich, when he describes this shrine as almost primitive ("Grenze zum Primitiven"):[30] No perspective and foreshortening are applied in the depiction of the figures or objects; the god and the workers are

FIG. 1.
Casa del Larario del Sarno (I.14.6/7), *aedicula* with niche in an open area at the back of the house. Sacrificing *genius* in the niche; on the socle on red background a scene with the river god Sarno and activities taking place at and on the river (FRÖHLICH, *Lararien- und Fassadenbilder*, L33, Taf. 6).

---

[30] *Ibid.*, p. 92; two statuettes of *Lares*, a bowl and a terracotta lamp were found there, see KAUFMANN-HEINIMANN, *Götter und Lararien*, fig. 157.

painted in a sketchy way; there is no coherence of proportions and little attention is paid to details, similar to that of the kitchen of the Casa di Sutoria Primigenia (I.13.2, Fig. 2). Another characteristic of *sacraria*-paintings are figures in frontal or profile view that stand parallel to the background as well as a symmetrical or paratactic composition, often assessed in qualitative terms as simple. However, behind the qualitative evaluations of such features, on the one hand, lies an art-historical, modern appraisal of what "art" is. Yet, ongoing research on "decor" as a multimodal phenomenon, and its artistic strategies and socio-historical value, is able to show the numerous layers of meaning, interrelations and significances of pictorial, sculptural and architectural imagery and forms, of surfaces and materials.[31] On the other hand, Fröhlich (1991), and others, acknowledge the vividness of the representations – the serpents, the vegetal decoration, *Lares*, sacrificial equipment – depicted on the walls with a few brush-strokes (Figs. 1-4). Precisely these pictorial strategies constitute the affordances for the particular effectiveness of the imagery as, for example, the easy-to-grasp positions of figures, a light, sketchy style, no visual 'ballast' through details (Fig. 1). These affordances through style have an immediate impact on the viewer.

---

[31] FRÖHLICH, *Lararien- und Fassadenbilder*, p. 31 and 56 declares the *sacraria* paintings as for the "unteren Gesellschaftsschichten," whereas the serpents were accepted in all societal strata, since they also appear in representative rooms, based on a too clear-cut functionality of spaces and status of dwellers. Even though he seems to be critical about the relation of "volkstümliche Kunst" and social position of the commissioners (p. 207-208), a general bourgeoise view of Bourdieuan habitus on what "dwelling" and "domestic art" is, lurks behind this statement; see P. ZANKER, "Die Villa als Vorbild des späten pompejanischen Wohngeschmacks," *Jahrbuch des Deutschen Archäologischen Instituts* 94 (1979), p. 513: regarding *decor* and equipment of houses the Pompeians looked for "eine möglichst prächtige, repräsentative Wirkung ... Tiefsinn, Bildung und Religiosität" are not to be expected. This view was broadened, e.g. by LORENZ, *Bilder*, and HAUG, *Decor-Räume* (e.g. p. 40: specific styles relate to "spezifischen Kommunikationsabsichten, nicht aber mit spezifischen sozialen Gruppen"). However, referring to *sacraria* (p. 408-412), she claims that early (Augustan) imagery in *sacraria* in kitchen areas was developed for the "Gesinde" and the (later) shrines in garden areas for the freeborn, she thus falls back on former interpretations. See in general B. AMIRI, *Religion romaine et esclavage au Haut-Empire: Rome, Latium et Campanie*, Rome, École française de Rome, 2021 (Collection de l'École française de Rome 581), ch. 6.

Fig. 2.
Casa di Sutoria Primigenia (I.13.2), kitchen-*sacrarium*. Image on the east wall with a group of people, flanked by *Lares*, sacrificing at an altar (www.pompeiiinpictures.com, I.13.2, part 2, © Jackie and Bob Dunn, by permission of the Ministero della Cultura – Parco Archeologico di Pompei, retrieved 25 May 2021, courtesy Johannes EBER).

The issue of style affects the composition, too. Even though many of the images are symmetrically composed with a central group or an object flanked by *Lares* or attendants (as in the Casa del Maiale IX.9.b/c, Fig. 3), they do not follow a strict system of panels and zones known from mythological and architectural paintings.[32] Yet, there is a distinction of a lower and an upper register, where *Lares* and deities are "at home" in the upper zone, while serpents are in the natural environment of the lower zone, as we can see in the Casa del Labirinto, VI.11.19 (L67) or the Casa dell'Efebo I.7.10-12 (L5).[33] In some cases, the serpents transgress the border between the registers, moving up from below, as in the image in the kitchen-yard of the Casa di Iulius Polybius, IX.13.1-3 (Fig. 4).[34]

---

[32] Inserted in the wall system is, e.g. painted *aedicula* for the *Lares* in the Casa di Pansa VI.6.1, L61.

[33] Serpents are a specificity of Campanian *sacraria* and a topic *per se*, beyond the recent book by FLOWER, *Dancing Lares*.

[34] L109, 4th style. Juno, *genius* and *Lares* are depicted, a sink or sewer is located at the bottom right corner of the image, to which the hearth adjoins. The *Lares* are addressed in a graffito (*AE* 1985, 285). Apparently original holes are at the height of the inner hands of the *Lares* to hold another real adornment.

Fig. 3.
Casa del Maiale (IX.9.b/c), kitchen-*sacrarium*. Two *lares* on their tip toes with blown-up dresses flank an altar with sacrificial goods, framed by garlands; in the lower zone two serpents approach an altar
(Fröhlich, *Lararien- und Fassadenbilder*, L108, Taf. 12,1-2).

The composition in the images of *Lares* and other deities rather "floats" on an often white background on the walls, or the scene continues around a corner like in the Casa di Sutoria Primigenia (I.13.2, Figs. 2 and 13) or Casa di Optatio VII.2.14/15 (Fig. 5),

Fig. 4.
Casa di Iulius Polybius (IX.13.1-3), kitchen-*sacrarium* with *lares* flanking symmetrically an altar; in the lower zone a serpent in vegetation moves upwards towards the altar (www.pompeiiinpictures.com, IX.13.1-3, part 14, © Jackie and Bob Dunn, by permission of the Ministero della Cultura – Parco Archeologico di Pompei, retrieved 25 May 2021, courtesy Nicolas MONTEIX).

thus making the viewer follow the scene.[35] White colour in Pompeian wall paintings is often used in socle zones (1st to 3rd style), in some cases in wall systems of rooms and halls (increasing in the 4th style) (Figs. 2-4). Moreover, white is the colour of many stuccoed columns or pilasters (as well as the painted architectural elements) and appears in the black and white mosaics of the floors (close to the *sacrarium* in V.4.3, L52). The neutral non-colour of these features allows for the hypothesis of white as an ordering feature: socle zones between horizontal and vertical surfaces, columns as vertical elements that order and stabilise, and backgrounds that do not distract the gaze, are strategies that facilitate orientation.

---

[35] Red was used for the *sacrarium* in the Casa del Larario del Sarno I.14.6/7 (Fig. 1), yellow in one of the *sacraria* in the Casa degli Amorini dorati VI.16.7 (L74), see MOORMANN, p. 213-214, and SFAMENI, p. 115-116 this volume. The colour effects are beyond the scope of this paper. The symmetry of the *Lares* is further emphasised in Casa del Maiale XI.9.b/c (Fig. 2) and I.12.3 (L24) by the mirrored colours of their dresses.

Fig. 5.
Casa di Optatio (VII.2.14/15). Open area at the rear of the house with a sacrificial scene with deities and helpers on the right wall, with an altar standing in the corner (left: a photograph, and right: a watercolour from the end of the 19th century) (Boyce, *Corpus*, Pl. 23,1 and water colour (anonymous?), DAI Rome, Archive, A-VII-32-119, http://arachne.uni-koeln.de/item/buchseite/949105).

The pictorial and compositional strategies of zoning and colour either bring an order into the depicted scene (background), or break up an order ("floating"). Both ways raise the beholder's attention to screen the image with their eyes.

Also, the size of the depicted figures has an effect on perception as we can see in the scenes with the tiny, sketchy figures of the Larario del Sarno (Fig. 1). Their small size requires closeness. Not all motifs can change their dimensions, though. *Lares* never grow as big as the image-objects of other deities.[36] They always remain graspable as in the "hand-held" format of their statuettes, whereas other deities that appear small in the household shrines (see the Minervae in house V.4.9, Fig. 11 and in the Casa di Sutoria Primi-

---

[36] Dimensions of only the *Lares* in images are rarely measured; however, assumably their height is between 15 cm to 40 cm. Statuettes are no larger than *c.* 20 cm, which allows for hands-on practices with them, see Hallett, *Miniature Cult Images*. They were also set up and stored away, see Amoroso, p. 67 and 68, p. 74, this volume.

genia I.13.2, Fig. 13) also have large-size counterparts in other realms of the city. People could carry the statuettes of the house gods and move them from spot to spot. After all, what could establish a closer connection to the protective deities than literally "grasping" them?

Pictorial and figurative representations – both mural images and statuettes – and their dimensions, as seen in the examples above, express and enable closeness to the beholders. *Sacraria* images "connect" easily to the human agent, and are thus easily implemented in behaviour, routines, and habits, which form the basis of religious rituals.

ii) Explicitness, detailedness, and recognisability

The immediateness of the paintings in the *sacraria* resulting from their style and composition is fostered by missing allegorical and mythological motifs known from other wall paintings. Even though the iconographies of the deities in the *sacraria* do not differ from mythological paintings in Pompeii, their explicitness and clearly layered ways of representing persons, objects and settings refer to practices and scenes people could recognise. This does not imply a one-to-one representation of "reality", as they still depict imagined counterintuitive beings such as *Lares* and *Genii*.[37] Yet, other items are rendered in great detail and bring them to the attention of the beholder through variances in brush-stroke, colour, and light spots. The fruits on the altars are clearly distinguishable and seem freshly picked, the flute is depicted in the hands of the *tibicen*, and attributes such as the *rhyta* or the dresses of the *Lares* are rendered realistically and in detail; the serpents' skin has visible scales, and the fat of the bacon rind can be distinguished from the meat, as, for example, in the *sacrarium* of the Casa del Maiale (IX.9.b/c, L108, Fig. 3).

The rather empty background of the scenes at altars often framed by garlands underpins the impression of detailedness, since all figures, items and equipment can be foregrounded. Only in the zones, where the serpents dwell, is "nature" explicitly

---

[37] Ancestors could also be depicted, probably in VI.1.1 (L55) or in the small busts in the Casa del Menandro I.10.4/14-17 (see MOORMANN, p. 149-154, this volume) and I.8 (L10).

Fig. 6.
Casa di Obellius Firmus (IX.14.2/4), kitchen-*sacrarium*. A serpent dwells in a natural environment below the niche, evoked by the green grass or shrubs (FRÖHLICH, *Lararien- und Fassadenbilder*, L111, Taf. 48,1).

evoked by – often oleander-like – shrubs, grass or other vegetation around the snakes and interspersed with the snakes' bodies. With a light, sketchy rendering of leaves and branches, as for example in IX.5.2/22 (L105), and in the kitchen *sacrarium* of the Casa di Obellius Firmus (IX.14.2/4, L111, Fig. 6), or with the pastose thicket in VI.16.40 (L77) and in the Casa del Maiale IX.9.b/c (Fig. 3), the situation in nature draws the viewer's attention to the contrast with the upper zone.

Recognisability is the main reason for developing iconographical schemes.[38] The core domestic gods, the *Lares*, match this perfectly. One of the most frequent themes in *sacraria* paintings is

---

[38] The iconography of the *sacraria* is not an unchangeable mould, but an open scheme with a set of protagonists, individually filled in each family and house. They were repainted – either by the same or successive families, see GIACOBELLO, *Larari*, p. 117 with n. 132 for examples.

the pairing of the *Lares* at the altar with or without a sacrificing *genius / paterfamilias*. The youthful bodies of these divine figures represent the well-being of the household. However, Pompeians could see the symmetrical composition all over the city, not only in the *sacraria*, but also in bars and in the streets.[39] Their appearance is schematised: They stand on their tiptoes; raise the *rhyta*, jugs, or *paterae*; wear short, blown-up dresses and long hair, as for example in the Casa di Iulius Polybius (IX.13.1-3, Fig. 4).

These compositorial, iconographic, stylistic, and size-related details described in i) and ii) increase the explicitness of the images and offer a perceptual framing that creates a closeness between represented motifs, presenting media, and viewing act and viewer. They establish links to the background of experiences of the viewers against which they see, order, or understand them, and internalise their aesthetic and content-related information.[40] They become meaningful by being looked at.

iii) Mimetic illusions and overlaps between reality and representation

The image in the kitchen of the Casa di Obellius Firmus (IX.14.2/4, Fig. 6) offers us another pictorial strategy – the mimesis:[41] The banquet scene in the lower left area of the composition is a reference to a real event – a *cena* at this or another house.[42] This is a rare motif as is the daily life scenery of workers we saw in the Casa del Larario del Sarno (Fig. 1), whereas others

---

[39] When the iconography crosses media, scales, and spaces it establishes even stronger ties of recognisability (see R. Raja, "Abstraction of religious symbols and objects in sacred architecture in the Roman Near East. The role of miniaturization" in E. Begemann, D. Pavel, G. Petridou, R. Raja, A.-K. Rieger, J. Rüpke (eds.), *Magnification and Miniaturization in Religious Communication in Antiquity and Modernity: Materialities and Meanings* (Contextualising the Sacred), Turnhout, Brepols, 2022.

[40] See above n. 20.

[41] On mimetic images and learning through mimesis see C. Wulf, "Gestures and Rituals. The Mimetic Creation of the Social," *Paragrana* 23 (2014), p. 111-121; R. Heersmink, "The Narrative Self, Distributed Memory, and Evocative Objects," *Philosophical Studies* 175 (2018), p. 1829-1849. The house has a second *sacrarium* in the front hall, see Boyce, *Lararia*, p. 30, no. 67.

[42] See W. Van Andringa, "Dal sacrificio al banchetto: Rituali e topografia della casa romana," in M. Bassani, F. Ghedini, Religionem significare, 2011, p. 91-98. A mimesis internal to the images is the figure of the servant in the background, who imitates the gesture of the *Lares* with the raised arm in the upper register.

are more common: The garlands and sacrificial goods on the altar also bridge the gap between real and represented objects by means of their mimetic characteristics.

The garlands are ubiquitous in the imagery of *sacraria* and refer to real ones hung up on various occasions: Garlands marked economic, political and religious events (markets, assemblies, rituals) space- and time-wise,[43] as for example, in the Casa del Maiale IX.9.b/c (Fig. 5). Comparable to their real counterparts, the garlands made from flowers, leaves, and fruit branches frame the scenes spatially with their elongated shape. Points in time and the passing of time are implied, as the garlands require advance preparation, and are only fixed in a specific moment (as part of, or shortly before the ritual practice). Finally, the fading of the flowers attests to the passing of time, to their transience, thus limiting their sacralising purpose.[44] Their mimetic capacities not only show in the depiction of the flower-stripes, but also in an often very vivid rendering of the softly flying ribbons with which they are knotted at the painted nails, evoking a light draught of air. In painted scenes this framing is "frozen" – the flowers never fade – as the scene in the frame of the religious practices.[45] However, the coincidence of real and depicted scenes reaches a next level of ambiguity, if there are painted nails and holes for real ones that held fresh garlands.[46] They are the mimetically rendered perpetuation as well as marker of repetition in the here and now of a religious act.[47]

---

[43] See the images of *forum* activities in the Praedia of Iulia Felix. The pig as mimetically rendered sacrificial animal and the processed meat as shown in many cases as well as the actual findings of piglet bones are not dealt with here, see for example, M. CIARALDI, J. RICHARDSON, "Food, Ritual and Rubbish in the Making of Pompeii," *Theoretical Roman Archaeology Journal* 99 (2000), p. 74-82.

[44] The making of garlands by amorini is shown in a frieze in VII.9.7. In two very different literary genres – Plautus, *Aulul.* 23-25 and Cato, *de Agric.* 143 – garlands as parts of religious rituals play a rôle. For a full discussion of these passages see FLOWER, *Dancing Lares*, p. 31-35 and 40-45.

[45] See KRÄMER, *Blickakte*, quote here n. 20.

[46] D. ROGERS, "The Hanging Garlands of Pompeii: Mimetic Acts of Ancient Lived Religion," *Arts* 9.2 (2020), p. 65 (19 p.); painted nails e.g. in Casa del Criptoportico I.6.2; nail holes in Casa dei capitelli colorati VII.4.31.51); Caupona di Soterius (I.12.3); bakery (VII.12.11).

[47] Cf. L. WEISS, "Perpetuated Action," in J. RÜPKE (ed.), *A Companion to the Archaeology of Religion in the Ancient World*, Malden, MA, Wiley Blackwell, 2015, p. 60-70 for depictions of sacrificial goods in Pharaonic Egyptian contexts transferred by ROGERS, *Garlands* to Pompeian garlands.

The act of viewing such imagery creates mimetic illusions and overlaps: In the moment of viewing, the medial character of the image (i.e. the painted surface with the motif of the pig) coincides with the imagined. The distance between the receiving and perceiving viewer and the image approaches zero, and the imagination is the affective and effective result of this situation.[48] The mimetically effective representation, implicitly referring to a real environment, constructs this environment (hence religious rituals) by being viewed.

The same perceptive, experiential, and mnemonic mechanisms operate, when, in addition to painted altars, three-dimensional ones are placed in the *sacraria* – often directly in front, below or beside the depicted ones[49] – occasionally bearing real gifts, while the depicted gifts never vanish from view.[50] The serpents add another layer of coincidence to the imaginary and the real: They often not only approach the real sacrificial items on the altars, opening their mouth to devour them, they also seem to come from (and disappear) into real holes in the wall, as the image in the shrine of I.12.16 (L28) shows.

This coincidence of a real and imagined world as well as the invisible world becoming visible makes images affective and effective at the same time. The imaginary of religious communication and former experiences are evoked by and presented in the image and have an impact on the beholders, thus gaining a particular meaning: a process which can be subsumed as the socio-historical specific viewing habit.[51] Real and depicted items shape the reli-

---

[48] Cf. KRÄMER, *Blickakte*; on mimesis, see above n. 27 and 41.

[49] e.g. BOYCE, *Lararia*, nos 103 (V.2. western side); 126 (V.4.13); 253 (VII.2.20); 291 (VII.6.28); 463 (IX.9.11). In addition, we can assume that statuettes of the *Lares* or the *Genius* as well as of other deities depicted in the painted image stood as statuettes in front of the painted ones, however both being representations; see e.g. the Casa delle pareti rosse VIII.5.37, L96; KAUFMANN-HEINIMANN, *Götter und Lararien*, fig. 169. See AMOROSO, this volume, p. 54-57.

[50] In another societal area in the Roman household, the symposium, mimetic overlaps are servants as statues and real acting people, see R. BIELFELDT, "Candelabrus and Trimalchio: Embodied Histories of Roman Lampstands and their Slaves," *Art History* 41.3 (2018), p. 420-443.

[51] Image-objects can "store" and trigger memories on which knowledge is grounded, see A.-K. RIEGER, "Pathways of religious experiences in the urban fabric of Roman Pompeii", in C. NORMAN, G. WOOLF (eds.), *Sanctuaries and Experience. Knowledge, practice and space in the Ancient World*, Cambridge: Cambridge University Press, 2022. HEERSMINK, *Narrative Self*.

gious knowledge and (re-)iterated religious practices in the Pompeian houses and families, because they are re-enacted on a daily basis.

2.2. Location, location, location – or how ritualisation of practices can take place through the spatial embedding of *sacraria* in the households' daily routines

If the main competence of the *Lares* and other deities was to provide protection for a fortunate economic and social life of the family and its individual members, such effective support required closeness to and embeddedness in the socio-spatial entity of the house. Against the backdrop of the affordances and effects of the image-objects and structures of *sacraria* (as presented above) their positions in the houses were crucial for their interaction with material and human agents in the house.[52] The physical closeness and connectedness through a location is augmented if we accept the gaze as a religious act and consider it as a daily religious practice that people in the households conducted habitually, or as a routine. We can link visibility and vision between sacralised "hubs" in the house and its agents.

To protect supplies, crops and other precious material that signified well-being and reproductive activity for the *familia*, people would place the *Lares* and other deities close to the stocks or where they were processed – in kitchens and service areas. These were often situated in less accessible spaces in the house (in basements, spaces under a staircase (*sottoscala*), or at the end of a corridor) and due to hearth installations (and latrines), also functionally determined (Figs. 2, 3, 6 and 13).[53] Other places where

---

[52] See G. SCHÖRNER, "Lokalisierung von Hauskulten im römischen Italien: Fremdbestimmte vs. individuelle Religion," in W. FRIESE, I. NIELSEN (eds.), *Persönliche Frömmigkeit: Funktion und Bedeutung individueller Gotteskontakte im interdisziplinären Dialog: Akten der Tagung am Archäologischen Institut der Universität Hamburg (25.-27. November 2010)*, Münster, Westf. Lit, 2011 (Hephaistos 28), fig. 1 for regio VI: gardens, followed by kitchens, front halls in the entry area, secondary courtyards without characterising the different spaces. Thoroughly on localisation see LAFORGE, *Religion privée*, p. 70-106, however, with rather generic activity determination (often based on standard houses/literary sources), see also BRANDT, *Sacra*.

[53] KASTENMEIER, *Luoghi di lavoro*, p. 46; VAN OYEN, *Storage*, p. 106.

the gods were best connected to people included entrance areas, front halls, courtyards as well as gardens or peristyles (Fig. 1), where the main functions were either passage, flow and connectivity or space-consuming activities.[54] Often accessible from a second entrance, areas such as peristyles, backyards, and gardens were also used for production and storage, commodity processing and redistribution and doing business, as findings of tools would also suggest; these spaces allowed for changing configurations of things and people.

i) Relations to locations of storage, business and idling

The Casa di Popidius Proculus with a bakery (VII.2.20.22.38.41, L81) possesses a *sacrarium* room with two niches above the image of the serpents at an altar in the basement of the house, which is accessible from the eastern side of the peristyle (Fig. 7). The niches with painted garlands around contain two *Lares* to the right and a *Genius* to the left; both niches show painted altars, the one showing the *Genius* also has a real one in front made of terracotta. The western wall of the small room shows a pair of serpents.[55] The room attached to this *sacrarium* room contained water-related installations, a tub and a well.[56] As regards accessibility and visibility, a *sacrarium* in this position is not comparable to one in the garden or a courtyard on the ground floor. It is located in the basement, at the end of a narrow thoroughfare to a storage place (Fig. 7). However, since the deities of the *sacraria* were responsible for protecting items necessary for the family's livelihood, it makes sense to locate them close to the kitchens and storage rooms: Spatial closeness means immediate, thus also better protection.[57]

---

[54] HAUG, *Decor-Räume*, p. 140-141, claims that in Late Republican and Augustan times courtyards or front halls were the only places with "cultic activities," which contradicts the remains of the *sacraria* in kitchens (p. 408-412).

[55] BOYCE, *Lararia*, p. 62, no. 253; KASTENMEIER, *Luoghi di lavoro*, p. 32, fig. 16 "non specificato".

[56] L. PEDRONI, "Pompei, Regio VII, Insula 2, pars occidentalis: le indagini dell'Institut für Archäologien dell'Universität Innsbruck," *Studi della Soprintendenza archeologica di Pompei* 25 (2008), esp. p. 239.

[57] Who exactly (entire family, the personnel in charge of storage) fulfilled (daily) rites there, remains open, see FOSS, *Watchful Lares*, p. 199-200.

FIG. 7.
Casa di Popidius Priscus (VII.2.20.22.38.41), *sacrarium* room (1.12 × 1.24 m) with two niches and serpents on the wall to the left in the basement room (dashed area) of the peristyle, seen from the adjacent larger room with water facilities (plan after E. POEHLER, *Pompeii Bibliography and Mapping Project* 2017; BOYCE, *Corpus*, pl. 41,2; underground room after PEDRONI, *Regio VII*).

In the Casa di Pupius Rufus (VI.15.5), the front hall was chosen for setting up an extra space to the right of the *fauces*. Being close to one of the entrances to the house through which many people would walk, and the hall where they would gather, with facilities for storage and redistribution activities, it was accessible and visible from the hall. It is adorned with three niches and two altars in front of them in the wall system of the 1st style (Fig. 8).[58] Another rectangular niche was positioned above the stucco entablature. Kitchen and storage rooms were located behind the recess with the altars and close to the *fauces*. In the front hall itself

---

[58] BASSANI, *Sacraria*, p. 113; HAUG, *Decor-Räume*, p. 140.

Fig. 8.
Casa di Pupius Rufus (VI.15.5), the *sacrarium* with multiple niches
and two situated in the front hall as place of business
(plan after POEHLER 2017; www.pompeiiinpictures.com, VI.15.5, part 2,
© Jackie and Bob Dunn, by permission of the Ministero della Cultura –
Parco Archeologico di Pompei).

and in a room accessible from it, various seals were found.[59] In the *sacrarium* with its many niches, a number of divine addressees might have been present. They observed the entire situation in the hall and the storage facilities behind it where documents or goods were stored, sealed and exchanged. However, the altars and three niches are at a handy height between 90 cm and 130 cm. Even

---

[59] See *NSc* 1896, p. 228-229 and *NSc* 1897, p. 22. The graffito *CIL* IV, 5380 from the front hall of IX.14.23-25, where a hearth and a *sacrarium* was situated, tells about work done by dwellers. H. SOLIN, P. CARUSO, "Memorandum sumptuarium pompeianum: Per una nuova lettura del graffito CIL IV 5380," *Vesuviana* 8 (2016), p. 105-127.

though we do not know anything about the imagery, the marked situation of the recess with two altars and three niches made this a focal point in the open space of the front hall.

Another example of the close connection between storage and sacralised places in the house is the Casa del forno (VI.3.3/27-28, L59),[60] which is a combined workshop and dwelling. The *sacrarium* of the bakery is painted immediately above the opening of the cistern – comparable to the houses with a *sacrarium* in the front hall, where *impluvia* were connected to cisterns, securing water availability.[61] The painting shows a woman seated on a throne (Vesta?) who is flanked by – supposedly – two *Lares*, while in the lower zone two serpents approach an altar. The position of the image at the two sinks where workers could get water is ideal for a recurring viewing and interaction with the workshop's staff.

Another way of interaction through location is the *sacrarium* in the corner of the garden area of the Casa di Optatio (VII 2, 14, L80): Two *Lares* are painted in an upper zone, between whom stands an altar (Fig. 5). The central scene is framed by Jupiter (left) and Minerva (right). In the lower zone, a serpent moves to the left, to the corner of the room, where a masonry altar stood, which served as the physical connection of the sacred image to the garden painting on the adjoining wall. At the far right of the painting, at the reveal of the window opening to the adjoining rooms, a man in a loincloth is painted. The imagery directs gazes from and to the core religious scenery by including adjoining walls. This location might rather have been a place of rest (with capacities of keeping things) than a place of work. This positioning is comparable to the *sacrarium* in the bakery and dwelling IX.3.19-20 where no *Lares* are visible, but a long serpent that curls at the rear of a long bench in a tiny garden area of the complex (Fig. 9, top right). It approaches an altar on whose right side a god lies comfortably on a rock – to judge by the bowl in his left hand, it is Bacchus (L104). A niche in the east wall of this open area might have contained an image of a deity. An altar stood in the large arched niche under the staircase in the southwest corner of the space, where some water pipes ran (receiving water from above?). Also from the

---

[60] Comparable to VII 12, 11 (L91).

[61] For the situation, see http://www.pompeiiinpictures.com/pompeiiinpictures/R6/6%2003%2003%20p2.htm.

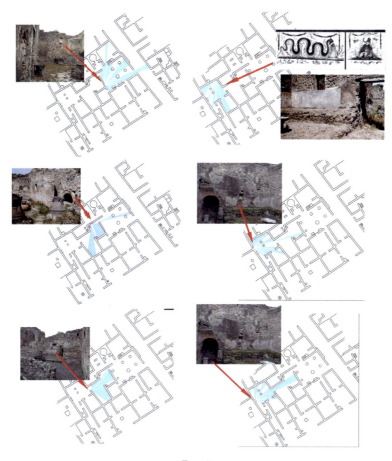

Fig. 9.
Bakery and dwelling (IX.3.19-20), isovists taken from the various niches and *sacraria* which show what areas the guarding gods on the walls and niches covered (software isovists.org/ based on plan after POEHLER 2017; www.pompeiiinpictures.com, IX.3.19-20, © Jackie and Bob Dunn, by permission of the Ministero della Cultura – Parco Archeologico di Pompei, retrieved 27 May 2021; FRÖHLICH, *Lararien- und Fassadenbilder*, L104, Taf. 43,2).

western side of the open area deities could guard the space (Fig. 9 centre and bottom right). Sitting and resting as a practice is connected to the presence of the deities in this part of the house, whereas in the other parts, work was done involving grain, flour and baking bread.[62]

---

[62] Cf. N. MONTEIX, S. AHO, A. COUTELAS, L. GARNIER, V. MATTERNE, S. ZANELLA, V. ALBANO, É. BUKOWIECKI, M. DERREUMAUX, C. HARTZ,

ii) A mesh of deities – a mesh of people: divine surveillance of rout(in)es

The fact that in many houses multiple *sacraria* – either for the *Lares*, the *genius*, the serpents or other deities – were in use at the same time has implications of how and where one could connect to the deities.[63]

The above-mentioned bakery IX.3.19-20 might serve as an example: In the room with the mills, a niche is located in the west wall approximately 1.70 m above the floor at the right side of the doorway to the next room (Fig. 9 top left).[64] When excavated, it showed the known scene of genius and *Lares*. Below the niche, a single serpent approaches an altar. In the northwest corner of the connecting room to the inner rooms of the workshop, another rectangular niche might have housed a set of protective deities that kept the tempering of the grain under their surveillance (Fig. 9 center left).[65] The isovists, or possible lines of sight from a certain point, taken from all niches of the dwelling (Fig. 9 bottom left), show the area that the deities covered in terms of visibility, and hence their presence in this dwelling and bakery.

In the Casa del Cenacolo V.2.h (Fig. 10) *Lares*, deities, and serpents were painted on the wall in three different places:[66] In the kitchen (room p, in the northeastern corner of the house, Fig. 10 top) we see a niche with serpents approaching the central altar from below on a white background. To the right of a small rectangular niche, there is a *tibicen* and further to the right, a *lar*,

---

É. Letellier, O. Mignot, S. Ranucci, "Pompéi, Pistrina recherches sur les boulangeries de l'Italie romaine," *Mélanges de l'École française de Rome – Antiquité* (2011), fig. 96 room 121.

[63] On "double lararia" see Giacobello, *Larari*, p. 59-60, where she distinguishes "larari" and "larari secondari" according to their position in the house, not according to audience (p. 114-115); see Dardenay, this volume, p. 211-222. It is not possible to distinguish different meanings of the deities at the locations and related routines (touching, giving, etc.).

[64] Boyce, *Lararia*, p. 84, no. 417.

[65] N. Monteix, "Contextualizing the Operational Sequence: Pompeian Bakeries as a Case Study," in A. Wilson, M. Flohr (eds.), *Urban craftsmen and traders in the Roman world*, Oxford, Oxford University Press, 2016 (Oxford studies in the Roman economy), p. 153-182.

[66] Sigges, *Ausstattung*, 339 doubts any connection to the Casa del Nozze d'argento.

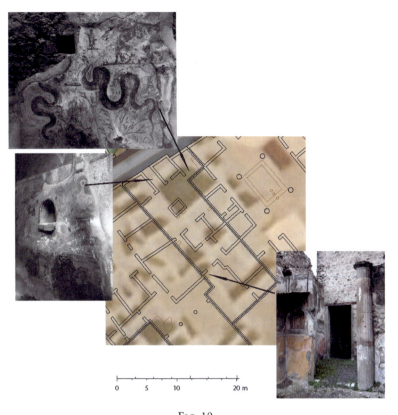

Fig. 10.
Casa del Cenacolo V.2.h, findings of religious routines and daily life activities (plan after POEHLER 2017; www.pompeiiinpictures.com, V.2.h, part 2, © Jackie and Bob Dunn, by permission of the Ministero della Cultura – Parco Archeologico di Pompei, retrieved 27 May 2021; BOYCE, *Corpus*, Pl. 17).

whose background must have shown a *popa* with a pig and a snake, but is no longer visible.

A single deity, or semi-god – Hercules – was painted in a vaulted niche of a room at the southern end of the house (room k, Fig. 10 bottom), directly to the right of the doorway to this room, which opens into a small garden/*viridarium* or backyard.[67] Hercules stands to the right of an altar in front of some vegetation, carrying the club and lion's skin on his left. With his right, he pours a libation onto the altar where a fire is burning. To his right stands a pig. A garland in the background marks the ritual

---

[67] L 46; KAUFMANN-HEINIMANN, *Götter und Lararien*, fig. 162.

setting. An entire set of objects for the ritual practices was found in the niche: a bronze statuette of Mercury, one of a kneeling woman with a palm branch, Minerva made of terracotta, a bronze, an amulet with dolphins, a head of a woman with wreath and lamp as well as two early imperial coins. A tiny terracotta *arula* still shows fire traces.[68] It seems that the open, architecturally rather undetermined spaces are of interest for setting up the household deities.

A third *sacrarium* was situated in the entrance area: a niche with a projecting shelf at the bottom covered with red stripes on white stucco (Fig. 10 centre). To the sides of the niches, two serpents curl around a bronze-like (portable) altar (brazier) of which the left one raises its head to the niche. They are depicted amongst the usual vegetation, and the top is framed by a hanging garland.[69] In the case of the Casa del Cenacolo (V.2.h) very different areas of action are marked, however, they are all relevant for getting into contact or having space for some activity.

Although the dwelling V.4.9 is not large, it possessed four *sacraria* (Fig. 11). In one of the *aedicula*-niches, fragments of an incense burner or box from the early first cent. BCE were found, so that we can assume that it was in use before Roman imperial times.[70]

An elaborate installation is still partly visible in the northeastern corner of the front hall with an *impluvium*: An arched niche with a pedestal inside watched over a "kitchenette" on the left side of an entrance to a larger room,[71] while a smaller rectangular niche on the right side and a stuccoed wreath decorated the right side of the doorway (Fig. 11 top right). Above this niche, another niche was visible at the moment of excavation. On the northern wall of the hall with a cistern was a small niche high above the

---

[68] Among the findings (*NSc* 1891, p. 376; *NSc* 1892, p. 30-31 and 56-57; *NSc* 1910, p. 329) are various sickles, fragments of mountings, and 14 amphorae in the *atrium*; A. D'AMBROSIO, M. R. BORRIELLO, *Arule e bruciaprofumi fittili da Pompei*, Napoli, Electa, 2001 (Studi della Soprintendenza Archeologica di Pompei 3), p. 42, no. 47: an incense burner or box with a snake curled around it (first cent. BCE) which is older than the paintings from early Augustan time.

[69] BOYCE, *Lararia*, p. 36, no. 106.

[70] D'AMBROSIO, BORRIELLO, *Arule e bruciaprofumi*, p. 40, no. 38.

[71] BOYCE, *Lararia*, p. 41 with descriptions of the step inside, a mark left by an oval object, and another cylindrical terracotta altar.

Fig. 11.
Workshop and dwelling V.4.9, findings of religious routines and daily life activities (plan after POEHLER 2017; photo Pierre GUSMAN and American Academy in Rome, Photographic Archive. Warsher collection no. 1585, after www.pompeiiinpictures.com, V.4.9, © Jackie and Bob Dunn, by permission of the Ministero della Cultura – Parco Archeologico di Pompei, retrieved 27 May 2021; *NSc* 1899, p. 346, Fig. 7).

ground with a high, stuccoed pediment and thick shelf and architrave inserted, overlooking the place (Fig. 11 left). The paint shows green and red stars inside the niche, and green, red and white accentuations on the protruding parts. Another religious item is a "patera umbellicata" with a wreath both, in stucco on the western edge of the southern wall of the central courtyard, of which we only have the description. In the southeast corner of the hall where a small, covered corner (*sottoscala*?) contained the latrine, a painted Fortuna was still visible when excavated (Fig. 11 right).[72] Cooking, food storage, as well as drawing water, washing and cleansing took place in the hall.[73] Only defecation was set apart, but even where consumption ends, Fortuna observes and protects this practice.[74]

In this dwelling with a number of tools, and instruments for cooking, storing, or filling, maybe also producing (the coloured plates), a kitchen and water facilities at four spots, a religious image or installation was present and visible mostly in the central courtyard. The isovists taken from the niches and stuccoed paintings demonstrate the complete visual coverage of the *sacraria* respectively the gods dwelling in them (Fig. 12). Only parts of the northeastern corner of the front hall were not seen by the eyes of the gods. Wherever a person was active – even when going to the toilet – he or she was in eye contact with divine beings (or their symbols).

In the Casa di Sutoria Primigenia (I.13.2) the divine beings were not only present in the kitchen and food processing area,[75] but in the front hall as well, where an *armarium* was situated (Figs. 2 and 13) with various items stored in it. A niche in a pilaster at the northeastern side of the front hall is located at a rather low level above the surface. A terracotta figurine of a lying woman – a so-called "Bona Dea a banchetto" – was found in its surroundings.[76]

---

[72] See *NSc* 1899, p. 103-104, 145-146 and 345-346 (on the *patera*); fig. 7. Minerva bust 17 cm, Venus (alabaster) 17.4 cm, Venus (ivory) too badly preserved, Venus (bronze) 8.9 cm. Another example for a (laurel) wreath as motif in a *sacrarium* is Casa del doppio larario (VII.3.13), *ibid.* no. 266, fig. 32,1 in the lower of the two niches where a curled serpent dwells in the wreath.

[73] *NSc* 1899, p. 103 and 145 lists these findings: bronze – baking form, ladle, rings, sticks; glass – 12 vessels, three pendants; terracotta – lamp, colour plates, cassaforte, abevoir, small vessels, two miniature altars; iron – knife, heel; in the niche with wreath: knife, hammer, small terracotta altar.

[74] The relation of the human waste under divine surveillance would be another topic in the frame of "social metabolism".

[75] See above, p. 284-285.

[76] G. Stefani, "Una particolare iconografia pompeiana. Bona Dea a banchetto," *Ostraka. Rivista di antichità* 9 (2000), p. 428, no. 6, fig. 12. Such a figurine was also found in the front hall of the Casa del'Efebo I.7.10-12 close to the *sacrarium* in the front hall and in VI.14.27, L5; Stefani, *Iconografia*, nos 8 and 10, fig. 15 and 18 connected to *Lares*.

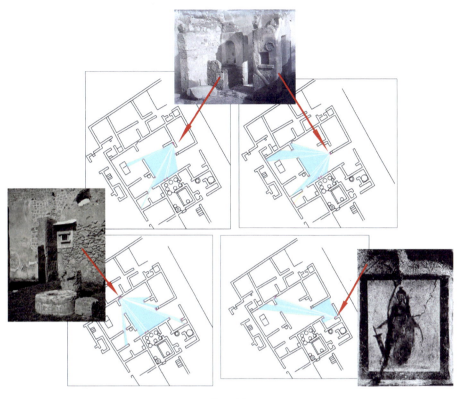

Fig. 12.
Workshop and dwelling V.4.9, isovists taken from the niches
(software /isovists.org, only the flat stuccoed image on the southern wall
is not included, since the angle of view is not discernible)
(plan after POEHLER 2017).

Very broadly speaking, this imagery relates to the female power in the house, whereas a bronze statuette of Minerva found in the niche in the garden of the same house (Fig. 13, bottom centre), represents a more general divine power, and belonged maybe to the niche-*sacrarium* in the rear wall behind the garden *triclinium*.[77]

---

[77] Minerva (PAP inv. 10560), 22.5 cm with base that carries an inscription to the *familia*. Other findings from the house: A. GALLO, *La casa di Lucio Elvio Severo a Pompei*, Napoli, Arte tipografica, 1994 (*Monumenti / Accademia di Archeologia, Lettere e Belle Arti di Napoli*): male herm, Hercules, two busts of deities; the box with metal objects containted spatula, tweezers, knife/cutter, box. KAUFMANN-HEINIMANN, *Götter und Lararien*, fig. 155. The tools do not point to an "Ärztehaus" according to B. GEISSLER, "Arzthäuser in Pompeji," *Kölner und Bonner Archaeologica* 1 (2011), p. 7-36.

Fig. 13.
Casa di Sutoria Primigenia (I.13.2), findings of religious routines and daily life activities (plan after POEHLER 2017; www.pompeiiinpictures.com, I.13.2, part 2, © Jackie and Bob Dunn, by permission of the Ministero della Cultura – Parco Archeologico di Pompei, retrieved 23 May 2021; GALLO, *Lucio Severo*, Tav. 7b; 22b; STEFANI, *Iconografia*, Fig. 12).

The pediment above the niche is decorated with a radiated sun. Whether the small room in the southeastern corner of the garden – with a basement in a corner – served as a *sacrarium* remains unclear.[78]

---

[78] STEFANI, *Iconografia*, p. 428, n. 39.

Whereas the *Lares* in the kitchen receive a sacrifice with many persons present, female deities of different competences and contexts are located at two places of the dwelling of I.13.2 where activities took place – the reclining woman in the front hall and Minerva in the garden area. The box with metal tools in the *armarium* – if for medical or other fine-mechanical usage – attest to some craft. Two larger weights of 1.18 kg in the central courtyard are of unclear purpose. However, spindles and loom weights suggest that weaving work was done in the house, while the purpose of the numerous glass containers is not clear.[79]

The described houses demonstrate that their *sacraria* marked areas of passage, of contact – often in working situations – and of specified activity. The connection of divinities to human agents worked easily in the front halls or courtyards – encounters by gazes, viewing and being looked at were unavoidable; in the kitchens, the human and the divine agents were closely entangled because of the limited space, and the clearer functionality. The mimetic effect of the feasting *familia* and the physically present people as well as the spatial closeness to storage facilities and food processing emphasised that connectedness.

3. *Routinized gazes and ritualised actions in Pompeian household religion*

People in the houses of Pompeii interacted on a daily and repeated base – often unconsciously – with the *Lares* and other deities in niches, wall paintings or as statuettes. With the concept of viewing act that embraces the multimodality of the media of religion – mimetic garlands, recognisable *Lares*, "frozen" sacrifices, vivid serpents in the Pompeian houses – and a practice-oriented approach to the socio-material environment, we were able to grasp how viewing the imagery and how patterned arrangements of image-objects worked, and how spatial and visual connections fostered the embedding of actions into daily routines. Perceiving and re-

---

[79] GEISSLER, *Arzthäuser*, p. 16-18. Some of the loom weights came to light in the kitchen area, whereas spindles have no clear find spot, GALLO, *Lucio Elvio*, p. 12; p. 123-124, no. 108, pl. 22 C-D and 29 G; p. 136-137, nno. 112-119, pl. 30 E-F, 31 B and 32 (loom weights); p. 158-164, without clear find spot, pl. 36 A-C, E-I and L-P (glass).

ceiving imagery as well as enacting or creating religious practices starts from the affordances and effectiveness of the image-objects, thus gaining closeness to the viewer and obtaining connectedness. Vision, visibility and relations of space and activities reconstructed from material culture are the archaeological parameters to unravel how iconographic, object-related and spatial patternedness generate visual and embodied routines; how the *sacraria* worked in human-divine communication and support. Pictorial and iconological strategies of the images and their location enable them to direct their unmediated presence, meaningfulness, and effect.[80] The imagery of divine figures and sacrificial scenes creates reality (a "world") in the act of viewing, reflecting it at the same time. Connectedness is the result of the effectiveness of the image-objects through style, size, explicitness, recognisability, mimetic overlaps, and location.

Whether viewing acts could become routinized and ritualised would largely depend on the position of the images, altars and niches: Surveillance of larger areas is given in some of the houses under investigation. In the limited spaces of food-processing areas or kitchens, people and images were close to each other. In courtyards, halls and gardens, interaction with the protective deities by gazes and movement was easily possible, while either idling on a bench or working. The imagery of *sacraria* was embedded in the practices of the users of the houses and dwellings spatially and by means of gazes. Moreover, these settings were closely related to the household resources, food, water and other belongings. To put everybody and everything belonging to various groupings in the nested households under the eyes of the deities in the houses or workshops is the foremost reason for the *sacraria*.

The spatial and embodied connectedness increases by a repeated act of viewing and passing by the patterned images and layout of the *sacraria* – through repetition of gaze and viewing, which is a criterion for ritualisation.

The patterns and types of images – *Lares* on tiptoes, *rhyta* in their raised hands, a *togatus capite velato*, serpents with their scaly skin, the garlands and altars, etc. as well as the three main positions

---

[80] Niches without paintings or findings of ritualised or ritualising objects are ubiquitous, see above, n. 4.

in the house (front hall, kitchen, open courtyard) establish a bundle of impressions that impact perception, reception, and cognition embedded in the (regular) activities in the house. Hence, they establish a direct link to the viewer and co-actant. Mimesis of what one sees and copies has a strong impact on individual orientation and social coordination; it produces and constructs a social environment.

These insights into what role such daily-life routines might have played in the creation of religious meanings, of social bonds, either in the core or extended family, in the neighbourhood or community, and the ritualisation of practices show that we should not underrate the religious activity of individuals "at home" and its socio-religious implications as basis of any religious knowledge and practices in a community or society.

Both the material of Pompeian household religion and the approach of image and practice theory reveal how religion with its social bonding capacities becomes accessible and tangible in the literal sense of the word. Spaces and groups in which the *sacraria* images or representations operate on a smaller daily scale are able to foster closeness and knowledge of the "what" and "why" of the depictions. These complex and far from consciously experienced or established interrelations and constructions of meaning crystallise materially in the household shrines. Their imagery – with deities and *numina* in the niches, on the walls, or above the hearth in Pompeian houses of the early first cent. CE, with the altars and gifts – and their compositorial and iconographical standardisation should be understood as a social practice, and the gaze on them as religious practice. From there, individuals learned about protective and dangerous powers, about alliances, communication, and reliability. These deities were closest to Pompeians in their everyday life during early Imperial times.

EMMANUEL PUI

LES PRATIQUES CULTUELLES DANS LES VILLAS GALLO-ROMAINES DU HAUT-EMPIRE

Nous nous écartons ici du cadre vésuvien, et même italique, pour nous intéresser à des contextes provinciaux. Plus spécifiquement, nous étudions les vestiges archéologiques témoignant de pratiques cultuelles domestiques au sein des villas implantées dans les provinces gauloises et germaniques de l'empire romain.

Ces grandes exploitations rurales ont été développées en Gaule et en Germanie, essentiellement à partir du Ier siècle ap. J.-C. Bien qu'ayant hérité d'une partie des caractéristiques formelles des grands établissements antérieurs à la conquête, elles témoignent d'une mutation économique sociale et culturelle de l'organisation de ces territoires. Les productions de ces vastes domaines ruraux étaient destinées à alimenter les réseaux commerciaux locaux mais également des marchés à l'échelle de l'empire. Les villas procuraient des revenus à leurs propriétaires citadins et leur fournissaient des résidences rurales bien équipées qu'ils occupaient épisodiquement, pour gérer leurs domaines et profiter d'une villégiature confortable. Ainsi sont-elles traditionnellement considérées par les chercheurs comme l'un des principaux marqueurs de l'adoption par les élites provinciales des valeurs culturelles et économiques portées par les Romains[1].

Existait-t-il, aux deux premiers siècles de notre ère, une opposition entre les cultes domestiques reconnus dans les villas et ceux pratiqués dans les établissements ruraux plus modestes ? En ma-

---

[1] P. GROS, *L'architecture romaine : du début du IIIe siècle av. J.-C. à la fin du Haut-Empire*, 1. *Les monuments publics*, Paris, A. et J. Picard, 3e édition mise à jour, 2011 (Les manuels d'art et d'archéologie antiques), p. 232.

tière cultuelle, les villas formaient-elles des « îlots de romanité » au sein de campagnes encore fortement imprégnées de culture gauloise[2] ?

Le recensement systématique des vestiges témoignant de pratiques cultuelles à l'intérieur des centres domaniaux de Gaule et de Germanie permet d'apporter des éléments de réponse à ces questions. D'une façon générale, les villas nous fournissent des contextes archéologiques privilégiés pour mener des études sur les cultes privés. Tout d'abord, elles formaient un maillage dense des territoires, et leur nombre compense en partie la rareté des découvertes liées aux pratiques cultuelles. Au total, sur l'ensemble des provinces gauloises et germaniques des Ier et IIe siècles, environ 230 villas ont livré de tels indices[3] (Fig. 1).

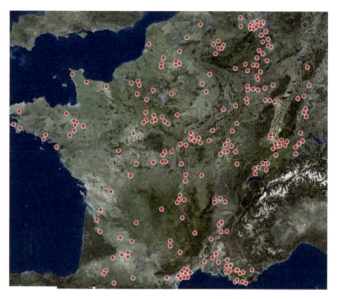

Fig. 1.
Localisation des villas de Gaule et de Germanie ayant livré des indices de pratiques cultuelles, datés des Ier et IIe siècles ap. J.-C.

---

[2] Pour une présentation de la vision dualiste des campagnes gallo-romaines : voir notamment P. OUZOULIAS, « Faut-il déromaniser l'archéologie des campagnes gallo-romaines ? », *Archéopages* 18 (2007), p. 21-25.

[3] Les données chiffrées sont extraites de la thèse soutenue le 04 mars 2022 à Aix-en-Provence par E. PUI, *Aménagements et pratiques cultuels dans les villas de Gaule et de Germanie durant le Haut-Empire*, Aix-Marseille Université, directeurs de thèse F. Quantin et C. Rousse.

Par ailleurs, lorsque du mobilier ou des aménagements sont découverts en contexte, ils le sont dans des espaces possédant des fonctions (résidentielles, agricoles ou artisanales) généralement bien identifiées. Les villas proposent en effet des structures extrêmement stables dans le temps, souvent sur une période de plusieurs siècles.

1. *Un mobilier cultuel varié reflétant les particularismes régionaux*

Le mobilier cultuel mis au jour, qu'il soit erratique ou associé à un contexte d'utilisation, fournit la part la plus importante des témoignages cultuels dans les villas. Ces objets, loin de former un groupe homogène sur l'ensemble du territoire, témoignent des mêmes particularismes régionaux que ceux découverts dans les autres contextes ruraux. Nous pouvons citer par exemple les hachettes votives du territoire helvète[4], les petites rouelles métalliques, essentiellement découvertes dans le quart nord-est de la Gaule et en Germanie[5] et les figurines

---

[4] Villas de Dietikon, Morat et Orbe (Suisse). K. Heid, *Repertorium zur Urgeschichte Dietikon und Umgebung*, Dietikon, Dietikon Verkehrsverein, 1965 (Neujahrsblatt von Dietikon 18), p. 3-29 ; C. Ebnöther, *Römischer Gutshof in Dietikon*, Dietikon, Dietikon Verkehrsverein (Neujahrsblatt von Dietikon 46), 1993, p. 4-72 ; E. Mouquin, E. Rossier, « Les haches miniatures du canton de Fribourg », *Cahiers d'Archéologie Fribourgeoise* 13 (2011), p. 112-125 ; E. Mouquin, « Morat : la villa de Combette et ses dépendances », *Cahiers d'Archéologie Fribourgeoise* 17 (2015), p. 126-129 ; D. Paunier, T. Luginbühl et al., *Urba I. La villa romaine d'Orbe-Boscéaz. Genèse et devenir d'un grand domaine rural*, 2 vol., Lausanne, 2016 (Cahiers d'Archéologie Romande 161-162).

[5] Villas de Brognon (Côte-d'Or), Corbeilles (Loiret), Damblain (Vosges), Gibloux (Fribourg), Juvigny (Marne), Matagne (Namur), Metz (Moselle) et Reinheim (Sarre-Palatinat). A. Cordier, *Sanctuaires et établissements ruraux aux abords de la voie Lyon – Trèves sur le territoire des Lingons*, Thèse de l'Université de Bourgogne, Dijon, 2015 ; M. Provost, R. Joly, M. Mangin, R. Goguey, G. Chouquet, *La Côte-d'Or*, 3 vol., Paris, Académie des Inscriptions et Belles-Lettres, 2009 (Carte archéologique de la Gaule 21) ; G. Poitevin, *Commune de Corbeilles (Loiret) « Franchambault »*, INRAP, 2007 (Rapport de fouille) ; G. Poitevin, « Corbeilles "Franchambault" », in *Les sites archéologiques de l'autoroute A19 (Loiret)*, Tours, FERACF, 2015, p. 361-364 ; K. Boulanger, *La villa à la Néréide. Un domaine agricole antique – pars urbana et pars rustica – réoccupé au premier Moyen Age*, Metz, INRAP GEN, 2012 (Rapport de fouille) ; K. Boulanger, « Mausolée cénotaphe ou temple ? Évolution des pôles funéraires et cultuels au sein du domaine bâti de la villa de Damblain

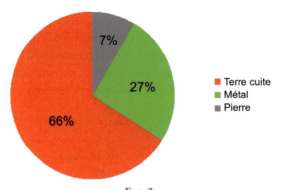

Fig. 2.
Répartition des figurines découvertes dans des villas du Haut-Empire,
de Gaule et de Germanie, selon leur type de matériau.

de type « Vénus à gaine », présentes dans le quart nord-ouest de la Gaule [6].

(Vosges) », in J.-N. Castorio, Y. Maligorne (coord.), *Mausolées et grands domaines ruraux à l'époque romaine dans le nord-est de la Gaule*, Bordeaux, Ausonius, 2016 (Scripta Antiqua 90), p. 123-144 ; P.-A. Vauthey, « Archéologie d'une vallée : la Sarine à contre-courant », *Archéologie Suisse* 30 (2007), p. 30-49 ; J. Monnier, « Un temple sort de terre : mise en valeur du fanum d'Estavayer-le-Gibloux », *Cahiers d'Archéologie Fribourgeoise* 13 (2011), p. 218 ; N. Achard-Corompt, *Juvigny « Les Monteux », les fouilles de 2008 et 2010*, Metz, INRAP Grand Est-Nord, 2012 (Rapport de fouille) ; N. Achard-Corompt, M. Kasprzyk, R. Durost, R. Bontrond, « Présence des élites en milieu rural en territoires rème et tricasse durant le Haut-Empire : l'apport dans les monuments funéraires », in Castorio, Maligorne, *Mausolées et grands domaines ruraux*, p. 35-64 ; G. De Boe, *Le sanctuaire gallo-romain dans la plaine de Bieure à Matagne-la-Petite*, Bruxelles, Service national des fouilles, 1982 (Archaelogia Belgica) ; R. Brulet, *Les Romains en Wallonie*, Bruxelles, Racine, 2008 ; G. Brkojewitsch *et al.*, « La *villa* gallo-romaine de Grigy à Metz (Ier s. apr. J.-C. - Ve s. apr. J.-C.) », *Gallia* 71.2 (2014), p. 261-305 ; A. Stinsky, *Die Villa von Reinheim*, Mainz, Nünnerich-Asmus Verlag, 2016 ; F. Müller, *Die Villenanlage von Reinheim – die Baugeschichte einer Großvilla vom längsaxialen Typus*, Thèse de l'Université de la Sarre, 2017.

[6] Villas de Saint-Germain du Puy (Cher), Bais (Ille-et-Vilaine), Saint-Patrice (Indre-et-Loire) et Pont-Croix (Finistère). M. Segard, *Saint-Germain-du-Puy – Cher (18) « Les Boubards »*, Chaponnay, Archedonum, 2012 (Rapport de fouille) ; D. Pouille, *Bais (Ille-et-Vilaine) – Bourg Saint-Pair. Un domaine rural de la campagne des Riedons*, INRAP GO, 2011 (Rapport de fouille) ; F. Le Boulanger, *Le bourg Saint-Pair. Une occupation antique au nord de la nécropole du haut Moyen Âge*, INRAP GO, 2006 (Rapport de diagnostic) ; T. Guiot, S. Raux, « La villa gallo-romaine de "Tiron" à Saint-Patrice (Indre-et-Loire) », *Revue Archéologique du Centre de la France* 42 (2003), p. 121-167 ; H. Le Carguet, « La statuette votive gallo-romaine de Kervénénec, en Pont-Croix », *Bulletin de la Société Archéologique du Finistère* 31 (1904), p. 104-110 ; P. Galliou, *Le Finistère*, Paris, Académie des Inscriptions et Belles Lettres, 1989 (Carte archéologique de la Gaule 29).

Les objets cultuels les plus fréquemment découverts dans les villas sont les figurines anthropomorphes ou zoomorphes. Nous en dénombrons près de 250 sur l'ensemble de la Gaule et de la Germanie romaines. Environ les deux tiers sont réalisées en terre cuite (Fig. 2).

TABLEAU 1.
Sujets représentés par des figurines découvertes dans des villas de Gaule et de Germanie, selon l'ordre décroissant de leur nombre d'occurrences.

Sujet	Céramique	Métal	Pierre	Total
Vénus	55	5	-	60
Nourrice assise[1]	35	-	-	35
Mercure	1	14	-	15
Minerve	4	2	-	6
Apollon	-	5	-	5
Amour	2	2	-	4
Fortune	1	-	2	3
Hercule	-	3	-	3
Jupiter	1	2	-	3
Bacchus	-	2	-	2
Cybèle	2	-	-	2
Épona	1	1	-	2
Junon	2	-	-	2
Mars	1	1	-	2
Sucellus	-	2	-	2
Victoire	1	1	-	2
Diane	-	1	-	1
Harpocrate	-	1	-	1
Isis	-	1	-	1
Risus	1	-	-	1
Personnage non identifié	41	10	13	64
Animal seul	13	13	1	27
Total	**161**	**65**	**16**	**242**

[1] Ce type iconographique est également nommé « déesse-mère », « déesse nourrice » ou « *Nutrix* ». Ces personnages sont traditionnellement identifiés à des divinités mais cette interprétation est actuellement remise en question (A. FERLUT, *Le culte des divinités féminines en Gaule Belgique et dans les Germanies sous le Haut-Empire romain*, soutenue à l'Université de Lyon, 2011, p. 40 ; A. BOSSARD, « Les terres (pas si blanches) de Vendeuil-Caply (Oise) », in *Figurines antiques d'ici et d'ailleurs itinéraire coroplastique de la Picardie au Bassin méditerranéen*, Amiens, Revue archéologique de Picardie, 2017, p. 45-62).

Les figurines réalisées en terre cuite représentent très majoritairement des personnages féminins et sont uniquement présentes dans la moitié nord de la Gaule et en Germanie (Fig. 3). Les Vénus et les nourrices assises sont les plus nombreuses et sont fréquemment associées dans les mêmes contextes (Fig. 4). Les quelques figurines en bronze représentant Vénus proviennent de villas de Narbonnaise. Ces aires de distribution régionales sont conformes à celles qui sont observées dans les autres contextes, qu'il s'agisse d'habitats, de sépultures ou de sanctuaires[7].

Naguère, ces petits objets en terre cuite étaient perçus comme des témoignages de cultes populaires, opposés dans leur forme à ceux pratiqués par les élites[8]. Cependant, certaines de ces figurines en céramique ont été découvertes, dans des espaces résidentiels d'établissements ruraux de prestige[9]. Ces objets constituaient un type d'offrande d'usage courant, dont la facture modeste ne préjuge pas du statut social du dévot.

Fréquemment, plusieurs figurines en terre cuite identiques (ou typologiquement très proches) sont présentes dans une même villa[10]. Elles sont même parfois associées entre-elles, au

---

[7] C. BÉMONT, M. ROUVIER-JEANLIN, C. LAHANIER (éd.), *Les figurines en terre cuite gallo-romaines*, Paris, Éditions de la Maison des sciences de l'homme, 1993 (DAF 38).

[8] Selon Alain Provost, ceux découverts dans le temple de la villa de Châtillon-sur-Seiche (Ille-et-Vilaine) « trahissent le culte éminemment populaire de la fécondité. L'absence de représentation en bronze et de grande statuaire plaident en faveur de la reconnaissance d'un édifice cultuel essentiellement à l'usage des populations laborieuses du *fundus* ». A. PROVOST, *Villa gallo-romaine de la Guyomerais, Chatillon-sur-Seiche (Ille-et-Vilaine)*, Rennes, Drac / Sra Bretagne, 1986, p. 46.

[9] Villa de Langon (Ille-et-Vilaine) et villa de Rodelle (Aveyron). R. SANQUER, « Circonscription de Bretagne », *Gallia* 31.2 (1973), p. 351-377 ; D. POUILLE, *Langon. « Le Balac »*, AFAN, SRA Bretagne, 1997 (Rapport de diagnostic) ; L. DAUSSE, « La villa romaine des Clapiès (Rodelle) », *Cahiers d'Archéologie Aveyronnaise* 6 (1992), p. 42-84 ; P. GRUAT, G. MALIGE, B. VIDAL, *L'Aveyron*, Paris, Académie des Inscriptions et Belles-Lettres, 2011 (Carte archéologique de la Gaule 12).

[10] Selongey (Côte-d'Or) : Vénus (NMI : 2), nourrices assises (NMI : 2), quadrupèdes (NMI : 5). Langon (Ille-et-Vilaine) : Vénus (NMI : 5), nourrices assises (NMI : 3). Mayen (Rhénanie-Palatinat) : personnages féminins (NMI : 7). Obermendig (Rhénanie-Palatinat) : personnages féminins assis (5). Rodelle (Aveyron) : têtes féminines (NMI : 4). Echternach (Luxembourg) : personnages féminins (NMI : 4). Habay (Virton, Be) : nourrices assises (2). Cesson-Sévigné

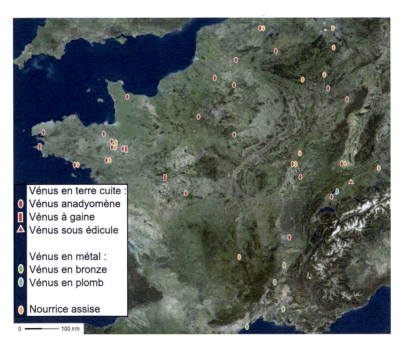

Fig. 3.
Localisation des villas ayant livré au moins une figurine de Vénus ou de nourrice assise.

Fig. 4.
Figurines en terre cuite représentant des nourrices assises et Vénus, découvertes dans le fanum de la villa de Carnac
(d'après J. MILN, *Fouilles faites à Carnac (Morbihan) les Bossenno et le Mont Saint-Michel*, Paris, Didier, 1877 D planches IV et V).

(Ille-et-Vilaine) : nourrices assises (2). Hoogeloon (Brabant P.-B.) : personnages féminins debouts sur un socle (2).

sein d'un même sanctuaire domestique. Ce type de répétition semble spécifique aux figurines en terre cuite[11]. Il témoigne de pratiques régulières, effectuées dans le cadre communautaire familial. Celles-ci marquaient très certainement des événements particuliers et récurrents (naissance, passage à l'âge adulte, mariage, etc.). La longue période de fréquentation des sanctuaires domestiques des villas entraînait une accumulation de ces petits objets de culte. Ils prenaient alors vraisemblablement une valeur générique. Leur profusion matérialisait ainsi l'existence d'une communauté stable, prospère et pieuse, reconnaissante envers les divinités du foyer.

D'une manière générale, une représentation divine fruste ou réalisée dans un matériau peu coûteux ne doit pas être considérée comme le reflet des faibles capacités financières du dédicant et surtout pas comme le témoignage d'un culte « indigène ». Il est probable que les objets les plus grossièrement façonnés ont été fabriqués sur place alors que les plus soignés provenaient d'ateliers spécialisés, parfois lointains. Cependant, une fabrication locale n'implique pas l'existence d'un culte local.

Par exemple, les figurines en pierre représentant des personnages féminins assis, découvertes dans les villas de Grimault (Yonne) (Fig. 5) et de Jonzac (Charente-Maritime), bien que massives et peu détaillées, reprennent les mêmes thèmes iconographiques et une partie des attributs des déesses romaines traditionnelles de la fertilité et de la fécondité. Leur style et leur mode de fabrication ne permettent pas d'identifier des divinités locales.

Ainsi, les villas nous livrent aussi bien des objets de culte particulièrement soignés que d'autres, plus grossièrement réalisés, comme l'illustrent les trois stèles suivantes, dont la première est aisément identifiable à Minerve (Fig. 6). Il serait périlleux de traduire les différences stylistiques en une opposition culturelle, censée illustrer l'existence d'un panthéon gaulois héritier de la protohistoire. Les limites de nos connaissances sur ce sujet doivent nous inciter à la prudence[12].

---

[11] Dans ce volume, N. Amoroso décrit des modalités d'association ou de dédoublement différents, concernant les figurines métalliques.

[12] S. Deyts, *Images des dieux de la Gaule*, Paris, Errance, 1992, p. 20.

FIG. 5.
Figurine en calcaire découverte dans la villa de Grimault (h : 0,18 m)
(R. MARTIN, « Circonscription de Dijon », *Gallia* 18.2 (1960),
p. 328-364, fig. 33).

a    b    c

FIG. 6.
Stèles découvertes dans les villas de St-Cyr-sur-Mer (Var), Téting (Moselle)
et Latresne (Gironde) (h. resp. : 0,14 m, 0,25 m et 0,26 m)
(É. ESPÉRANDIEU, *Recueil général des bas-reliefs de la Gaule romaine*,
Paris, Imprimerie nationale, 1907, vol. 10, n° 7534 et vol. 1 n.° 42 ;
J. COUPRY, « IXe Circonscription », *Gallia* 13 (1955), p. 190-192, p. 192).

Certaines divinités romaines « rustiques » se prêtaient également bien à des représentations plus frustes, exécutées par les habitants eux-mêmes. Généralement, les statues de Priape étaient réalisées en bois. Dans la villa de Martial, c'est le *vilicus* lui-même qui avait construit l'autel dédié à Silvain[13]. Les images cultuelles de facture modeste, ou anciennes, pouvaient se voir attribuer un surcroît de valeur symbolique. Elles permettaient notamment d'associer la piété envers les Lares à celle due aux aïeux[14]. Ainsi, comme partout ailleurs, y compris à Pompéi, les figurines présentes dans les sanctuaires domestiques formaient des groupes « très hétérogènes, sans unité de matériaux ni de taille ni de qualité »[15]. Par exemple, dans la villa de Vallon, dans le même ensemble de figurines métalliques découvert dans une pièce d'apparat richement décorée, se côtoyaient deux représentations très différentes de la même déesse (Fig. 7)[16].

Des statues lithiques de grande qualité, reprenant des types classiques gréco-romains, sont parfois mises au jour dans les villas les plus importantes. Ces découvertes sont notamment nombreuses en Narbonnaise. Cependant, la plupart de ces objets de luxe constituaient probablement des éléments décoratifs et non des supports de culte. Plusieurs ont été ainsi découverts près de bassins d'agrément ou dans des espaces thermaux[17]. La plupart du temps, les fragments statuaires importants proviennent de colonnes votives ou d'un temple associé à la villa. Or, ces derniers, plutôt rares, ne participaient probablement pas du culte domestique. Ils possé-

---

[13] Martial, *Épigrammes* X, 92.

[14] « Ah ! Protégez-moi, Lares de mes pères : c'est vous aussi qui m'avez nourri, lorsque, petit enfant, je courais à vos pieds. Et ne rougissez pas d'être taillés dans un vieux tronc : ainsi vous habitâtes l'antique demeure de mon aïeul. » Tibulle, *Élégies* I, 10, 15-21 (Paris, Les Belles Lettres, 1967 ; traduction M. Ponchont).

[15] A. KAUFMANN-HEINIMANN, « Statuettes de laraire et religion domestique à Pompéi », in *Contributi di archeologia vesuviana III : I culti di Pompei*, Roma, « L'Erma » di Bretschneider, 2007 (Studi della Soprintendenza archeologica di Pompei), p. 151-157, part. p. 153.

[16] Sur ces dédoublements, voir la contribution de N. Amoroso dans ce volume.

[17] Pour ce qui concerne les découvertes récentes : une statue d'Harpocrate en marbre dans le comblement d'un bassin dans la villa de Peltre (Moselle) et une tête d'Éros en marbre dans le niveau de comblement d'une fontaine à Aspiran (Hérault). M. FELLER, « Peltre (Moselle) '*Les Rouaux*' », Metz, INRAP GEN, 2006 (Rapport de fouille) ; information orale, S. Mauné 2020.

Fig. 7.
Figurine en bronze et plaquette en plomb, représentant Diane, découvertes à Vallon (d'après M. E. Fuchs, « Témoignages du culte domestique en Suisse romaine », in *Sacrum facere*, Edizioni Università di Trieste, 2016 (Polymnia. Studi di archeologia), p. 99-131, p. 130 ; M. Bouyer, G. Bougarel, J.-L. Boisaubert, « Époque romaine », *Chron. Archéologique* (1985),p. 28-65, p. 63).

daient vraisemblablement un caractère communautaire plus large et ne sont pas traités ici.

2. *Des sanctuaires domestiques accueillant toutes les divinités du territoire*

Les figurines en métal sont majoritairement celles de dieux et de déesses issus du panthéon traditionnel romain, mais certaines divinités plus spécifiquement gauloises sont également représentées[18].

---

[18] Épona et Sucellus dans la villa de Buvilly (Jura) et Sucellus dans la villa de Lépine (Pas-de-Calais). M.-P. Rothé, *Le Jura*, Paris, Académie des Inscriptions et Belles-Lettres, 2001 (Carte archéologique de la Gaule 39), p. 254 ; C. Pietri, « Circonscription du Nord », *Gallia* 31.2 (1973), p. 313-321 ; A. Kaufmann-Heinimann, « Ikonographie und Stil. Zu Tracht und Ausstattung einheimischer Gottheiten in den Nordwestprovinzen », in *Collections électroniques de l'INHA. Actes de colloques et livres en ligne de l'Institut national d'histoire de l'art*, INHA, 2017, fig. 8-9.

TABLEAU 2.
Pourcentage du nombre total de figurines en métal représenté par les divinités les plus souvent attestées.

Divinité	Villas de Gaule et de Germanie (42 figurines)	Sanctuaires domestiques des provinces de Gaule, Germanie, Rhétie et Norique[1]
Mercure	31%	30%
Vénus	12%	5%
Apollon	12%	5%
Hercule	7%	< 5%
Jupiter	5%	8%
Minerve	5%	7%
Mars	< 5%	7%
Divinités plus rarement attestées	Bacchus, Diane, Épona, Fortune, Harpocrate, Isis, Sucellus	

[1] A. KAUFMANN-HEINIMANN, *Götter und Lararien aus Augusta Raurica : Herstellung, Fundzusammenhänge und sakrale Funktion figürlicher Bronzen in einer römischen Stadt*, Basel, Suisse, Augst, 1998, p. 163.

Mercure, comme le rappelle William Van Andringa, étant le garant des activités lucratives et commerciales, était honoré souvent et en tout lieu[19]. Logiquement, les villas, à la fois complexes résidentiels, productifs et commerciaux, en accueillaient fréquemment des représentations. Celles-ci prenaient très souvent la forme de figurines en bronze. Mercure représente environ un tiers du total des objets de ce type découverts lors des fouilles des centres domaniaux[20].

Il est cependant à noter que parmi les 65 figurines en bronze découvertes dans les villas de Gaule et de Germanie, aucune ne représente un Lare. Nous possédons uniquement une plaquette épigraphique votive dédiée à des Lares[21]. Par ailleurs, il n'existe

---

[19] W. VAN ANDRINGA, « La religion – cultes et sanctuaires », in A. FERDIÈRE, *La Gaule Lyonnaise*, Paris, 2011, p. 107-108.

[20] Sur la présence récurrente de Mercure en contexte domestique, voir la contribution de N. Amoroso, dans ce volume.

[21] Dans la villa de Pontaix (Drôme) (*CIL*, XII 1564). J. PLANCHON, M. BOIS, P. CONJARD-RÉTHORÉ, *La Drôme*, Paris, Académie des Inscriptions et Belles-Lettres, 2010 (Carte archéologique de la Gaule 26), p. 494-496.

en contexte domanial qu'un seul autel dédié à un *Genius* et une seule figurine en bronze représentant vraisemblablement le *Genius* du *paterfamilias*[22].

Ce résultat peut sembler surprenant. À Pompéi, par exemple, parmi les 117 figurines métalliques dont le sujet a été identifié, 23 représentent un Lare[23]. Cependant, si l'on se restreint aux ensembles découverts dans les villas de cette région, nous retrouvons cette absence des Lares[24]. Le groupe de figurines de la villa de Vallon en Suisse, qui nous est parvenu entièrement, n'en compte pas non plus[25]. Ceci peut s'expliquer par le fait que les centres domaniaux ne constituaient pas la résidence principale du propriétaire, celle qui traditionnellement accueillait les Lares familiaux[26]. Columelle note pourtant que les repas du personnel de la villa doivent se tenir à proximité des Lares du maître et Caton exhorte la femme de l'intendant à prier les Lares familiaux les jours de fête[27]. Il est cependant probable que ces divinités, autant attachées à la famille qu'à la maison[28],

---

[22] Dans la villa de Plassac (Gironde) et dans la villa de Rognac (Bouches-du-Rhône) (*LGN*, 658). J. COUPRY, « Circonscription de Bordeaux », *Gallia* 23.2 (1965), p. 413-442 ; H. SION, *La Gironde*, Paris, Académie des Inscriptions et Belles-Lettres, 1994 (Carte archéologique de la Gaule 33), p. 101-106 ; H. DE GÉRIN-RICARD, « Autel magique de Rognac », *Provincia* IX (1929), p. 31-37 ; F. GÂTEAU, *L'étang-de-Berre*, Paris, Académie des Inscriptions et Belles-Lettres, 1996 (Carte archéologique de la Gaule 13/1), p. 276.

[23] M.-O. LAFORGE, *La religion privée à Pompéi*, Naples, Centre Jean Bérard, 2009, p. 88.

[24] Villa de Fondo d'Acunzo à Boscoreale, villa de Fondo Imperiali à Boscoreale et villa de Fondo Aconfora à Scafati : d'après les données de KAUFMANN-HEINIMANN, *Statuettes de laraire*. Voir, dans ce volume, les remarques de C. Sfameni.

[25] M. E. FUCHS, « Témoignages du culte domestique en Suisse romaine », in F. FONTANA, E. MURGIA (éd.), Sacrum facere. *Lo spazio del 'sacro' : ambienti e gesti del rito, Atti del III Seminario di Archeologia del Sacro (Trieste, 3-4 ottobre 2014)*, Trieste, Edizioni Università di Trieste, 2016 (Polymnia. Studi di archeologia 7), p. 99-131.

[26] A. DURAND, W. VAN ANDRINGA, « To live or not to Live. The Lares and the Transfer of the *domicilium* in a Roman Town », in R. BERG (dir.), *Tangible Religion. Materiality of Domestic Cult Practices from Antiquity to Early Modern Era*, Rome, Quasar, 2021 (Acta Instituti Romani Finlandiae), p. 85-91, part. p. 90.

[27] Columelle, *De l'agriculture* XI.I.19 ; Caton, *De l'agriculture* 143.

[28] M.-O. CHARLES-LAFORGE, « Les cultes privés chez les Romains (IIIe s. avant - IIIe s. après J.-C.) », *Pallas* 111 (2019), p. 171-197.

étaient déplacées lorsque le propriétaire cédait un bien immobilier [29].

D'une façon générale, dans les sanctuaires domestiques des villas, comme dans ceux des *domus* [30], se côtoyaient des divinités locales, romaines ou d'origine étrangère. Le lot d'objets cultuels découvert dans la villa de Vallon en Suisse illustre cette diversité. Il est essentiellement composé de 13 figurines en bronze (dont Mercure, Diane, Hercule, Mars, Apollon, Harpocrate et Isis) et d'un calice en bronze portant une dédicace aux *Suleviae* [31], qui sont des divinités féminines essentiellement attestées en Gaule et en Germanie. Ces artefacts gisaient sur le sol d'une pièce d'apparat, détruite par un violent incendie.

Les quelques autels inscrits qui nous sont parvenus, majoritairement issus de la partie méridionale de la Gaule, nous renseignent sur l'identité de certaines des divinités honorées dans les villas. Jupiter [32], Silvain [33], Castor [34] et à nouveau les *Suleviae* [35]

---

[29] Voir, dans ce volume, la contribution d'A. Durand.

[30] Voir, dans ce volume, la figure 6 de la contribution de N. Amoroso.

[31] *AE*, 2002, 1058 ; FUCHS, *Témoignages du culte domestique*.

[32] Dans la villa de Niefern (Bade-Wurtemberg), associé à la famille impériale (*AE*, 1923, 31) ; W. FISCHER, « Römischer Altar und Bruchstücke einer Jupitergigantensäule von Oeschelbronn », *Germania* 6 (1922), p. 43-45 ; P. STEMMERMANN, « Römischer Gutshof in Öschelbronn », *Badische Fundberichte Amtliches Nachrichtenblatt für die ur- frühgeschichtliche Forschung Badens* 3 (1936), p. 321-329.

[33] Dans la villa de Lacoste (Vaucluse). J. MOURARET, *Lacoste – Les Viginières (Vaucluse)*, Avignon, Association archéologique vauclusienne, 2009 (Rapport de fouille).

[34] Dans la villa de Domazan (Gard) (*AE*, 1959, 195) et dans celle de La Cadière-d'Azur (Var) (*AE*, 2010, 853). F. BENOIT, « Un autel des Dioscures au fouet à Domazan (Gard) », *OGAM* IX (1957), p. 249-254 ; M. PROVOST, J.-M. PÈNE, H. PETITOT, *Le Gard*, Paris, Académie des Inscriptions et Belles-Lettres, 1999 (Carte archéologique de la Gaule 30), p. 354-355 ; M. BORRÉANI, *Fouille préventive nécessitée par l'urgence absolue au domaine des Salettes (La Cadière-d'Azur)*, Toulon, Centre archéologique du Var, 2006 (Rapport de fouille) ; M. BORRÉANI, F. LAURIER, « La *villa* antique des Salettes (commune de La Cadière-d'Azur, Var) », *Bulletin Archéologique de Provence* 33 (2010), p. 27-48.

[35] Dans la villa de Lambesc (Bouches-du-Rhône) (*ILN* III, 256). J. GASCOU, *Inscriptions latines de Narbonnaise III. Aix-en-Provence*, Paris, CNRS, 1995 (Supplément à Gallia), p. 322 ; F. MOCCI, N. NIN, *Aix-en-Provence, Pays d'Aix, Val de Durance*, Paris, Académie des Inscriptions et Belles-Lettres, 2006 (Carte archéologique de la Gaule 13/4), p. 571-572.

sont mentionnés. Notons également la présence de deux divinités topiques, Laha[36] et Abnoba[37].

Laha n'est connue que par quatre autres inscriptions, toutes découvertes dans un rayon de 10 km (Fig. 8). Il s'agit certainement d'une divinité d'un petit territoire du piémont pyrénéen[38]. Dans cette région, ce sont environ quarante divinités locales qui ont été identifiées grâce à la découverte de nombreux autels votifs[39].

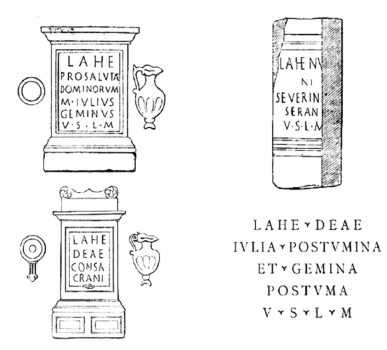

FIG. 8.
Reproductions des inscriptions mentionnant la déesse Laha
(J. SACAZE, M. A. LEBÈGUE, *Inscriptions antiques des Pyrénées*, E. Privat, 1892).

---

[36] Dans la villa de Sana (Haute-Garonne). J. SACAZE, M. A. LEBÈGUE, *Inscriptions antiques des Pyrénées*, Toulouse, E. Privat, 1892, p. 298-299 ; J. MASSENDARI, *La Haute-Garonne (hormis le Comminges et Toulouse)*, Paris, Académie des Inscriptions et Belles-Lettres, 2006 (Carte archéologique de la Gaule 31/1), p. 336-339.

[37] Dans la villa de Pforzheim (Bade-Wurtemberg) (*CIL*, XIII, 06332).

[38] J.-L. SCHENCK-DAVID, « Le panthéon pyrénéen », in *Autels votifs*, Toulouse, Conseil général de la Haute-Garonne, 1990, p. 33-57.

[39] L. RODRIGUEZ, R. SABLAYROLLES, *Les autels votifs du musée Saint-Raymond, musée des Antiques de Toulouse*, Toulouse, Musée Saint-Raymond, musée des Antiques de Toulouse, 2008, p. 28.

La présence de la déesse Abnoba est uniquement attestée dans la région de la Forêt Noire. Il est d'ailleurs possible que le nom même d'Abnoba ait désigné ce massif durant l'Antiquité[40]. Plusieurs autres inscriptions indiquent que cette déesse était parfois identifiée à Diane[41].

À partir de deux stèles découvertes en contexte rural, Raphaël Golosetti évoque l'existence d'un possible culte aux Mères et/ou aux Proxsumes qui aurait été développé dans des villas du sud-est de la Gaule[42]. Ce second groupe de divinités est essentiellement attesté dans la basse vallée du Rhône et surtout en contexte privé[43].

Non seulement les divinités d'origine locale ou romaine ne se distinguaient pas nécessairement par leurs modes de représentation, mais elles prenaient place dans des mêmes panthéons publics, mis en place progressivement à l'échelle des cités, comme l'a montré W. Van Andringa dans sa synthèse consacrée aux cultes publics en Gaule[44]. Dans ce cadre, les divinités anciennement présentes sur le territoire patronnaient fréquemment des parties de celui-ci, ou différentes communautés, suivant les subdivisions administratives de la cité. Dans un *pagus*, un *vicus*, une *curia* ou une *regio*, les habitants honoraient leurs divinités tutélaires. Si ces cultes constituaient une affirmation de leur appartenance à un groupe territorial ou social bien défini, celle-ci ne se construisait pas en opposition avec le reste de la communauté civique mais comme une composante celle-ci.

---

[40] H. Horn, « Abnoba. Eine Zusammenfassung alter und neuer Forschungserkenntnisse », *Die Ortenau. Zeitschrift des Historischen Vereins für Mittelbaden* 94 (2014), p. 434-464.

[41] W. Heinz, « Der Altar der Diana Abnoba in Badenweiler », *Archäologische Nachrichten aus Baden* 27 (1981), p. 13-20.

[42] R. Golosetti, « Deux lieux de culte de domaine foncier sous le regard croisé de l'archéologie, de la sculpture et de l'épigraphie : Saint-Vincent (Saint-Paul-Trois-Châteaux) et Beauvoir (Allan) », in S. Agusta-Boularot, E. Rosso (dir.), Signa et tituli. *Monuments et espaces de représentation en Gaule méridionale sous le regard croisé de la sculpture et de l'épigraphie*, Paris, Errance, 2014 (Bibliothèque d'Archéologie Méditerranéenne et Africaine 18), p. 221-237.

[43] A. Buisson, « Un monument dédié aux *Proxsumae* retrouvé dans la vallée du Rhône », *Revue Archéologique de Narbonnaise* 30.1 (1997), p. 269-275.

[44] W. Van Andringa, *La religion en Gaule romaine. Piété et politique (Ier-IIIe siècle apr. J.-C.)*, Paris, Errance, 2017, p. 257-261.

À une échelle plus locale encore, les domaines ruraux, occupant de vastes espaces, abritaient diverses divinités topiques. Les façons de les nommer, de les représenter et de les honorer ont évolué au cours du temps. Cependant, qu'elles aient été identifiées ou non par les habitants, leur accord devait être sollicité pour exploiter les terrains où elles résidaient[45]. De façon complémentaire, les propriétaires sacrifiaient à la fois aux divinités anciennement présentes sur le territoire et à celles, plus universelles, dont le pouvoir d'action s'étendait aux éléments naturels et aux travaux des champs.

Ainsi, non seulement le mobilier cultuel découvert dans les villas n'est pas spécifique à ce type d'établissement, mais les divinités qui y étaient honorées ne se distinguent pas de celles présentes sur le territoire, ou le micro-territoire, qui accueillait le domaine.

3. *Des aménagements cultuels fonctionnels*

Les aménagements cultuels des villas, du moins durant les deux premiers siècles de notre ère, étaient toujours modestes. Le plus souvent, nous peinons d'ailleurs à les identifier archéologiquement. L'état d'arasement des vestiges ne permet notamment pas de restituer les équipements placés en hauteur, tels les niches ou les peintures murales, dont nous savons grâce aux découvertes effectuées dans la région de Pompéi qu'ils constituaient souvent les seuls aménagements cultuels fixes dans les habitations. Dans la villa de Vallon, par exemple, les figurines étaient exposées ou rangées dans un simple meuble en bois[46].

Nous pouvons dans certains cas identifier de petites structures maçonnées ayant servi à présenter des objets cultuels[47], ou des espaces destinés à accueillir un sanctuaire domestique. Il peut s'agir

---

[45] « Qui que tu sois, dieu ou déesse, à qui ce bois est consacré, comme tu as droit que l'on te sacrifie un porc en expiation... » Caton, *De l'agriculture*, 139 (Paris, Les Belles Lettres CUF, 1975 ; traduction : R. Goujard).

[46] J.-B. GARDIOL, S. REBETEZ, F. SABY, « La villa gallo-romaine de Vallon FR : une seconde mosaïque figurée et un laraire », *Archéologie Suisse* 13 (1990), p. 169-184.

[47] Dans les villas de Langon (Ille-et-Vilaine) et de La Cadière-d'Azur (Var). Cf. notes 10 et 33.

dans ce cas d'un simple renfoncement [48] ou d'une petite pièce, parfois de forme absidiale, s'ouvrant généralement sur un espace ouvert, atrium ou péristyle [49].

Ces équipements ne présentaient jamais un aspect ostentatoire mais semblent avoir essentiellement obéi à des considérations fonctionnelles. Parmi celles-ci, la valeur symbolique de l'emplacement choisi et la visibilité jouaient un rôle primordial. En effet, en certaines occasions, les cérémonies cultuelles devaient pouvoir être effectuées en présence de nombreux participants ou spectateurs. Le besoin de visibilité fonctionnait d'ailleurs dans les deux sens. Les divinités devaient également assurer un contrôle visuel sur l'ensemble des activités domestiques, dont elles assuraient la réussite, mais aussi la surveillance [50]. C'est ainsi que nous observons à Pompéi que leurs représentations étaient parfois placées à l'entrée des celliers, ou que le coffre-fort de la maison était fréquemment installé à proximité du laraire [51].

Les installations agricoles de certaines villas permettent de mettre en évidence cette recherche d'un emplacement optimal pour bénéficier d'une action divine bienfaisante. Dans la villa Regina de Boscoreale, par exemple, la niche qui accueillait une représentation de Bacchus se trouve à côté de la porte de la cuisine et fait face au chai (Fig. 9). Un autel surmonté de fresques, ren-

---

[48] Dans la villa de Bad-Neuenahr (Rhénanie-Palatinat). H. FEHR, *Römervilla : Führer durch die Ausgrabungen und Ausstellung am Silberberg Bad Neuenahr-Ahrweiler*, Koblenz, Archäologische Denkmalpflege des Landesamtes für Denkmalpflege Rheinland-Pfalz, Amt Koblenz, 1993 (Archäologie an Mittelrhein und Mosel).

[49] Dans les villas de Darnets (Corrèze), Rodelle (Aveyron) et Tourves (Var). P.-F. FOURNIER, « Circonscription de Clermont-Ferrand », *Gallia* 17.2 (1959), p. 363-377 ; G. LINTZ, *La Corrèze*, Paris, Académie des inscriptions et Belles-Lettres, 1992 (Carte archéologique de la Gaule 19), p. 128 ; DAUSSE, *Villa romaine des Clapiès* ; P. GRUAT, G. MALIGE, B. VIDAL, *L'Aveyron*, Paris, Académie des Inscriptions et Belles-Lettres, 2011 (Carte archéologique de la Gaule 12), p. 363-364 ; F. BENOIT, « Circonscription d'Aix-en-Provence (Partie Sud) », *Gallia* 16.2 (1958), p. 412-447 ; J.-P. BRUN, *Le Var*, Paris, Académie des Inscriptions et Belles-Lettres, 1999 (Carte archéologique de la Gaule 83/1), p. 835-840.

[50] Voir, dans ce volume, la contribution de M. Mauger.

[51] W. VAN ANDRINGA, *Quotidien des dieux et des hommes. La vie religieuse dans les cités du Vésuve à l'époque romaine*, Rome, École Française de Rome, 2009 (BEFAR 337), p. 227 et 240.

Fig. 9.
Aménagements cultuels de la Villa Regina : autel installé à proximité du réceptacle du moût et niche faisant face au chai (clichés E. Pui 2019).

voyant également à l'univers bacchique, était implanté à proximité du réceptacle du moût[52]. Un aménagement similaire existe dans la villa de N. Popidius Narcissus Maior, à Scafati.

L'importance symbolique du récipient destiné à accueillir le liquide obtenu par pressage est également illustrée dans l'établissement oléicole de La Garde (Var), par le dépôt d'un jeune porcin sous le sol de l'huilerie, au contact du cuveau de réception de l'huile d'olive (Fig. 10).

Dans la villa vinicole de La Cadière-d'Azur (Var), un autel se trouvait dans la couche d'effondrement d'une pièce contiguë au pressoir. Il était vraisemblablement installé sur le massif maçonné adossé à un mur, présent à proximité. Les bassins de réception du moût étaient visibles depuis cet aménagement. L'espace qui l'accueillait ne communiquait pas avec la partie centrale de la villa mais s'ouvrait sur une cour secondaire, utilisée pour les activités viticoles. De cette position « stratégique », la divinité occupant ce petit sanctuaire, Castor en l'occurrence, pouvait assurer sa fonction de protection et de surveillance du pressoir, mais aussi de l'entrée du chai (Fig. 11).

---

[52] S. De Caro, *La villa rustica in località Villa Regina a Boscoreale*, Roma, G. Bretschneider, 1994.

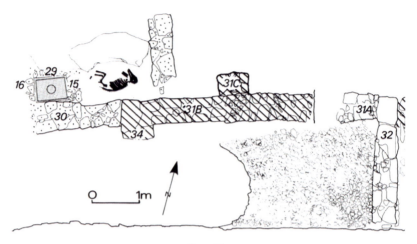

Fig. 10.
Plan du dépôt faunique de l'établissement gallo-romain précoce de La Garde
(d'après J.-P. Brun, G. B. Rogers, P. Columeau, M. Thinon, M. Gérard,
« La villa gallo-romaine de Saint-Michel à La Garde (Var).
Un domaine oléicole au Haut-Empire », *Gallia* 46.1 (1989), p. 103-162, p. 108).

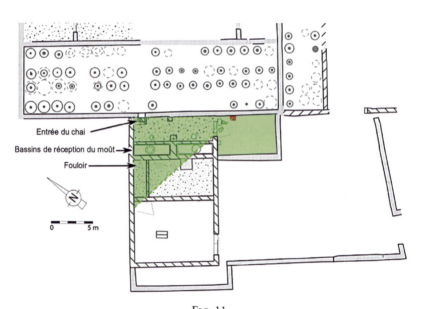

Fig. 11.
Représentation de l'espace visible (en vert) depuis le probable aménagement
cultuel (en rouge) de la villa de La Cadière (d'après M. Borréani, F. Laurier,
« La villa antique des Salettes (commune de La Cadière-d'Azur, Var) »,
Bull. Archéologique Provence (2010), p. 27-48, p. 31).

Signalons également le cas du petit espace cultuel de la villa de Pouzac (Hautes-Pyrénées) qui était implanté dans une cour de service de la partie thermale de l'établissement. Trois autels, dont un inscrit, ont été découverts à côté de leurs bases respectives encore en place. L'emplacement de ce petit sanctuaire, difficilement accessible et non visible pour les visiteurs, a très certainement été choisi pour une raison pratique liée à sa fonction. Selon l'interprétation qu'en propose Jean-Luc Schenck-David, il s'agirait à l'origine d'un *fulgur conditum* installé près d'un lieu touché par la foudre [53]. La divinité, ici Jupiter, se serait symboliquement approprié cet espace.

L'évolution du sanctuaire domestique de la villa de Rodelle (Aveyron) montre que ceux-ci étaient également porteurs de l'histoire de la maison. L'aménagement cultuel initial, implanté à proximité immédiate de la cuisine, a été maintenu après le déplacement de cette dernière et la réalisation d'importants réaménagements modifiant l'ensemble du plan de la villa. Ce petit sanctuaire a été plusieurs fois reconstruit, embelli et agrandi. Au IIe siècle, il a notamment pris la forme d'une pièce à abside, conforme aux innovations architecturales de cette période [54]. Cependant, son emplacement original, qui marquait celui du foyer de la maison, n'a pas été modifié durant la très longue durée d'occupation de [55].

La vocation première de ces aménagements cultuels n'était pas l'affirmation ou l'affichage d'une identité culturelle ou sociale du propriétaire vis-à-vis de ses visiteurs. Chacun de ces petits sanctuaires possédait une fonction concrète précise. Ils étaient implantés, équipés et honorés de façon à pouvoir jouer au mieux leur rôle spécifique dans le bon fonctionnement de la villa et le bien-être de ses habitants.

Chaque villa était dotée d'une très grande diversité d'aménagements et de dispositifs de protection spécifiques et com-

---

[53] J.-L. SCHENCK-DAVID, « À propos d'un nouvel autel votif découvert à Saint-Pé-d'Ardet en Haute-Garonne », *Aquitania* 22 (2006), p. 171-204.

[54] E. MORVILLEZ, « Apparition et développement des absides dans l'architecture domestique gallo-romaine », in C. BALMELLE, H. ERISTOV, F. MONIER (éd.), *Décor et architecture en Gaule entre l'Antiquité et le haut Moyen Âge. Actes du Colloque international. Université de Toulouse II-Le Mirail, 9-12 octobre 2008*, Bordeaux, Aquitania, 2011, p. 257-278.

[55] DAUSSE, *Villa romaine des Clapiès*.

plémentaires, adaptés à tous les types d'activités et d'espaces. Ils prenaient des formes parfois très visibles[56] et parfois réduites à un unique objet scellé[57]. Ensemble ils formaient un « maillage protecteur étroit »[58] permettant d'assurer les garanties divines nécessaires au bon fonctionnement de l'établissement. Chaque propriétaire jouissait d'une très grande liberté d'initiative tant pour la mise en place des aménagements cultuels de son domaine que pour l'organisation et la réalisation des pratiques rituelles. Chacun construisait une topographie rituelle unique et personnalisée pour sa maison[59].

4. *Des rituels adaptés aux cultes romains mais empreints des traditions locales*

Il existe des différences formelles importantes entre les pratiques rituelles qui avaient cours en Gaule et en Germanie à la période protohistorique et celles issues de la culture méditerranéenne gréco-latine. Elles se distinguent notamment par des types d'offrandes différents. Or, la nature de ces dernières a connu une évolution importante, amorcée dès le début du Ier siècle av. J.-C.[60]. Gérard Bataille relève que la principale nouveauté apparue à cette période est l'introduction d'objets cultuels par nature, « totalement inconnus dans la Gaule indépendante », et non plus

---

[56] Une vingtaine de colonnes joviennes sont attestées au sein de villas, essentiellement en Germanie, mais également dans le Massif-Central.

[57] Dans les villas de Paulhan et de Sauvian, dans l'Hérault, il s'agit d'une monnaie scellée dans la maçonnerie d'un mur. G. BARRUOL, « Circonscription de Languedoc-Roussillon », *Gallia* 33.2 (1975), p. 491-528 ; I. BERMOND, M. FEUGÈRE, « Un dépôt de fondation (monnaies gauloises) sur le site de Marinesque Combe-Rouge à Loupian (Hérault) », *Cahiers Numismatiques* 213 (2017), p. 5-11 ; M. CLAVEL, *Béziers et son territoire dans l'antiquité*, Paris, Les Belles Lettres, 1970 (Annales littéraires de l'université de Besançon 112), p. 109 ; D. UGOLINI, C. OLIVE, *Le Biterrois*, Paris, Académie des Inscriptions et Belles-Lettres, 2003 (Carte archéologique de la Gaule 34/5), p. 496-499.

[58] VAN ANDRINGA, *Quotidien des dieux et des hommes*, p. 261.

[59] P. FOSS, « Watchful Lares : Roman household organization and the rituals of cooking and dining », in R. LAURENCE, A. WALLACE-HADRILL (éd.), *Domestic space in the roman world : Pompeii and Beyond*, Portsmouth, RI, JRA, 1997 (Journal of Roman Archaeology Suppl. 22), p. 197.

[60] É. GOUSSARD, « Produire pour offrir. L'offrande par destination chez les Celtes », *Techniques et Cultures* 70 (2018), p. 200-213.

uniquement d'objets utilitaires[61]. Ce changement témoigne de profondes transformations des pratiques rituelles dans le monde celtique, découlant d'une mutation des sociétés, liée à une influence grandissante de la culture gréco-romaine[62]. Cependant, ce processus est antérieur à la diffusion du modèle de la villa dans ces provinces, voire à la conquête romaine. Les centres domaniaux ont donc pris place dans des territoires dont les formes rituelles étaient déjà en grande partie renouvelées.

Les principaux indices matériels dont nous disposons pour tenter de percevoir les modalités d'exercice des pratiques cultuelles domestiques sont les dépotoirs contenant des objets utilisés lors des cérémonies, et les dépôts rituels. Or, de ce point de vue non plus, les villas ne se distinguent pas des autres habitats ruraux ou des sanctuaires implantés dans les mêmes territoires. Nous en détaillons quelques exemples.

Les gobelets datés des Ier et IIe siècles, découverts en nombre important dans le dépotoir du sanctuaire domestique de la villa de Rodelle (Aveyron), sont identiques à ceux utilisés dans les différents sanctuaires du territoire rutène. Il s'agit de récipients en terre cuite, à pied étroit, recouverts le plus souvent d'un engobe blanc. Ils servaient de contenants pour de petites offrandes alimentaires, solides ou liquides.

Certains des dépôts en fosse mis au jour dans des espaces extérieurs contenaient une partie d'un vaisselier céramique et, fréquemment, des reliefs de nourriture[63]. Ils sont le résultat de l'en-

---

[61] G. BATAILLE, « Principes d'évolution des ensembles de mobiliers métalliques issus de sanctuaires dans le quart est de la Gaule, entre les IIIe s. av. - IIe s. apr. J.-C. », in M. REDDÉ et al. (dir.), *Aspects de la Romanisation dans l'Est de la Gaule*, Glux-en-Glenne, 2011 (Bibracte), vol. 2, p. 660.

[62] GOUSSARD, *Produire pour offrir*, p. 203.

[63] Dans les villas de Cernay-lès-Reims (Marne), Corbeilles (Loiret), Dury (Somme) et Hamois (Province de Namur). A. KOEHLER, Cernay-lès-Reims (Marne) *« Les Petits Didris » : Villa gallo-romaine : Barreau est de Reims, itinéraire de substitution – Contournement de Witry-les-Reims*, Metz, INRAP GEN, 2004 (Rapport de fouille) ; POITEVIN, *Commune de Corbeilles* ; POITEVIN, *Franchambault* ; P. QUÉREL, M. FEUGÈRE, *L'établissement rural antique de Dury (Somme) et son dépôt de bronzes (IIIe s. av. J.-C. - IVe s. apr. J.-C.)*, Villeneuve d'Ascq, Revue du Nord, Université Charles-de-Gaulle – Lille 3, 2000 (Revue du Nord, hors-série, Collection Art et Archéologie 6) ; S. LEFERT, *La villa gallo-romaine du Hody, à Hamois : un modèle original*, Namur, Société archéologique de Namur, 2018 (*Namur*. Archéologie 1).

fouissement rituel des restes d'un repas cérémoniel. Ce type de dépôt est également documenté dans des sanctuaires et dans des établissements ruraux beaucoup plus modestes[64].

Les dépôts aviaires des villas de Loupian (Hérault)[65] et de Castillon-du-Gard (Gard)[66] semblent s'inscrire dans une tradition locale attestée depuis au moins le IVe siècle av. J.-C., en Occitanie et en Catalogne. Sous le sol des habitats, on découvre fréquemment un ou plusieurs pots contenant un œuf ou un serpent[67]. L'exemple de Castillon-du-Gard montre que ce rituel régional a perduré au moins jusqu'au IIIe siècle ap. J.-C.

Qui ordonnait et réalisait ce type de petits rituels ? En théorie, comme le rappellent les auteurs des traités d'agronomie antique, notamment Columelle, seul le *dominus*, responsable de la communauté familiale, était en charge des cultes au sein de la villa. L'intendant ne possédait théoriquement aucune autonomie en la matière. L'auteur rejette d'ailleurs les superstitions populaires qui pourraient guider les actions du *vilicus* et qui seraient préjudiciables au bon fonctionnement de l'exploitation. Cependant, comme le relève Stéphanie Wyler, Columelle prend soin, dans un souci de pragmatisme, de rappeler au propriétaire l'intérêt de s'appuyer sur les savoirs empiriques des habitants des campagnes, notamment pour lutter contre les prodiges[68]. De la même façon,

---

[64] Comme par exemple dans l'établissement rural de Saint-Zacharie (Var) : P. Digelmann, I. Rodet-Belarbi, « Pratiques rituelles en milieu rural. Note sur un dépôt d'offrandes dans un établissement agropastoral du Haut-Empire (Saint-Zacharie, Var) », *Bulletin Archéologique de Provence* 38 (2017), p. 65-75.

[65] C. Pellecuer, *La* villa *des Près-Bas (Loupian, Hérault) dans son environnement. Contribution à l'étude des* villae *et de l'économie domaniale en Narbonnaise*, 2 vol., Aix-en-Provence, Thèse de l'Université Aix-Marseille I-Université de Provence, 2000.

[66] N. Rovira, « La *villa* de La Gramière (Castillon-du-Gard) Premier bilan de la recherche », *Revue Archéologique de Narbonnaise* 42 (2009), p. 115-216.

[67] V. Fabre, V. Forest, J. Kotarba, « Dépôts cultuels domestiques dans la ferme d'époque romaine du Pla de l'Aïgo », *Revue Archéologique de Narbonnaise* 33 (1999), p. 271-292 ; J. Cazas, J. Ruiz de Arbulo, « Ritos domésticos y cultos funerarios. Ofrendas de huevos y gallináceas en villas romanas del territorio emporitano (S. III d.C.) », *Pyrenae* 28 (1997), p. 211-227.

[68] S. Wyler, « Pratiques et représentations religieuses dans les villas de Campanie à l'époque néronienne », in O. Devillers (éd.), *La villégiature dans le monde romain de Tibère à Hadrien*, Bordeaux, Ausonius, 2014 (*Neronia* IX ; Scripta Antiqua 62), p. 61.

tout en rappelant sa méfiance envers l'astrologie, il concède qu'il peut être bénéfique d'utiliser les connaissances acquises par le *vilicus* sur ce sujet[69].

La tablette de défixion en plomb découverte dans la villa de Flavin (Aveyron) montre que, le cas échéant, le propriétaire pouvait avoir recours à des rituels encore plus marginaux, ici de type « magique », pour assurer la sécurité de son domaine. Le texte gravé est daté stylistiquement du Ier siècle ap. J.-C. Il est rédigé en latin mais contient des formules en langue gauloise[70]. Il est mentionné que le demandeur usait de ce procédé dans le but d'interdire l'accès de son domaine à un individu précis.

Il n'existait visiblement pas d'opposition entre ces différentes pratiques. Elles pouvaient être mises en œuvre de façon simultanée et complémentaire pour offrir la protection la plus complète possible aux installations du domaine et à ses habitants.

5. *Conclusion*

Ni les découvertes archéologiques effectuées en Gaule et en Germanie romaines, ni nos connaissances sur l'organisation cultuelle des territoires ne nous autorisent à considérer qu'il existait des pratiques cultuelles domestiques différentes entre les membres de l'élite occupant les villas et les autres habitants des campagnes. Ce que nous pouvons en restituer s'apparente essentiellement à un ensemble de dispositifs et de gestes « utiles » au bon fonctionnement du domaine et à la protection de ses habitants. Partout, ces pratiques paraissent conformes aux usages en cours dans un territoire donné et à une période donnée.

Les propriétaires de ces villas, membres des élites locales, étaient probablement en partie les mêmes que ceux qui, investis de fonctions municipales, avaient la charge de la gestion des cultes publics. Cependant, rien de ce que nous observons ne nous permet de supposer que leurs résidences rurales avaient vocation à servir de relais locaux à la diffusion du culte civique, ni même

---

[69] Columelle, *De l'agriculture* X, 337-341.
[70] M. MARTIN, « Les plombs magiques de la Gaule méridionale », *Ephesia Grammata* 5 (2012), online.

à celle d'une religion romaine qui se serait opposée à des traditions cultuelles anciennes.

Ainsi, nous ne percevons pas d'enjeux de « romanité » en matière de cultes domestiques dans les villas de Gaule et de Germanie. Les propriétaires les plus aisés disposaient de nombreux autres moyens de témoigner de leur adhésion à la culture romaine. Ils pouvaient notamment le faire par l'architecture et la décoration de leur centre domanial, ainsi que par la construction de tombeaux monumentaux de style classique, ce qui était fréquemment le cas. En revanche, ils n'avaient probablement aucune raison de se démarquer des pratiques cultuelles qui avaient cours sur le territoire, voire sur le micro-territoire dans lequel leurs établissements étaient installés. Dans le cadre privé comme public, toutes les divinités, locales ou non, avaient vocation à patronner les diverses activités humaines, conformément à leurs compétences spécifiques et à leurs places respectives dans les panthéons civiques et domestiques. En aucune façon, les indices de pratiques cultuelles présents dans les villas ne nous autorisent à identifier une hypothétique origine ethnique ou culturelle du propriétaire, ni un degré d'assimilation plus ou moins grand des élites provinciales à la culture romaine. Les cultes domestiques puisaient essentiellement leurs formes dans une tradition culturelle locale, qui transcendait les classes sociales, mêlant à la fois des éléments indigènes et romains.

AUDE DURAND

RÉFLEXION SUR LE DEVENIR ET LA PROPRIÉTÉ DES *SACRARIA* EN CONTEXTE DOMESTIQUE *

« Rien de ce qui est sacré ou religieux ne peut être vendu[1] ! » Cette clause de Sabinus, relative aux contrats de vente et rapportée par Ulpien, illustre bien le caractère indisponible, en droit sacré et en droit public, de certaines *res* à l'époque impériale[2]. En l'occurrence, il s'agit ici des *res sacrae* et des *res religiosae*, mais cela concernait également les *res sanctae* ainsi que les *res publicae*[3]. Ces choses, retranchées du commerce des hommes[4], étaient affectées pour toujours à la cité ou aux dieux. En particulier, un espace ou un bâtiment, une fois consacré, devenait la propriété de la (ou des) divinité(s) auquel il était dédié ; cette procédure, impliquant des rites réalisés par un magistrat, le rendait dès lors perpétuellement indisponible.

À l'inverse, les *res priuatae* étaient patrimoniales, appropriables donc, et, à ce titre, pouvaient être vendues, données, héritées, transformées ... En contexte domestique, les laraires ou tout autre espace de culte, n'ayant pas été consacrés par un magistrat,

---

* Sauf mention contraire, les photographies sont de l'auteur et ont été réalisées avec l'aimable autorisation du *Parco archeologico di Pompei*.

[1] *Digeste*, XVIII, 1, 22 : *Si quid sacri, uel religiosi est, eius uenit nihil*.

[2] Plusieurs témoignages textuels prouvent que, dès l'époque républicaine, les *res diuinae* et les *res publicae* étaient déjà caractérisées par leur inappropriabilité et leur inaliénabilité, mais ce n'est qu'à l'époque impériale, à Rome, que certains auteurs ont formalisé un tel régime.

[3] Y. Thomas, « La valeur des choses. Le droit romain hors la religion », *Annales HSS* 6 (2002), p. 1431-1462.

[4] Commerce est ici à entendre au sens large d'échange, aussi bien onéreux (une vente) que gratuit (donation, legs, succession ...).

n'étaient pas, du point de vue du droit, « sacrés ». Au contraire, relevant des *sacra priuata*, ils faisaient partie du patrimoine (*pecunia*) du *paterfamilias*. Celui-ci pouvait donc *a priori* en disposer à sa guise.

Pourtant certains passages littéraires ou juridiques manifestent une certaine ambiguïté attachée à ce que, en contexte domestique, nous appelons *sacraria*. Par exemple, Festus précise que, suivant les rites accomplis, les espaces de culte privés pouvaient être « considérés comme sacrés[5] ». À qui donc appartient le *sacrarium* installé dans un lieu de métier ou dans une habitation ? Qu'advient-il de lui lorsque change le propriétaire de l'édifice où il se trouve ? Est-il conservé, modifié ou condamné à l'occasion d'un déménagement, d'une vente, d'une donation, d'un legs ou d'un héritage ? Sans même envisager de changement de propriétaire, dans quelle mesure était-il possible d'apporter des modifications (des réfections ou des ajouts) à un espace sacré privé ?

Bien que les textes conservés soient peu prolixes sur le sujet, ils fournissent un point de départ essentiel pour émettre certaines hypothèses. Celles-ci confrontées à un ensemble de données matérielles pompéiennes – qu'il conviendrait d'étoffer à l'avenir –, permettent de réfléchir sur la propriété et le devenir des *sacraria* domestiques. Minces, ces éléments laissent entrevoir des jeux d'échange et de redistribution des domaines urbains, notamment des établissements marchands et artisanaux, ce qui témoigne, une fois de plus, de l'impact des configurations sociales et économiques sur les pratiques religieuses des particuliers.

1. *Des sources textuelles peu disertes*

Les sources antiques sont très peu bavardes sur le sujet. À ma connaissance, il n'existe aucune mention sur la propriété ou le devenir des *sacraria* privés dans la jurisprudence latine. Parmi le corpus imposant des sources juridiques relatives à la propriété

---

[5] Festus (éd. Lindsay), p. 424. La polémique relative au caractère sacré ou non de la maison de Cicéron montre également que les catégories du droit public et du droit sacré n'étaient pas en pratique toujours perçues par les particuliers (Cicéron, *Lettres à Atticus*, IV, 2, 3 et IV, 2, 7).

immobilière rassemblées par Julien Dubouloz[6], il n'est jamais fait état des aménagements religieux ; tout au plus est-il question de statues, mais celles-ci, faisant partie des *ornamenta*, doivent être entendues comme des statues décoratives, non cultuelles. Cela s'explique d'une part par le fait que, dès l'époque républicaine, il s'opère une scission entre le droit civil (*ius ciuile*) et le droit religieux (*ius pontificum* ou *ius sacrum*)[7]. D'autre part, les lois relatives aux *res sacrae* concernaient essentiellement la religion publique puisque, comme les pontifes ne pouvaient gérer directement l'ensemble des *sacra priuata*, ceux-ci étaient laissés à la discrétion du responsable de la communauté concernée (père de famille en contexte domestique, *magister collegii* en contexte associatif …).

Finalement seules quelques très rares allusions dans les textes littéraires constituent un point de départ aux hypothèses que les données matérielles permettent d'émettre. Par exemple, un passage du *Trinummus* de Plaute nous apprend que, à l'occasion d'un changement de domicile, il était d'usage d'offrir une couronne aux Lares familiaux ; cette offrande, accompagnée de prières, visait à assurer la prospérité et le bonheur au sein de la nouvelle demeure[8]. Ces Lares, comme les divinités domestiques d'une manière générale, étaient propres à chaque *familia* ; ils semblent en outre avoir marqué le *domicilium*, c'est-à-dire la résidence administrative principale du père de famille, celle d'où il gérait son patrimoine et ses affaires civiques[9]. Étudier le devenir des *sacraria*

---

[6] J. Dubouloz, *La propriété immobilière à Rome et en Italie (I{er}–V{e} siècles). Organisation et transmission des* praedia urbana, Rome, École française de Rome, 2011 (BEFAR 343).

[7] Cette scission, dont la publication en 304 av. J.-C. du *Ius Flauianum* de Appius Claudius Caecus et de son secrétaire Cnaeus Flauius constitue une étape importante (Tite-Live, *Ab Vrbe Condita*, IX, 46, 5 ; Valère Maxime, *Des faits et des paroles mémorables*, II, 5, 2 ; *Digeste*, I, 2, 2, 7), est bien marquée à l'époque de Cicéron (Cicéron, *Lettres à Brutus*, 156), mais n'est définitivement scellée que sous le Principat. Sur ce point : A. Maiuri, Sacra privata. *Rituali domestici e istituti giuridici in Roma antica*, Roma, « L'Erma » di Bretschneider, 2013 (Storia delle religioni 19), p. 11-12.

[8] Un personnage de cette comédie de Plaute, Calliclès, après avoir acheté la maison de son ami Charmide, s'adresse à son épouse en ces termes (Plaute, *Trinummus*, 39-42) : *Larem corona nostrum decorari uolo. | Vxor, uenerare ut nobis haec habitatio | bona fausta felix fortunataque euenat.*

[9] A. Durand, W. Van Andringa, « To live or not to live : The Lares and the transfer of the *domicilium* in a Roman Town », in R. Berg (dir.), *Tangible Religion. Materiality of Domestic Cult Practices from Antiquity to Early Modern Era*, Rome, Quasar, 2021 (Acta Instituti Romani Finlandiae), p. 85-91.

présents dans un édifice nécessite donc *a priori* de distinguer les cas où l'édifice passait entre les mains d'un propriétaire extérieur à la famille initiale de ceux où il restait à un membre de celle-ci.

1.1. Legs, donation, vente d'un édifice à un propriétaire extérieur à la *familia* initiale

Compte tenu de l'unicité des *sacra priuata* et de l'exclusion d'étrangers à une *familia* au cours de ses rites domestiques[10], lorsqu'un bâtiment résidentiel ou économique devenait la propriété d'un individu extérieur à la famille initialement installée – ce qui était possible dans le cas d'une vente, d'un legs ou d'une donation –, alors le Lare mentionné dans le *Trinummus* de Plaute et, plus généralement, l'ensemble des divinités dorénavant honorées étaient celles de la *familia* du nouveau propriétaire : ces divinités devenaient les nouveaux dieux protecteurs de l'édifice et de ses occupants. À l'inverse, les dieux anciennement présents dans la maison, spécifiques aux propriétaires antérieurs, ne recevaient plus de témoignages de dévotion. Il semblerait donc que, lors d'un changement de domicile, les anciens propriétaires (ou leurs héritiers dans le cas d'un legs) s'en allaient avec leurs statuettes cultuelles, tandis que les nouveaux arrivaient avec les leurs. C'est l'image qui transparaît à travers plusieurs passages littéraires dont les plus célèbres sont certainement ceux qui mentionnent Énée ayant quitté Troie en emportant les statuettes de ses Pénates[11], c'est-à-dire de ses dieux familiaux.

Il paraît assez probable, sans qu'il soit facile de le démontrer, qu'il en allait de même du mobilier cultuel. Dans son étude sur la propriété immobilière à l'époque impériale, J. Dubouloz montre que le droit des successions et le droit des ventes distinguent clai-

---

[10] L'étude des sources littéraires et juridiques permet de mettre en évidence trois caractéristiques majeures des *sacra privata* : 1. Ils étaient uniques, propres à chaque noyau familial (choisis en fonction de l'histoire et de l'activité économique de la famille) ; 2. Ils excluaient des cérémonies domestiques les individus extérieurs à la *familia* ; 3. Ils se transmettaient par voie masculine, conjointement au patrimoine familial. Ces éléments ont été mis en évidence par l'analyse des données textuelles faite par A. Maiuri (MAIURI, Sacra privata) et clairement résumés par M. Bassani. Voir M. BASSANI, Sacraria. *Ambienti e piccoli edifici per il culto domestico in area vesuviana*, Rome, Edizioni Quasar, 2008 (Antenor quaderni 9).

[11] Virgile, *L'Énéide*, I, 378-379 ; II, 717-749.

rement, dans la dotation mobilière, les *res aedium*, c'est-à-dire les objets immobilisés dans la propriété[12] – ceux que le *Code civil* français qualifierait d'« attachés à perpétuelle demeure » –, de la *supellex*, soit le mobilier personnel du père de famille servant à son usage quotidien[13]. Comme le *paterfamilias* se servait régulièrement de l'*instrumentum* rituel, étant l'acteur principal officiant lors des cérémonies religieuses domestiques, on peut envisager sans trop d'hésitation que celui-ci faisait partie de sa *supellex* et était donc emporté lors d'un changement de domicile. *A contrario*, les aménagements cultuels bâtis (niches, édicules, autels maçonnés ...) devaient être rattachés à l'immobilier ; ils étaient probablement entendus comme *pars domus* et surtout, à la manière des *ornamenta*, ils devaient – au moins pour les *sacraria* les plus imposants – participer à la qualification sociale et familiale de l'habitation (éventuellement du local artisanal ou commercial).

1.2. Legs, donation, vente d'un édifice à un membre de la même *familia* et cas des héritiers

Des réflexions similaires peuvent être menées dans le cas où le changement de propriétaire se faisait au sein d'une même *familia*. Il pouvait là encore s'agir d'une vente[14] ou – et ce devait être plus fréquent – d'un legs[15] ou d'une donation[16]. En outre, bien

---

[12] Cela concerne bien entendu des éléments constitutifs de l'édifice (charpente, tuiles, système de fermeture ou d'alimentation en eau, ...) mais aussi le décor (*ornatus* ou *ornamenta*) qui, reflétant le statut et la volonté du *paterfamilias*, jouait un rôle symbolique majeur dans la définition sociale et familiale d'une propriété ; c'est « ce qui fait d'une *aedes* une *domus* » (DUBOULOZ, *La propriété immobilière*, p. 79-87, en part. p. 85).

[13] Sur la dotation mobilière : DUBOULOZ, *La propriété immobilière*, p. 63-104 et p. 589-595 (en part. p. 66 et p. 90-97).

[14] Par exemple, si un esclave obtenait la liberté du vivant de son maître, on peut imaginer des clauses dans le contrat d'affranchissement par lesquelles le *libertus* achetait le local où il travaillait avant d'acquérir son nouveau statut.

[15] Ainsi il n'était pas rare qu'un *dominus* prévoit, dans son testament, d'affranchir certains de ses esclaves, en leur léguant – éventuellement sous conditions (un certain nombre de jours dus, versement d'une partie de leur chiffre d'affaires à l'héritier, ...) – la boutique ou l'atelier dans lequel ils avaient travaillé du vivant de leur maître. Finalement le quotidien de ces *liberti* devait souvent rester très proche de celui avant leur manumission, réalisant à l'égard de leur *patronus*, ce qu'il faisait auparavant pour leur *dominus*.

[16] La note précédente peut facilement se transposer à une situation de donation, en imaginant simplement que l'affranchissement et la dotation mobilière se

que l'héritage pût concerner un individu extérieur à la famille du défunt, la loi imposait l'adoption des *sacra priuata* de ce dernier. Les dispositions testamentaires visaient en effet à garantir la continuité du *nomen* et de la lignée familiale du défunt[17] ; les *heredes* devaient dès lors, en acceptant tout ou partie des biens familiaux (*pecunia*) du testateur, adopter (ou conserver) les *sacra priuata* de ce dernier, constitutifs de l'identité familiale et entendus comme partie intégrante du patrimoine de chaque *familia* romaine.

À la mort du *paterfamilias*, aussi bien dans le cas d'un legs au sein de la *familia* que d'un héritage, il ne paraît pas impossible que l'ensemble du *sacrarium* (aussi bien les aménagements religieux, maçonnés ou non, que le mobilier rituel, statues de culte et objets liturgiques) ait été conservé tel quel au sein de l'habitation ou du local légué ou hérité. Quand bien même l'on laisserait de côté des questions purement pratiques évidentes, le fait de sacrifier aux mêmes divinités, dans le même espace sacré et avec les mêmes équipements cultuels, n'était-ce pas symboliquement la manière la plus efficace de faire perdurer l'identité familiale ?

Enfin, dans le cas d'une vente ou d'une donation à un membre de la *familia*, s'il paraît probable que les aménagements bâtis restaient à demeure, il est plus délicat de savoir à qui revenait le mobilier rituel : statuettes et éléments liturgiques partaient-ils avec le père de famille, à charge dès lors du nouveau propriétaire de « ré-équiper » son espace de culte ?

En définitive, les textes antiques conservés ne fournissent que très peu d'éléments pour connaître le devenir des *sacraria* privés au cours de l'histoire du bâtiment dans lequel ils étaient établis. Le droit des ventes et des successions, couplé à l'analyse

---

faisaient, non plus à la mort du donateur, mais de son vivant. Néanmoins, soulignons que la manumission par testament restait le mode d'affranchissement le plus fréquent.

[17] Le fils (naturel ou adopté) ou l'affranchi héritait des divinités du père ou de l'ancien maître. Tous les dieux du *paterfamilias* étaient alors conservés d'une génération à l'autre ou suite à un affranchissement ; tout au plus, de nouvelles divinités pouvaient être ajoutées, suivant le principe d'agglomération des cultes propre au polythéisme, particulièrement fréquent dans la religion romaine. Les divinités familiales étant liées à l'histoire et aux activités de la *familia*, on imagine aisément qu'un événement particulier ou de nouvelles activités, économiques notamment, pouvaient entraîner l'adoption de nouvelles divinités, plus à même de définir et protéger le noyau familial.

de quelques rares allusions littéraires ou juridiques sur les *sacra priuata*, permet d'émettre quelques hypothèses sur les éléments qui, à l'occasion d'un changement de propriétaire, soit partaient avec l'ancien *dominus*, soit restaient sur place.

En revanche, rien dans la jurisprudence latine ne permet d'envisager ce qu'il advenait de ces aménagements religieux bâtis, une fois la propriété passée entre de nouvelles mains : étaient-ils réutilisés en l'état par les nouveaux propriétaires ? Tout en étant maintenus, étaient-ils repeints ? Subissaient-ils des ajouts ou tout autre réfection avant d'accueillir les nouvelles divinités tutélaires de l'édifice ? Au contraire, pouvaient-ils perdre leur fonction religieuse en étant soit condamnés (voire détruits), soit détournés de leur rôle initial ?

Si les sources textuelles à disposition sont muettes à ce sujet, plusieurs témoignages archéologiques pompéiens prouvent que certains *sacraria* domestiques furent condamnés à un moment donné de l'histoire du bâtiment dans lequel ils avaient été installés. Même si un tel moment est souvent difficile à préciser et, surtout, bien que les raisons d'une telle transformation demeurent en général une énigme, l'étude du bâti permet parfois de proposer quelques hypothèses[18].

2. *Des observations archéologiques à multiplier*

2.1. Des indices de réfections régulières

Notons en premier lieu que divers exemples pompéiens attestent des entretiens relativement réguliers que purent recevoir certains *sacraria* privés. À plusieurs reprises en effet, la chute des couches d'enduit les plus récentes laisse entrevoir, sous certaines peintures religieuses, les traces d'images sacrées plus anciennes : ceci est vrai pour les autels de carrefour[19] ; ceci se retrouve aussi dans les habi-

---

[18] Seule la répétition d'observations semblables sur cette question pourra permettre de confirmer les conjectures émises.

[19] C'est le cas pour l'autel de carrefour n° 14, localisé au croisement des îlots IX 7 et IX 11 ou encore pour celui (n° 16) situé au sud-est de l'*insula* IX 12. W. VAN ANDRINGA, « Autels de carrefour, organisation vicinale et rapports de voisinage à Pompéi », *Rivista di Studi Pompeiani* XI (2000), p. 54-58 ; W. VAN

tations[20]. Plutôt que des réfections, il s'agirait dans ces cas-là de simples restaurations d'aménagements cultuels plus anciens, restaurations révélatrices du soin et de l'attention qui étaient portés aux *sacraria*.

Dans le commerce alimentaire en I 8, 8.9, ouvert sur la *Via dell'Abbondanza*, le célèbre laraire figurant, dans un pseudo-édicule avec tympan en stuc, la scène traditionnelle du *paterfamilias* effectuant une libation, encadré par les Lares, eux-mêmes accompagnés de Bacchus et de Mercure, repose sur un précédent aménagement sacré. La chute de l'enduit le plus récent dévoile en effet, au-dessus du laraire, les restes d'un autre tympan en stuc, deux fois plus petit que le nouveau et désaxé par rapport à celui-ci (Fig. 1) : en effet, si le nouveau laraire se trouve au centre des deux ouver-

FIG. 1.
Le *sacrarium* du commerce alimentaire en I, 8, 8.9. Dans les dernières années de la vie de la cité pompéienne, un laraire fut aménagé dans l'axe du comptoir de vente. Sous le dernier laraire apparaît un *sacrarium* plus ancien.

ANDRINGA, *Quotidien des dieux et des hommes : la vie religieuse dans les cités du Vésuve à l'époque romaine*, Rome, École française de Rome, 2009 (BEFAR 337), p. 172-174.

[20] Par exemple, le laraire de la maison de C. Iulius Philippus (IX 1, 1-3) est une peinture circonstanciée, réalisée à un moment précis de l'histoire de la famille, pour le retour sans encombre du *dominus* (VAN ANDRINGA, *Quotidien des dieux et des hommes*, p. 249-253).

tures vers les espaces arrière, l'ancien pseudo-édicule avait été réalisé directement à droite de la porte menant à l'arrière-boutique. Cette réfection du *sacrarium* doit-elle être mise en relation avec un changement d'activité au sein du lieu de métier – par exemple avec l'installation du commerce alimentaire, éventuellement associé à un changement de propriétaire ? Ou peut-être simplement cette réfection participe-t-elle à l'ensemble des réaménagements subis par le bâtiment, en particulier sur sa façade nord, suite aux épisodes sismiques quelques années avant l'éruption[21]. En tout cas, elle prend clairement en compte la fonction de l'établissement commercial puisque le nouveau *sacrarium* se trouve désormais parfaitement aligné avec l'un des bras du comptoir maçonné (l'*instrumentum* de l'établissement)[22].

2.2. Changement d'activité économique d'un établissement et condamnation d'un *sacrarium*

Dans quelques cas, la condamnation d'un aménagement religieux semble pouvoir être mise en relation avec un changement d'activité du lieu, éventuellement associé à un changement de propriétaire de l'établissement. À ce titre, l'exemple de l'atelier de production de *garum* des *Umbricii* (I, 12, 8) paraît assez significatif. En effet, tout en conservant des espaces résidentiels, le laboratoire fut installé au sein d'une ancienne habitation dans la dernière décennie de la vie de Pompéi (Fig. 2a). À ce moment, il possédait plusieurs espaces sacrés : un laraire était peint au-dessus du foyer de la cuisine et le *viridarium*, où étaient stockés les amphores et

---

[21] Plusieurs ouvertures des édifices de l'*insula* I 8 présentent des montants tantôt en *opus vittatum*, tantôt en brique, attribués aux restaurations menées dans le quartier suite au tremblement de terre de 62/63 apr. J.-C. Par ailleurs, si quelques pièces en I 8, 8.9 conservent en partie une décoration du IIème style (tel le sol du *cubiculum* ouvert sur l'atrium ou le pan méridional de l'arrière-boutique), une majorité des espaces (commerce alimentaire et arrière-boutique, ainsi que *xystus, tablinum, triclinium, oecus, cubiculum* dans la partie résidentielle du bâtiment) ont reçu de nouveaux décors dans une phase ultérieure, leurs sols ou leurs murs étant attribués à la phase IIB du IIIème style.

[22] Signalons que la niche aménagée dans le *cubiculum* n'était probablement pas destinée à des fins cultuelles. En effet, outre le fait qu'il s'agirait d'un emplacement peu usuel pour un *sacrarium*, l'absence de mobilier religieux et l'enduit blanc dans et tout autour de la niche, suggèrent qu'elle devait plutôt servir à des fins pratiques, notamment au dépôt d'une lampe pour éclairer cette pièce relativement sombre.

les *dolia* semi-enterrés contenant le *garum*, comportait un autel à l'extrémité septentrionale du *pluteus*. Si laraire et autel ont pu dater d'une époque antérieure à l'installation de l'atelier, notons que ces aménagements furent maintenus quand on y produisit et stocka la précieuse sauce de poisson. En revanche, une niche présente dans le mur ouest de l'atrium – probablement un *sacrarium* également – fut condamnée : cette niche, bien que murée, laisse encore percevoir un fin liseré d'enduit qui ornait ses parois latérales (Fig. 2b). L'éventuelle décoration associée n'est, bien entendu, pas visible ; de même l'absence d'enduit conservé tout autour de la niche empêche d'assurer sa destination cultuelle. Toutefois, son emplacement, au centre du mur ouest de l'atrium de l'habitation préexistante, usuel pour des chapelles domestiques, laisse assez peu de doute sur la fonction initiale de cette construction[23]. Il semble envisageable de dater la condamnation de cette niche du moment où l'atrium et le vestibule de la maison antérieure connurent d'importants remaniements pour permettre l'installation des trois espaces en façade, à l'époque où le bâtiment fut transformé en atelier de *garum*[24]. Sans doute est-ce le changement de propriétaire de l'édifice (plus qu'un simple changement d'activité) qui généra la désaffectation de ce probable *sacrarium* originel. Malheureusement, si les *tituli picti* retrouvés sur différents contenants de l'atelier permettent de supposer que le propriétaire de l'établissement était A. Umbricius Scaurus[25], pour lequel travaillaient de nombreux *liberti*, l'identité de la famille occupant la demeure préexistante reste inconnue.

---

[23] En effet, la fonction cultuelle de niches présentes dans les *atria* pompéiens a fréquemment pu être mise en évidence (VAN ANDRINGA, *Quotidien des dieux et des hommes*, p. 220-222).

[24] La destination de ces pièces demeure incertaine (servait-elle à la vente du produit ? à son stockage avant expédition ?) ; notons en tout cas que celle la plus à l'est, dotée d'un seuil à rainure et ouverte, non sur la rue, mais sur la pièce d'entrée du bâtiment, présentait dans son mur nord une niche, fonctionnelle au moment de l'éruption. Faut-il y voir un nouveau *sacrarium*, aménagé au sein d'un espace commercial afin de remplacer l'ancienne niche de l'atrium qui était associée à l'habitation précédente ? Aucun élément conservé ne permet de confirmer cette hypothèse.

[25] La *domus* de celui-ci a été localisée en VII 16, 12-16, grâce à une inscription réalisée dans le pavement en mosaïque de l'atrium (au n. 15). L'exemple de A. Umbricius Scaurus illustre bien la possible dispersion des domaines urbains d'un *dominus*, même au sein d'une cité de la taille de Pompéi.

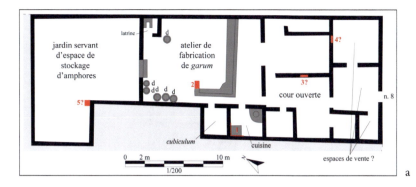

Fig. 2.
L'atelier de *garum* des *Umbricii* (I 12, 8).
a. Plan de l'atelier et localisation des (potentiels) aménagements religieux.
b. La niche de l'ancien atrium était murée dans les dernières années avant l'éruption.

De manière analogue, quoiqu'avec des indices plus ténus, il paraît probable que la niche présente en face du four (Fig. 3) d'une petite boulangerie en I 8, 15.16 ait été murée suite à la conversion de la salle de cuisson en un nouvel atelier, conversion peut-être liée à un changement de propriétaire. Ces éléments demeurent là encore très hypothétiques. D'une part, la fonction cultuelle de la niche ne s'imagine que par comparaison avec d'autres boulangeries, les *sacraria* de ce type d'établissement étant en effet régulière-

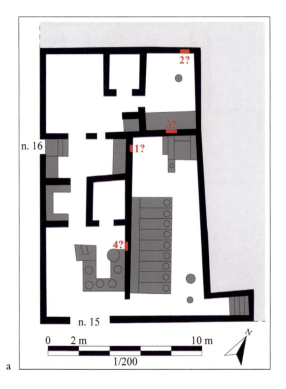

Fig. 3.
Le commerce alimentaire avec *pistrinum* en I 8, 15.16.
a. Plan de l'établissement et localisation des (potentiels) aménagements religieux.
b. En face du four, une niche pourrait avoir servi de *sacrarium*.

ment aménagés à proximité du four. D'autre part, le changement d'activité est lui aussi sujet à interrogations : s'il est clair que la partie occidentale de l'édifice, ouverte sur la rue aux n. 15 et n. 16, servait de commerce alimentaire, la fonction de la pièce située à l'est, accessible uniquement depuis la salle de vente au n. 15, paraît moins évidente. La présence de deux meules à corps cylindrique et d'un four à voûte, certes de petites dimensions, permettent de l'identifier à une boulangerie, mais les aménagements au sol – bassin et ensemble de petites cuves circulaires recouvertes de feuilles de plomb et dont la fonction demeure pour l'heure énigmatique [26] – invitent à penser que cette pièce connut d'autres activités productives, de manière contemporaine ou non au fonctionnement de la *pistrina*. Bien qu'aucun élément disponible ne permette d'assurer une désaffectation de la boulangerie en 79 apr. J.-C., on peut se demander pourquoi la niche pariétale en face du four, contemporaine de la construction du mur et ne semblant pas menacer la solidité de celui-ci, fut condamnée à un certain moment de l'histoire de l'édifice. Quel intérêt y aurait-il à murer une simple « étagère », alors que les besoins en lumière de la pièce restaient *a priori* les mêmes ? Ce choix se comprend en revanche s'il s'agissait d'un espace sacré ayant accueilli les divinités familiales d'un ancien propriétaire ; l'activité religieuse d'une nouvelle *familia* établie dans le commerce pourrait avoir eu lieu dans les espaces de réception de la clientèle où ont été identifiés de potentiels espaces sacrés [27]. Si certains de ces aménagements semblent avoir été entretenus jusque lors de la dernière

---

[26] N. Monteix rejette, à juste titre, le rôle d'*officina pigmentaria* proposée en premier lieu par M. Della Corte en raison de l'absence de trace de pigments dans le local. En revanche, les feuilles de plomb recouvrant le dispositif l'amènent à l'associer éventuellement à la production fromagère. Voir N. MONTEIX, *Les lieux de métier : boutiques et ateliers d'Herculanum*, Rome, École française de Rome, 2010 (BEFAR 344), p. 142, n. 48.

[27] Deux niches se trouvaient dans l'espace arrière servant sans doute pour le repas des clients ; la fréquente présence de *sacraria* au-dessus des *triclinia* d'été laisse envisager, quoique de manière incertaine, la fonction cultuelle de l'une ou l'autre de ces deux niches. Quant à celle aménagée dans le mur oriental de la salle de vente, au-dessus du comptoir, il semble moins probable qu'elle ait constitué un espace sacré, par comparaison avec les niches retrouvées en des emplacements similaires au sein de commerces alimentaires.

phase de la vie de l'édifice[28], l'ensemble du bâtiment nécessiterait une étude approfondie des différentes phases constructives. Cet exemple, comme les précédents, fait ressortir l'importance tant de la stratigraphie que de l'analyse fine du bâti, essentielles pour permettre la restitution de la chronologie relative des espaces ainsi que des aménagements associés les uns par rapport aux autres, et donc des activités liées à chacune des phases mises en évidence.

2.3. Évolution du bâti entraînant la condamnation d'un *sacrarium*

À côté de ces premiers exemples, on relève toute une série de niches murées dont la condamnation paraît pouvoir être mise en relation, là encore, avec un changement de propriétaire. Toutefois, ce changement de *dominus* semble transparaître, non plus à travers une mutation des activités réalisées au sein de l'édifice en question, mais à travers une évolution du bâti (une ouverture sur de nouveaux espaces « annexés » ou à l'inverse la fermeture d'une porte, l'ajout d'un mur de refend ...).

Non loin de la *Porta Marina*, l'établissement VII 15, 4.5 résulte de la fusion de deux bâtiments (l'un au n. 4, l'autre au n. 5), formant, au moment de l'éruption, un tout unitaire, à en juger par la peinture uniforme en façade et les différentes ouvertures internes (Fig. 4a). Il comportait un commerce alimentaire[29], des espaces de réception de la clientèle et des espaces résidentiels, notamment à l'étage. Outre une peinture de Mercure, réalisée sur le pilier auquel s'adossait le comptoir de vente, un espace sacré avait été aménagé dans le *viridarium* en arrière de l'établissement. Celui-ci consistait en une niche rectangulaire, précédée d'un autel maçonné, creusée dans le mur nord de la cour et encadrée par deux larges montants d'enduit rouge sur lesquels étaient peints des serpents (Fig. 4b). Au fond de la niche, un personnage féminin (?), identifiée par G. Fiorelli à *Libera* en raison de la couronne de lierre

---

[28] En particulier l'enduit couvrant la niche septentrionale de l'espace situé à l'angle nord-est du commerce alimentaire semble correspondre à l'ultime revêtement pariétal de la pièce.

[29] Une salle de vente dotée d'un comptoir était ouverte sur la rue au n. 5 ; derrière elle, dans une petite pièce située à l'ouest (un ancien *cubiculum* ?), était aménagée une cuisine.

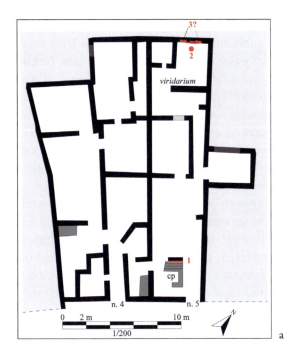

Fig. 4.
Le commerce alimentaire en VII 15, 4.5.
a. Plan de l'établissement et localisation des *sacraria*.
b. Dans le *viridarium*, un *sacrarium* s'est superposé à deux niches antérieures.
Au moment du dégagement de l'établissement, seul le *sacrarium*
le plus récent était visible.

la coiffant, figurait allongé sur un lit, abrité par une tente et précédé d'une table sur laquelle étaient posés trois verres, un écho, une fois n'est pas coutume, à l'activité du lieu. La chute progressive de l'enduit a fait apparaître deux niches de dimensions semblables et situées à une même hauteur par rapport au sol [30] ; ces « niches jumelles » correspondent très probablement à un *sacrarium* antérieur, si l'on en juge par des aménagements similaires, en principe destinés aux Lares d'une part et au *Genius paterfamiliaris* d'autre part [31]. En outre, l'emplacement de ce *sacrarium* antérieur (dans un *viridarium*) ne serait guère surprenant.

Cet exemple est intéressant dans le sens où il semble être l'un des rares témoignages où l'on pourrait préciser que le changement de chapelle domestique s'est accompagné d'un changement de divinités honorées. Si nos hypothèses sont correctes, nous aurions donc la manifestation du départ d'une première *familia* avec ses divinités domestiques [32]. À ce moment-là, le nouveau propriétaire, au lieu de réutiliser l'ancien *sacrarium*, aménage un nouvel espace sacré pour ses propres divinités familiales, non sans lien avec ses sphères d'activité. Impossible en revanche de dire si c'est la *familia* partante qui, éventuellement au cours d'une cérémonie spécifique, a condamné les niches de sa chapelle ou si c'est la nouvelle famille qui, en s'installant, mure les niches antérieures pour édifier par-dessus son *sacrarium*. Quoi qu'il en soit, le symbole est fort et lourd de sens : il s'agirait d'effacer l'emprise des divinités domestiques antérieures, marqueurs topographiques d'appartenance d'un édifice au patrimoine (*pecunia*) d'une *familia*, pour y installer d'autres dieux familiaux, qui témoignent désormais du rattachement du bâtiment aux domaines urbains des nouveaux propriétaires.

---

[30] La photographie de G. K. Boyce ne permet pas de deviner les niches sous-jacentes. Voir G. K. BOYCE, *Corpus of the Lararia of Pompeii*, Rome, American Academy in Rome, 1937 (Memoirs of the American Academy in Rome, 14), pl. 12, n° 3. Celle des *PPM*, réalisée après la chute du montant peint à l'ouest de la niche, laisse clairement voir la niche orientale, même si la seconde est encore difficilement décelable (*PPM*, VII, p. 789, fig. 16).

[31] Les niches jumelles ayant révélé des peintures de divinités montrent cette répartition. L'un des plus beaux exemples est probablement le laraire souterrain en VII 2, 20.22.41.

[32] Compte tenu de ce que révèlent les sources textuelles, ce changement de propriétaire pourrait être lié à une vente, à une donation ou à un legs mais pas à un héritage qui nécessiterait d'acquérir, en même temps que le bien, les *sacra priuata* du testateur.

Ce témoignage invite à émettre des hypothèses similaires lorsque l'on observe des niches murées à proximité immédiate d'aménagements sacrés (ou potentiels aménagements sacrés). C'est le cas par exemple dans l'habitation VII 11, 8, localisée au nord de la Maison du Labyrinthe (VII 11, 9.10) et reliée à celle-ci dans les dernières années de la vie de Pompéi (Fig. 5a). La cour à atrium de cette petite résidence présentait, dans son mur nord, un pseudo-édicule peint d'un décor végétal. À l'extérieur de la niche, figuraient un paon et, au-dessous, les deux serpents s'avançant vers un autel. L'exemple précédemment étudié amène à se demander si l'installation de ce *sacrarium* ne suit pas la fermeture de la niche de la paroi située juste à côté, à l'angle nord-est de l'atrium (Fig. 5b), et si cette fermeture ne serait pas liée éventuellement à un changement de propriétaire, par exemple lorsque l'habitation fut reliée à la Maison du Labyrinthe.

De même, le bouchage de potentielles niches jumelles, peut-être un *sacrarium* destiné aux Lares et au *Genius paterfamiliaris*[33], dans le mur sud de la cuisine localisée en arrière d'une officine de lavage de toisons (IX 3, 13) correspond-il à un nouveau *dominus tabernae* qui aurait installé, toujours dans la même pièce, une autre niche dans le mur nord[34] (Fig. 6) ?

Une pratique similaire ne pourrait-elle pas aussi expliquer la présence d'une niche murée dans le mur oriental du commerce alimentaire en VII 3, 3.38, juste à côté d'une seconde niche, non murée quant à elle[35] (Fig. 7) ?

---

[33] Voir la note 31 sur les niches jumelles.

[34] G. K. Boyce recense également la peinture d'un Génie du père de famille sacrifiant, encadré par des Lares, « on the wall of the shop » (BOYCE, *Corpus of the Lararia of Pompeii*, p. 183-184, n° 411).

[35] Des hypothèses analogues peuvent être émises dans le cas des laraires de carrefour, dont l'organisation et les célébrations associées étaient orchestrées par les familles les plus en vue du quartier en question. À côté de simples restaurations consistant à repeindre quasiment à l'identique la peinture précédente (comme pour l'autel n° 16, situé à l'angle sud-est de l'*insula* IX 12 ; VAN ANDRINGA, *Autels de carrefour*, p. 57-58), on peut se demander s'il n'existait pas des réfections liées à un changement de familles prééminentes. Ainsi à l'extérieur de la maison en IX 7, 20, la chute de l'enduit à droite de l'entrée a révélé une niche ; or, c'est à cet emplacement qu'avait été repérée et dessinée au XIXe siècle une peinture de laraire. Celle-ci daterait-elle de l'installation du dernier propriétaire de la maison, peut-être un certain D. Caprasius Felix ?

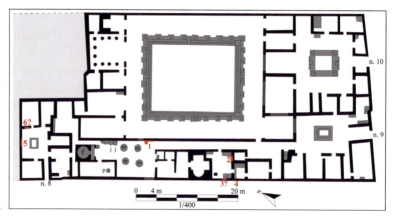

Fig. 5.
La Maison du Labyrinthe (VI 11, 8-10).
a. La petite habitation en VI 11, 8 communiquait, en 79 apr. J.-C.,
avec la Maison dite du Labyrinthe (VI 11, 9.10).
b. La niche murée à l'angle nord-est de l'atrium était-elle un ancien *sacrarium* ?
(© Jackie et Bob Dunn, www.pompeiiinpictures.com ;
sur concession du MiBAC – Parco Archeologico di Pompei).

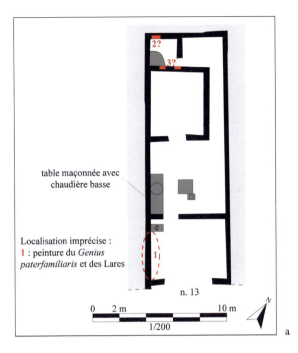

Fig. 6.
Les (potentielles) niches de l'officine de lavage de toisons en IX 3, 13.
a. Plan de l'officine de lavage de toisons avec espaces résidentiels.
b. La niche au-dessus du foyer de la cuisine pourrait avoir servi de *sacrarium*.
c. Potentielles niches jumelles du mur sud de la cuisine.

Fig. 7.
Vue du commerce alimentaire en VII 3, 3.38 depuis la *Via della Fortuna*.
Deux niches, dont l'une murée, sont visibles dans le mur oriental de la boutique.

À nouveau, il paraît difficile de comprendre l'intérêt de colmater des niches si elles n'avaient qu'une fonction pratique, surtout pour en reconstruire une à proximité[36] ; cet intérêt se comprend en revanche dans le cas d'une fermeture symbolique d'un espace sacré pour permettre l'installation d'un nouveau *sacrarium*.

Des évolutions plus marquées du bâti, sans doute fréquemment liées à un changement de propriétaire, semblent parfois expliquer le déplacement d'un espace sacré. Dans le jardin de l'habitation en I 10, 1, servant tant pour la cuisine que pour le stockage de denrées, la construction d'un muret à côté du foyer est venue obturer une niche dont la fonction cultuelle originelle paraît assez certaine (Fig. 8). En effet, d'une part elle semble avoir fonctionné avec la niche voisine, de dimensions semblables, et d'autre part, une corniche en stuc courait sous l'ensemble des trois niches du mur sud ; la niche orientale, peut-être agrandie lorsque fut construit le mur de refend, a livré un buste en terre-cuite archaïsant de Cérès.

---

[36] À condition, bien entendu, de pouvoir établir un tel phasage dans l'histoire des murs.

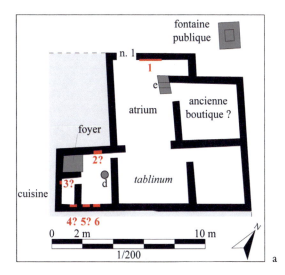

Fig. 8.
L'habitation en I 10, 1.
a. Plan de l'habitation et localisation des (potentiels) *sacraria*.
b. Les trois niches du mur sud : la niche occidentale, de dimensions semblables à celle au centre, fut obturée par la construction du mur de refend. Cette niche a conservé la moulure en stuc qui courait le long du mur.

En revanche, il est plus difficile d'attribuer une fonction religieuse à la petite niche semi-circulaire réalisée dans le mur ouest, à côté de l'espace de cuisson ou encore à celle construite dans le mur

Fig. 9.
Mur oriental du jardin de l'habitation en VI 11, 3, dans lequel furent creusées trois niches à des époques différentes. La petite niche à l'aplomb d'un muret fut aménagée après la fermeture des niches jumelles.

nord, à côté de la porte vers l'atrium. Cette dernière, semblant dater d'une phase constructive postérieure à l'élévation du mur[37], conservait encore, au moment de son dégagement, son enduit interne jaune, bordé de rouge.

De façon analogue, dans une habitation située au nord de la ville (en VI 11, 3), la reconfiguration de l'espace, par l'ajout d'un muret, semble concomitante du déplacement du *sacrarium* : dans le mur oriental du jardin, deux niches jumelles furent condamnées et le mur reçut un enduit blanc. Postérieurement, mais peut-être dans un laps de temps très court, l'on construisit contre ce pan un muret au-dessus duquel fut installée une nouvelle niche (Fig. 9).

De même, on peut se demander si la fermeture de la niche du commerce alimentaire en VI 4, 3 est contemporaine de l'ouverture de cette salle de vente sur l'habitation voisine (VI 4, 4), dotée

---

[37] Sous la niche, le parement est essentiellement composé de pierres de basalte gris à peine équarris et disposés sans assises régulières apparentes. En revanche, à partir de la hauteur où est aménagée la niche, les pierres utilisées sont principalement du tuf calcaire jaune, disposées en arc autour de la niche.

Fig. 10.
En 79 apr. J.-C., une petite niche était murée dans le mur du fond de l'arrière-boutique en VIII 3, 19, reliée à la maison voisine (au n. 18) dans les dernières années de Pompéi.

d'un laraire peint juste à droite de la porte reliant les deux bâtiments. Également, est-ce au moment où une communication est établie entre l'atrium de la maison en VIII 3, 16.18 et la boutique adjacente (au n. 19) qu'est murée la petite niche située en arrière de l'espace de vente (Fig. 10) [38] ?

Si ces exemples demeurent des hypothèses [39], le changement de propriétaire est avéré dans un cas un peu particulier. À l'époque

---

[38] Les montants en brique de la porte donnant accès à l'atrium de la maison semblent en effet indiquer que l'ouverture fut pratiquée dans un second temps de la vie de l'édifice.

[39] En particulier, il faut garder à l'esprit que l'on manque en général d'arguments pour assurer le caractère sacré de ces niches. C'est en multipliant les comparaisons et les études de cas qu'il sera possible de mieux interpréter les pratiques (religieuses ou non) associées aux niches murées.

augustéenne, M. Tullius donne à la cité une partie de ses *praedia urbana*[40] (*solo*) et finance (*pequnia sua*) l'érection d'un temple public dédié à la Fortune Auguste[41]. La consécration d'un tel temple nécessite au préalable le passage du terrain privé dans la propriété publique[42]. Or, la fouille a mis en évidence l'existence d'une niche murée, un ancien *sacrarium*, dans le petit local situé à l'est, à l'arrière du temple. Le message était clair : les divinités familiales de M. Tullius ne pouvaient demeurer dans cette chapelle, le terrain étant passé aux mains de la municipalité, avant d'être cédé, à jamais cette fois, à la Fortune Auguste.

Ces changements de propriétaires devaient, au moins dans certains cas, s'accompagner de cérémonies rituelles, mais celles-ci n'ont que rarement été mises en évidence. Des dépôts de fondation ont parfois été enregistrés : par exemple, trois monnaies furent placées dans le sol en béton de tuileau datant du réaménagement des boutiques de la parfumerie en VII 4, 24-25, suite au tremblement de terre de 62/63 apr. J.-C.[43]. L'analyse de restes anthracologiques et carpologiques formant le comblement supérieur d'un des trous de poteaux liés à la construction du temple de la Fortune Auguste a révélé qu'un rituel spécifique, impliquant la combustion d'un

---

[40] Les fouilles menées sur le temple et ses annexes par l'équipe archéologique de W. Van Andringa, de 2008 à 2013, ont révélé que le sanctuaire fut aménagé sur un ensemble d'habitations et boutiques datant de l'époque républicaine et ayant été arasées. Voir W. Van Andringa *et al.*, « M. Tullius et le temple de Fortune Auguste à Pompéi (campagnes de fouille et d'étude 2008-2010) », *MEFRA* 123/1 (2011), p. 364-365.

[41] *CIL*, X, 820 : *M(arcus) Tullius M(arci) f(ilius) d(uum)v(ir) i(ure) d(icundo) ter(tium) quinq(uennalis) augur tr(ibunus) mil(itum) / a pop(ulo) aedem Fortunae August(ae)* **solo et peq(unia) sua**.

[42] Thomas, *La valeur des choses*, p. 1437 (en part. n. 11 pour les références littéraires et juridiques) ; W. Van Andringa, « *M. Tullius ... aedem Fortunae August(ae) solo et peq(unia) sua*. Private Foundation and Public Cult in a Roman Colony », in C. Ando, J. Rüpke (éd.), *Public and Private in Ancient Mediterranean Law and Religion*, Berlin, De Gruyter, 2015 (Religionsgeschichtliche Versuche und Vorarbeiten 65), p. 99-113.

[43] J.-B. Brun, N. Monteix, « Les parfumeries en Campanie antique », in J.-B. Brun (dir.), *Artisanats antiques d'Italie et de Gaule. Mélanges offerts à Maria Francesca Buonaiuto*, Naples, Centre Jean Bérard, 2009 (Collection du Centre Jean Bérard 32), p. 125. Ce geste rappelle les dépôts de fondation enregistrés dans plusieurs maisons pompéiennes, vraisemblablement liés à un changement de propriétaire (Bassani, Sacraria, p. 24, n. 7).

ensemble de fruits sur un foyer, a marqué la fin du chantier de construction[44]. Seules de telles observations, couplées à une analyse fine de la stratigraphie et du bâti, permettront de mettre en évidence les pratiques religieuses, ou au moins rituelles, qui étaient associées à un changement de propriétaire et de mieux connaître le devenir des espaces sacrés en contexte domestique.

---

[44] L'étude carpologique a été réalisée par V. Matterne (VAN ANDRINGA *et al.*, *M. Tullius*, p. 365).

INDEX RERUM

Aedes 173, 183, 195
Aedicula 54, 76, 113, 115, 117-119, 126, 141, 147, 167, 172-173, 175, 177, 183, 187, 194, 200, 210, 214-215, 217-219, 222-223, 227, 235-236, 273, 279, 298
Ala 142
Altar *passim*
Andron 27, 30, 38, 48
Antrum 156
Ara/arula 184, 190, 297
Armarium 67, 300-301
Atrium 53-54, 56, 64, 76, 78, 112-114, 116, 118, 142-145, 148, 152-153, 184, 187-188, 190, 200, 214, 216, 218, 224-225, 227-229, 231, 234, 260-261, 263-264, 266, 324, 342-343, 349-350, 354-355

Biclinium 56, 62, 76

Caupona 57, 115
Cenaculum 215, 218-219, 221, 224-225, 227
Compitum 97, 183, 185
Compluvium 261
Cornucopia 60, 63-64, 110
Corridor 217, 259-261, 263, 290
Courtyard 31-33, 36-38, 60, 89, 147, 165, 167, 182-184, 190-191, 195, 214, 270, 291, 298, 300-301, 303-305, 325, 327, 346, 349
Crypta 91
Cubiculum 56, 78, 112-113, 120, 188

Dominus 12, 74, 110, 153, 177-178, 188, 203, 211, 229, 330, 339, 346, 349
Domus passim
Door 16, 70, 77, 146, 154, 156, 165, 185, 216, 218, 231-236, 242-266, 324, 341, 346, 354

Entrance 15-17, 156-157, 162, 178, 183-191, 194-195, 200, 203, 218, 231-236, 241-266, 291-292, 297-298, 325-326
Externa sacra 174

Facade 112, 145, 152, 167, 185, 261, 278, 341-342, 346
Familia 11-12, 85, 92, 102, 110, 139-140, 142-143, 145-146, 211, 272, 290, 303, 336-338, 345, 348
Fauces 76, 231, 263, 292
Fons 200

Garden 90, 145-146, 148, 154, 156-157, 161, 163-165, 168, 191, 195-196, 206-207, 214, 224, 232, 253, 291, 294, 296, 300, 304, 352, 354
Gynaikon 38-39

Hermes 22-23, 152-153, 177, 197, 200, 228, 263
Hortus 77, 84, 91, 121, 230, 233-234
Household *passim*

Imagines maiorum 142-143, 152-153, 180, 189, 206-207, 245
Incense burner 143, 269, 298
Insula 78, 84, 89, 92, 98, 102, 185, 215-216, 222, 224, 226-227, 274

Kitchen 17, 60, 76, 109-110, 115, 119-120, 143-145, 156, 194, 213, 217-221, 224, 254, 280-283, 286-287, 290-292, 298, 300-301, 303-304, 324, 327, 341, 349, 351-352
Kline 30, 116

Lararium passim
Latrines 290
Lekythos 43-44

Mithraea 14, 83-92, 97-102, 127, 200
Mosaic 33, 66, 165-166, 177, 191, 199, 204, 233, 262-263, 283

Niche 15, 54, 68, 106, 113, 126, 134, 142, 144, 146-153, 157, 160, 162, 164-165, 167-168, 172, 175, 177, 183-191, 200, 210-211, 219-220, 222-226, 253, 262-263, 269-270, 272-273, 276, 279, 286, 291-305, 323-325, 337, 342-356

Ostiarius 264

Painting 33, 42-43, 51, 57, 60, 106, 109-110, 113-115, 123, 132, 141, 144, 148, 156, 160, 162, 164, 168, 177, 186, 213, 217-226, 250, 258, 260, 265, 276, 278-283, 285-286, 294, 300, 303, 323, 339, 346
Palatium 84, 91
Paterfamilias 10-15, 85, 88, 111, 174, 257, 263, 287, 319, 334, 337-338, 340, 348-349
Peristylium 32-34, 36-38, 49, 56, 58, 76, 112-113, 115, 126, 130, 144, 147, 149, 151, 153, 156, 178, 190-196, 202-203, 214, 219, 253, 266, 291-292, 324

Pinax 229-230
Pluteus 342
Porticus 191, 206
Pyxis 43-44

Reception room 36, 66, 115, 217, 234, 261, 266
Rhyton 110, 218, 285, 287, 304

Sacellum 89, 115, 134, 146, 165, 172-173, 178, 183, 185, 190, 195-198, 204, 219
Sacra 100, 184, 190, 207
Sacra privata 9-12, 171-208, 219, 222, 235-236, 335-336, 338-339
Sacra publica 11, 101, 171
Sacrarium 15-17, 56, 134, 139-169, 173, 176, 187-195, 198, 200, 203-204, 210, 277-283, 285-304, 334-356
Shrine 13-16, 24, 42, 105-135, 214, 236, 241-243, 250, 252-254, 258, 261, 265, 267, 277, 279, 284, 289, 305
Simulacrum 176-178, 193, 197, 207
Staircase 216, 221, 233, 290, 294
Statue(tte) *passim*

Taberna 52, 78, 89, 267, 351
Tablinum 78, 188-189, 198, 234, 263
Temple 7, 15, 54, 57, 62, 67, 89, 101-102, 140, 145-146, 160, 168, 172-173, 178, 184, 194-197, 201, 251-253, 260, 316, 356
Thymiaterion 28, 34, 184
Tituli picti 261, 342
Triclinium 230, 233, 265, 300

Vestibule 70, 77, 112, 156, 188, 342
Villa passim
Viridarium 146, 156, 162, 164, 233-234, 296, 341, 346-348

Window 17, 294

INDEX DEORUM

Abnoba 321-322
Abundantia 70, 77
Anubis 115-116, 161
Aphrodite 17, 21-50, 61, 79, 125, 127, 134, 203
    Euploia 48
    Limenia 48
    Ourania 23, 48
    Pandemos 48
    Pseliumene 40-41
Apis 72, 121
Apollo 55, 57, 67, 76-78, 113, 121, 123, 127, 130, 197, 311, 318, 320
    Patroos 22
Artemis 33, 130
Asclepius 63, 75-76, 79, 119, 125, 128, 130, 134
Astarte 25, 40
Athena 119, 121, 126

Baal 95
Bacchus 54, 57, 66, 115, 156, 167, 294, 311, 318, 324, 340
Bona Mens 147

Caelus 96-97
    Aeternus 96-97
Cardea 255
Carna 255
Castor 320, 325
Cernunnos 70, 77
Concordia 133
    Augusta 133

Cupid 118, 124
Cybele 125, 127, 129, 134-135, 311

Demeter 127, 130
Deverra 256
Diana 59, 63, 67-68, 70, 76-78, 120, 124, 151, 178, 197, 311, 317-318, 320, 322
Dionysus 23-24, 36, 125, 127, 130, 151, 154, 168, 202, 204
Dioscuri 76, 260

Epona 311, 318
Eros 25, 28, 30, 32-34, 37-38, 43, 46, 49, 54, 69, 78, 125, 311
Europe 130

Forculus 255
Fortuna 54, 63, 69-70, 73, 76-78, 115, 118-125, 127, 134, 145, 199, 258, 277, 298-299, 311, 318, 356

Genius 13, 53-54, 57, 59-60, 69-72, 76-78, 106, 108-109, 111, 113, 117-118, 120-123, 132, 134, 139, 148, 167, 189, 200, 211, 223, 277, 279, 285, 291, 295-296, 319, 348-349

Harpocrates 59, 63, 67, 76, 78, 114-116, 119-120, 125-126, 161, 312, 318, 320

INDEX DEORUM

Helios 76, 120
Heracles/Hercules 54-55, 57, 67, 77-78, 113, 117-118, 121, 124, 126-127, 130, 167, 172-173, 186-187, 199, 201, 225, 277, 296, 311, 318, 320
Hermaphrodite 22
Hermes 22
Hestia 22
Horus 115, 127
Hygieia 125, 130

Intercidona 256
IOM Dolichenus 87, 97
Isis 25-26, 59-62, 67-68, 72, 75-79, 112, 114-116, 120, 125-128, 130, 133-134, 160-161, 312, 318, 320
    Aphrodite 40-41, 125
    Demeter 125
    Fortuna 115, 120, 126, 142
    Lactans 125
    Panthea 126
    Tyche 125

Janus 146, 253-255
Juno 62, 64, 78, 96, 113, 115, 124, 311
    Regina 96
Jupiter 54, 60, 62-63, 69, 71, 76-78, 87, 95-97, 99, 113, 115, 118-120, 122-123, 134, 163, 251, 277, 294, 311, 320-321, 327

Laha 321
Lares 54-57, 59-60, 63-64, 66, 68, 76, 78, 105-106, 108-111, 113, 115-125, 127, 130, 132-135, 139-140, 142, 148, 152, 154, 163, 167, 172-176, 181, 183, 185, 189, 192, 197, 209-212, 215, 217-219, 223, 226, 231, 242, 245, 249, 267, 272, 276-277, 280-287, 290-291, 294-296, 301, 303-304, 316, 318-319, 335, 340, 348-349
Latona 197
Leda 127

Liber 135, 204
Libera 348
Limentinus 255-256
Luna 71, 77, 95, 123

Magna Mater 128
Mars 75, 77-79, 123, 125-126, 134, 191, 311, 318, 320
    Ultor 70
Matres 70
Mercury 10, 54-55, 57, 59-60, 63-64, 67-71, 73, 76-78, 97, 113, 117-118, 120-124, 127-128, 133, 135, 145, 156, 186-187, 201, 258, 272, 277, 296, 311, 318, 320, 340, 346
Minerva 54, 57-59, 62-65, 69, 76-79, 96, 113, 115, 118, 120-121, 123-124, 134, 163, 272, 277, 284, 294, 296, 300, 311, 314, 318
Mithras 10, 14-15, 81-103

Nechbet 25
Neptune 77, 120, 201, 233, 254

Ouranos 47

Pan 45, 124, 130
Pankrates 128
Penates 7, 10, 15, 105-106, 108-109, 127, 135, 139, 142, 181, 189, 209-211, 223-224, 226, 231, 236, 261, 336
Pilumnus 256
Priapus 156, 316
Proxsumae 322
Psyche 34

Risus 1

Saturn 96
Serapis 59, 76, 115, 120, 126, 134, 161
Silvanus 124, 130, 256, 316, 320
Sol 60, 95, 100-101, 135
Somnus 68, 78, 124
Sucellus 70, 77, 311, 318
Suleviae 68, 320

Taranis 70
Telesphorus 125
Tutela 77, 123
Tyche 75, 79, 125

Venus 25-27, 54, 57, 61, 69, 72, 75-77, 113, 115-116, 118-121, 123, 130, 134, 151, 156, 163, 165, 197, 201, 221, 272, 277, 310-313, 318

Vesta 7, 108, 115, 135, 146, 254, 294
Victoria 54, 64, 77-78, 118, 123-124, 134, 311

Zeus 22
    Herkeios 22
    Ktesios 22

INDEX LOCORUM

Ager Pompeianus
    Boscoreale, villa de Fondo d'Acunzo 60, 76, 120, 319
    Boscoreale, villa de Contrada Civita di Nitto 59, 76
    Boscoreale, villa de Fondo Giovanni Imperiali 319
    Boscoreale, villa Regina 325
    Boscoreale, villa in Contrada Giuliana (Fondo Zurlo) 195
    Scafati, villa di Cn. Domitius Auctus 72, 120
    Scafati, villa di N. Popidius Narcissus Maior 325
Acholla, casa di M. Asinius Rufinus Sabinianus 200, 203
Aosta (*Augusta Praetoria*), Casa di Tito Vareno 200
Arezzo, domus di San Lorenzo 122
Athens
    Agora 26, 124-125
    House of Proclus 128-129
Augst (*Augusta Raurica*) 51, 68, 78, 124
Avenches 64-65, 78

Bezonnes (Rodelle, Aveyron), villa des Clapiès 327, 329
Bilbilis, domus de la Fortuna 124
Brèves 73, 77, 123
Brioni island, villa of the *Laecanii* 201-202

Clermont-Ferrand 70-71, 77
Corinth, locality of Panaya 130
Cos, House of the Bronzes 56, 74, 79, 125, 205

Delos 23, 27, 32-34, 39, 47, 106, 186, 189-190
    House of the Herms 32-33
    House of the Dolphins 186
    House I C 187
    House Th VI 0 33
Dion, House of Dionysus 204

Ephesos 33-37, 39, 47
    Terrace House 1 34-35, 49
    Terrace House 2 36-37, 126, 202-203
Eraclea Minoa 190

Finziade 190
Flavin, villa de Mas Marcou 331

Gerona, villa de Vilauba 124
Grimault, villa 314-315

Herculaneum 13, 25, 53, 56, 118-120, 132, 209-237, 267
    Casa del Bicentenario (V, 13-16) 119, 219-222
    Casa a Graticcio (III 13-15) 56, 62, 76, 120, 215

Casa di Nettuno ed Anfitrite (V, 6-7) 119, 213, 216-219, 227-235
Casa del Rilievo di Telefo (Ins. Or. I, 2-3) 214
Casa del Sacello di Legno (V, 31) 67, 214, 227, 232
Casa del Salone Nero (VI, 11) 214
Cenaculum V, 13-14 219-220
Cenaculum V, 18 215
Villa dei Papiri 192-193

Jonzac, villa 314

La Cadière-d'Azur, villa 321, 325-326
La Garde, villa Saint Michel 325-326
Latresne 315
Loupian, villa 330
Lucus Feroniae, villa dei Volusii Saturnini 191-192

Mâcon 71-72, 77, 123
Murlo, archaic palace 182

Nea Paphos, villa of Theseus 130-131

Oberwinterthur (*Vitudurum*) 69, 78
Olynthus 23
Oplontis, villa 194
Ostia 88-91, 98, 102-103, 123
    Mitreo degli Animali 89
    Mitreo di Menandro 89
    Mitreo delle Pareti dipinti 88
    Mitreo delle Sette Sfere 89
    Sacello delle Tre Navate 89

Palombara Sabina (Rome), villa in loc. Formello 195-196, 201
Pergamon, Peristyle House II 126
Piazza Armerina, villa del Casale 203
Pompeii
    Casa degli Amorini dorati (VI 26, 7) 62, 115-116, 142, 144, 161, 213-214

Casa di L. Caecilius Iucundus (V 1, 26) 148, 229-232, 252-253, 260-265
Casa di M. Caesius Blandus (VII 1, 40) 185-186
Casa del Cenacolo (V 2, h) 57, 117, 296-298
Casa del Citarista (I 4, 5) 57-58, 62, 76, 189
Casa dei Dioscuri (VI 9, 6-7) 258-261
Casa dell'Efebo (I 7, 10-12) 281, 300
Casa di M. Epidius Rufus (IX 1, 20) 200
Casa di un Flamine (V 4, 3) 53, 118
Casa del Forno (VI 3, 3) 294
Casa del Gallo (VIII 5, 2-5) 190
Casa di Iulius Polybius (IX 13, 1-3) 111-112, 281-283, 287
Casa del Labirinto (VI 11, 9-10) 281
Casa di Marcus Lucretius (IX 3, 5-24) 233-234
Casa del Maiale (IX 9, b-c) 281-288
Casa di Marcus Memmius Auctus (VI 14, 27) 116
Casa del Menandro (I 10, 4) 149-151, 168, 189, 214, 229, 285
Casa di Obellius Firmus (IX 14, 2-4) 286-287
Casa di Optatio (VII 2, 13-15) 162-165
Casa delle Pareti rosse (VIII 5, 37) 54-57, 76, 113-114, 289
Casa del Principe di Napoli (VI 15, 7.8) 232
Casa di Popidius Priscus (VII 2, 20) 291-292
Casa di M. Pupius Rufus (VI 15, 5) 188-189, 292-293
Casa della Regina Carolina (VIII 3, 14) 196

Casa del Larario del Sarno (I 14, 7)   232, 279, 284, 287
Casa di M. Spurius Saturninus (VII 6, 3)   178-179, 196
Casa di Sutoria Primigenia (I 13, 2)   280-284, 300-302
Casa del Torello (V 1, 7)   187-188
Casa della Venere in Conchiglia (II 3, 3)   165, 191
Casa I 10, 1   352-353
Casa I 12, 11   186
Casa I 12, 16   289
Casa II 1, 1   186
Casa II 2, 4   251
Casa V 4, 9   298
Casa VI 11, 3   354
Casa VI 16, 40   286
Casa VII 6, 3   179, 196, 252
Casa IX 3, 19-20   294
Caupona I 8, 8   57
Complesso dei Riti magici («Casa di Sabazios») (I 2, 12)   154-157
Shop I 8, 8-9   340
Shop I 8, 15-16   343-344
Shop I 12, 8   341, 343
Shop VI 4, 3   354
Shop VII 3, 3   349, 352
Shop VII 4, 24-25   356
Shop VII 11, 8   349
Shop VII 15, 4-5   346-347
Shop VIII 3, 16-18   355
Shop IX 3, 13   349, 351
Praedia di Iulia Felix (II 4, 2)   116-117, 143, 157-163, 167-168, 288

Villa delle Colonne a mosaico   165-167
Villa dei Misteri   193
Pola, domus in S. Teodorus area   199
Pouzac, villa   327
Priene   23, 27, 28-31, 39, 47
    House 13   30
    House 29   31
    House 33   28-30

Rezé   123
Rome
    Casa di Augusto   197, 251
    Domus degli Aradii   127-128, 135
    Domus di via G. Lanza   86-87, 126
    Horti Domitiae   59, 77, 121
    Horti Sallustiani   91
    Mitreo dei Nummii Albini   86, 102
    Mitreo dei Olympii   84, 86, 88, 99-101
    Mitreo de l'Ospedale San Giovanni   85
    Mitreo di Palazzo Barberini   85-87
    Mitreo di Santa Prisca   84-87

Saarlouis-Fraulautern   68, 78
Saint-Cyr-sur-Mer, villa   315
Setteville (Rome, via Tiburtina), villa dei Galloni   172

Téting, villa   315

Vallon, villa   66-68, 78, 316-317, 319-320, 323